ITAN

ting
e l and
oductive

Aging

Primary Prevention of Psychopathology

George W. Albee and Justin M. Joffe
General Editors

VOLUMES IN THIS SERIES:

Prevention of Delinquent Behavior, 1987
John D. Burchard and Sara N. Burchard, *Editors*
VOLUME X

Families in Transition, 1988
Lynne A. Bond and Barry M. Wagner, *Editors*
VOLUME XI

Primary Prevention and Promotion in the Schools, 1989
Lynne A. Bond and Bruce E. Compas, *Editors*
VOLUME XII

Primary Prevention of AIDS, 1989
Vickie M. Mays, George W. Albee, and Stanley F. Schneider, *Editors*
VOLUME XIII

Improving Children's Lives, 1992
George W. Albee, Lynne A. Bond, and Toni V. Cook Monsey, *Editors*
VOLUME XIV

The Present and Future of Prevention, 1992
Marc Kessler, Stephen E. Goldston, and Justin M. Joffe, *Editors*
VOLUME XV

Promoting Successful and Productive Aging, 1995
Lynne A. Bond, Stephen J. Cutler, and Armin Grams, *Editors*
VOLUME XVI

Volumes I-IX are available from
University Press of New England
3 Lebanon Street, Hanover, New Hampshire 03755

Promoting
Successful and
Productive
Aging

Editors

Lynne A. Bond
Stephen J. Cutler
Armin Grams

Primary Prevention of Psychopathology XVI

SAGE Publications
International Educational and Professional Publisher
Thousand Oaks London New Delhi

For information address:

SAGE Publications, Inc.
2455 Teller Road
Thousand Oaks, California 91320

SAGE Publications Ltd.
6 Bonhill Street
London EC2A 4PU
United Kingdom

SAGE Publications India Pvt. Ltd.
M-32 Market
Greater Kailash I
New Delhi 110 048 India

Printed in the United States of America

Library of Congress Cataloging-in-Publication Data

Main entry under title:

Promoting successful and productive aging / edited by Lynne A. Bond,
    Stephen J. Cutler, Armin Grams.
        p. cm. — (Primary prevention of psychopathology; v. 16)
    Outgrowth of the Sixteenth Vermont Conference on Primary
 Prevention of Psychopathology, held June 1993 at the University of
Vermont.
    Includes bibliographical references and index.
    ISBN 0-8039-7171-0 (acid-free paper). — ISBN 0-8039-7172-9 (pbk.
: acid-free paper).
    1. Aging—Congresses. 2. Aged—Health and hygiene—Congresses.
3. Aged—Psychology—Congresses. 4. Aged—Social conditions—
Congresses. I. Bond, Lynne A., 1949-   .II. Cutler, Stephen J.
III. Grams, Armin. IV. Vermont Conference on the Primary Prevention
of Psychopathology (16th : 1993 : University of Vermont) V. Series.
RC454.P683   vol. 16
[HQ1061]
305.26—dc 20   94-42212

This book is printed on acid-free paper.

95 96 97 98 99 10 9 8 7 6 5 4 3 2 1

Sage Production Editor: Diane S. Foster

Contents

Preface

This book grew in large part from the 16th Vermont Conference on the Primary Prevention of Psychopathology (VCPPP) convened in June 1993, and part of a series of annual meetings held at the University of Vermont since 1975. This Vermont Conference, like so many before it, was made possible, in part, by generous support from the National Institute of Mental Health (NIMH).

Since 1975, the VCPPP has brought together scholars, practitioners, social policy makers, community activists, and others to examine research, theory, policy and practice in varied domains of the primary prevention of psychopathology and the promotion of healthy functioning. Although VCPPP had long expressed interest in convening a group to examine prevention efforts in support of successful and productive aging, the conference on which this book is based came to fruition as a result of a collaboration between the University of Vermont's Center for the Study of Aging (with leadership from editors Cutler and Grams) and the VCPPP (with leadership from editor Bond). Primary prevention remains a relatively young field within mental health; ironically, the study of aging is similarly "young." Yet in the past couple of decades, both fields have matured considerably; thus it is particularly fitting to see them drawn together at this time, both in the form of this book as well as in the ideas and accomplishments reported here.

The reader will find that this volume includes reflections and analyses of experts from a wide range of disciplines, including psychology, psychiatry, gerontology, sociology, anthropology, public health, education, and medicine. Together they consider a series of questions and perspectives that underlie efforts to promote successful and productive aging. For example:

- Who are older adults? What are their characteristics, strengths, needs, and vulnerabilities? In what ways can we best consider the growth of the oldest old, individual differences, cohort effects, and lifelong versus late-onset issues in aging?
- What are the special risks related to aging, particularly in terms of cognitive conditions, comorbidity issues, and disability?
- What is successful and productive aging, for surely it is more than avoiding disability and disease; and as we recognize the social construction of aging,

can we go beyond culturally bound definitions of success and productivity in the later years?

- What are the preventive goals we should strive for as we consider successful and productive aging? Four areas that have been identified are (a) health, (b) financial security, (c) independence, and (d) sense of meaning, ego integrity, and vital involvement.

- How can we cultivate and communicate strategies for effective prevention programs? Here we consider the content of preventive and promotive interventions as well as the procedures they employ, focusing on matters such as context, timing, participant recruitment and involvement in program design, and the choice of individually based versus community-based approaches.

The focus of this volume is not to prevent aging, although some in our society would have us adopt such a goal; rather, the intent is to understand and prevent unnecessary disturbance and pathology that can be associated with aging and to promote a higher quality of life and productivity throughout the later years. This volume provides an opportunity to reflect on certain important accomplishments toward this end as well as to identify challenges and guideposts for future primary prevention and promotion efforts in support of successful aging.

The VCPPP is a nonprofit educational foundation incorporated in the state of Vermont and based at the Department of Psychology of the University of Vermont. Its board members include George W. Albee, Ph.D., Lynne A. Bond, Ph.D., John D. Burchard, Ph.D., Marc Kessler, Ph.D., and Justin M. Joffe, Ph.D., professors of psychology.

The Center for the Study of Aging at the University of Vermont is dedicated to promoting greater understanding of the aging process and its implications for individuals and society. It seeks to integrate the study of aging into the instructional, research, and service activities surrounding every major discipline at the university, and offers educational programs centered in the field of gerontology.

Special recognition and thanks go to the staff of VCPPP. During the planning and organizing of the 1993 conference, Kimberly Ryan-Finn served as conference coordinator as she completed coursework at the University of Vermont. Gisele Lizewski in the Psychology Department made invaluable contributions to conference organization, operations, correspondence, and information management. Sarah Gilmore in the Department of Sociology deserves special thanks and recognition for her diligent assistance in the preparation of manuscripts for this volume.

We would like to express our special gratitude to the National Institute of Mental Health and, in particular, to Juan Ramos, Associate Director for Prevention, and Edward Kelty, Assistant Director for International Programs. This year, as well as in previous years, they have provided critically valuable technical and financial assistance that have made the VCPPP conferences and volumes the successes they have been.

Lynne A. Bond
Stephen J. Cutler
Armin Grams

PART I

INTRODUCTORY CONSIDERATIONS

Documentation of interest in human aging appears sporadically throughout recorded history. The obvious and not so obvious changes individuals' experience during the course of a lifetime, but especially during the "third age," as well as the ingenious and not so ingenious adaptations that aging persons make to such changes, have captured the attention and imagination of many observers of the human condition for centuries.

Scholarly study of the aging process, on the other hand, is confined almost exclusively to the 20th century. For the most part, the evolving study of human development paralleled its subject. Only after the establishment of studies of infancy, childhood, adolescence, and young adulthood as respected developmental disciplines did the study of adult development and aging fill out the final phase of what is now known as life span human development.

Like its younger counterparts, gerontology is a multidisciplinary field. It is difficult to imagine an arena of human experience into which the study of aging does not venture. A student of the literature in this field soon learns that scholars in gerontology have roots not only in the physical, biological, behavioral, and social sciences, but in the humanities as well. The field attracts basic scientists as well as those who identify with applied and clinical issues. Such multidisciplinary breadth is modestly represented in the array of chapters that constitute this volume.

One of the most consistent findings to emerge from the study of aging is that the range of individual differences in almost all measures of status, performance, and productivity increases with the age of the sample. This fact gives rise to heuristic correlates such as certain of those in the title of this book: "successful" versus "usual" aging, "productive" aging, and "promoting" such development during the final third of life. "Prevention," the dominant theme of this entire series of volumes, is clearly implied when one considers the unachieved developmental potential revealed by adult development and aging research. What intervention strategies emerge that contribute to promoting successful and productive aging? What can we learn from the study of aging that will reduce the incidence of dysfunctional aging?

Although the four chapters that constitute the initial section of this book are relatively autonomous, they each address fundamental issues that surface in many of the subsequent chapters. The first, by Armin Grams and George W. Albee, draws upon Albee's schematic description of the basic elements of primary prevention to preview and analyze issues and strategies in supporting successful and productive aging. For the reader who may be less familiar with the language of prevention, this chapter provides a helpful orientation to this approach. For those who have a more limited acquaintance with gerontology but familiarity with the field of primary prevention, Grams and Albee's analysis introduces ways in which well established principles of primary prevention can be extrapolated to address issues in aging.

After defining primary prevention within a life span perspective, Grams and Albee summarize conditions that put elders in our society at risk for serious difficulties as well as certain variables that are associated with experiences of high quality of life during the "third age." The authors then proceed through a systematic analysis of classes of variables that can be manipulated in order to foster successful and productive aging, referring to examples from subsequent chapters of this volume as well as from the literature at large. Their concluding examination of public policy implications foreshadows some of the critical questions raised by the author of the chapter that follows.

In Chapter 2, Margaret Gatz presents a challenge not only to her fellow psychologists but to all professionals concerned with primary prevention. Recognizing that our readers may represent a broad range of disciplines but are likely to have in common an interest in prevention, Gatz poses those common questions that articulate our two principal themes: aging and prevention. In her discussion of why preventionists may have been a bit tardy in examining aging, Gatz paves the way for the major discussion of ageism that follows in the Hendricks chapter. Similarly, her reference to demographics puts the Simonsick chapter in proper perspective.

Of particular value is Gatz's deft interweaving of the components of prevention with those of the aging process. Because this is the first VCPPP volume to focus on development in old age, her analysis provides a framework for the ensuing discussions. Pervading the discussion of risk factors on the one hand and autonomy and social support on the other is the clear mandate to look beyond the results of systematic investigation to the implications for public policy and clinical practice. Her thesis is clear: If the goal of prevention is to foster continuing productive pursuit of human potential in old age, it must recruit both individual initiative and community action. The latter is of special importance, and it will not surprise the reader to find that it is the first of three clusters of preventive programs identified by Gatz. The second cluster calls attention to a major risk factor in aging, the potential for depression. Her chapter concludes with reference to a third approach, namely that of preventing dependency by fostering autonomy. This is again easier said than done, and the author cautions against a simplistic view, challenging us to appreciate the subtleties that research in this arena continues to elucidate.

Chapter 3 by Jon Hendricks also emphasizes the influence of social policy, both in the evolution of ageism and in considering intervention programs. Studies of two analogous phenomena, racism and sexism, indicate that although individual prejudice against minorities and women is alive and well, institutionalized prejudice is more pervasive and damaging. Hendricks acknowledges as well that some ageist attitudes stem from personal experiences, but insists that the juggernaut here is the socially constructed, read "institutionalized," prejudice against oldness.

Although the bulk of the chapter is devoted to the institutionalization of ageism, Hendricks begins, in good pedagogical form, with a concise discussion of the constructionist perspective. He argues that we have applied a constructionist perspective to the life course, with particular attention to old age. It may be that old age is what we make of it, but Hendricks believes that what we make of it is powerfully influenced by the prevailing ethos. We have here an example again of how the old (expectations) both colors and is colored by the new (individual aging experiences). Yet the dice are loaded on the side of expectations. The very language we use to consider and discuss developmental issues during the last third of life is a powerful tool that serves to maintain imbedded societal meanings—for example, should we have said "latter" instead of "last" in order to blunt the reality of the end of life?

Hendricks explores at length the links between ageism and the meso-, exo-, and macrosystem within which lives unfold. The complexity increases as the moral and ethical dilemmas created by the growing numbers of old people are added into the mix. Finally, the heart of the chapter, an extended discussion of the biomedicalization of aging, integrates the earlier theoretical material with the real-life issues of successful versus usual aging, autonomy and control, aging and illness, and value judgments and ethical issues that demand our prompt attention.

Chapter 4, by Eleanor Simonsick, on the demographics of aging, provides detailed documentation for what is sometimes referred to as the "aging imperative." Simonsick begins with a presentation of information about people in the United States 65 years of age and older, including characteristics that impinge on productive aging such as educational attainment and health status. A consistent finding is that large numbers of people over the age of 65 are indeed productive, that they want to continue to be productive, and that, in general, the health status and level of educational attainment of the "young-old" members of the population are sufficient to support such intentions. In the second section of the chapter, the author presents information about traditionally defined productive activity. These data indicate that older people confront a variety of barriers as they seek to lead productive lives, a clear challenge to local and national policy makers. Data on leisure and recreational activities, reported in the chapter's closing section, reveal widespread participation in such forms of personal productivity, although there is a decline with age in participation in those activities that require higher levels of energy and the availability of transportation.

1

Primary Prevention in the Service of Aging

Armin Grams
George W. Albee

There is little disagreement that, at least in the area of human development, preventing problems before they arise is preferable to eliminating them once they have occurred. People concerned with guiding the development of children do whatever they can to remove barriers that impede growth and to encourage the development of self-confidence because they believe that intervention can make a difference in the future life experience of their charges. We see the same belief expressed in educational, vocational, and training programs that we provide, if not mandate, for youth, young adults, and many members of the workforce. Whenever we employ preventive measures designed to help individuals achieve their maximum potential, we practice the principles of primary prevention.

But what about old people? Is there any point in applying these principles to them? Do they still have potential to be realized? In his poem *Rabbi Ben Ezra,* written in 1864, Browning said, "Grow old along with me! / The best is yet to be, / the last of life for which the first was made" (1911, lines 1-3). Did he recognize, well in advance of primary preventionists and gerontologists, that lifestyles adopted in the first half of life play a major role in how the second half unfolds? What do we know about human development that we can apply to the practice of primary prevention in the service of aging? Exploring this question is a goal of this volume.

Aging is an inexorable, lifelong process that, to our present knowledge, cannot be prevented. The only alternative to growing old is dying young, and for most people such an option is unacceptable. How we age, however, is in large part determined by what happens to us, and by what we are able to do about it, in the years that precede the "last of life." In addition, of course, the way we interpret the last act in life's drama and, as a consequence, the way we play our role bear heavily on its outcome for each of us.

We support the notion that successful and productive aging can be the experience of increasing numbers of elders because we hold in common the belief that development across the life span can be managed so that our potential for productive and successful aging is more fully realized. In other words, we believe that the principles of primary prevention are indeed relevant to the experience of aging. In this opening chapter we present a formula for primary prevention (Albee, 1984) that will serve as the framework for our ensuing discussions.

First we define *primary prevention,* with particular attention to the way that it applies to human development in the last period of life. We then illustrate the elements that comprise the primary prevention formula with data derived from the study of aging, and refer, where appropriate, to later chapters that embody extensive elaborations on these matters. Finally, we examine some of the implications of our findings for public policy. We hope in this way to begin to address certain questions that Gatz raises in Chapter 2. This volume breaks new ground by establishing the importance of primary prevention in the field of aging and by suggesting intervention programs that can enhance the quality of life for that significant number of persons who already are old, and for that great company waiting in the wings, whose last act will begin in the early decades of the next century.

Defining Primary Prevention

It is important, at the outset, to be clear about the meaning of the term *primary prevention.* The strategy is to take action in the present with the goal of reducing the incidence of future problems. The term *incidence* means the number of new cases of whatever it is we seek to prevent in the future. It must be clearly understood that incidence reduction is the goal. *Incidence* should not be confused with *prevalence,* the latter term being applied to the total number of cases in the population at a given time. Reducing incidence has the effect of ultimately reducing prevalence, but intervening with treatment for people who are already afflicted with an undesirable condition does nothing to reduce incidence. An example may make this distinction clear. Depression occurs with significant frequency in old people. Treating people currently depressed, though an admirable and humane activity, does little or nothing to reduce the number of new cases of depression. The only way to accomplish the latter is to intervene with groups not yet depressed, but perhaps at high risk, to prevent them from becoming depressed in the future.

Because our goal is to reduce the rate of mental and emotional disorders among older persons or, conversely, to increase their quality of life, it is important that we consider preventive strategies with demonstrated effectiveness in the field of public health.

It has long been clearly understood in public health circles that one-to-one treatment does not reduce the incidence of illness or debilitating conditions; only successful efforts at primary prevention can do so. Treating individual children who had diseases such as diphtheria, polio, and measles did nothing to reduce the incidence of these conditions. But successful efforts at immunization of healthy children before they were affected has had dramatic success in reducing the rate of these conditions.

Effective prevention efforts are frequently addressed to high-risk groups, those who would otherwise have a high likelihood of subsequent affliction. For example, older persons are at greater risk for serious reactions to influenza (flu), so public health strategy urges older groups to have a flu shot in the fall before the influenza virus makes its extended annual appearance. Again, it is clear that individual treatment of flu sufferers does little to reduce the number of new cases but that widespread immunization is effective at reducing incidence.

Although traditionally public health efforts have been directed at the prevention of physical diseases, these strategies have also been used effectively in the prevention of mental and emotional disorders. Briefly, there are three strategies. The first is to *remove or neutralize the noxious agent* or agents responsible for the condition to be prevented. The second is to *strengthen the resistance of the host* to the noxious agent. The third is to *prevent transmission* of the noxious agent to the host. These simple strategies (often difficult to achieve in practice) have had remarkable success in reducing or eliminating many of the great plagues that have afflicted humankind in the past. Efforts at removing or neutralizing toxic agents in the water supply have reduced or eliminated diseases such as cholera, influenza, typhoid, and various forms of diarrhea. Strengthening the resistance of the host through immunization, for example, has eliminated smallpox worldwide. And interrupting transmission of yellow fever and malaria by eliminating the mosquitoes that transmit them has had demonstrable success.

Because our focus is on reducing or eliminating mental and emotional disorders, we can adapt the methods used by the field of public health to prevent physical diseases to our goal of reducing psychopathology in the aged. Here, for example, a noxious agent often is uncontrolled stress. Stress may take several forms, including the stress of loneliness and social isolation, the stress of poverty and associated inadequate housing and health care, and the stress of living in a culture that emphasizes youth and physical attractiveness and rejects older persons who are defined as unattractive and burdensome. Therefore one course of prevention efforts takes the form of stress reduction through programs whose goals are aimed at counteracting these stresses. Strengthening the resistance of older persons to stresses may take the form of improving social skills, fostering better self-esteem, and providing support groups. The third strategy, preventing transmission, may be accomplished by efforts at eliminating cultural messages that lead to ageist, sexist, racist, and other pathological attitudes prevalent in the culture.

Life Span Primary Prevention

A recent major epidemiological study organized by the National Institute of Mental Health (see Regier et al., 1984), involving careful interviews with thousands of adult Americans, found 19% affected by a diagnosable mental condition. This means that a total of one in five adult Americans exhibits a disorder such as alcoholism, drug abuse, depression, anxiety and phobic conditions, or antisocial behavior. The study did not include homeless people or people in institutions like hospitals and nursing homes, who would probably have increased prevalence rates even more. Obviously, the number of professionals available to provide treatment for this vast group is minuscule and will never be sufficient. The only logical answer to dealing with the problem is effective prevention.

A first step in any prevention effort must involve the identification of the problem behaviors to be targeted for reduction. Next, it is necessary to determine the number of people affected by these (preventable) problems, and then to discover the strategies available for reducing their incidence. Finally, these strategies must be evaluated to determine their ongoing effectiveness in reducing the targeted conditions and then modified in response to the findings.

One of the problems in defining the primary prevention of mental and emotional disturbances is that often we cannot be sure of the actual time of onset of an emotional disturbance. It is relatively easy to define the onset of a specific disease like syphilis or strep throat, or the beginning of a discontinuous process like pregnancy or a fractured bone. But when does a person first become emotionally disturbed? Who can point to the moment of onset of schizophrenia, depression, or even Alzheimer's disease? Even abnormal organic mental processes are slow and insidious. When does normal forgetfulness become dementia?

It is clear that we can decide arbitrarily to define *primary prevention* as a program that is instituted before the onset of the condition to be prevented. When the time of onset is unclear and ambiguous, however, primary prevention may blend into early intervention.

Also, the pathology associated with most traditional diseases is, at least temporarily, the exclusive property of the individual affected. Although others may be indirectly affected (often seriously) by the suffering or incapacity of an individual with a physical illness, the actual physical pain associated with arthritis, for example, is not experienced directly by anyone else. But mental and emotional distress is shared by the other parties to one's disturbed interpersonal relationships. People become neurotic or psychotic in significant measure in their relationships with other people. Often, it is the relationships that are disturbed. When do these disturbances begin? Are disturbed relationships with elderly parents a "developmental emergent," or are they likely to be a continuation of the long-standing interaction pattern between parents and offspring? In their investigation of midlife crises, Farrell and Rosenberg (1981) suggested that the negative traits some of their subjects exhibited did not newly emerge in response to their current life situation but were a part of their continuous pattern of adjustment. This is congruent with other reports in the area of human relationships—learned patterns of adjustment are relatively stable across the years (Costa & McCrae, 1980; Tuddenham, 1971). The quality of the interaction between parents and offspring across time is a topic that has received inadequate research attention (Hagestad, 1984; McCrae & Costa, 1984). Yet insofar as the elements of interpersonal behavior, personality traits, and other learned behavior patterns show remarkable consistency over time, we feel safe in suggesting that parent-offspring interaction patterns do not ordinarily change as a function of increased age. Patterns of control, whether on the part of the younger or older individual, are overlearned and persist because, for the most part, they have worked to the benefit of the individual involved. The belief that these idiosyncratic behaviors will change when "the children are grown up and gone" or "when we are on our own" often proves to be cruel illusion. Interestingly, McCrae and Costa (1984) stated that interview studies of parent-child relationships "seem unanimously to suggest that the intrapsychic rate of change by no means keeps pace with the behavioral. Years after moving away from home and taking financial responsibility for themselves, adults often seem curiously tied to the approval and opinions of their parents" (p. 114). Self-serving and demanding old people were probably always that way, and the passage of time does little to alleviate the stress that such characteristics may generate (Brubaker & Brubaker, 1981). Primary prevention of later life adjustment problems appears to be best accomplished by creating early on the settings and circumstances conducive to more effective patterns of adjustment.

Elders at Risk:
Reflections on Selected Demographic,
Environmental, and Societal Changes

Before effective primary prevention programs can be initiated, it is essential to understand how selected demographic, environmental, and societal changes effectively put many elders at risk. In this volume, Simonsick (Chapter 4) makes the point that many older people now are less productive than they would like to be, but that for a host of reasons our society does not provide opportunities for them to participate more fully. This productive loss will, of course, intensify substantially when the "baby boomers" born between 1946 and 1964 reach "retirement age" in the early decades of the next century. Later in this chapter, we underscore the importance to one's mental health of making a significant contribution to one's world, but unless we open new avenues for such participation, we place an enormous number of "new-olds" at risk for "unsuccessful" aging.

The picture is made more complex when the over-65 population is broken down by race and gender. The life expectancy, for example, of migrant farm workers, whose plight is described in searing detail in the report of the President's Commission on Mental Health (1978), is only about two thirds of that for Caucasians in the United States. Life expectancy for women, on the other hand, is on average about 7 years more than for men, so they constitute an ever-increasing proportion of the very old. Because their median income is substantially lower than that of their male counterparts, they are most vulnerable to the financial strain that is the focus of most of Krause's chapter (Chapter 11) in this book. The full complexity of these issues is nicely presented in Gibson's chapter on minority elders (Chapter 15), in that she clearly portrays the triple jeopardy in which many black elderly females find themselves but also focuses our attention on their resourcefulness, their continuing contribution, the resulting recognition they receive, and the appropriate sense of pride and personal worth derived from such activities.

Kramer (1989) introduced a success/failure dilemma in his discussion of a rising pandemic of mental disorders. Advances in medical care (successes) ensure that many more people survive illnesses and live into advanced old age. One result, however (failure), is that the prevalence of chronic mental disturbances and physical diseases increases as the number of very old people at high risk for such conditions grows. These older adult consumers account for a major share of our national health expenditures. Some suggest that these expenses, if unchecked, will pose a serious threat to our nation's standard of living. Kramer submitted that our major hope is research into methods of effective prevention of physical and mental disorders.

A clear demographic shift that has posed interesting challenges for an aging world is continuing urbanization. As young adults and their children migrate to larger population centers in response to the shift from an agrarian to an industrial and, most recently, to an information society, more old people live alone. Although this places some elders at risk, young children of emotionally disturbed parents may be at greater risk, in that there are no surrogate nurturant grandparents to deflect or dilute the damage such parents can inflict. Some elders, left to fend for themselves at a time that they may need the additional support, subject themselves as well as their offspring to increased stress by requiring assistance that is often not within the ability of their daughters or daughters-in-law (who in addition to spouses/partners are the major family caregivers of elders) to provide. Chapter 9 by Chappell and Chapter 14 by Markson elaborate on this "woman in the middle" issue. It is an ironic accompaniment to this increasing need of some elders for assistance from family members that a growing proportion of women occupy paid positions of employment outside the home. The cost of providing effective care for elders, when added, for many families, to the cost of day care for their children, is prompting a reexamination of adult role choices.

It is equally important to recognize, however, that although the nuclear family ordinarily does not allow for the co-residence of three or more generations, this is not necessarily negative. Most elders report that they enjoy their independence from offspring and grandchildren and strive to maintain it as long as they are able. At the same time, this has not led to isolation and loneliness. The myth of abandonment of the old is just that. Shanas (1979) published convincing evidence of continued close ties between generations often despite living in quite disparate locations. Thus both salutary and distressing relationships within families can and do continue in our largely postrural society.

At the same time, we must guard against the growing belief that our increasing population of old people represents a potentially insuperable burden to "the sandwich generation," those caught between the need to provide for their college-age daughters and sons and the need to care for their failing parents. The gerontological literature on caregiving is exploding, and casual perusal of the contents of current journals would support the conclusion that old people are indeed an increasing burden to their families. The attention being given, and appropriately so, to dementias, particularly to Alzheimer's disease, accounts, of course, for this spate of literature. In its wake, it is all too easy to forget that this is not what happens to most old people and their families. Quite to the contrary, a growing but largely unnoticed group of elders is serving as a resource to the younger members of their families. The principal direction of the flow of resources across generations continues to be from the oldest to the younger ones. This view of elders as having strength and resources is essential to the notion of successful and productive aging, and we are well advised not to lose it in our compassion for those who are severely limited.

Unfortunately, implanting such a positive view of elders represents an uphill battle. Ageism, the prejudice against individuals based solely on their being old, is alive and well, and has a substantial head start. The development of mandatory retirement in 19th-century America was spurred by the wide-spread perception of older workers as less efficient and less productive. Efficiency experts joined forces with industrial philosophers to prove that older workers had to be replaced by younger ones. Where pension plans were developed to tide over the newly unemployed older person, they were administered by company executives and often perceived by management as a benevolent gift from industry rather than a right earned by the worker. Such treatment added another negative quality, that of financial dependency, to the common contemporary perception of elders as slow, inefficient, incompetent, and needing to be retired because they were physically incapable of productive work. The situation was as bad if not worse for women. Poverty was widespread among widows and older unmarried females, and their portrayal as the most helpless and needy people in society further established the stereotype of the old as useless and consequently worthless.

A current issue that confronts us today is the impact of the "information highway" on the employment scene as well as on interpersonal relationships both within the family and in the broader spheres of social and political interaction. Just as social and technological changes surface that will permit greater flexibility in work schedules, including the part-time employment for which many elders express a preference, many employers make no effort to retain valuable experienced older workers. Our industrial society has been replaced by an information society, one in which data are urgently needed and thus marketable commodities. The growing volume of information available seems to parallel our burgeoning ability to store and transmit it. Personal computers and modems are transforming our means of interpersonal dialogue. Families in increasing numbers are communicating electronically, and although slower to take advantage of our growing capacity, business and industry are beginning to accommodate to remote workstations that permit individuals to regain family time lost as increasing numbers of family members joined the workforce. How this will affect the interchange of resources between generations is an intriguing question. If we are indeed moving toward a "global village," will we become more like "villagers"?

Only an impractical dreamer would suggest that there is any possibility of returning to the family farm, or, for that matter, to the breadwinner/home-maker model of the industrial society, despite their attractiveness, for some, as a way of life. The factory farm, with its mechanization, its chemical pesticides, its carefully engineered tasteless tomatoes, and its 5 million migrant farm laborers, is far more efficient and more profitable. But is there not some room for creative thinking based on these observations?

One of the best known, and most controversial, industrial psychologists in America is Frederick Herzberg. His research on job satisfaction led him to formulate what he called a "motivation-hygiene theory" of human behavior. Much of this is spelled out in his book *Work and the Nature of Man* (1966). When Herzberg asked people to think back to a time when they were particularly unhappy in their work or their lives, they invariably reported their memories of bad working conditions, low pay, long hours, insensitive bosses—in short, negative work environments, pressures, and discomforts. On the other hand, when people were asked to remember a time in their lives when they especially enjoyed their work, or their life experience, they rarely mentioned things like good pay, good working conditions, and attractive surroundings. Instead, they reported those zestful times when they were doing something they enjoyed, something creative, challenging, and exciting. Solving a problem, doing something well with all of one's might, stands out in people's memory as a source of great satisfaction. From repeated observations of this sort, Herzberg concluded that unpleasant environmental (hygiene) factors can make people miserable but that changing them cannot make people happy. His view is that happiness and satisfaction come from throwing oneself into interesting, challenging, difficult, satisfying tasks (motivator factors) in which one can see that one is making a difference.

What is the relevance of Herzberg's research for our concern about older persons? Simply that we must not only attend to environmental factors, like adequate housing, health care, nutrition, and safety, but also remember that a life worth living is one in which we have some challenges, some goals, and some control over our environment. Research clearly links life satisfaction in old age to living as independently as possible. Like everyone else, elders need to feel that the things they do make a difference. We who are interested in reducing the risk to elders of unproductive aging need to concentrate our attention and our efforts on enhancing the opportunities for older persons, not only to feel secure and safe but also to experience opportunities to feel competent.

In many respects the information society lends itself admirably to this challenge. We are, for example, rediscovering the value of information shared between generations. Many old people are veritable treasure troves in this regard. Although much of the history of their times is, of course, recorded in books, we are warming again to personal histories that add a dimension not found in history books. To be asked to tell one's life story so that it might be captured in writing or on videotape is a powerful tribute to one's self-worth. In a day when stories of the lives of "superstars" clog the media, it is easy to devalue ourselves. Our life experience seems mundane in comparison. Yet introducing elders in an organized way into the lives of children and youth provides an opportunity for such older persons to make a contribution that has genuine significance. The autobiographical resources of people of advanced age are so abundant that they defy depletion. Our challenge is to make them available to succeeding generations.

Unfortunately, in much of the modern world, efforts along these lines do not seem to have high priority. The effective environment of many old people does not provide them opportunity for significant engagement. In his study of factors associated with the quality of life in persons at age 70, Flanagan (1979) and his associates interviewed 500 men and 500 women across the United States. One of the important areas explored, relevant to our present reflections, was the large amount in older persons' lives of *passive recreation* (rather than active involvement). Although some respondents said that reading, radio programs, and listening to music were for them important recreational resources, a great many older people, especially the homebound, indicated major dependence on television for daily entertainment. Flanagan's wry suggestion was that life quality for most Americans would be enhanced by improving the quality of television programs. In general, the media are only rarely kind to older persons. Signorielli (1983) showed the negative way in which older persons are presented and the consequent damaging effects on self-esteem. The portrayal of elders on TV, though gradually improving, perpetuates many myths about aging for viewers, including the aging themselves.

In striking contrast to the negative media stereotypes of old people as incompetent complainers, Flanagan reported that a large proportion of elders are healthy, mobile, socially active, and not at all lacking in lust for life. A full 85%, when asked to look back and assess their lives, reported them to be good or better. At least 70% reported feeling on top of the world often, or at least some of the time. But 15% to 30% were not happy according to their self-report, and this represents a higher degree of dissatisfaction than that found in other age groups. It is quite clear from these studies that wealth and health, rather than age, are major determinants of the quality of life. When correlations were calculated between quality of life and predictors, material wealth and health correlated most highly with overall life quality. Surprisingly, support groups composed of neighbors and friends were more influential than one's own children in determining the felt quality of life.

Flanagan's results, though correct and often replicated, unfortunately overlook the insights provided by Herzberg, who noted how important it was for elders to be zestfully engaged. Health and wealth are indeed correlates of self-reported life satisfaction in old age, but our findings are often compromised to the extent that we fail to include questions about participation in significant endeavors in our homes and communities. The Alameda County California study (Berkman & Syme, 1979) of the association of social networks with lower mortality rates alerted us to this possibility a long time ago. Most healthy elders remain engaged. And from the point of view of personality development, such engagement is the principal avenue for the interchange of competence, talent, and strength with human weakness and need. Future research will be well served by the incorporation of measures of such variables.

A Prevention Schematic and Its Application to the Study of Aging

As we have indicated earlier, some of the fundamental strategies for preventing later psychopathology and reducing the incidence of mental and emotional disorders involve intervention strategies long understood and applied in the field of public health. These strategies can be conceptualized as follows (see Albee, 1982, 1984):

$$\frac{\text{Changing}}{\text{incidence}} = \frac{\text{Debilitating organic conditions} + \text{Stress} + \text{Exploitation}}{\text{Social skills, competence} + \text{Self-esteem} + \text{Support systems}}$$

This schematic attempts to interrelate the elements in primary prevention. As individuals are helped to increase the variables in the denominator and to decrease those in the numerator, we would expect the incidence of disorders to decrease. In other words, to the extent that individuals and society can work together to reduce susceptibility to disease and chronic disorders, to eliminate distress and exploitation, to increase individuals' repertoire of social skills and overall competence, to enhance self-esteem, and to create more formal and informal structures that can provide the social support we all require, they increase the likelihood that people will realize a successful and productive old age. The following portion of this chapter is devoted to a more detailed discussion of each of the six component elements.

The Reduction of Organic Damage and Provision of Health-Promoting Programs

The first strategy is to minimize or reduce various organic factors that can cause problems for elders. Although the focus of this volume is not on preventing specific diseases, it is clear that the deterioration of physical health is often accompanied by serious emotional problems. To be physically incapacitated or handicapped, to be damaged by an inadequate diet, to believe that exercise is dangerous or, if not, to have no access to opportunities for such activities, to be the victim of a physically damaging work environment, or to be lacking adequate iron or calcium as a result of nutritional neglect, to name just a few conditions, results in debilitation that often leads to mental and emotional problems. Clearly, a salutary prevention program would include ensuring a regular and adequate diet, comfortable and safe housing, and a barrier-free and physically safe environment. The importance of preventive health care measures and health promotion for elders is highlighted in the Spring 1994 issue of the journal *Generations*. One contributor, Pearl German (1994), makes it clear in that article and also in Chapter 5 of this book that although prevention and health promotion are not unheard of in the gerontological literature, neither have they received the attention they deserve. Later in this book, both Poehlman (Chapter 6) and Mortimer (Chapter 7) address preventing debilitating organic conditions and their consequences.

One serious but preventable chronic illness in old age is osteoporosis. Because many of the falls so feared by people over age 65 are actually caused by, rather than the cause of, bone fracture, maintaining bone density should be a high priority for adults. The loss of bone density is a universal developmental phenomenon that begins around age 30 and continues at a steady pace for the remainder of life. Early screening can detect individuals who are at risk and allow for counteraction. Poor health habits like smoking and excessive use of alcohol contribute to an individual's vulnerability to excessive loss of bone. Weight-bearing exercise, in which stress is placed on the bone, results in increased calcium content in bone, with the concomitant increased resistance to fracture.

Although it is clear that as a nation we are exercising more than we have in the past, it is a practice seen more among younger than older adults. Some elderly individuals mistakenly believe that due to their frailty they endanger themselves by exercise, yet it is clear that appropriate regular exercise is beneficial throughout the life span. A report from the Mayo Clinic suggests that, as with everything else, there are risks involved that result from exercising "too much, too vigorously, and with too little previous activity," but it is instructive to remember that most heart attacks do not occur during exercise, but rather when the individual is at rest ("Exercise," 1994, p. 3). Just as it is never too late to stop smoking, it is never too late to begin exercising. Taking regular walks is simple and effective, but even people who are not ambulatory or who can walk only a limited amount can profit from health-enhancing forms of bodily exercise. A carefully controlled study of exercise training (Fiatarone et al., 1994) involving 100 frail nursing home residents further supports this view. So valuable is this activity that it has often been said that if the benefits of exercise could be put in a pill, it would be the most widely prescribed medication in the world.

The Reduction of Unnecessary Stress

No longer are simple cause-and-effect relationships clear. Stress takes many forms. Reducing stress may require changes in the social environment and in deeply ingrained cultural values. Loneliness and social isolation are major factors that are subject to prevention efforts. Some groups are far more at risk for stress than others. Flanagan's study revealed that older people with significant wealth and financial security are more likely to report a satisfactory lifestyle than those without economic advantages. Chapter 11 by Krause discusses this in detail. Clearly, an income continuum shows a linear relationship for nearly every type of illness (including mental illness). The same is true for death rates. It is not just the very poor who are at risk, with everyone else doing very well. Interestingly, universal health care, long available in England and also in Canada, does not change this situation (Wolfson, Rowe, Gentleman, & Tomiak, 1993). There is still a linear relationship between social class and rates of both morbidity and mortality. Mirowsky and Ross (1989) showed that 85% of all stress occurs among those below the median level of income. Although stress is caused by a variety of conditions (see also Kimmel, Chapter 16 of this volume), it is still strongly correlated with economic security. In a somewhat broader context, Ikels and her colleagues, in Chapter 17 lend the additional support of cross-cultural research to the important role that health and material well-being play in a satisfying old age.

One stressor deserves particular consideration in a volume dedicated to a better understanding of aging. Lack of knowledge about what will happen in our later years is a significant source of stress. We are all more anxious when we do not understand what is happening to us in the present and what the future holds. For example, one of the benefits of Head Start programs is the reduction of apprehensiveness in both children and their parents about what school will be like. Moreover, we provide orientation programs for individuals entering a variety of different roles or settings. Although some employers provide preretirement programs, and the self-help books are appearing in increasing numbers, we are a long way from helping middle-aged adults to overcome their anxiety about growing old. We know that knowing what to expect significantly allays fears and reduces unnecessary stress, but as with so many other things, we know a lot better than we act.

Exploitation

Exploitation differs from the other components in the schematic in an important way. Variations in the degree or type of exploitation have significant interaction effects with all the other variables in the formula: stress, coping skills, self-esteem, the nature and type of support groups available, and even the incidence of organic factors. For example, in a society in which a power elite exploits the environment for personal profit without regard to the social costs, the incidence of organic conditions may be increased by environmental contamination or malnutrition, further threatening the physical health of older persons. Because exploitation encompasses all the other variables, as well as being something that in itself, with its many faces, contributes to psychopathology, it needs to be considered in both its broader and its specific senses.

Persons who are victims of any form of exploitation often suffer serious emotional damage. The exploitation often involves the use of excessive power by the exploiter to force the victims to conform or to behave in ways that are degrading, demeaning, dehumanizing, and/or dangerous. Although the experience may well be both stressful and damaging to self-esteem, there is a qualitative difference that justifies separate analysis of this factor. There are many subtle ways that people can be subject to daily humiliations.

It is important, when we try to learn about a society, or any other group sharing a common culture, to look as well at things often taken for granted (like gender roles and class position). What are the unquestioned assumptions, the accepted ways of understanding reality, that never rise above the threshold of conscious awareness because no one feels that these can be questioned or examined? In Chapter 3, Hendricks' extensive discussion of institutionalized ageism emphasizes the subtle and pervasive power inherent in the way society constructs the realities of aging. Once accepted, such ageist constructs can oppress victims far more than ageist individuals may do in the course of their interaction with others. Chapter 14 by Markson and Chapter 15 by Gibson provide substantial amplification of this phenomenon in the areas of gender roles and class positions, respectively.

Damage done through exploitation—economic, sexual, media generated—causes increased incidence of emotional pathology. The exploited groups are not responsive to exhortations or to other quick-fix solutions. Certain types of exploitation result in low self-esteem and become a kind of self-fulfilling prophecy. Older members of ethnic minorities, women, and elders in general learn from childhood that their condition or characteristics are regarded as inferior by the dominant youthful culture. They suffer loss of self-esteem that may be exceedingly difficult to change. Feelings of powerlessness are a major form of stress. Intervention here, as we will suggest in the conclusion of this chapter, may have to take the form of laws to ensure equal opportunity, public education, changes in the way the mass media portray these groups, and pervasive value system changes.

Because many elders are vulnerable in a dangerous society, they are common victims of exploitation. Of those who live alone, many live in fear of attack, behind barred doors. They are subject to endless types of fraud. A few examples from a depressingly long list provided by Barrow and Smith (1992) are mail order products promising magical ways to maintain health and overcome common chronic diseases, door-to-door sales of shoddy repairs, and especially expensive cancer cures that tempt the desperate. On the other hand, those who live with children or other relatives may suffer abuse and/or neglect. Clearly, the number of elders at risk for exploitation by the unscrupulous is very great and growing. To reduce the rate of such exploitation must be a target for primary prevention of emotional disorders among persons of advanced age.

Having concluded our discussion of the three categories of variables that reduce the likelihood that individuals will experience successful and productive aging, let us consider the factors in the denominator of the formula given earlier, namely, three areas in which preventive efforts can serve to *strengthen the resistance of the host.* Because there is increased variance in the observed performance of elders on a wide array of tasks, attainment of successful and productive aging involves efforts to enhance competency so that individuals may realize more fully their potential for continued growth and development in what in France is known as the "third age."

Social Skills and Competence Training

Just as learning about what to expect as one ages can reduce stress and anxiety, learning how to deal more effectively with age-related changes in ourselves and our surroundings adds to the resources that we bring to our "third age." There are clear universal changes that occur with aging—among them, changes in body composition, loss of reserve capacity, and loss of efficiency in response to stress. Differing degrees of decline in various organ systems begin rather insidiously after age 30 and change steadily across the ensuing years. Fortunately, for many reasons, most individuals are untroubled by these alterations because people are often comfortable with the adaptations that they make to accommodate the changes. Enhancing competence and skill in the face of inevitable changes requires more than acquiescence, however. Successful adaptation involves a number of processes that permit aging individuals to maintain a sense of personal integrity and dignity. Baltes and Baltes (1990) suggested that selection, optimization, and compensation are three such processes. They combined selective disengagement with channeled and focused activity within the broad limits of the potential revealed in the variance that studies of "usual" aging (namely, normative research) report. Dixon develops the concept of compensation at some length in Chapter 12. What we confront, then, is the challenge to accept limitations beyond our ability to affect, while dedicating continuing effort to maintain and even to improve performance in arenas still open to us. To paraphrase the well-known supplication, we need the serenity to accept those things that we cannot change, the courage to change what we can, and the wisdom to know the difference.

At the age of 85, Malcolm Cowley (1985), the distinguished journalist, urged his compatriots to learn gracefully to accept help whenever it is offered. An equally important corollary skill that men, in particular, are well advised to cultivate in the middle and later years is to ask for help as well. Unfortunately, this is difficult for many individuals who have bought into the notion that "grown-ups" are people who can "stand on their own two feet and make it by themselves." Yet learning to ask for help from others and to accept it when it is offered does not indicate immaturity and weakness, but rather testifies to our understanding of our true nature as human beings— namely, our interdependence.

Of all the important social skills that we acquire over the life course, competence in balancing our strengths and weaknesses at different times and under differing circumstances is truly crucial. Human development does not proceed from dependency in infancy to independence in adulthood, but rather consists of appropriately juxtaposing these essential elements of human relations across the life span. Admitting to weakness, admitting that we do not know something and that consequently we need help, fosters social interchange. It provides others with an opportunity to make a contribution, to use their strength and "know-how" on our behalf. By the same token, continuing to hone our strengths and cultivate skills and abilities provides us with a ready supply of resources to draw on in contributing to the needs of others. Without a clear appreciation of the importance of this reciprocal arrangement, we may see no reason to pursue further competence training (selective optimization) and dread unduly allowing others to help in those areas where we have chosen to withdraw and disengage.

To this end, primary *intervention* calls for the support of programs designed to stimulate and challenge those abilities that aging individuals elect to sharpen and those interests that they wish to pursue. Opportunities for socialization sufficiently inviting to engage elders contribute to the prevention of loneliness and accompanying depression—conditions that are not endemic to aging, but whose prevalence is greater than ordinarily acknowledged. Many community organizations provide opportunities for elders to socialize, to participate in group recreational pursuits and exercise, and to volunteer their time and talents in a variety of service activities. Such programs can reflect the variety of social skills and needs that elders possess and can incorporate further learning opportunities and training as needed. Among those with particular promise are the many educational opportunities for older people that are beginning to emerge. Elderhostel, one of the best known, combines exposure to outstanding teachers with travel, recreation, and socialization. Many colleges and universities are developing institutes for more serious educational pursuits on their campuses and are experiencing a substantial increase in the number of old people enrolling in regular course work, certification, or degree programs. But there are also less ambitious programs that teach people who can no longer drive to use public transportation, to budget, to shop wisely for food and clothing, and to organize the physical and social environment to minimize problems. A book by Skinner and Vaughan (1983), *Enjoy Old Age*, is full of suggestions for improving the competence and social skills of older persons.

Self-Esteem

The development of competence is, of course, closely linked to one's feelings of worth and value, which are, in turn, important components of self-esteem. The relationship, of course, is not perfect. There will always be a few highly accomplished individuals who suffer low self-esteem, who view themselves as failures because they have not lived up to their self-imposed standards of excellence. ("I used to be a perfectionist, but I gave it up. I wasn't good enough at it.") If this book is to contribute to promoting successful and productive aging, we probably cannot overemphasize the importance of the development of competencies and the correlative growth of one's sense of personal worth.

For most individuals, productivity must be recognized and acknowledged in order to contribute to self-esteem. There are very few Emily Dickinsons in the world whose productive output can continue unabated without the reinforcement of public acceptance and acclaim. One obvious reason that older people may experience difficulty in maintaining their self-esteem is that the role of contributing members of society becomes progressively more difficult to play. Even if one has all the competence in the world, if it has no outlet, it will gradually "die on the vine." The ubiquitous "needs assessments" carried out by countless agencies dedicated to the well-being of elders consistently validate the notion that older people are in need of assistance that compassionate younger people can define and provide. Very few such interview schedules question elders about their competencies. The concept of need has been that of weakness, infirmity, and incompetence. The need of people of advanced age to be "needed" has been for the most part overlooked. Yet a major component of life satisfaction is the sense that one is contributing something of significance to one's world. If productive aging is to become widespread, bona fide opportunities to use one's talents in ways that benefit others are essential, and elders must be seen as resources to be accessed to meet such opportunities.

The failure to see elders as resources can be variously illustrated. The many skilled blue-collar as well as white-collar employees who are being encouraged to opt for early retirement represent a large and growing pool of talent that our society can ill afford to ignore. Technical and vocational schools, small businesses, and day care facilities for people of all ages represent just a few of the available arenas where their particular gifts could be utilized. A few imaginative employers, recognizing the costly loss of such productive individuals, are turning to retired workers when they are in need of temporary employees. The Service Corps of Retired Executives (SCORE) offers significant assistance to individuals struggling to found and nurture new enterprises in many different fields. An example close to home for many of our readers would be the virtual disregard of retired faculty and administrative officers at colleges and universities. Only very recently have such institutions begun to study how they might tap the potential that continues to reside in that retired population. Although it is true that some of these individuals, for a host of reasons, have no desire to continue to use what talent they have in the service of educational institutions, continued involvement of those who do could benefit students and younger colleagues and prove profitable to older academics in many respects, not the least of which would be financial rewards, still considered in many societies to be the requisite symbol of importance and value. This last suggestion is important because there is a prevalent view that elders are an important source of volunteer effort. Indeed, a substantial portion of Chapter 13, by Moen, deals with the role of volunteering in the lives of elders. And elders do indeed constitute a formidable army in service to their communities. Opportunities such as these are also important sources of self-esteem, especially when the true talents of the volunteer are matched with the work to be done. When this does not occur, many rightly feel that the jobs they are asked to perform, rather than being self-enhancing, are a bit demeaning. Basically, what is most important here is not the form of compensation but a genuine recognition of the older people as individuals who can contribute importantly to the well-being of others and thus to their own sense of self-esteem.

Another important source of positive self-evaluation is the extent to which we feel in control of our lives. For whatever reason, persons who feel powerless, who feel that their life is merely happening to them, are vulnerable to psychologically unhealthy conclusions about themselves. Yet a study by Langer and Rodin (1976) of quite frail and physically limited elders demonstrated how encouraging personal decision making can counteract such feelings of helplessness, enhance self-concept, and restore a healthier sense of worth. Although this experiment was set in a nursing home, people who reside in the community are not immune from self-devaluation when they experience a substantial insult to their sense of competence. Nor is this just the case with older people. Studies of the experiences of families during the Depression years of the early 1930s document the loss of self-esteem on the part of breadwinner fathers subsequent to being laid off (Elder, 1974). To complicate matters further, these men tended to fault themselves for their failure, an opinion that came unfortunately to be shared by their families.

All that will be said in this volume about productive activity and competence must ultimately lead to a consideration of what happens as a host of biopsychosocial processes gradually converge to reduce such sources of feelings of well-being and self-esteem. Is it possible to maintain a positive self-image in the face of gradually diminishing instrumental capacity, particularly in advanced old age? Our position is congruent with that advanced by Dixon in Chapter 12 of this volume: Compensation is a psychologically sound way to promote competence and support productive aging.

Making a distinction between primary and secondary ways of remaining in control (Schulz, 1986) is helpful here. For the most part healthy adults exercise the former in their lives. They make decisions and carry them out. They are "doers" who deal effectively with their environment. They take appropriate pride in being "in charge." As most realistic adults also realize, however, this is not without cost. Such responsible behavior requires considerable energy expenditure, is often accompanied by heightened tension, and can be draining. Yet many are loath to relinquish such primary control for fear that they will suffer loss of status and consequently an increased sense of personal inadequacy. We are all acquainted with individuals who have clung tenaciously to power at considerable expense to themselves and others. Schulz suggests that primary control probably peaks between ages 50 and 60, at which point one's compensatory secondary control grows to replace primary and continues to provide a healthy sense of personal power. Whereas in primary control we say, "I'm in charge, I directly control what is happening," in secondary control we retain a sense of power because we have made the arrangements needed so that we can say, "Things are under control."

Brim (1992) provided a beautiful illustration of how self-esteem can be preserved in the face of growing infirmity. He described what Baltes and Baltes (1990) called selective optimization with compensation by recounting how his father, a retired academician, selectively reduced, over a very long retirement life, his effective environment. From caring, at first, for an extensive piece of rural property, he continued to preserve his sense of responsible stewardship for decades by systematically reducing the area of his "tending" to fewer fields and smaller gardens until it encompassed a single window box. Productive and successful aging at its best!

Social Support

We now proceed to social support, the last element in our prevention schematic. This transition is handily illustrated in Chapter 8 by Zautra and his colleagues. In discussing the importance to elders' mental health of being able to maintain control and autonomy, they make a particular point of examining the role of the social network in this process.

Given our interdependent nature, it should come as no surprise that individuals who are enmeshed in social relationships tend, on average, to live longer than those who have few if any friends. The salutary consequences of living in community are evident in a number of ways. For example, old people who live with a partner report higher life satisfaction than other older persons. Because it is the wife who most often orchestrates their social and community involvement, recently widowed men are, at least temporarily, at sea. The fact that they tend to remarry with far greater frequency than widows is probably not unrelated to their desire to, among other things, restore their social support. The fact that older persons who have never married are almost equally high in self-reported life satisfaction is an additional interesting commentary on the importance of social support. Certainly a reasonable explanation of this apparent contradiction is that single individuals cultivate over a lifetime a network of friends and acquaintances that serves to provide them with many of the same psychological benefits that married couples derive from their companionship. Although much of the above is based on studies of heterosexual couples, we are aware that individuals with a homosexual orientation have similar need for and experience with social support. In Chapter 16, Kimmel asserts that older gay people report levels of life satisfaction comparable to those of people whose orientation is reported as heterosexual. Drawing extensively on his own research, he underscores the importance of, among other things, a network of social support for older lesbians and gay men (Kimmel, Raphael, Catalano, & Robinson, 1984).

Although most life satisfaction studies are subject to criticism because they utilize self-report data, the follow-up study of older people in Alameda County, California (Berkman & Syme, 1979), as mentioned earlier, established a direct relationship between the presence of a social support network in the lives of the subjects and their mortality rate. People who had both informal and formal ties to other individuals and to community organizations outlived whose who did not. Although the underlying mechanism here is not entirely clear, it seems safe to suggest that being a part of groups provides a support network that aids the individual to resist stress and other noxious agents. These findings underscore the importance for older people of a sense of belonging, whether to a family or to a special group or community.

Facilitating the establishment of interpersonal, organizational, and societal forms of social support for elders is perhaps the most important of all forms of primary intervention in the promotion of successful and productive aging.

Earlier in this chapter we discussed the extensive life span support that family members provide to each other. Because recently so much attention has focused on the strains of coping with elders suffering from dementia, we feel obliged once more to emphasize the fact that much social support in the family continues to flow from the oldest generation downward. These same old people who jealously guard their independence by maintaining their own homes and private lives are also guardians of their family's cohesiveness (Troll, 1983) and willingly lend to younger members what help they can where needed to smooth the way. However, given the persisting stereotypes of frail, dependent elders, it is not surprising that there has been little empirical research reported about the contributions that they continue to make to their offspring and others (Morgan, Schuster, & Butler, 1991). This latter cross-sectional study failed to find any significant crossover effect in social support (where help received exceeded help given) in samples younger than 85 years of age. What they did find was an age-associated decline in both help given and help received. Similar findings were reported by Depner and Ingersoll-Dayton (1988), who suggested that the former decline may be more a function of lack of opportunity than lack of resources. They recommended that as the need for old people to provide support for members of their immediate family declines, we take steps to create additional outlets for older adults to contribute to society.

The decline in reported help received may reflect the disinclination of many people to admit dependence and their corresponding effort to appear self-sufficient. Because it may be somewhat easier for people to accept help when they are confronted with more serious problems such as divorce and substance abuse, we would expect that, under such circumstances, parents of advanced age would be asked for assistance by their sons, daughters, and grandchildren. Indeed, this is what Greenberg and Becker (1988) reported. Although they recommended that their work be replicated with a larger, more representative sample, they made a strong case in challenging gerontologists to study the ways that elders serve as family resources, particularly when their offspring experience substantial stress.

Obviously the ability and opportunity to make such a contribution to younger family members is a significant component in successful and productive aging. Families in which the recognition of our mutual need for assistance is comfortably acknowledged are strongholds of mental health. They provide the two basic elements of human complementarity: strength and weakness. These two elements can also be called resources and needs, or can be referred to as competence and the opportunity for its utilization.

This reciprocity in family social support alerts us to another consideration that bears on successful and productive aging: the important distinction between caring about people and caring for them. We referred above to the desire of most people of advanced age to live independently in the community. Generally, offspring and other family members who care *about* them support that decision. When, however, chronic illness, increasing frailty, or the death of an elder companion intervenes, the inclination of family to care *for* them grows. The balance between "caring about" that involves trusting the older person's judgment and "caring for" by taking over decision-making responsibility for the elder is often a precarious one. Well-meaning people with the best of intentions can unwittingly contribute to the erosion of the sense of control so crucial to the maintenance of self-esteem. Overkill in "caring for" can rapidly reduce anyone's level of competence. The corrosive effect of learned helplessness is amply demonstrated in the often precipitous decline seen in individuals who are transplanted from risky independent community residence to the shelter of an institutional setting. Frequently, truly caring about someone requires that we do not care for them. Although such a choice can be a bit scary for the caring offspring, and can, of course, be reviewed over time, it is a decision congruent with the best principles of primary intervention aimed at fostering successful and productive aging.

But the family is not the sole source of social support available to individuals. Indeed, it never was. The notion that organizational and societal support has emerged in relatively recent history largely in response to families "abandoning" their responsibilities is based not in fact but rather on a nostalgic, romanticized view of "the way things were." Organizations like the Grange in rural communities, the Policemen's Benevolent Societies in cities, and similar fraternal organizations that came to the aid of widows, orphans, and other persons and groups in need were already significant sources of support in this country in the 19th century. Churches, mosques, synagogues, auxiliaries, civic organizations, and community support groups have through the years provided the opportunity for the strengths of some individuals to find an outlet in service to others. Many such organizations sponsor support groups that figure importantly in the ability of persons under stress to cope successfully. Diet and exercise, bereavement support, and widow-to-widow programs are but a few examples of services designed to meet the needs of particular groups. At the same time, home-delivered meals and visitation programs for home-bound individuals make significant use of the talents of more successful and productive volunteers.

Both Chapter 9 by Chappell and Chapter 10 by Smyer make extensive contributions to this discussion. Some, but not all, of the programs we refer to above are formally organized by their community sponsors. Many, however, resemble the community care with informal support that Chappell refers to as a major component in the Canadian health care system. Smyer reminds us of the heterogeneity of old people that calls for diverse forms of support, and points to such formal systems as continuing care retirement communities that in one location attempt to provide a wide variety of forms of social support as illustrations worth further study. Although Chappell advises caution as we move toward the development of public policy to ensure an aging citizenry's adequate support, we will argue next that there are some policies already in place that can serve as models in this regard.

Beyond family networks and community organizations, there is a place for support programs provided by agencies of the federal, state, and local governments. The provision of appropriate social support is so critical a component in the healthy development of its citizenry that governments failing to ensure it do so at their peril. Unfortunately, the United States has lagged far behind other developed countries in assuring its people such benefits. The enactment of Social Security in 1935 was indeed a step of monumental importance, and the system still serves as a model of efficiency and cost-effectiveness to this day. Thirty years elapsed, however, before any further federal social policy measures designed to support older individuals were adopted. The passage of the Older Americans Act in 1965 was heralded as an important new beginning, but through its many subsequent revisions and its failure to keep pace with the growing needs of those whom it was designed to serve, it pales as social policy in comparison to the enactment of Titles XVIII and XIX of the Social Security Act (Medicare and Medicaid, respectively). The fate of the Older Americans Act is not incongruent, however, with our current health and welfare policy priorities. All the preventive programs that might assist elders to avoid or postpone encroaching disabilities are found in Title III—Grants for State and Community Programs on Aging. And this title, along with the act in general, has historically been underfunded and is the consistent target of budget-cutting programs. Medicare, on the other hand, was established on a fee-for-service basis, and thus encourages and rewards services designed to "treat" and to "cure" once the individual has become acutely ill or incapacitated. For preventive health services, it provides next to no support.

The Age Discrimination in Employment Act (ADEA) does represent a step in the right direction. By prohibiting the utilization of age as a criterion of eligibility for employment, it guarantees important rights to persons who wish to continue to utilize their capacities by engaging in gainful employment. Although the term *productive aging* does not signify productivity in the workplace in the usual sense, it certainly does not exclude that possibility. The ADEA is an example of the sort of public policy that informed and responsible public officials must continue to fashion if we as a society are to fulfill our commitment to elders so eloquently articulated in the Declaration of Objectives (Title I) of the Older Americans Act (see Appendix A).

Educational and Mandated Prevention Programs

The above illustrations of how the prevention model can be adapted to the field of gerontology serve to emphasize that preparation for successful aging is a lifelong process. They also remind us that there are two quite different approaches to primary prevention. We can ask and encourage people to change their lifestyle, and sometimes they do. Or we can pass laws requiring changes. Educating people about the dangers of tobacco has lowered consumption; mandating higher taxes on tobacco products or forbidding smoking in public places yields similar results. Educational programs encourage people to assume responsibility for their own health care. Although compliance with such recommendations is, of course, less than perfect, providing people with information about maintaining and enhancing their health can have widespread, positive results. In contrast, mandated programs often involve legislative or regulatory action designed to benefit entire populations. The above mentioned ADEA is an example of a federal mandate aimed at preventing the exploitation of older workers; the nearly universal coverage under Social Security is another.

In a major review of the primary prevention literature over a decade, Cowen (1986) divided prevention strategies into those that occur at a *systems level* (often mandated) and those that are *person centered* (usually voluntary/ educational). He suggested that *systems-level* strategies basically seek to empower those who are socially disadvantaged. These approaches involve social action, social reform, and policy changes that are based on concepts such as universal justice and equal opportunity. Not surprisingly, these *system-change* approaches are frequently opposed by powerful political groups that support the established order of things. The suggestion, for example, that older women need to be empowered to reduce their risk for depression often elicits extreme positions among groups favoring or opposing social changes in the status of women. So do programs that reduce the exploitation of older persons or that provide for protection against involuntary unemployment. Yet, as Cowen noted, many leaders in the field of primary prevention believe that empowerment is the essential strategy. Much of this thinking is based on the work of a South African physician, John Cassel, who later became a leader in the public health movement in the United States. Cassel took the position that a major factor in producing both physical illness and psychological disorder is social marginality. Cassel (1976) accumulated and reported extensive evidence to support his view that persons who are socially isolated and marginal in their society are at high risk for a variety of disturbances. His solution: to work toward the elimination of social marginality through political action and social change.

Obviously this is a much more controversial strategy than prevention programs that work within the existing social order. Cowen reviewed a number of examples of systems-level strategy changes, including attempts at building "competent communities." Recent regulations requiring that individuals, upon admission to hospitals and long-term care institutions, be informed of their right to implement "advance directives" represent such strategy changes. If the person already has documents such as a living will or durable power of attorney for health care, copies and other appropriate notes are placed in the file. If not, and they wish to, individuals may specify what should or should not be done in the event that they are later not in a position to make such judgments. This is clearly a strategy that empowers individuals and that by establishing such secondary controls enhances their sense of dignity and worth. These, then, are important systems-level strategies that we as a concerned community, rapidly growing older, must continue to support, implement, and augment.

Cowen's second area for prevention programming he called *person-centered* strategies. The first type of person-centered intervention strategy relates certain stressful life situations and events to subsequent psychological problems. Here efforts are developed to intervene with people who are likely to experience such negative life events in order to forestall their probable negative psychological consequences. This is a clear example of an educational endeavor, and we will return to this important and widely applied method of intervention shortly. Actually, most of the prevention programs mentioned in the extensive review by Buckner, Trickett, and Course (1985) are educational and voluntary in content. Because our traditions strongly support autonomy and free choice, this should not surprise us. Also, not surprisingly, because choice is involved, such prevention programs are not as effective as one might wish. It is possible, of course, that in the future important educational efforts may be imposed on us, just as certain public health practices are. Over the objections of a few iconoclasts, we steadfastly maintain compulsory vaccination, fluoridation of water supplies, and restrictions on smoking. A more controversial mandate in the future might include raising the age of eligibility for Social Security in the next century, beyond the current approved age of 67 to age 70 or beyond. Another might be restrictions on demeaning stereotypic representation of older persons in the media.

A second type of person-centered strategy is aimed at developing competencies and skills in unaffected people to strengthen their capacity for adapting to stressful events. Cowan called these *competency-enhancing* approaches. Obviously, we will want to do all we can to reduce the likelihood of stressful life events (eliminating noxious elements), but in the current context, we will want to make every effort to give individuals coping skills so that they can deal more effectively with such stressful events (strengthening the host). Not uncommon in the life experiences of elders are burdening demands that can extract a heavy toll. Having to care for a spouse or partner who is becoming increasingly demented, witnessing the dissolving marriage and subsequent divorce of one's daughter or son, losing a loved one in death, suffering inexorable impoverishment, and being ill and hospitalized are situations that lend themselves to preventive intervention. Individuals can learn skills that make living with a person who is cognitively impaired more bearable, and in the case of offspring with partner problems, they can learn how to listen sympathetically and avoid being judgmental.

There is considerable evidence that the trauma of hospitalization and surgery has both short-term and long-term negative consequences on people. Cowen reviewed a variety of work that has led to the development, in many hospitals, of preventive measures for people headed for hospitalization and surgery. Orientation hospital tours and opportunities for them to talk with others in the hospital, an opportunity to talk over fantasies with a sympathetic social group worker, providing unlimited visiting hours for the relatives, and so forth have been demonstrated to reduce the damaging consequences of the stress of hospitalization. Similar stress reduction methods apply to a wide variety of comparable situations. Some stress situations are not acute crises (like hospitalization) but are more chronic and continuing. One effective preventive program taught highly stressed and impoverished widows life coping and stress management skills, simultaneously providing psychological support and improved self-concepts (Tableman, Marciniak, Johnson, & Rodgers, 1982). The bottom line is clear: Wherever possible, provide opportunities for people to develop skills, to become more competent, to acquire a better understanding of self and others, and thereby to sense the accompanying empowerment.

One of the most effective preparations for a successful and productive old age is enhanced understanding that the course of human development in later life is in large part a continuation of its course during earlier years. Much of what has been said about reducing the effects of noxious elements, stress, and exploitation has equal validity at any point in the life span. Just as the increasing life expectancy we witness today is first and foremost a result of a much greater number of individuals outliving childhood, namely, benefiting from improved sanitation and immunization against the killer diseases of the past, so do opportunities for continuing one's education to enhance one's competence, the establishment of social support systems, and the adoption of a healthy lifestyle serve as effective preparations for one's older years. Although intervention even in advanced old age can make important differences in how we will experience what remains of life, clearly the sooner both person-centered and systems-level programs are initiated, the better for all concerned.

It should come as no surprise that, as suggested earlier, morbidity and mortality are correlated with socioeconomic status, educational attainment, and "zestful engagement" with one's world. Individuals who better understand what makes for more successful and productive aging, and are in a position to capitalize on such knowledge, are at a distinct advantage. The continuing development of competence broadens our coping repertory and permits us to select from a wider range of options when some of the losses of aging deprive us of certain others. Retirement experiences illustrate this quite well. Persons with numerous interests and many different skills and abilities cultivated over their lifetime are at much less risk of boredom, feelings of uselessness, and their possible depressive consequences. Individuals with good "people skills" are at some advantage when deprived of long-time companions and confidants. Those with sufficient self-esteem to be able to follow Malcolm Cowley's (1985, p. 58) advice to "accept, accept, accept" have a leg up on those who dread the possible devaluation by others that they believe open admission of some incompetence would bring.

It has been suggested that "old age is not for sissies." We agree, but insist that strengthening the resistance of the host by implementing effective person-centered strategies and by supporting sound existing public policy and evolving new mandated programs as needed is an approach to old age that can bring out the best in us all.

References

Albee, G. W. (1982). Preventing psychopathology and promoting human potential. *American Psychologist, 37,* 1043-1057.

Albee, G. W. (1984). Prologue: A model for classifying prevention programs. In J. M. Joffe, G. W. Albee, & L. M. Kelly (Eds.), *Readings in primary prevention of psychopathology* (pp. viii-xviii). Hanover, NH: University Press of New England.

Baltes, P. B., & Baltes, M. M. (1990). Psychological perspectives on successful aging: The model with selective optimization and compensation. In P. B. Baltes & M. M. Baltes (Eds.), *Successful aging: Perspectives from the behavioral sciences* (pp. 1-34). Cambridge, UK: Cambridge University Press.

Barrow, G. M., & Smith, P. A. (1992). The aged as victims. In *Aging, the individual, and society* (2nd ed., pp. 297-323). St. Paul, MN: West.

Berkman, L. F., & Syme, S. L. (1979). Social networks, host resistance, and mortality: A nine-year follow-up study of Alameda County residents. *American Journal of Epidemiology, 109,* 186-204.

Brim, O. G. (1992). *Ambition.* New York: Basic Books.

Browning, R. (1911). *Rabbi Ben Ezra.* Philadelphia: D. McKay.

Brubaker, T. H., & Brubaker, E. (1981). Adult child and elderly parent household: Issues in stress for theory and practice. *Alternative Lifestyles, 4,* 242-256.

Buckner, J. C., Trickett, E. J., & Course, S. J. (1985). *Primary prevention in mental health: An annotated bibliography* (DHHS Publication No. ADM 85-1405). Washington, DC: Government Printing Office.

Cassel, J. (1976). The contribution of the social environment to host resistance. *American Journal of Epidemiology, 104,* 107-123.

Costa, P. T., Jr., & McCrae, R. R. (1980). Still stable after all these years: Personality as a key to some issues in adulthood and old age. In P. B. Baltes & O. G. Brim, Jr. (Eds.), *Life-span development and behavior* (Vol. 3, pp. 65-102). New York: Academic Press.

Cowen, E. L. (1986). Primary prevention in mental health: Ten years of retrospect and ten years of prospect. In M. Kessler & S. E. Goldston (Eds.), *A decade of progress in primary prevention* (pp. 3-45). Hanover, NH: University Press of New England.

Cowley, M. (1985, May 26). Being old. *New York Times Magazine,* p. 58.

Depner, E. E., & Ingersoll-Dayton, B. (1988). Supportive relationships in later life. *Psychology and Aging, 3,* 348-357.

Elder, G. H., Jr. (1974). *Children of the Great Depression.* Chicago: University of Chicago Press.

Exercise: Are the risks underplayed and the benefits overdone? (1994). *Mayo Clinic Health Letter, 12*(6), 1-3.

Farrell, M. P., & Rosenberg, S. D. (1981). *Men at midlife.* Boston: Auburn House.

Fiatarone, M. A., O'Neill, E. F., Ryan, N. D., Clements, K. M., Solares, G. R., Nelson, M. E., Roberts, S. B., Kehayias, J. J., Lipsitz, L. A., & Evans, W. J. (1994). Exercise training and nutritional supplementation for physical frailty in very elderly people. *New England Journal of Medicine, 330,* 1769-1775.

Flanagan, J. C. (1979). *Identifying opportunities for improving the quality of life of older age groups.* Final report submitted to the Administration on Aging. Palo Alto: American Institutes for Research.

German, P. S. (1994). The meaning of prevention for older people: Changing common perceptions. *Generations, 18*(1), 28-32.

Greenberg, J. S., & Becker, M. (1988). Aging parents as family resources. *The Gerontologist, 28,* 786-791.

Hagestad, G. O. (1984). The continuous bond: A dynamic multigenerational perspective on parent-child relations. *Minnesota Symposium on Child Psychology, 17,* 129-158.

Herzberg, F. (1966). *Work and the nature of man.* New York: Thomas Y. Crowell.

Kimmel, D., Raphael, S., Catalano, D., & Robinson, M. (1984). Gerontology: Older lesbians and gay men. In F. H. Schwaber & M. Shernoff (Eds.), *Sourcebook on lesbian/gay healthcare* (pp. 69-72). New York: National Gay Health Education Foundation, Inc.

Kramer, M. (1989). Barriers to prevention. In B. Cooper & T. Helgason (Eds.), *Epidemiology and the prevention of mental disorders* (pp. 30-55). London: Routledge.

Langer, E. J., & Rodin, J. (1976). The effects of choice and enhanced personal responsibility for the aged: A field experiment in an institutionalized setting. *Journal of Personality and Social Psychology, 34,* 191-198.

McCrae, R. R., & Costa, P. T., Jr. (1984). *Emerging lives, enduring dispositions: Personality in adulthood.* Boston: Little, Brown.

Mirowsky, J., & Ross, C. E. (1989). *Social causes of psychological distress.* New York: Aldine.

Morgan, D. L., Schuster, T. L., & Butler, E. W. (1991). Role reversals in the exchange of social support. *Journal of Gerontology: Social Sciences, 46,* S278-S287.

President's Commission on Mental Health. (1978). *Report to the President.* Washington, DC: Government Printing Office.

Regier, D. A., Myers, J. K., Kramer, M., Robins, L. N., Blazer, D. G., Hough, R. I., Eaton, W. W., & Locke, B. Z. (1984). The NIMH epidemiological catchment area program. *Archives of General Psychiatry, 41,* 934-941.

Schulz, R. (1986). Successful aging: Balancing primary and secondary control. *Adult Development and Aging News: Newsletter of Division 20, American Psychological Association, 13*(3), 2-5.

Shanas, E. (1979). Social myth as hypothesis: The case of the family relationships of old people. *The Gerontologist, 19,* 3-9.

Signorielli, N. (1983). Health, prevention, and television: Images of the elderly and perceptions of social reality. In S. Simson, L. B. Wilson, J. Hermalin, & E. R. Hess (Eds.), *Aging and prevention* (pp. 97-117). New York: Haworth.

Skinner, B. F., & Vaughan, M. E. (1983). *Enjoy old age: A program of self management.* New York: Norton.

Tableman, B., Marciniak, D., Johnson, D., & Rodgers, R. (1982). Stress management training for women on public assistance. *American Journal of Community Psychology, 10*(3), 333-345.

Troll, L. E. (1983). Grandparents: The family watchdogs. In T. Brubaker (Ed.), *Family relationship in later life* (pp. 63-76). Beverly Hills, CA: Sage.

Tuddenham, R. D. (1971). The constancy of personality ratings over two decades. In M. C. Jones, N. Bayley, J. W. McFarlane, & M. P. Honzik (Eds.), *The course of human development* (pp. 395-403). Waltham, MA: Xerox College Publishing.

Wolfson, M., Rowe, G., Gentleman, J. F., & Tomiak, M. (1993). Career earnings and death: A longitudinal analysis of older Canadian men. *Journal of Gerontology: Social Sciences, 48,* S167-S179.

Appendix A

Older Americans Act of 1965 (Public Law 89-73)

AN ACT To provide assistance in the development of new or improved programs to help older persons through grants to the States for community planning and services and for training, through research, development, or training project grants, and to establish within the Department of Health, Education, and Welfare an operating agency to be designated as the "Administration on Aging".

Be it enacted by the Senate and House of Representatives of the United States of America in Congress assembled, That this Act may be cited as the "Older Americans Act of 1965".

(42 U.S.C. 3001 note)

TITLE 1—DECLARATION OF OBJECTIVES; DEFINITIONS

DECLARATION OF OBJECTIVES FOR OLDER AMERICANS

SEC. 101. The Congress hereby finds and declares that, in keeping with the traditional American concept of the inherent dignity of the individual in our democratic society, the older people of our Nation are entitled to, and it is the joint and several duty and responsibility of the governments of the United States, of the several States and their political subdivisions, and of Indian tribes to assist our older people to secure equal opportunity to the full and free enjoyment of the following objectives:

(1) An adequate income in retirement in accordance with the American standard of living.

(2) The best possible physical and mental health which science can make available and without regard to economic status.

(3) Obtaining and maintaining suitable housing, independently selected, designed and located with reference to special needs and available at costs which older citizens can afford.

(4) Full restorative services for those who require institutional care, and a comprehensive array of community-based, long-term care services adequate to appropriately sustain older people in their communities and in their homes, including support to family members and other persons

providing voluntary care to older individuals and needing long-term care services.

(5) Opportunity for employment with no discriminatory personnel practices because of age.

(6) Retirement in health, honor, dignity—after years of contribution to the economy.

(7) Participating in and contributing to meaningful activity within the widest range of civic, cultural, educational and training, and recreational opportunities.

(8) Efficient community services, including access to low-cost transportation, which provide a choice in supported living arrangements and social assistance in a coordinated manner and which are readily available when needed, with emphasis on maintaining a continuum of care for vulnerable older individuals.

(9) Immediate benefit from proven research knowledge which can sustain and improve health and happiness.

(10) Freedom, independence, and the free exercise of individual initiative in planning and managing their own lives, full participation in the planning and operation of community-based services and programs provided for their benefit, and protection against abuse, neglect, and exploitation.

2

Questions That Aging
Puts to Preventionists

Margaret Gatz

There are at least two reasons that older adults should be attractive to mental health professionals concerned with prevention. First, dialectic theories of human development can offer a theoretical basis for prevention. Life span developmental theories encompass nonpathological models of change and attention to the role of interacting influences, compatible with community psychology's ecological approach to understanding problems. Second, older adults fit into community psychology's definition of an underrepresented population. Elders are subjected to stereotyping processes that are used systematically to discriminate against them at both individual and institutional levels. Apparently, these lines of thinking have not proved compelling, for older adults have been relatively neglected in the prevention literature.

Can we simply take primary prevention as it has been understood in younger populations and transfer the precepts to old age? If not, what factors complicate the definition of prevention for older adults?

I confess to a lurking suspicion that younger people are favored targets for prevention because (a) they seem easier to change—more flexible and not as likely to talk back, (b) cost-benefit calculations would point to the fact that children have a longer future in which to benefit from the effects of change, (c) young children are cute, whereas old people are not, and (d) scientists and professionals are not free of countertransferential issues concerning their parents or their own aging. However, it is unnecessary to pit preventive efforts for one age group against preventive efforts for another. Society is multigenerational, and there is overlap among groups in need. Those who promote preventive interventions, above all others, need to move beyond fragmented advocacy to greater collective social responsibility.

AUTHOR'S NOTE: The support of National Institute on Aging Grant No. R01 AG08724 is gratefully acknowledged, as is the assistance of Donna Polisar.

Who Are Older Adults?

Older adults, in contrast to many other target groups, are a group to which we all will or do already belong.

It is obligatory to review a few familiar facts. First, the proportion of the American population who are over age 65 has grown in the last several decades and is projected to continue to grow (U.S. Bureau of the Census, 1986). This change in population distribution is both a function of changes in the size of birth cohorts (baby booms and baby busts) and a function of increased longevity (see Figure 2.1). Note that life expectancy at age 65 is increasing as well as life expectancy from birth (U.S. Department of Health and Human Services, 1991). The implications of this growth remain controversial in terms of how much the increase represents more unhealthy persons surviving for a longer time and requiring more health care resources, and how much it represents people staying well for longer. What is clear is that the fastest growing segment are the oldest old, defined as those aged 85 and older (Suzman & Riley, 1985).

Second, there is substantial variability among older adults. Those aged 65 and older are not a unitary target group, but rather are heterogeneous. As we have just seen, they are heterogeneous as regards age. In addition, people bring with them to old age all the differences that they were born with, such as gender and race, and all the differences that they have accumulated over their lives, such as education and attitudes and stressful life experiences.

Third, cohort effects must be kept in mind. People who are aged 50 today will be 75 in 2018. They represent the leading edge of the baby boom; they would have attended college in the early 1960s. One cannot expect them to be the same as 75-year-olds of today. Thus both age and cohort must be weighed in characterizing older persons.

Fourth, a key distinction for gerontologists has always been between lifelong difficulties and difficulties of late life onset. A subset of those with lifelong difficulties might be of interest for prevention. Specifically, those at greatest risk of having difficulty with the transitions of later life may be those who have a lifelong pattern of high neuroticism (Costa & McCrae, 1978) but have not previously come to the particular attention of any formal system of intervention. However, those with difficulties of late life onset may be of most interest for preventive intervention. These are typically individuals who have been successfully adjusted their entire life until encountering an unusually demanding situation in later life—for example, dementia in a close relative or a debilitating physical illness.

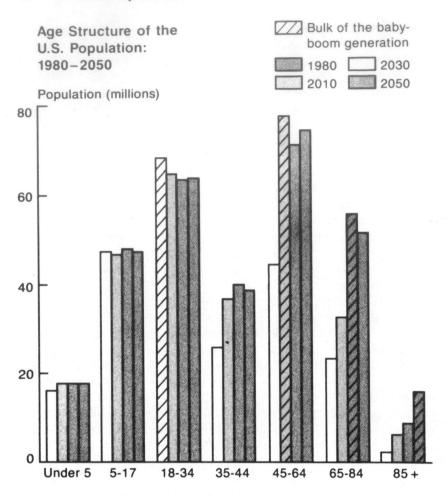

Figure 2.1. Age Structure of the U.S. Population in the 21st Century
SOURCE: U.S. Bureau of the Census, 1986.

What Are the Special Risks of Old Age?

The key notion to bear in mind is that aging is a biopsychosocial phenomenon. Biological, psychological, and social factors are all important, and these factors are profoundly interrelated.

Three special perils of old age can be identified, each illustrating an aspect of the biopsychosocial mix. First, in older adults, both cognitive and functional conditions are the targets for preventive mental health interventions.

Second, with age there is an increase in comorbidity. Third, in old age there is an acceleration of dependency on family support.

The most important mental disorders in the elderly include dementia, delirium, depression, and anxiety. Epidemiologic Catchment Area (ECA) survey data suggest that older adults have lower rates of major depressive disorder and of all diagnoses other than cognitive impairment, but higher rates of cognitive disorders, compared with other age groups (Regier et al., 1988). Dementing disorders—defined as progressive impairment of memory and other cognitive abilities—include both dementia of the Alzheimer's type and vascular dementia. In the ECA data, prevalence of moderate to severe dementias in those aged 65 and older was 5.1% (Regier et al., 1988). However, rates of dementia escalate with age, essentially doubling every 5.1 years (Jorm, Korten, & Henderson, 1987). Older adults are also the age group at greatest risk for delirium. Delirium is an acute disruption of brain physiology, involving confusion, and often accompanied by disorientation, delusions, and agitation. Possible causes include any interference with oxygen supply to the brain, such as toxic effects of medications, infections and fever, and postanesthesia reactions (Caine & Grossman, 1992; Raskind & Peskind, 1992). Thus, in contrast with other age groups, older adults are more likely to suffer from brain changes, some reversible and some not, raising the special problem of the prevention of dementia and delirium.

Comorbidity refers to the simultaneous experience of various disorders. Comorbidity is the rule rather than the exception in old age. Data from the Swedish Adoption/Twin Study of Aging give some idea of the scope of comorbidity. For example, in women under age 55, well over half have either no chronic condition or only one condition from a list of 13 disease categories, including cardiovascular disorder, sensory impairments, arthritis, cancer, and various neurological and cognitive disorders. In contrast, among those aged 75 and older, nearly half have at least three chronic conditions (Gatz, Harris, & Turk-Charles, in press). Mental disorders are part of the picture of comorbidity, with prevalence of certain mental disorders, especially delirium and depression, notably higher in those who have a co-occurring physical illness, and medical treatments themselves may introduce additional problems—for example, certain heart medications can be depressogenic (Cohen, 1992). Up to half of hip surgery patients have been reported to develop delirium (Cummings & Benson, 1992). Moreover, ailments cascade, and treatments for one condition may exacerbate another condition, or certain treatments may be precluded due to comorbid conditions and their treatments. In short, older adults inevitably experience physical decrements; thus interaction between physical and mental health is particularly common and consequential among older adults.

Chronic illnesses often lead to physical disability and conceivably to cognitive decrement. These impairments, in turn, put large numbers of elders at risk of needing assistance. It is possible, at least hypothetically, to divide the life span into years of active life expectancy and years of disability (Guralnik, 1991; Manton, 1991). As shown in Figure 2.2, active life expectancy refers to the proportion of life that can be lived without serious disability, either free of disease (A) or with chronic disease but unimpaired (B). There is considerable debate over which of these lines are movable. In the compression of morbidity scenario (Fries, 1983, 1989), active life expectancy would increase because longevity (C) would be constant and morbidity (A and B) would be compressed. In a stable morbidity scenario in which morbidity was neither compressed nor expanded, active life expectancy would increase if longevity increased (Guralnik, 1991).

In actuality, the data are not clear-cut, because detection of the onset of chronic diseases is not perfectly calibrated and because the sort of decline that necessitates a need for assistance is often gradual. Recent data from Manton, Corder, and Stallard (1993) indicate a proportional decline in rates of disability when the increase in the oldest population is taken into account. On the other hand, Guralnik (1991) found more years of disability prior to death, and Kaplan (1991) reported an increase in age-specific prevalence rates for many chronic conditions. Independent of this controversy, prevention has an evident role in reducing the weight of morbidity. Theoretically, as suggested by Abeles (1993), successful aging could be defined in terms of expanding active life expectancy. Along these lines, the Gerontological Society of America employed the phrase "adding life to years" as the theme of the 46th annual meeting.

Disability tends to be measured using activities of daily living (ADLs), such as whether people are able to walk, bathe, dress, shop, and perform housework (Cornoni-Huntley et al., 1985). The number of activities for which assistance is required can be calculated for each person, with impairment on two or more ADLs often used as a criterion for need for long-term care services.

The vast majority of elders reside in the community, not in institutions. Consequently, when there is disability, family members inevitably are the first individuals to whom these elders turn for help, or who make themselves available to provide assistance. The ability of family members to provide care may be affected by demographic trends such as increasing rates of divorce and remarriage, variability in the age of bearing children, voluntary childlessness, and women's commitment to the workplace. For example, single parents or working women may have less time available for caregiving, and stepfamilies may have a diluted sense of responsibility for older relatives and an increased number of older in-laws and former in-laws

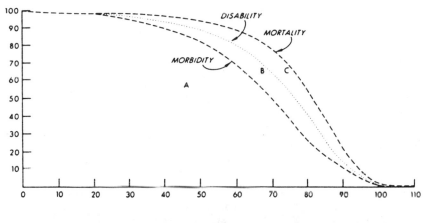

Figure 2.2. Graph illustrating the risk of three age-controlled outcomes: How the possibility of surviving (vertical axis) without one of three health events (disease, disability, death) changes as a function of age.

SOURCE: Manton, 1985, p. 623. Reprinted from the *New York State Journal of Medicine*, vol. 85, November 1985. Copyright 1985 by the Medical Society of New York and reprinted by permission of the copyright owner.

(Smyer & Hofland, 1982). Whether family are available and willing, and whether other informal or formal sources of support might fill a similar role, become key risk factors, and loss of autonomy becomes a major threat that is especially relevant in old age.

What Are the Central Preventive Goals for Older Adults?

Drawing in large part on the above list of special risks of old age, in combination with the larger literature on adult development and aging, I believe that four preventive goals could be suggested for older adults:

1. *Health.* Here, health is multifaceted, encompassing physical health and mental health, especially an intact memory.
2. *Financial security.*
3. *Independence and enhanced functional status.* Decreasing the duration of dependence and preventing institutionalization are frequent operationalizations of this goal. For elders, a key element lies in not being a burden.
4. *Sense of meaning or ego integrity or "vital involvement"* (Kivnick, 1993).

What Are Special Considerations
in Preventive Interventions With Older Adults?

In primary prevention, the goal of the intervention is to prevent disorder. This can be achieved through altering characteristics of the individual (e.g., teaching new skills to the person), altering characteristics of the environment (e.g., eliminating sources of stress), or placing vulnerable individuals into environments that will counteract the predisposition to disorder (e.g., creating supportive social networks). Whereas primary prevention is aimed at preventing onset, secondary prevention is aimed at preventing maintenance of disorder, including prevention of recurrence.

These notions are readily applicable to the latter half of the life span. In order to explore the special concerns raised by an aging population, I first apply to prevention the idea of postponing morbidity or expanding active life expectancy. Second, I critically examine the premises of existing prevention efforts. Two general points to reiterate are that preventive interventions must be construed as biopsychosocial, because these elements are so profoundly interwoven, and that prevention is a life span undertaking.

Prevention as the Expansion of Active Life Expectancy

If the life span is divided into active life expectancy and years of disability, and prevention is defined as expanding the years of active life, prevention may be accomplished through delaying age of onset of chronic diseases. The chronic illnesses typical of old age are commonly associated with risk factors that increase the potential of their occurrence and may accelerate their progression. Moreover, the changes tend to be age related, with the disease diagnosed when the decrements are sufficiently severe, referred to as "crossing a threshold." As shown in Figure 2.3, modification of risk factors could result in prevention or postponement of significant disability through slowing progression and delaying age at onset of chronic disease through the time at which the clinical threshold is crossed and the disease is diagnosed (Fries, 1989). Delaying onset is significant in old age because sufficient delay means that the individual may die of other causes before the disorder has the opportunity to manifest itself.

Although this logic has characteristically been applied to physical illnesses, it can be extended to dementia (Gatz, Lowe, Berg, Mortimer, & Pedersen, 1994; Henderson, 1988; Mortimer, 1994; Roth, 1986). For Alzheimer's disease, family history has been the most noticeable risk, and mutations have been identified in different families along with markers linked to several chromosomes. Gene therapy cannot be ruled out as a far distant future scenario, and efforts directly to correct the neurochemical pathways are conceivable.

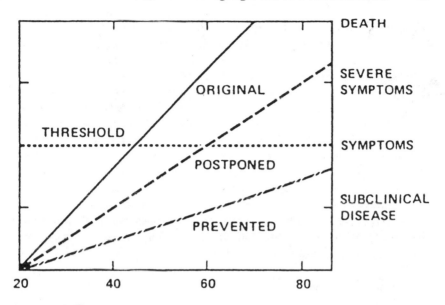

Figure 2.3. The clinical course of chronic disease. The universal, chronic diseases begin early in life, progress through a clinical threshold, and eventuate in disability or death. An important strategy for their control is to alter the rate (slope) at which they develop, thus postponing the clinical illness or even "preventing" it.

SOURCE: Reprinted with permission from *Vitality and Aging*, Fries, J. F., & Crapo, L. M. (1981), p. 82. San Francisco: W. H. Freeman.

Evidence for any one environmental risk factor has been elusive. However, theoretically, any combination of factors that reduce the cerebral capacity could contribute to disease. Accordingly, applying preventive models to Alzheimer's disease would entail delaying age of onset by modifying environmental exposures that impinge upon the brain's reserve capacity, whether or not they are directly causal of the pathological changes associated with Alzheimer's disease. Candidates that have the most empirical support to date include head trauma, hypothyroidism, aluminum, possibly other workplace exposures such as organic solvents, and alcohol (Fratiglioni, Ahlbom, Viitanen, & Winblad, 1993; Mortimer, 1994). Preventive strategies follow readily from several of these factors—for example, preventing head injury through wearing a helmet while bicycling. Aluminum exposure could occur through such diverse means as use of antacids or antiperspirants, industrial welding, other occupational exposures to aluminum, or drinking water, again leading to methods of prevention through avoiding aluminum-containing compounds.

Research has also identified education as a possible protective factor (Mortimer, 1994). Although the mechanism remains speculative, at least one line of thinking is that exercising and stimulating the brain may have a positive influence on cerebral capacity (Swaab, 1991).

Because vascular dementias share risk factors with other cardiovascular diseases, there is even more reason to believe that primary prevention can be effective, via improved diet and exercise (Rabins, 1992). With conditions such as cerebrovascular disease, earlier detection can permit secondary prevention efforts, such as an aspirin regimen following an initial stroke (Olshansky, Rudberg, Carnes, Cassel, & Brody, 1991). This framework for prevention is perhaps uniquely applicable to old age, that is, expanding disability-free years. For the most part, mental health professionals and researchers concerned with prevention are not accustomed to the centrality of organic conditions. But the strategies are familiar: altering health behaviors and eliminating neurotoxic exposures.

From Socialization to Empowerment

Preventive programs for older adults have tended to fit into three clusters (Stacey-Konnert & Gatz, in press). First are programs designed to increase social support. Second are programs aimed at preventing symptoms of depression. Third are programs with the goal of decreasing dependency, and especially preventing institutionalization. We discuss each in turn. Admittedly, there is some overlap among these categories insofar as reduction in symptoms of depression is often used as an outcome in measuring the effect of social support programs, and increasing older adults' social support has been viewed as relevant to preventing institutional placement.

As to the first set of programs, social support is probably the major theme in community programs for older adults. Programs are sometimes targeted to lonely (or to presumably lonely) individuals; sometimes the timing of the intervention is subsequent to a stressful life situation such as bereavement; sometimes older adults serve as the providers of the support. Although I do not want to argue that social support is a misguided goal, I do urge that it is irresponsible not to incorporate into interventions what is known about the role of support (see Antonucci & Jackson, 1987; Rook, 1984). We know that it is relevant to differentiate quality and quantity of support. We know that there are different types of support—emotional, instrumental, and informational. We know that social networks can have negative as well as beneficial effects. And we need to be careful not to frame programs in a fashion that may inadvertently be patronizing.

Two examples may help. The first is from Maggie Kuhn's (1991) autobiography. She is concerned about reliance on recreation by program planners. She writes:

> In one of our early efforts to establish a patients' rights committee in a Philadelphia nursing home, the administrators of the home, unable to understand that we were taking their patients seriously, asked that our first project be to help the residents make Easter baskets. What the patients really needed was to gain a place at the board table where the decisions about their lives were made. They needed freedom, spending money, respect, and fresh vegetables—not Easter baskets! (p. 144)

The second example is from the program from Heller, Thompson, Trueba, Hogg, and Vlachos-Weber (1991) in which they developed peer telephone dyads for elderly women with low perceived social support. In this carefully designed and evaluated intervention, the authors did not find that the program resulted in significant effects on increased morale or reduced symptoms of depression. Among the post hoc explanations for less than expected success were that (a) some types of losses of social support are not readily filled by other relationships, (b) useful social roles may be more important than companionship, and (c) with increased age, people may become more selective about choosing social partners in order to conserve their resources (Barrera, 1991; Carstensen, 1992; Heller et al., 1991; Hobfoll & Jackson, 1991; Rook, 1991; Stein, 1991).

In short, the meaning of the social support, and whether it is in fact efficacy enhancing, must remain a critical concern.

The second set of programs is aimed at reducing symptoms of depression. Outcome variables tend to encompass both increasing well-being and decreasing symptoms. An intriguing question here is what the proper outcome variable should be. On the positive well-being side, at the age of 80, Malcolm Cowley (1980) wrote about distrusting the word *happy,* preferring goals like esteem and working on projects, often that have something to do with transmitting knowledge or something of value to the next generations. Similarly, Kivnick (1993), working with the Eriksons, made the case for vital involvement.

On the symptom side, the greatest attention has been to symptoms of depression, although some have suggested that anxiety and stress reduction have been overlooked as targets. Depressive syndromes in older adults are not common, but symptoms are frequent (Blazer, Hughes, & George, 1987). Depression scales are often used as outcome measures in programs designed generally to enhance the quality of life of older adults. Most of these programs probably should not properly be considered as primary prevention of depression. Indeed, it is not clear how often episodes of major depressive disorder occur in older adults who do not have a history of depression from earlier in life and who have not suffered from a medical condition. Secondary prevention might focus on warning signs such as listlessness in medical patients, a group among whom risk of depression is known to be elevated (Rabins, 1992).

In sum, some grasp of the meaning of well-being in later life and some knowledge about the epidemiology of mental disorders in later life are necessary in designing programs.

The third set of programs concern prevention of dependency. Prevention of institutionalization is a goal that is unique to older adults compared to those in other phases of the life span. Issues related to dependency and autonomy are crystallized around older adults' need for assistance and eventually, perhaps, an institutional living situation. The goal should be to optimize autonomy within the context of whatever level of support is needed. To the extent possible, the older adult with functional impairments should be in charge of negotiating the nature of the support, and provision of unnecessarily restrictive alternatives should be eliminated.

One important avenue to fostering autonomy despite impairment can be found in the increased use of assistive devices, from velcro fasteners on clothes to wheelchairs to electronic medical alert systems (Manton et al., 1993). This is an example of adjusting the environment to the vulnerabilities of the individual. Cognitive compensatory strategies have also been explored, involving skills training with the older individual (Hultsch & Dixon, 1990).

In the face of frailty, sense of control becomes an especially important aspect of the quality of life (Abeles, 1991), embodied in notions of empowerment (Rappaport, 1981). A large amount of data support the positive effects of enhanced sense of control for older adults in institutions and in the community (Rodin, Cashman, & Desiderato, 1987). Central to the idea of fostering a sense of control is giving people choices and creating situations in which people will experience that their efforts do matter.

I find myself wanting to warn against false empowerment. False empowerment would be appearing to offer a choice when in fact all important matters have been predetermined. Rappaport (1981) recognized this danger when he described artificial programs in which everyone knows who is truly in charge.

Another version of false empowerment is presenting a choice when a person does not want to make a choice, or establishing situations in which people will experience that their efforts are futile. Carobeth Laird (1985) described a bump on the floor in the corridor of the nursing home where she resided.

Wheelchairs could easily become stuck. Residents were encouraged to deal with the bump by themselves. For some, having successfully negotiated the bump engendered a small sense of mastery. Illustrating individual differences, for other residents, the bump was too much to manage. For them, the staff's refusal to give them a push was dependency promoting because they resigned themselves to not using the corridor. The challenge is to design interventions that genuinely maintain autonomy and empower older adults. In summary, across the range of preventive interventions, being sensitive to older adults means taking into account the knowledge base in adult development and aging and respecting the integrity of the intended program recipients.

Conclusion

Julian Rappaport (1981) taught us to look for two-sided solutions. There is in the literature a struggle over the image of the older adult. Is she or he a dependent person to be helped, trained in various skills, or made the target of prevention programs, or is she or he an individual to be assured of rights and choices? In the former instance, the elderly are a population at risk whose needs can be identified. In the latter instance, rights are preeminent. Rappaport argued that both rights and needs may be proper to consider.

Gesten and Jason (1987) proposed further that there were two elements to empowering: fostering a sense of control, and establishing a more symmetrical helping relationship. Older adults, who often have a lifetime of experience being competent, make us more aware of the dilemmas of helping. To do professional psychology with older adults in a way that truly enhances autonomy requires entertaining models in which there is a changed relationship between the helper and the helped. Obviously, this objective becomes more complex when the older adult has an impaired memory and his or her competency is dubious. However, not taking these dilemmas into account risks engendering dependency through our very efforts to help.

If we succeed in transferring the precepts of prevention and empowerment to old age, we may change the definition of prevention itself.

References

Abeles, R. P. (1991). Sense of control, quality of life, and frail older people. In J. E. Birren, D. E. Deutchman, J. Lubben, & J. Rowe (Eds.), *The concept and measurement of quality of life in the frail elderly* (pp. 297-314). New York: Academic Press.

Abeles, R. P. (1993, May). *Research directions in behavioral and social research at NIA.* Paper presented at the University of Southern California, Ethel Percy Andrus Gerontology Center, Multidisciplinary Research Colloquium Series in Aging, Los Angeles.

Antonucci, T. C., & Jackson, J. S. (1987). Social support, interpersonal efficacy, and health: A life course perspective. In L. L. Carstensen & B. A. Edelstein (Eds.), *Handbook of clinical gerontology* (pp. 291-311). New York: Pergamon.

Barrera, M., Jr. (1991). Support interventions and the third law of ecology. *American Journal of Community Psychology, 19,* 133-138.

Blazer, D., Hughes, D. C., & George, L. K. (1987). The epidemiology of depression in an elderly community population. *The Gerontologist, 27,* 281-287.

Caine, E. D., & Grossman, H. T. (1992). Neuropsychiatric assessment. In J. E. Birren, R. B. Sloane, & G. D. Cohen (Eds.), *Handbook of mental health and aging* (2nd ed., pp. 603-642). San Diego: Academic Press.

Carstensen, L. L. (1992). Social and emotional patterns in adulthood: Support for socioemotional selectivity theory. *Psychology and Aging, 7,* 331-338.

Cohen, G. D. (1992). The future of mental health and aging. In J. E. Birren, R. B. Sloane, & G. D. Cohen (Eds.), *Handbook of mental health and aging* (2nd ed., pp. 893-912). San Diego: Academic Press.

Cornoni-Huntley, J. C., Foley, D. J., White, L. R., Suzman, R., Berkman, L. F., Evans, D. A., & Wallace, R. B. (1985). Epidemiology and disability in the oldest old: Methodologic issues and preliminary findings. *Milbank Quarterly, 63,* 350-376.

Costa, P. T., Jr., & McCrae, R. R. (1978). Objective personality assessment. In M. Storandt, I. C. Siegler, & M. F. Elias (Eds.), *The clinical psychology of aging* (pp. 119-143). New York: Plenum.

Cowley, M. (1980). *The view from 80.* New York: Penguin.

Cummings, J. L., & Benson, D. F. (1992). *Dementia: A clinical approach* (2nd ed.). Boston: Butterworth-Heinemann.

Fratiglioni, L., Ahlbom, A., Viitanen, M., & Winblad, B. (1993). Risk factors for late-onset Alzheimer's disease: A population-based case-control study. *Annals of Neurology, 33,* 258-256.

Fries, J. F. (1983). The compression of morbidity. *Milbank Quarterly, 61,* 397-419.

Fries, J. F. (1989). The compression of morbidity: Near or far? *Milbank Quarterly, 67,* 208-232.

Fries, J. F., & Crapo, L. M. (1981). *Vitality and aging.* San Francisco: W. H. Freeman.

Gatz, M., Harris, J., & Turk-Charles, S. (in press). Older women and health. In A. L. Stanton & S. J. Gallant (Eds.), *Women's psychological and physical health: A scholarly and social agenda.* Washington, DC: American Psychological Association.

Gatz, M., Lowe, B., Berg, S., Mortimer, J., & Pedersen, N. (1994). Dementia: Not just a search for the gene. *The Gerontologist, 34,* 251-255.

Gesten, E. L., & Jason, L. A. (1987). Social and community interventions. *Annual Review of Psychology, 38,* 427-460.

Guralnik, J. M. (1991). Prospects for the compression of morbidity: The challenge posed by increasing disability in the years prior to death. *Journal of Aging and Health, 3,* 138-154.

Heller, K., Thompson, M. G., Trueba, P. E., Hogg, J. R., & Vlachos-Weber, I. (1991). Peer support telephone dyads for elderly women: Was this the wrong intervention? *American Journal of Community Psychology, 19,* 75-84.

Henderson, A. S. (1988). The risk factors for Alzheimer's disease: A review and a hypothesis. *Acta Psychiatrica Scandinavica, 78,* 257-275.

Hobfoll, S. E., & Jackson, A. P. (1991). Conservation of resources in community intervention. *American Journal of Community Psychology, 19,* 111-122.

Hultsch, D. F., & Dixon, R. A. (1990). Learning and memory in aging. In J. E. Birren & K. W. Schaie (Eds.), *Handbook of the psychology of aging* (3rd ed., pp. 258-274). San Diego: Academic Press.

Jorm, A. F., Korten, A. E., & Henderson, A. S. (1987). The prevalence of dementia: A quantitative integration of the literature. *Acta Psychiatrica Scandinavica, 76,* 456-479.

Kaplan, G. A. (1991). Epidemiologic observations on the compression of morbidity: Evidence from the Alameda County study. *Journal of Aging and Health, 3,* 155-171.

Kivnick, H. Q. (1993). Everyday mental health: A guide to assessing life strengths. *Generations, 17,* 13-20.

Kuhn, M. (1991). *No stone unturned.* New York: Ballantine.

Laird, C. (1985). *Limbo.* Novato, CA: Chandler & Sharp.

Manton, K. G. (1985). Future patterns of chronic disease incidence, disability, and mortality among the elderly: Implications for the demand for acute and long-term health care. *New York State Journal of Medicine, 85,* 623-633.

Manton, K. G. (1991). The dynamics of population aging: Demography and policy analysis. *Milbank Quarterly, 69,* 309-338.

Manton, K. G., Corder, L., & Stallard, E. (1993). Changes in the use of personal assistance and special equipment from 1982 to 1989: Results from the 1982 and 1989 NLTCS. *The Gerontologist, 33,* 168-176.

Mortimer, J. A. (1994). What are the risk factors for dementia? In F. Huppert, C. Brayne, & D. O'Connor (Eds.), *Dementia and normal aging* (pp. 208-229). Cambridge, UK: Cambridge University Press.

Olshansky, S. J., Rudberg, M. A., Carnes, B. A., Cassel, D. K., & Brody, J. A. (1991). Trading off longer life for worsening health: The expansion of morbidity hypothesis. *Journal of Aging and Health, 3,* 194-216.

Rabins, P. V. (1992). Prevention of mental disorder in the elderly: Current perspectives and future prospects. *Journal of the American Geriatrics Society, 40,* 727-733.

Rappaport, J. (1981). In praise of paradox: A social policy of empowerment over prevention. *American Journal of Community Psychology, 9,* 1-26.

Raskind, M. A., & Peskind, E. R. (1992). Alzheimer's disease and other dementing disorders. In J. E. Birren, R. B. Sloane, & G. D. Cohen (Eds.), *Handbook of mental health and aging* (2nd ed., pp. 478-515). San Diego: Academic Press.

Regier, D. A., Boyd, J. H., Burke, J. D., Rae, D. S., Myers, J. K., Kramer, M., Robins, L. N., George, L. K., Karno, M., & Locke, B. Z. (1988). One-month prevalence of mental disorders in the United States. *Archives of General Psychiatry, 45,* 977-986.

Rodin, J., Cashman, C., & Desiderato, L. (1987). Intervention and aging: Enrichment and prevention. In M. W. Riley, J. D. Matarazzo, & A. Baum (Eds.), *Perspectives in behavioral medicine: The aging dimension* (pp. 149-172). Hillsdale, NJ: Lawrence Erlbaum.

Rook, K. S. (1984). The negative side of social interaction: Impact on psychological well-being. *Journal of Personality and Social Psychology, 46,* 1097-1108.

Rook, K. S. (1991). Facilitating friendship formation in late life: Puzzles and challenges. *American Journal of Community Psychology, 19,* 103-110.

Roth, M. (1986). The association of clinical and neurological findings and its bearing on the classification and aetiology of Alzheimer's disease. *British Medical Bulletin, 42,* 42-50.

Smyer, M. A., & Hofland, B. F. (1982). Divorce and family support in later life: Emerging concerns. *Journal of Family Issues, 3,* 61-77.

Stacey-Konnert, C., & Gatz, M. (in press). Community and preventive interventions for normative occurrences of later life. In J. Rappaport & E. Seidman (Eds.), *Handbook of community psychology.* New York: Plenum.

Stein, C. H. (1991). Peer support telephone dyads for elderly women: The wrong intervention or the wrong research? *American Journal of Community Psychology, 19,* 91-98.

Suzman, R., & Riley, M. W. (1985). Introducing the "oldest old." *Milbank Quarterly, 63,* 177-186.

Swaab, D. F. (1991). Brain aging and Alzheimer's disease, "wear and tear" versus "use it or lose it." *Neurobiology of Aging, 12,* 317-324.

U.S. Bureau of the Census. (1986, December). *Age structure of the U.S. population in the 21st century* (SB-1-86). Washington, DC: Government Printing Office.

U.S. Department of Health and Human Services. (1991). *Healthy people 2000* (DHHS Publication No. [PHS] 91-50212). Washington, DC: Government Printing Office.

3

The Social Construction of Ageism

Jon Hendricks

All too frequently, old age appears to be that territory across an unseen chasm from the rest of life. Younger people, and sometimes representatives of the older generation as well, attribute all types of differences to those they see as old simply by virtue of their being on the other side of the great divide. To many people, being old is equated with decline, dependency, and disability. Why is this image as pervasive as it is? What prompts us to think that those who are old are somehow different from those who are not?

Paradoxical as it may seem, it may be a combination of our very successes and the shared values of our culture that has set older persons apart. We have made old age what it is and we have shaped our attitudes about it at the same time. The very segregation of people on either end of the life cycle from those in the middle grows out of the way society has been organized and from changes in the conditions of production, changes in values, and the advent of specialized forms of care provision. It should come as no surprise that the societal arrangements under which we live foster discriminative attitudes. In fact, an orienting premise of sociology is that individual attitudes are part and parcel of a collective orientation toward the phenomena in question rather than being somehow unique to the individual expressing those attitudes. To fail to recognize the extent to which both individual aging and attitudes about aging are correlative with many collective patterns beyond the ken of individuals is to ensure an incomplete explanation for why people encounter the things they do and feel about them as they do.

In Western societies, visible signs—gray hair, wrinkles, hearing aids, and the like—often connote changing age and/or social status. Whether or not the same cosmetic changes reflect physical or mental capacities, they have meanings rooted in socially shared perceptions—pejorative imagery or stereotypes not necessarily derived from the experience of daily life. The same is as true of benign ageism or even positive ageism as it is for their negative opposites (Palmore, 1990). Compassionate ageism, the "poor dear" syndrome, is no less dehumanizing than its negative antithesis. Whether positive or negative, the fact is that imputed characteristics often take precedence over actual personal attributes (Schmidt & Boland, 1986; Stoller & Gibson, 1994). They may even subvert personal attributes to the point where these become invisible, or worse, are beside the point as far as interpersonal interaction or evaluation is concerned. The important point is that the images themselves are pernicious and often so subtle as to go unrecognized as stereotypes. For example, electronic and print media have recently featured images of white-haired models who are exercise whizzes, with bodies that could easily be that of someone many years their junior. In fact, their appearance is presented as proof positive for whatever is being hawked. Does the fact that their bodies are not acceptable in their normative age-true characteristics ever strike you as incongruous? Is it possible such images are either elitist or ageist, take your pick (Stoller & Gibson, 1994)?

The purpose of this chapter is to look at ageism, not simply as stereotypic attitudes about old people but as something more suggestive of societal norms than any type of narrow individual or group bias. It may be comforting to the rest of us to label those who hold stereotypical views about old age as narrow-minded and ill informed, and they may be, yet at the same time they may only be expressing views derived from broader social currents. I begin by summarizing what is called a constructionist perspective and by providing an example of its application to the life course. To establish the context in which ageist attitudes find root, I then focus on how the world is given meaning through the influence of language, group membership, and underlying societal values. Each of these, plus the biomedicalization of the human condition, underpins how any one of us evaluates aging and the aged. Having discussed these social forces in turn, I conclude that it is an error to dismiss ageism as some type of individual myopia or aberration. If we are to ameliorate ageism in its more virulent forms, we must look beyond individuals to the nature of societal organization and institutions.

To equate ageism with a type of gerontophobia may be convenient but not entirely accurate—the latter is customarily said to be a psychological characteristic of individuals (Palmore, 1972). In point of fact, ageism is a societal attribute expressed not only by individuals but in political priorities and in social policies and arrangements. Butler (1987), who coined the term in the first place, stated that the institutional foundations of ageism were a way to sidestep responsibility and a means of discounting the strengths, skills, and resources of older people as beside the point. Of course, in an absolute sense, ageist attitudes do not have to be just about old people; they can focus on any age group. Like racist or sexist attitudes, they discount the primary characteristics of people as irrelevant to what others regard as central.

A Constructionist Perspective

Suppose I forget a word in the process of speaking with you. Am I distracted, preoccupied, thinking ahead of or behind my mouth? Suppose an 85-year-old with whom you interact forgets a word—lots of words. Do labels like *forgetful, senile, foggy, demented* come to mind? Through the simple words used to describe someone who is forgetful, a whole realm of meaning starts to be constructed.

The idea I am after here is not new, far from it. I will skip an exposition of the etiology and hope it suffices to say we are in pursuit of something that is at the core of much of social science, something near and dear to the hearts of many a social scientist regardless of species type. I refer to the "social construction of reality" thesis, the contention that the worldview individuals call their own, and defend to the hilt, also serves to link them to others of like mind. It is through the process of their interaction that reality is given shape. Of course there is an opposition camp, which contends that the whole cognitive process works the other way around—that an event, behavior, or stimulus of any type contains within it the impetus by which it is categorized. A response is a response is a response, according to those who see human beings primarily as reactors and only secondarily as creators.

There is a major epistemological puzzle implied by the two points of view. Is there such a thing as "truth"? The constructionists concede there is, but say it may not lie in an event but in the perception of an event that stems from the act of following conceptual rules. It sounds more complicated than it is. One camp, the positivists, say "truth" is out "there" to be discovered. The other camp, the constructionists, say we make our own truth collectively. Two conceptions of truth—a correspondence and a consensus model— emerge from these grossly simplified characterizations of the two camps.

The constructionists cite any number of variable responses to a common stimulus and maintain that the meaning of an object or event derives from tacit agreements negotiated between participants. Implicit in the assertion is what may be called a "prescriptive thesis," which, in the extreme, directs individuals to respond, behave, or perceive according to certain principles and rules (Armon-Jones, 1986, p. 33). In other words, for the construction-ists, perception of any sort is always laden with concepts, responses mediated by and descriptions rooted in the sociocultural milieu (Averill, 1980). A constructionist perspective goes on to contend that the meaning of things, events, or people has no ontological status of its own, even when it feels as if it does. Whatever an object means, that meaning is purposive, socially negotiated, and learned by others. I have encapsulated an entire epistemo-logical debate, but believe it or not, it is very relevant to how we approach aging and how those whom we study or care for experience life.

Social Construction of the Life Course

What any of us regards as objective reality is only grudgingly open to challenge. In many respects it is analogous to the shopworn example of a fish not knowing it is wet because that is all it does "know." As sentient beings, humans know we draw oxygen from air whereas fish extract it from water—situations easily recognized as two different realities. Yet when it comes to entertaining other possible realities for what it is we "do," we are not necessarily more enlightened than the fish. Surely we can appreciate, if only at an intellectual level, that many factors influence the way we experience life. Part of what defines our species is that we reflect on those experiences and attempt either to discover or create patterns of meaning.

As noted earlier, the process of interpretation is not simply a matter of individual volition. That is part of it, no doubt, but the parameters of the social constructionist argument are found in shared language and shared practice, both resting on a set of shared assumptions and values. It is through these mechanisms that shared meanings are created and our reality becomes for us what water is for the fish—it is all we know. As the discussion progresses, the interconnectedness of each of these realms should become apparent.

Social gerontology has examined the life course from a multitude of perspectives (Gubrium, Holstein, & Buckholdt, in press). Most have added to our understanding of and made a contribution to the way we explain aging. What a social constructionist perspective adds is an appreciation for the profundity of the claim that age is what we make it.

In their exposition of the constructionist perspective on life course development, Gubrium et al. (in press) underscore the role conceptual frameworks play in helping define the meaning of phenomena. Perhaps the best way to clarify the point is by an example. There have been any number of academic treatises and popularized accounts of the turning points that connote transition from what is described as one phase, period, season, or stage of life to another. Regardless of how real these phases or stages may feel, their practical utility lies in providing a framework that helps individuals interpret things. To the extent that we conceive of life as a trajectory, we incorporate what that implies as a thematic dimension of our self-concept. In fact, conceiving of life as a passage through time becomes a "self-fulfilling prophecy" that, in effect, helps us sort out what we experience. The nature of the intervals, the stages, or the phases varies according to shared beliefs about important things in the life of that culture.

The notion of a "constructed life course" may run counter to the way we think we experience things. But we also think of history as a process even though we recognize that history is in the writing and is not inherent in the unfolding of events. There is an important difference, however. History is not conscious; people are, and people create patterns and meanings—that is what it means to be human. To a greater or lesser extent, part of our pattern making is the creation of a pattern for ourselves, a pattern to tell us where we are and where we might be going. It is not an inappropriate exaggeration to say that the way we conceive life's script will surely color the way we live it (Hendricks, 1984). For those who conceive of life as a trajectory, the meaning of their life, of themselves, derives from their interpretation of the forward-looking relationship between the present and some future state. For those who conceive of life not as a trajectory but merely as one day following another, more or less statically, there is still meaning and interpretation, even if it is that particular events, acts, and behaviors do not mean much of anything.

The living of life, like the writing of history, is an unrelenting act of interpretation. We react to and categorize the welter of events of our lives in terms of what is meaningful to us. The word *interpretation* may sound like an act that implies language and words, but interpretation can also be behavioral. The act of interacting with others is interpretive, and in so doing the participants create shared meanings. Similarly, social practice and social policy are interpretive and create meanings by providing a framework by which the phenomena in question are categorized. Once something, anything, is interpreted, once meanings are established, consequent activity is undertaken and interpreted in light of the precedent of the original interpretive act.

Think for a moment of how "senseless" certain behaviors are, how chaotic or pointless, until we define them as part of, say, a game, and then define the game in terms of rules—formal or informal. Suddenly the behaviors previously thought of as meaningless take on a complex of meanings in light of the rules and the nature of the game. Children's word games, or even the codes used to transmit encrypted messages, are a ready case in point. Spontaneously created games may provide an even better example of how meanings are created. To the outsider, to one who does not know the code or is not "in" on the game, the behavior has little meaning. Once one is versed in the minutiae, however, patterns become clear, breaches evident, and meaning no longer questioned.

Language and the Power of Suggestion

"When *I* use a word it means just what I choose it to mean—neither more nor less," says Humpty Dumpty, in a rather scornful tone, to Alice in *Through the Looking Glass*. Is that so? Probably not, but certainly we should not underestimate the connection between the ways we express ourselves and the way we perceive the world. Once established, the taken-for-granted assumptions with which we orient ourselves to the world of experience are nearly indelible. Furthermore, our sense of either belonging to a larger collectivity or being an outsider is, in part, a result of knowing the meanings of certain signs and symbols. A few examples may help make the point. Suppose I held up a button with a pink triangle and asked you to describe it. What would you say? Would you focus on what you saw, or would you refer to the current meaning of the symbol? Knowing what category that symbol fits into is an example of the type of sorting strategy used to create categories of meaning and to separate insiders from outsiders. Suppose I refer to a person as "born again," a "pinko," a "hockey nut," a "bimbo," a "woman-izer"? Would you start to develop an image, an impression, a *read* on the person in question? What if I described someone as an "old codger," an "old biddy," "over the hill," a "sundowner"? Would your perception of that person be likely to incorporate the label? In every realm of life, categories provide a cognitive schema through which experience is filtered. As we attach labels we create meaning—an impression, an expectation—not only in our own minds but commonly in the minds of others as well.

The words used as illustrations in the preceding paragraph are fairly accessible examples of the power of language and symbols to shape our perception of a person, place, or thing. The same process is operative in all spheres of activity. Language is a powerful influence, one that shapes all subsequent perception. In fact, it is not an exaggeration to say that language is a naive form of "theorizing" insofar as it provides our first, and largely unexamined, conceptual framework. When you purchase an expensive item, is it spendy, pricey, or dear? Do you drink your coffee regular or black? Do you like milkshakes, malteds, or frappes with your hamburger? Eat dark toast or whole wheat? Without my pushing the analogy to the point where you start to think more about snacks than my comments, you are probably begin-ning to get my drift but beginning to ask what is my point. The categories of everyday languages are everywhere. If you listen closely, you will hear the differences and begin to appreciate how they affect behavior and how they define membership in one or another social group.

Group Membership, Social Practice, and Worldviews

It is comforting to think we would personally hold off a bit before jumping to conclusions, but it may only be because I have drawn attention to the tendency. The power of suggestion is not limited to the innuendos that advertisers wish to attach to cereal, new cars, or some fragrance. If you will permit me continue to refer to it as the power of suggestion for a while longer, I will say it evolves from language but also from our membership in social categories and ethnic groups and from our gender, professional, and yes, even educational status.

As we move away from simple words to social practices, the power of presuppositions, predilections, and sanctions to shape our worldview may get a little fuzzier, but is no less real (Harre, 1986, p. 5). The imperatives of practice and group norms are like the power of words. It is difficult to imagine that the world could be other than "just so" once we begin doing something in any particular way. Consider for a moment what we call "legal precedent." In law the role of precedent is a little clearer than it is in common sense or in science. Precedents point to conclusions; as long as a case is sufficiently like an earlier case, the determination should be the same. What is at issue in law is a question of how similar the cases are. The more global the sorting strategy, the more similarity is thought to reside in the antecedent. In law, extenuating circumstances are sought as a means of asserting that two acts are not alike and should not be judged alike. It is not until the sorting strategy is fine-tuned that differentiation and a proliferation of categories occur.

In life, membership in social classes, in ethnic, racial, or geographically identifiable groups, or in any of the other collectivities to which a person might belong serves to provide what amounts to precedent for an interpretation of many of the things a person experiences. Until an exception is suggested, similarity is assumed. Each membership group creates in the minds of its participants what the constructionist perspective refers to as a "natural attitude" toward the world. That is to say, these groupings instill in their members a characteristic worldview that constitutes the "filter" through which they look out on the rest of the world. In so doing they channel lifestyles, shape values, suggest priorities, and influence any number of other behavioral or attitudinal traits.

When images of anything are generally accepted by all likely participants, we say the image has been "institutionalized." Not unlike norms, with which they share a number of key features, institutionalized images are taken as the standard against which reality is measured. The adjectives used to label a category are customarily taken as both description and explanation, a reification fallacy if ever there was one.

Many psychologists say that coming to terms with the processes accompanying aging is an adaptive response, whereas struggling against them is maladaptive. What they may not take into account is that gender, race, social class, and myriad other qualifiers all affect how adaptive or maladaptive behaviors are given voice. When we, as social scientists, offer descriptive comments concerning ethnic or racial minorities, contrasting them, even benignly, to idealized mainstream norms, the potential is that differences will be stressed over similarities and those differences imbued with particular meaning. Social science itself is remarkably blind to the latent biases implicit in its own formulations. As practitioners, we must constantly guard against facile but myopic generalizations lest we demonstrate a type of ageism embedded in "just so" descriptions. It is potentially even more damaging that many elders themselves share taken-for-granted assumptions about aging, based on the power of the stereotype, and, in assuming its veracity, denigrate themselves or their age peers if they do not measure up to the idealized version.

Moral Judgments and Just Deserts

With aging, elderly persons, and social policy very much in the news these days, social perceptions of older persons are being cast in bold relief. As Crews (1993) reminded us, the rectangularization of the survival curve has outstripped cultural definitions of and attitudes about elderly people. When only a small proportion of those who live into adulthood continue to live into old age, attitudes concerning old people can be charitable without having to be reconciled with scarcities. During times of plenty it is also easy to proclaim that all disadvantaged persons should benefit from public largesse. With either increases in the proportion of elderly persons in a population, or a diminution of resources, attitudes about previously "deserving populations" are soon challenged by new realities.

Despite a certain organic interconnectedness of the life course in undifferentiated cultures, the valence of public sentiments is not as clear-cut as we might think. As Sokolovsky (1993) pointed out, discussions of changes in images of old people must avoid the trap of an overly simplistic dichotomy between pre- and postindustrialization, and must couch any such deliberation in the context of available resources. Following Glascock and Feinman (1981), Sokolovsky provided a needed perspective in that he reminded us that the social definition of what it means to be old is always contingent on changes in social/economic roles, changes in capabilities linked to chronology, and shifts toward incapacity that distinguish among those already thought of as old. I would add that each of these, in turn, rests on an underlying moral economy that, as the term implies, is based on the interplay between public attitudes and economics.

Underlying the shifting valuation of elders that results in a negative ageism are intertwining themes of moral and political economy. In a nutshell, moral economy provides the rationale for our notions of distributive justice.

In its relevance for the present discussion, moral economy is the determination of what is a fair shake for any member of a category, based on that person's presumed worth and contributions to social priorities. Lurking behind a concern with debilitation, dependency, and social justice is a larger question: Is the situation of old people in general—or even a single older person—entirely of their own making? Furthermore, are old people to be judged on the basis of current contributions only, and by what criteria? If social gerontologists agree on anything, it is that there is a dialectical relationship between structural arrangements, public policy, and individual life worlds (Estes, 1979; Townsend, 1981). The case for created dependencies has been well presented and need not be reiterated here. Suffice it to say, proponents of what is often called a political economic approach to understanding aging assert that people age the way they do as a consequence of either deliberate or unanticipated consequences of social and political decision making. For one reason or another, the ideology of the marketplace has informed the way we have chosen to see and deal with old age.

Gramsci's (1971) concept of hegemony is relevant here in that it provides a means to appreciate how the ideology of the marketplace constitutes a virtually "taken-for-granted" assumption about old age. The same ideology provides the underpinning for the delivery of social services and is a component in the evaluation of those who have reasons to claim those services. As intended by Gramsci, *hegemony* is a term used to define taking for one's own ideological position the ideology of a dominant social category or group. The ideology of the marketplace has become part of our value system not by coercion but by virtue of the active consent of all participants. Our culture has normalized the valuation of people and services in terms of "cost-benefit ratios" and "bottom lines" in such a way that anyone who issues a challenge is branded a heretic and dismissed as a "lefty" socialist.

Because of the moral economy implicit in our norms and ideals, we have designed entitlements and accommodations for nonaffluent elders in terms of their presumed personal worth as reflected in their work history, or in terms of a welfare mentality that requires near-destitution to claim public largesse. Estes (1979) in the United States and Walker (1980) and Townsend (1981) in England were among the first to draw attention to the impact on older people of age-based public policies and how the latter are implicated in many of the social problems associated with old age. Olson (1982) joined them to focus attention on how the negative effects of market, class, gender, and race relations throughout life have a cumulative impact in even more adverse conditions in old age. As differential opportunities are created by societal arrangements, so too are justifications created and incorporated into our ideas of fair play in the realm of intergenerational justice (Greene, 1989).

All socially recognized categories, whether of people, the meaning of an event, or some aspect of the environment, incorporate societal priorities. People or things that do not reflect those priorities, or that do not explicitly contribute to the realization of those priorities, are frequently saddled with pejorative labels and defined by negative terms that are often mirror images of whatever is esteemed for its centrality to those priorities. Ageism, defined by Butler (1969) as the "systematic stereotyping of and discrimination against people because they are old" (p. 243), is one dimension of this perceptual predisposition. As Butler (1987) noted, one effect is that younger persons view old people as different from themselves, not just chronologically but in qualitative terms as well. As a consequence, a "we-them" mind-set develops that is far more permissive of discrimination than would be a mind-set that viewed elders as young people grown old. Regardless of verbal claims to the contrary—"some of my best friends are old" and the like—when recessions come, populations benefiting from public benevolence, older persons in particular, come in for increased scrutiny and criticism. The stereotypes of "welfare chiselers" and "greedy geezers" are dusted off and trotted out for the full effect of media attention. Present-moment relative contributions to national priorities are defined in the utilitarian terms of "exchange value," with nary a nod to earlier contributions or the humanitarian ideals of "use value" and the rights of citizenship (Hendricks & Leedham, 1992; Myles, 1984). In every arena, from access to health care to access to the centers of power, all forms of cold shouldering are justified in terms of near-term potential contributions to the prioritized agenda. The paradox is that as a society we pump untold resources into amelioration and cure to thwart the early-life causes of mortality, only to label elderly survivors as an onerous burden (Butler, 1993).

What is taking place is that a vernacular of crises, war, and cheating is replacing one of equity, well-being and fair play. Trial balloons do not have to fly in order to succeed. With each attempt, the dialogue is gradually recast so that the sacred cow of a generation ago can be relabeled the ruinous overgrazer of today. The power of public policy, like that of verbal imagery (Cirillo, 1993), is long-term, caustic, and effective in pernicious ways because it creates a mind-set that gives license where none may have existed previously.

Biomedicalization and
Social Construction of Ageism

Estes and her colleagues (Estes, 1979; Estes & Binney, 1989; Estes, Gerard, Zones, & Swan, 1984) first drew the attention of the gerontological community to some of the consequences of casting all manner of aging issues as biomedical problems. It seems to have been nearly inevitable because "the high profile of biological theories and perspectives in gerontology has resulted in a perceived general association between age and (ill) health. To be old is to be, of necessity, unhealthy" (Victor, 1991, p. 23). The result is a clear example of the management of meaning by and through the medical enterprise. Not only is the analytic framework one that revolves around individualized organic pathologies, but attention is diverted from other possible causes so that all explanations are formulated in terms of "biomedical" resolutions (Estes & Binney, 1989, p. 587). This construction of aging as a medical problem carries with it a clear-cut focus on clinical-like intervention and secondary prevention. Perhaps as important, it either fosters or reinforces lay conceptions of the process of aging as a process of physical and mental decline and of old people as denizens of one or another type of hospital or long-term care institution.

A number of dimensions of the biomedicalization of aging are germane to this discussion of the social construction of ageism. On one hand, there is the tendency to relegate many problems associated with aging to the medical arena and to look to the medical establishment for amelioration.[1] Once this is done, everyone else is relieved of responsibility for helping "solve" the problems. In a society that prides itself on specialization, well-defined divisions of labor, and the merits of a "techno-fix" for whatever is wrong, we "medicalize" many types of social problems, thus avoiding serious scrutiny of how societal arrangements themselves, lauded for their benefits and defended for their rationality, have helped create the problems that now need resolution. To fully understand all the ramifications of this medicalization, we must also consider whether there is any evidence that the delivery of medical care is in any way biased. Still another consideration is the micro-level issue of what happens, interpersonally, in the process of providing medical care.

Part of the impetus for the promulgation of a biomedical model stems from the undeniably important advances medicine has made in treating previously debilitating and crippling conditions. There is no gainsaying how important a role modern medicine plays in our lives and well-being. Neither can we deny that sickness and health are central to the aging process. Yet the very successes medicine has wrought have also created a mind-set in which other possible antecedents to the problems identified are subjugated to those thought to be related to biomedical mechanisms. As diagnostic categories are defined and treatment strategies explicated, new "sufferers" and their symptoms proliferate. As the dimensions of the problem are "recognized," official pronouncements are forthcoming, clinical protocols specified, treatment regimes tried, and appropriate pharmaceuticals put to the test. Like the proverbial fish in the water, we do not seem to recognize another way, or any other reality.

Obviously not all the "problems of living" that elders encounter have their roots in physiological or medical substrates; seldom do we think that is the case for other age ranges.[2] A vocabulary of medicalization has become an expedient way to think about the problems of old age because it helps absolve the rest of us from any responsibility while relegating concerns to the medical arena (Estes & Binney, 1989; Estes et al., 1984). As Pitts (1968) asserted over 25 years ago, "It would seem that medicalization is one of the most effective means of social control and that it is destined increasingly to become the main mode of *formal* social control" (p. 391). Seemingly, anything that affects the body, and that includes the mind too, is first and foremost relegated to the purview of medicine (Friedson, 1970, p. 251).

Of course, the process is a two-edged sword. The medicalization of problems of living is facilitated by a complex set of cultural values and social priorities. Still, none but the most heartless wants others to suffer—if medical intervention can ameliorate, then medical attention is appropriate. If the treatment is successful, it provides its own justification. But as we treat, so too do we insulate problems of living from many other aspects of our lives. Furthermore, what we treat is what we see as a cause for concern. Some have suggested that to really understand health patterns among older persons, it is helpful to distinguish between disease, illness, and sickness. The first is a pathological condition, the second a subjective feeling, the third a social definition (Twaddle & Hessler, 1986). Whereas the first and last definitions may be considered by health care policy, the second is roundly criticized as being beyond the pale and much too capricious for inclusion. Among the wide array of possible afflictions affecting individuals, there are significant definitional gaps between underlying biomedical mechanisms or diseases, how people feel, and how they are labeled by others.

In their original critique, Estes and Binney (1989) pointed out that Medicare's reimbursable conditions are defined in terms of the acute maladies not only of younger persons but also of those likely to affect societal economic well-being and potential contributions to Gross Domestic Product. Functional criteria, vested in economic more than in social functioning, inform the pattern of coverage. In the interval since Estes and Binney stated their case, the situation not only has not improved but has been subjected to a further politicization.

One consequence of this politicization is that government bureaucrats have taken an active part in deciding what is a medical condition, who is eligible for insurance protection, and what and who fall outside the bounds of public policies. National well-being and the common good are used to defend health care policy and proposals for rationing, but the nature of that well-being is never clearly defined. Those with "definitional power" exercise it to assign responsibility, eligibility, exclusion. In our society we look to our lawmakers, at times to our technical experts, and on occasion to our spiritual leaders or other sages for definition. For the most part, however, the medical and the political establishments have an undeniable suzerainty over how we categorize and how we perceive the process of aging. What is occurring now is that revisions to the implied social contract are redefining the terms of citizenship. There is no shortage of examples of the de facto consequences of the political-medical definition of worthy causes. From proposals to ration health care based on contributions to national well-being (Callahan, 1987), to the lack of coverage for long-term care (Hendricks, 1994b), to the pattern of medical attention to minority populations (Escarce, Epstein, Colby, & Schwartz, 1993; U.S. Department of Health and Human Services, 1986), one can discern a fairly clear-cut list of priorities. Even the pattern of protection offered by the much-discussed prospective payments system (DRGs) points to the relationship between health and public policy. As patients are released from hospitals "quicker and sicker," what are the realistic prospects of cost cutting as opposed to cost shifting?

A second dimension of the medicalization issue that deserves consideration is the possibility of bias in the delivery of medical care. Generally, the medical establishment operates as best it can and does not practice bias. Still, there may be unintended and unrecognized patterns of differential treatment that once identified will undoubtedly be corrected. A case in point is demonstrated by Escarce et al. (1993). They identified a pattern of racial differences in utilization patterns among older persons that persists even when level and type of third-party payment and health conditions are taken into account. As these authors maintained, it is not really a question of access, for access to health care is by now fairly universal among poor and elderly persons. Rather, it is a question of what type of access is available; are high-tech and specialized procedures equally available and utilized? Using a national sample of Medicare records, Escarce et al. examined 32 medical procedures or diagnostic tests and discovered a vexing pattern of differential treatment. What they found were statistically significant differences between white and black levels of medical attention. A pattern of differential care, diagnostic procedures, and mortality rates has long been identified in the research literature (Blendon, Aiken, Freeman, & Corey, 1989; Syme & Berkman, 1990; U.S. Department of Health and Human Services, 1986). What is relevant here is the authors' contention that elderly whites are notably better served when it comes to newer and more technologically sophisticated procedures. They assert that the differences are unlikely to be related to prevalence rates—if anything, prevalence rates would predict the opposite findings—and they conclude that there is considerable unmet need among elderly blacks.

Escarce et al. asserted that once type and level of Medicare-Medicaid coverage are considered and controlled, racial disparities persist even when controls for financial parity are exercised. Among the possible responsible factors they identified are organizational barriers reflecting proximity to knowledge of different types of medical attention and differential treatment within the same type of facility. Their analysis indicates that race may well be a factor affecting physician and institutional decision making—a troubling finding, to be sure, and one that will be carefully examined by other researchers and concerned citizens alike.

Although their research speaks only to racial differences among those who claim Medicare benefits, Escarce et al.'s findings are interesting because one may infer that the possibility of bias is fairly evident in patterns of treatment and that the differences are unrelated to financial considerations or prevalence rates. If this is so, are there other types of possible biases that might affect the receipt of medical care? The specter of a "geriatric challenge" (Jahnigen & Binstock, 1991), based on presumed "overloads" brought by the expected growth in the number of older persons, and especially the oldest old, suggests that additional biases may come to undermine the quality of care available to older persons.

Gekoski and Knox (1990) offered still another issue relevant for this discussion of the interaction of ageism and health. They suggested that a significant component of what usually passes as simple ageism may, in fact, be a form of "healthism"—a tendency to discount anyone who manifests poor health—especially old people. Victor (1991) hit the issue squarely when she asserted that healthism not only is ageist in the extreme but lumps all elderly persons into a single category without entertaining any possibility of significant variation. As she pointed out, health status among the retired varies by age, social class, and gender, and one commits what amounts to a composition fallacy by defining all elderly persons as heavy users of the health care system. Not coincidentally, Victor averred that in many respects, the differences in health status observed among older persons represent little more than a continuation of inequities found earlier in life.

One additional aspect of the medicalization of old age needs to be considered here. As has already been said, many ageist notions lurk in the language used by and about older persons. Williams and Giles (1991) provided a much-needed amplification of this issue in their efforts to consider not just the meanings of words but the way they are spoken, the voice used for their utterance, and how verbal exchange patterns communicate ageist attitudes. Imagine for a moment how question and response in a health care setting can extend beyond a simple two-way informational interaction to communicate disadvantage, power, influence, decision-making authority, and compliance. I wonder what an analysis of the intonation structure of the spoken phrases would suggest about control and definition of the situation. Add the possibility of age bias as another complication to what is hardly a simple interaction and we can begin to appreciate how ageism can be implicit in the dynamics of the situation (Adelman, Greene, & Charon, 1991).

Conclusion

The concept of ageism is far more complex than an individual bias. Without an understanding of the conditions that have shaped the situation in which older people now find themselves, it is unlikely that any serious inroads can be made in abolishing ageism or lessening its impact on older persons. The thesis of this chapter has been that ageism is socially constructed and is endemic to the social organization of our society.

What has been missing in previous discussions of ageism is an appreciation of the ethical and moral underpinnings that allow it to flourish. It is easy to point a finger at individuals who ply bias and discrimination as part of their daily routine and to dismiss them as a lower order of life. It is far more difficult to appreciate that there is something in the warp and woof of a culture that gives license to such sentiments. No doubt, whatever that something is, it is a latent consequence of the price of doing business as we have decided to do it.

My thesis has been that the constitutive elements, the underpinnings of what we label ageism, are part and parcel of social organization because the meaning of people, places, and things is socially created through interaction. I have identified what is generally labeled a constructionist perspective as a means of shedding more light on the question of ageism while trying to dissipate some of the heat that the term conjures up when it is applied to individuals as the sole agents of their own behavior and attitudes. The constructionist perspective maintains that meanings are not inherent but are always socially negotiated, that meanings are conveyed by the descriptive terminology and everyday language used to describe phenomena, and that worldviews are intrinsic to our membership in diverse social categories. In either instance, rhetoric provides both description and explanation.

For the most part, socially responsible people want to be just, but in deciding whether they are, they rely on the taken-for-granted assumptions of their sense of morality. Moral economy has been described as the ideological infrastructure of our collective values that help manage meaning. It derives from and provides the rationale for justifying societal arrangements, social policies, and the treatment accorded groups and individuals in terms of their participation in the priorities of a culture. We observe the outcome of the moral valuations in the nature of entitlement programs, public policies stipulating what is fair and equitable treatment, and our own deliberations of who is deserving and what constitutes a fair shake.

The biomedicalization of social problems is a tendency that seems to characterize modern industrialized societies; the United States is no exception. By turning responsibility for solving significant problems of living over to medical experts, we simultaneously insulate as we seek relief and provide solace. Within the medical establishment, we must wrestle with an array of possible biases. It would be an error to assume that those biases are any more deliberate than they are in society in general; rather, they stem from the fact that those who deliver health care are members of broader social groups and carry those identities with them to the practice of medicine. Like society in general, the organizational structure of medical care is such that unintended consequences create unanticipated outcomes. Neither in health care nor in life is the injustice of ageism likely to be an intended result.

Notes

1. The equation of old age with disease is hardly a new phenomenon. In Egypt, references to old age as a time of failing vitality and mental deterioration can be found as early as 2500 B.C. (De Beauvoir, 1985). As early as 161 B.C., the Romans were also referring to old age as a disease; see Terence's *Phormio,* for example. Certainly Cicero (Hendricks, 1994a) saw it as a disease, albeit one amenable to certain modifications by lifestyle changes. Actually, Quetelet (1796-1874), who established the statistical foundation of much of modern social science, also, through his observations, helped define today's concept of old age as beginning between the ages of 60 and 65. Quetelet's comments about declining viability can legitimately be said to be part of the impetus for the biomedicalization of the later years. In reviewing the history and growth of geriatric medicine, Kirk (1992) reviewed the increase in biologically based concepts of old age that occurred during the course of the 18th and 19th centuries.

2. There are exceptions of course; an outstanding example is the evolution of hyperkinesis as a medical diagnosis among children (Conrad, 1975).

References

Adelman, R., Greene, M., & Charon, R. (1991). Issues in physician-elderly patient interaction. *Ageing and Society, 11,* 127-148.

Armon-Jones, C. (1986). The thesis of constructionism. In R. Harré (Ed.), *The social construction of emotions* (pp. 32-56). Oxford, UK: Basil Blackwell.

Averill, J. (1980). A constructivist view of emotion. In P. Plutchik & H. Kellerman (Eds.), *Emotion theory, research, and experience* (Vol. 1, pp. 305-339). New York: Academic Press.

Blendon, R., Aiken, L., Freeman, H., & Corey, C. (1989). Access to medical care for black and white Americans: A matter of continuing concern. *Journal of the American Medical Association, 261,* 278-281.

Butler, R. N. (1969). Ageism: Another form of bigotry. *The Gerontologist, 9,* 243-246.

Butler, R. N. (1987). Ageism. In G. L. Maddox (Ed.), *Encyclopedia of aging* (pp. 22-23). New York: Springer.

Butler, R. N. (1993). Dispelling ageism: The cross-cutting intervention. *Generations, 17,* 75-78.

Callahan, D. (1987). *Setting limits: Medical goals in an aging society.* New York: Simon & Schuster.

Cirillo, L. (1993). Verbal imagery of aging in the news magazines. *Generations, 27,* 91-93.

Conrad, P. (1975). The discovery of hyperkinesis: Notes on the medicalization of deviant behavior. *Social Problems, 23,* 12-21.

Crews, D. E. (1993). Cultural lags in social perceptions of the aged. *Generations, 17,* 29-33.

De Beauvoir, S. (1985). *Old age.* New York: Penguin.

Escarce, J. J., Epstein, K. R., Colby, D. C., & Schwartz, J. S. (1993). Racial differences in the elderly's use of medical procedures and diagnostic procedures. *American Journal of Public Health, 83,* 948-954.

Estes, C. (1979). *The aging enterprise.* San Francisco: Jossey-Bass.

Estes, C., & Binney, E. A. (1989). The biomedicalization of aging: Dangers and dilemmas. *The Gerontologist, 29,* 589-596.

Estes, C., Gerard, L. E., Zones, J. S., & Swan, J. H. (1984). *Political economy, health, and aging.* Boston: Little, Brown.

Friedson, E. (1970). *Profession of medicine.* New York: Harper & Row.

Gekoski, W. L., & Knox, V. J. (1990). Ageism or healthism? Perceptions based on age and health statistics. *Journal of Ageing and Health, 2,* 15-27.

Glascock, A., & Feinman, S. (1981). Social asset or social burden: An analysis of the treatment of the aged in non-industrial societies. In C. Fry (Ed.), *Dimensions: Aging, culture and health* (pp. 13-32). New York: Praeger.

Gramsci, V. (1971). *Selections from the prison notebooks* (Q. Hoare & C. N. Smith, Eds. and Trans.). London: Laurence & Wishart.

Greene, V. (1989). Human capitalism and intergenerational justice. *The Gerontologist, 29,* 723-724.

Gubrium, J. F., Holstein, J. A., & Buckholdt, D. R. (in press). *Constructing the life course.* Dix Hills, NY: General Hall.

Harre, R. (1986). An outline of the social constructionist viewpoint. In R. Harre (Ed.), *The social construction of emotions* (pp. 2-14). Oxford, UK: Basil Blackwell.

Hendricks, J. (1984). Lifecourse and structure: The fate of the art. *Ageing and Society, 4,* 93-98.

Hendricks, J. (1994a). Cicero and social gerontology: Context and interpretation of a classic. *Journal of Aging Studies,* 255-285.

Hendricks, J. (1994b). Governmental responsibility: Adequacy or dependency for the elderly. In S. Ingman & D. Gill (Eds.), *Distributive justice and geriatric care* (pp. 255-285). Albany: SUNY Press.

Hendricks, J., & Leedham, C. (1992). Toward a political and moral economy of aging: An alternative perspective. *International Journal of Health Services, 22,* 125-137.

Jahnigen, D. W., & Binstock, R. H. (1991). Economic and clinical realities: Health care for elderly people. In R. H. Binstock & S. G. Post (Eds.), *Too old for health care?* (pp. 13-43). Baltimore: Johns Hopkins University Press.

Kirk, H. (1992). Medicine and the categorization of old age—the historical linkage. *Ageing and Society, 12*, 483-497.

Myles, J. (1984). *Old age in the welfare state.* Boston: Little, Brown.

Olson, L. K. (1982). *The political economy of aging: The state, private power, and social welfare.* New York: Columbia University Press.

Palmore, E. B. (1972). Gerontophobia versus ageism. *The Gerontologist, 12,* 213.

Palmore, E. B. (1990). *Ageism: Negative and positive.* New York: Springer.

Pitts, J. (1968). Social control: The concept. In *International encyclopedia of the social sciences* (Vol. 14, pp. 381-396). New York: Macmillan.

Schmidt, D., & Boland, S. (1986). Structure of perceptions of older adults: Evidence for multiple stereotypes. *Psychology and Aging, 1,* 255-260.

Sokolovsky, J. (1993). Images of aging: A cross-cultural perspective. *Generations, 17,* 51-54.

Stoller, E., & Gibson, R. (1994). *Worlds of difference: Inequality in the aging experience.* Newbury Park, CA: Sage.

Syme, S., & Berkman, L. (1990). Social class, susceptibility, and sickness. In P. Conrad & R. Kern (Eds.), *The sociology of health and illness* (pp. 28-34). New York: St. Martin's.

Townsend, P. (1981). The structured dependency of the elderly: A creation of social policy in the twentieth century. *Ageing and Society, 1,* 5-28.

Twaddle, A., & Hessler, R. (1986). *A sociology of health* (2nd ed.). New York: Macmillan.

U.S. Department of Health and Human Services. (1986). *Report of the Secretary's Task Force on Black and Minority Health.* Washington, DC: Government Printing Office.

Victor, C. (1991). Continuity or change: Inequality in health in later life. *Ageing and Society, 11,* 23-39.

Walker, A. (1980). The social creation of poverty and dependency in old age. *Journal of Social Policy, 9,* 49-75.

Williams, A., & Giles, H. (1991). Sociopsychological perspectives on older people's language and communication. *Ageing and Society, 11,* 103-126.

4

Demography of
Productive Aging

Eleanor M. Simonsick

In 1990 there were over 31 million Americans aged 65 years and older, representing 12.6% of the total U.S. population (U.S. Bureau of the Census, 1992). Both the absolute number of elders and their relative size will increase dramatically over the next three decades to a projected 52 million persons, 17.7% of the total U.S. population (Spencer, 1989). With the increasing size of the aged population, there has been increased interest in the social and economic costs associated with an aging society. This concern stems from the commonly held misperception of the aged as largely unproductive and as high consumers of government-provided services and resources.

Although it is well established that persons aged 65 years and older are the largest per capita consumers of health care and the primary beneficiaries of the Social Security pension plan, the majority lead healthy and productive lives. The literature is rich with data and discourse on dependency in old age; however, few address productivity in old age.

Existing population-based data provide an incomplete description of the productivity of the aged population. First, the scope and range of activities ascertained is often limited to paid work and volunteer pursuits, excluding homemaking and caregiving activities. This is particularly problematic when women make up a large majority of American elders. Moreover, the current population of older women reached adulthood in the 1940s, when work outside the home was discouraged. Second, whereas paid work is often measured in terms of hours per week and weeks per year employed, participation in other productive activities is not generally as finely measured.

This chapter presents data on the productive activities of persons aged 65 years and older. The concept of productivity, although commonly used, has not been defined in a consistent manner and has been rarely applied to the aged. The most simplistic definition of productivity centers on the economic value of goods and services produced and equates productivity with paid work. Some have expanded the definition to include unpaid but nevertheless economically valued activities, such as child care, household tasks (e.g., meal preparation, laundry, and housekeeping) and volunteer services. For this report, I have further expanded the concept of productivity to include leisure and recreational activities, and label them *personally productive activities*.

Personally productive activities, though they do not directly produce a good or provide a service, serve at least two important functions in American society. First, these activities contribute substantially to the health of the U.S. economy by creating and supporting businesses and jobs. The golf and travel and resort industries, for example, are highly dependent on a retired clientele. Similarly, symphony orchestras and other cultural arts rank high in the leisure pursuits of older adults, so the aged population represents a major source of their financial support. Second, involvement in leisure and recreational activities contributes to the health and well-being of the older adult. Maintained health and functioning in old age lowers the need for medical and long-term care services and reduces strain on economic resources.

This chapter is organized in three parts. The first provides an overview of the basic demographic characteristics of the U.S. population aged 65 years and older, including educational attainment and health status, factors that might be considered the "raw materials" of productivity. The second part presents data on traditionally defined productivity, including paid work, volunteer work, caregiving, and homemaking and household maintenance activities. The last section covers personally productive activities, primarily leisure and recreational pursuits.

The demographic information contained in this report comes from a variety of sources. A major consideration in selecting data sources was adequate measurement of productivity as well as the inclusion of health status indicators and an assessment of educational attainment. Thus, in addition to the Current Population Reports conducted by the U.S. Census Bureau, the 1984 National Health Interview Survey's Supplement on Aging (SOA) (Fitti & Kovar, 1987) served as a major source of information. Two independent surveys of volunteerism in the United States supplement data on volunteer activities, and published tables from the 1986 survey of Americans' Changing Lives (ACL) (see Herzog et al., 1989) provide data on caregiving. Data on leisure and recreational activities come from individual sites of the Established Populations for Epidemiologic Studies of the Elderly (EPESE) (see Cornoni-Huntley, Brock, Ostfeld, Taylor, & Wallace, 1986) conducted by the National Institute on Aging.

Most surveys that include measures of productivity exclude persons residing in institutions. Thus this report focuses on the community resident

Table 4.1   Marital Status and Living Arrangements

	65-74 Years		75-84 Years		85+ Years	
	Men	*Women*	*Men*	*Women*	*Men*	*Women*
Married	80.2	53.1	73.9	29.2	51.2	10.6
Spouse present	78.2	51.1	71.2	27.7	47.0	10.2
Spouse absent	2.0	2.1	2.6	1.4	4.2	0.5
Unmarried	19.8	46.8	26.1	70.8	48.9	89.4
Never	4.7	4.6	3.3	5.2	3.6	6.2
Divorced	6.0	6.2	3.3	3.6	2.0	3.4
Widowed	9.1	36.1	19.5	62.0	43.4	79.8
Lives:						
Alone	13.0	32.2	19.3	53.3	28.1	56.8
With spouse	78.2	51.1	71.2	27.7	47.0	10.2
With other relatives	6.6	14.1	7.4	16.8	21.1	27.5
With nonrelatives only	2.2	1.7	2.0	2.2	3.8	5.5

SOURCE: U.S. Bureau of the Census, 1991a.

population. Exclusion of persons in long-term care settings, where a substantial proportion may be described as nonproductive, produces an overestimate of productivity levels. This overestimate is small for the total population aged 65 years and older and for the younger age groups through age 80 years, but increases markedly above age 85 years, especially for women, of whom 25% reside in nursing homes (Hing, 1987).

Basic Demographic Characteristics

Age, Sex, Marital Status, and Living Arrangements

The majority of American old are young-old. In 1990, of the 31.1 million U.S. persons aged 65 years and older, nearly one third were younger than 70 years of age, and five sixths were below 80 years (Figure 4.1). Women vastly outnumber men, particularly in very old age. For every 100 women aged 65 years and older there are 67 men. By age 85 there are only 39 men for every 100 women. The predominance of women is reflected in the marital status and living arrangements of the older population. Between age 65 and 74 years, 80% of men and 53% of women are married; by age 85 years, 51% of men and only 11% of women have a living spouse (Table 4.1). The majority of older Americans live with a spouse or alone (Table 4.1). The proportion who live alone increases with increasing age for both men and women to 28% and 57%, respectively, by age 85 years. The proportion who live with nonspouse relatives also increases with increasing age to about 25% by age 85 years. Very few older Americans live with nonrelatives.

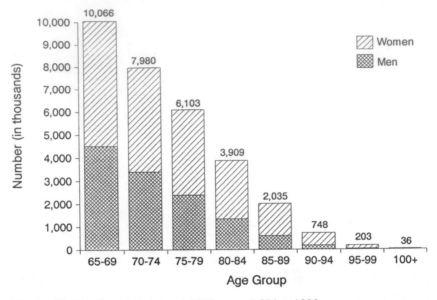

Figure 4.1. U.S. Population Aged 65 Years and Older: 1990
SOURCE: U.S. Bureau of the Census, 1991b.

Health Status

Health status can be measured in numerous ways. In considering productivity or capacity for productive activity, health and physical function are
important dimensions. For this report, two categories of health status were
created. Persons in the *good* category rate their health good to excellent and
have no difficulty in any of the following activities of daily living (ADLs):
eating, dressing, bathing, transferring, using the toilet, and walking. Persons
in the *poor* category rate their health poor or fair or have difficulty in one or
more ADLs. This categorization is used to illustrate the relationship between
health and productivity and to demonstrate that poor health does not preclude
engagement in productive activities. Figure 4.2 gives the distribution of
persons in good health by age and gender. The two youngest age groups are
included for comparison purposes. About two thirds of persons aged 65 to
69 years have good health, but this declines markedly with increasing age to
about 50% in persons aged 80 to 84 years. Women report marginally poorer
health than men.

Cognitive Status

Cognitive status is also an important dimension of productive capacity.
Analyses of data from the Seattle Longitudinal Study (Schaie, 1991) on the

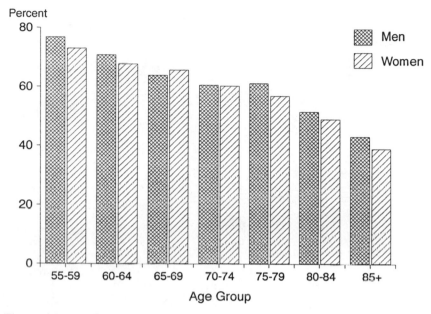

Figure 4.2. U.S. Population Aged 55 Years and Older Who Report Good Health and No Difficulty in Activities of Daily Living: 1984
SOURCE: Fitti & Kovar, 1987.

maintenance of performance over 7 years on tests tapping 5 primary mental abilities (word comprehension, spatial orientation, inductive reasoning, addition, and recall vocabulary) show that although some intellectual capacity is lost, the loss is small and usually limited to one or two areas. Even in the eighth decade, 80% of individuals maintain performance in at least three abilities. Clearly, much of higher order cognitive function is maintained well into late life. Even though dementia and dementing illnesses receive a great deal of attention and represent major health care concerns in the elderly population, dementia is not a major cause of lost productivity.

Educational Attainment

Educational attainment, as measured by years of school completed, has increased dramatically over the past 50 years, as illustrated in Figure 4.3. Although the proportion who have postcollegiate training has remained relatively constant, the proportion completing high school has increased dramatically for both men and women. Each cohort of elders is increasingly better educated: 55% of men aged 65 to 69 years graduated high school in contrast to 30% of men aged 85 years and older. Women in the oldest age

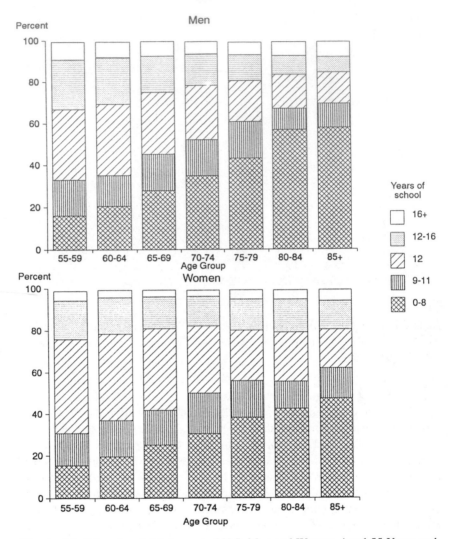

Figure 4.3. Educational Attainment of U.S. Men and Women Aged 55 Years and Older: 1984

SOURCE: Fitti & Kovar, 1987.

groups have higher educational attainment than men; rates of high school graduation are more similar below age 70 years. Data from 1991 (Kominski & Adams, 1992) show a tapering of the high school graduation rate and a modest increase in the proportion attending college. In 1991, 50% of persons aged 35 to 44 years completed one or more years of college in comparison to 25% of persons aged 65 to 74 years.

Educational Attainment and Health Status

Health and educational attainment are strongly related, particularly in the young-old (Figure 4.4). Men and women with at least a high school education consistently rate their health better than those with less education. Up to age 80 years, men and women who have more than a high school education consistently have the best health. This strong relationship between education and health is important to remember in interpreting the relationship between both education and health and productivity presented later in this chapter.

Paid Work and Volunteer Activities

Paid Work

Many barriers and disincentives exist for older Americans to maintain high levels of work-related productivity. Few organizations offer alternative work schedules, and pension plans and early retirement packages often render continued employment financially unattractive. Ageism in hiring practices makes it difficult for retired or released older individuals to find other work. Lastly, retirement is a highly valued and long-anticipated transition in American society. Retirement is considered an entitlement—a deserved rest and opportunity to pursue personal interests. Thus current levels of productivity, as measured by paid work, grossly underrepresent potential productivity in terms of both capacity and desire.

Figure 4.5 presents the work status of men and women as reported in the 1984 SOA. Participants were asked the number of weeks they worked in the preceding 12 months and the number of hours worked per week. The four categories of work in Figure 4.5 represent the average number of hours worked per week over the past year. Between age 55 and 59 years, 83% of men worked for pay; only 70% worked full time, at least 35 hours per week. In the cohort 10 years older, aged 65 to 69 years, only 32% worked at all, and the majority worked part time. With increasing age, rates of participation in the workforce declined steeply. Of those who continued to work, the proportion working part time increased with age. Beyond age 70, few men worked full time. Nevertheless, 5% to 8% of men 80 years and older still engaged in paid work.

The participation of women in the workforce is lower than that of men in each age group, although patterns of decline in participation with increasing age are similar. About 50% of women aged 55 to 59 years work for pay, with

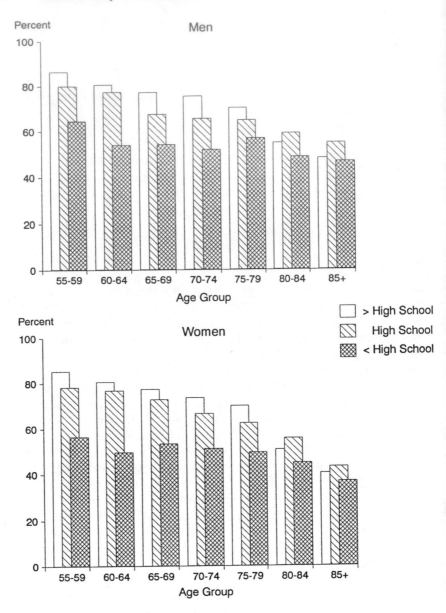

Figure 4.4. U.S. Population Aged 55 Years and Older Who Report Good Health and No Difficulty in Activities of Daily Living by Educational Attainment: 1984
SOURCE: Fitti & Kovar, 1987.

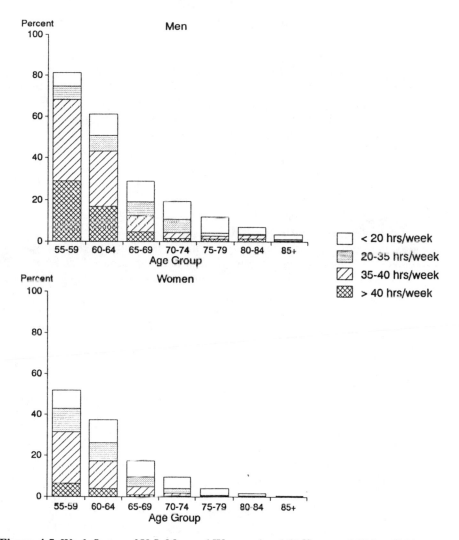

Figure 4.5. Work Status of U.S. Men and Women Aged 55 Years and Older: 1984
SOURCE: Fitti & Kovar, 1987.

about 30% employed full time. In the age group 65 to 69 years, fewer than 20% work and only 5% work full time. Of women who work, a higher proportion work less than 35 hours per week than of men who work. Participation in paid work among older women, however, is likely to increase substantially over the next 20 years and beyond because each successive cohort of young and middle-aged women has had greater participation in the workforce than the one before.

In addition to historical trends and societal and personal expectations, a variety of factors, including health and educational attainment, influence participation in paid work among the elderly. Figure 4.6 presents the work status of men and women aged 55 years and older by health status. Clearly, persons in poor health are less likely to work than persons in good or better health at all ages. A major reason for less than full participation in the workforce among men aged 55 and 59 years is poor health or disability. Still, among men in good health, only 70% aged 60 to 64 years work, and fewer than 35% aged 65 to 69 years continue to work. Although men in poor health or with disabilities are less likely to work than their healthy counterparts, 15% of those 65 to 74 still work. Although, on the basis of health status, many would not consider this group successfully aged (e.g., Rowe & Kahn, 1987), they are nonetheless productive in the traditional sense. The picture is similar for women, although the overall rates of employment are much lower.

Figure 4.7 presents work status of men and women by level of educational attainment. Rates of employment are substantially higher among the most educated across the age span for both men and women. Among women aged 75 years and older, rates of paid work do not vary by educational level, as very few women work.

Volunteer Activities

As with participation in paid work, actual levels of volunteerism under-represent desired levels. The Marriott's Seniors Volunteerism Study conducted in 1991 found that 41% of Americans aged 60 years and older performed a volunteer service in the past year. An additional 38% reported a willingness to volunteer, if asked, and among current volunteers, 26% would have volunteered more time. On average, these seniors volunteered 64 days per year and averaged 3.6 hours per day. Rates of volunteering declined with increasing age but still remained high at 27.3% of persons aged 80 years and older responding to the Marriott Study. Participation in volunteer activities also varied greatly by education and income. Among college graduates aged 60 years and older, 66.2% had volunteered in the past year versus 37.5% of persons graduating high school only. Over half of persons earning $40,000 or more had volunteered versus one third of persons earning less than $15,000. Most volunteer activities are affiliated with church, religious, or social service organizations, and most frequently concern the provision of companionship, transportation, advisory services, and instruction.

Figure 4.8 presents data on volunteer activities from the 1984 SOA. Respondents were asked whether they had done volunteer work in the past

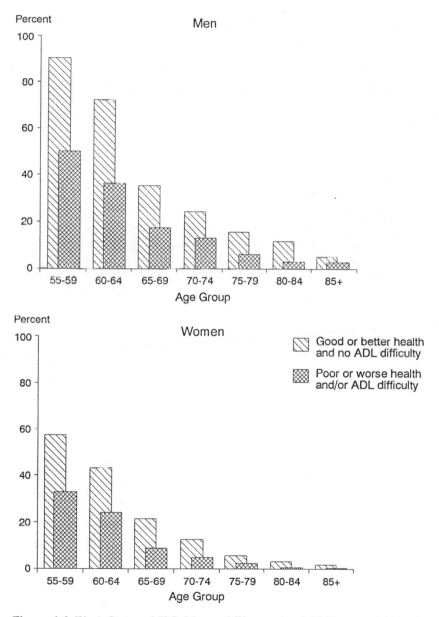

Figure 4.6. Work Status of U.S. Men and Women Aged 55 Years and Older by Health Status: 1984
SOURCE: Fitti & Kovar, 1987.

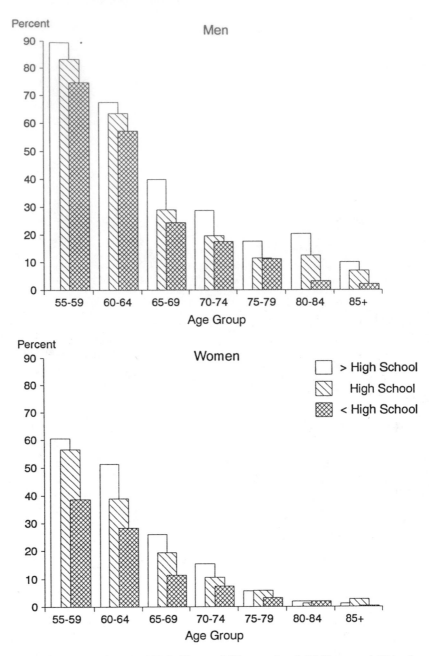

Figure 4.7. Work Status of U.S. Men and Women Aged 55 Years and Older by Educational Attainment: 1984

SOURCE: Fitti & Kovar, 1987.

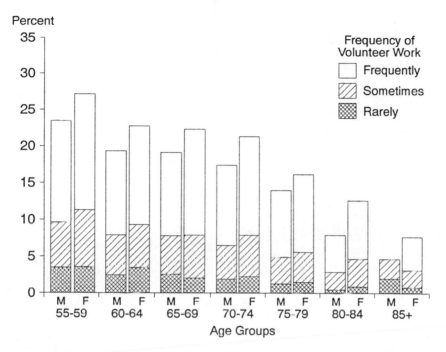

Figure 4.8. Volunteerism of U.S. Men and Women Aged 55 Years and Older: 1984
SOURCE: Fitti & Kovar, 1987.

12 months and if yes, how often. The overall participation rate among persons aged 65 years and older of 20% was much lower than the rates found in the Marriott Study and by the Independent Sector (1992) in their annual national survey of giving and volunteering. This large difference probably stems from the different purposes of the surveys, with the SOA a general survey of health and functioning and the Marriott and Independent Sector studies focused specifically on volunteering. Estimates from the SOA most likely exclude infrequent volunteers, for the majority of those volunteering worked frequently (Figure 4.8).

Participation in volunteer activities varies by health status, with persons in poor health or disabled less likely to report volunteer work (Figure 4.9). However, despite health problems, 15% of both men and women aged 65 to 69 years performed some volunteer work. As with paid work, persons whom many would not consider successfully aged are nonetheless productive, even among the oldest old.

The relationship between volunteerism and educational attainment is more striking than that observed for work, with upwards of 30% of men aged

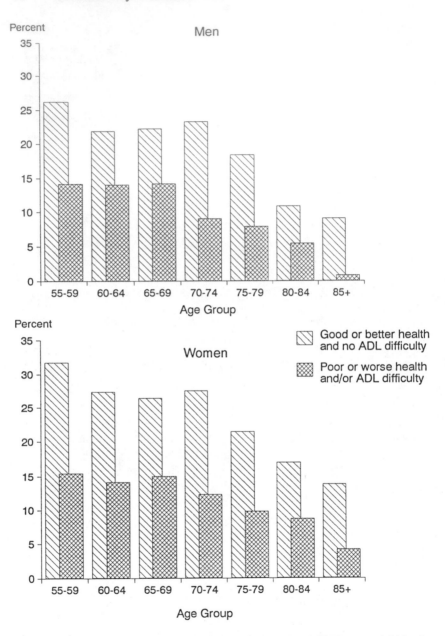

Figure 4.9. Volunteerism of U.S. Men and Women Aged 55 Years and Older by Health Status: 1984

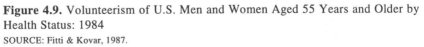
SOURCE: Fitti & Kovar, 1987.

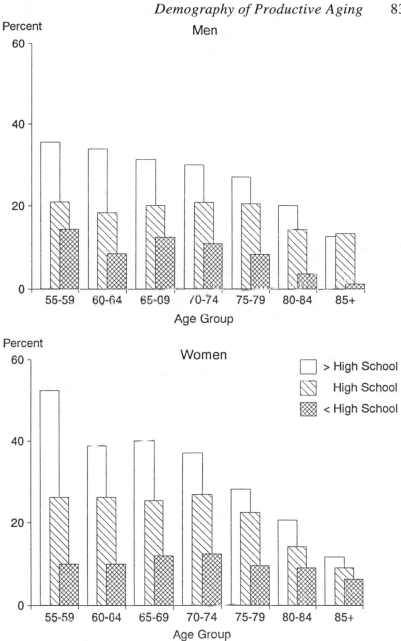

Figure 4.10. Volunteerism of U.S. Men and Women Aged 55 Years and Older by Educational Attainment: 1984
SOURCE: Fitti & Kovar, 1987.

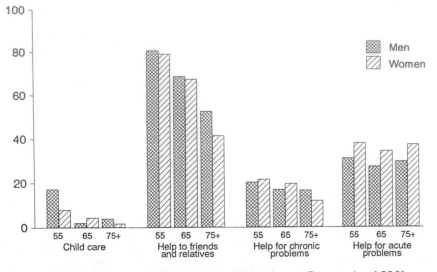

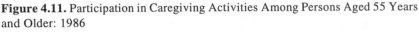

Figure 4.11. Participation in Caregiving Activities Among Persons Aged 55 Years and Older: 1986

SOURCE: Adapted from Herzog et al., 1989.

65 to 79 years and 40% of women aged 60 to 74 years with greater than a high school education engaging in volunteer activities (Figure 4.10).

Caregiving Activities

Providing care and assistance to children or a sick friend or relative, including one's spouse, is an important productive activity that is often overlooked and is not typically captured in assessments of volunteer activity. For instance, an older women caring for her incapacitated husband probably would not consider her care to him volunteer work—yet she provides an essential service. The survey of Americans' Changing Lives conducted in 1986 provides an estimate of caregiving activities among persons aged 55 years and older. Figure 4.11 shows that a very small proportion of older adults do child care but that a large majority provide help to friends and relatives. The proportion giving such help drops precipitously after age 74 years, from 70% among persons aged 65 to 74 years to 35% of persons aged 75 years and older. Nearly 20% report providing help to persons with chronic problems, and about one third provide help when acute problems arise. The proportions providing help to persons with chronic or acute problems decline very little with increasing age.

Personally Productive Activities

Personally productive activities are recreational and leisure pursuits engaged in primarily for personal enrichment and fulfillment. The data come from the New Haven and Iowa sites of the EPESE baseline conducted between 1982 and 1983 (Cornoni-Huntley et al., 1986). These surveys, though not specifically designed to characterize activity patterns of elders, included several questions on social and physical activities not available in other studies.

Figure 4.12 presents the proportion of men and women in the New Haven EPESE who engaged in each of three social activities within the month preceding the survey by health status. A majority of healthy older men and women go out to a movie, restaurant or sporting event at least monthly, up to age 80 years; just under half of those in poor health also get out for dinner or a show at least monthly. Overnight and day trips are also very common, with about one third traveling at least monthly. Card games and bingo are slightly more popular than travel, with participation varying only moderately by health. Participation in all three activities declines markedly with increasing age even among the healthy.

Figure 4.13 presents the proportion of men and women with at least weekly participation in each of three recreational activities and at least monthly participation in sports, golf, or hunting by health status from the Iowa EPESE. Nearly 60% of men and about 50% of women engage in some physical exercise, primarily walking, at least weekly. Even higher proportions engage in garden or home projects, with men more active than women. Involvement in gardening or home projects drops steeply with age, more so than involvement in physical exercise. Virtually all women bake, sew, or make crafts until age 85 years. Still, 70% of the oldest old women in good health and 50% of women in poor health bake, sew, or do crafts. Fewer than 20% of men are involved in this activity, but this does not change much with age or health. Sports, golf, or hunting is popular among young-old men, with 50% participating between the ages of 65 and 69 years. Although participation declines steeply with age, down to 30% among men 85 years and older, a sizable proportion, including even those in poor health, engage in sporting activities well into old age.

Even with a limited number of items, these data indicate that older adults have very high levels of social and recreational activity. However, without data on the number of hours spent per day or per week in these and similar activities, comparisons with time spent in traditionally defined productive activity is not possible.

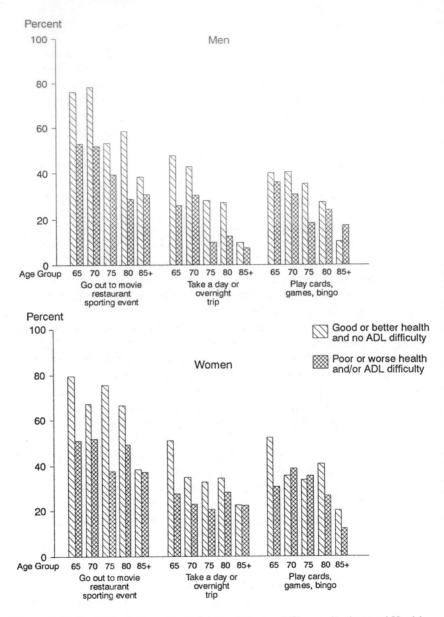

Figure 4.12. Social Activity in Past Month of Men and Women by Age and Health Status, New Haven EPESE: 1982-1983

SOURCE: Cornoni-Huntley et al., 1986.

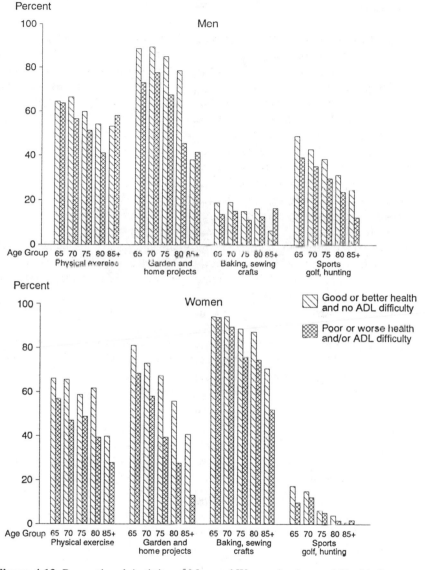

Figure 4.13. Recreational Activity of Men and Women by Age and Health Status, Iowa EPESE: 1982-1983

SOURCE: Cornoni-Huntley et al., 1986.

Summary

The U.S. population aged 65 years and older appears to be highly engaged in many forms of productive activity, including paid work, volunteering, caregiving, and social and recreational activities. There is evidence that a sizable proportion of this population desires to do more in many different realms. Education and health seem to promote productivity in that the most educated and those in good health have the highest levels of participation in both paid and volunteer work. Given the increasing levels of educational attainment in younger cohorts, we should expect to see higher levels of productive activity in future elderly cohorts.

There appears to be substantial unmet need with regard to opportunities for productive activity among older adults. The identification of barriers to increased productivity would be a fruitful area of inquiry. The barriers encountered probably vary by age, with the young-old, for instance, beset with social incentives to retire, economic disincentives to continue work, and limited opportunity for alternative work arrangements. The oldest old, on the other hand, may face barriers to volunteer work, for example, related to mobility and transportation problems.

As the population aged 65 years and older becomes a larger proportion of the total adult population, their contribution to a productive society becomes increasingly important. We still know very little about the productivity of older adults. Although this report gives an incomplete sketch of productivity of aged Americans, it is evident that persons aged 65 years and older contribute a great deal and possess the desire and capacity to do more.

References

Cornoni-Huntley, J., Brock, D. B., Ostfeld, A. M., Taylor, J. O., & Wallace, R. B. (1986). *Established Populations for Epidemiologic Studies of the Elderly [EPESE]: Resource data book* (USDHHS/PHS/NIH/NIA NIH Pub. No. 86-2443). Washington, DC: Government Printing Office.

Fitti, J. E., & Kovar, M. G. (1987). *The supplement on aging to the National Health Interview Survey* (Vital and Health Statistics, Vol. 1, No. 21). Washington, DC: Government Printing Office.

Herzog, A. R., et al. (1989). Age differences in productive activities. *Journal of Gerontology, 44,* S129-S138.

Hing, E. (1987). *Use of nursing homes by the elderly: Preliminary data from the 1985 National Nursing Home Survey* (Advance Data from Vital and Health Statistics, No. 135). Washington, DC: Government Printing Office.

Independent Sector. (1992). *Giving and volunteering in the United States.* Washington, DC: Author.

Kominski, R., & Adams, A. (1992). *Educational attainment in the United States: March 1991 and 1990* (Current Population Reports, Series P-20, No. 462). Washington, DC: Government Printing Office.

Marriott's Seniors Volunteerism Study. (1991). Commissioned by Marriott Senior Living Services and United States Administration on Aging. Washington, DC: Marriott Senior Living Services.

Rowe, J. W., & Kahn, R. L. (1987). Human aging: Usual and successful. *Science, 237,* 143-149.

Schaie, K. W. (1991). The optimization of cognitive functioning in old age: Predictions based on cohort-sequential and longitudinal data. In P. B. Baltes & M. M. Baltes (Eds.), *Successful aging* (pp. 94-117). Cambridge, UK: Cambridge University Press.

Spencer, G. (1989). *Projections of the population of the United States, by age, sex, and race: 1988 to 2080* (Current Population Reports, Series P-25, No. 1018). Washington, DC: Government Printing Office.

U.S. Bureau of the Census. (1991a). *Marital status and living arrangements: March 1990* (Current Population Reports, Series P-20). Washington, DC: Government Printing Office.

U.S. Bureau of the Census. (1991b). *1990 census of population and housing: Modified and actual age, sex, race, and Hispanic origin data* (Series CPH-L-74). Washington, DC: Government Printing Office.

U.S. Bureau of the Census. (1992). *Sixty-five plus in America* (Current Population Reports, Special Studies, P23-178). Washington, DC: Government Printing Office.

PART II

SUCCESSFUL AND PRODUCTIVE AGING: ORGANIC FACTORS

Many of the changes to the human organism that manifest themselves over the course of the life span are universally experienced indices of the aging process. In societies in which the outward appearances of youthfulness are highly valued, those changes that are visible to others are often dreaded. Many individuals go to great lengths (and great expense) to ward off these changes, and many others profit handsomely from such efforts.

It is unfortunate that such cosmetic changes are a source of discomfort to so many. But the good news is that these most dreaded signs of aging are least likely to do us any harm in the long run. For that matter, research clearly indicates that, given freedom from disease, the human organism sustains itself exceedingly well with age. Human organ systems, though losing some efficiency over time, are capable of supporting life beyond the life expectancy of the individual. The problem, of course, is that these systems are often compromised by unhealthy lifestyles that result in both chronic and acute diseases. The conditions or diseases common to individuals in the middle and later years are widely recognized; unfortunately, their effects on organ systems are often erroneously attributed to the aging process per se. Distinguishing between illness and aging is prerequisite to an appropriate understanding of the role prevention can play in promoting successful and productive aging.

Chronic diseases are ubiquitous among old people in part because, until recently, little attention has been directed at attempting to prevent them. The authors in this section of the book focus on specific areas of chronic disease prevention. They explore how disease compromises the integrity of human organ systems and thus reduces the potential of older individuals to function optimally. Pearl S. German begins Chapter 5 with a review of the implications of the demographic aging imperative for the prevalence, incidence, and distribution of chronic disease in the United States. It is clear that without major initiatives aimed at disease prevention and health promotion, the task of treating the diseases of our burgeoning older population will soon prove undoable. An important argument in her chapter deals with the likely success of primary prevention as a strategy here in the light of her observation that elders in the past have not readily identified with such programs. Though encouraging continued efforts to involve and recruit elders, German sees the need to include secondary and even tertiary prevention in our overall approach to the treatment of chronic disease in old people.

Eric Poehlman's work on energy expenditure in elderly people relates directly to two key factors in disease prevention and health promotion: diet and exercise. It has been suggested that if the benefits of exercise could be made available in capsule form, it would be today's most widely recommended health supplement. Yet the literature about exercise benefits among older groups of people is not unequivocal.

Similarly, although the importance of proper nutrition to the promotion of good health has long been known, the value of various dietary regimens in promoting health is far from agreed upon. Of central importance here is the whole issue of required dietary allowances for older people. What guidelines we have are extrapolated from data on younger subjects; it has been argued that, compared to younger adults, old people need the same nutritional components but fewer calories. Important as we believe nutrition to be, we are only beginning to study energy expenditure and nutritional correlates in elders.

In Chapter 6, Poehlman reviews data, including his own, that relate to energy requirements in old people, and in particular to the interplay between endurance exercise and energy metabolism. A significant finding, further buttressing the notion of increased heterogeneity with age, is that caloric expenditure varies substantially in older subjects and consequently makes estimation of energy requirements for individuals a difficult undertaking.

Chapter 7, by James Mortimer, explores the possibility of preventing one of the most dreaded diseases of old age. Research on Alzheimer's disease continues apace, and it is well that it does, for the course of the disease threatens to disrupt the lives of the victims and family members who believe that Alzheimer's is, as the author puts it, "a slow death of the mind," "a nightmare that never ends." With the pervasive view that this is an illness with no known cause or cure, such pessimism is understandable. Our author, however, believes that the future may not be quite so hopeless.

Mortimer argues that primary and secondary prevention of dementing conditions is a future possibility. One model he advances reflects the redundancy of brain components. There is substantial reserve capacity that permits normal functioning even in the presence of extensive damage. The difficulty with the threshold model at this time is that we do not get early warning signals that such damage is occurring in amounts large enough to warrant additional preventive measures. Another preventive approach builds on the fact that dementia is a multifactorial condition. Identifiable factors that can contribute to dementia may be controllable or even eliminated, with a resultant slowing of the disease progression. Mortimer identifies known risk factors, particularly in Alzheimer's disease, and modestly suggests that reduction of exposure to them, as well as continued research findings in areas such as molecular genetics, may lead to modification in the course of the disease.

5

Prevention and Chronic Disease in Older Individuals

Pearl S. German

The demographic trend that has "aged" the U.S. population, and indeed populations of most industrialized nations, began soon after the end of World War II and has persisted and intensified. This "aging" characterization of the current population has become commonplace and is de rigueur to any discussion of demography or chronic disease. Known as the "demographic imperative," it runs as follows: This country's older population is increasing in absolute numbers and proportionally, and is doing so at an accelerating rate. Life expectancy is rising as well, causing a particularly rapid rise of "old-olds," those 75 and over (U.S. Bureau of the Census, 1992). This confluence of facts, when included in a variety of gerontologic presentations, is accompanied by concerns, dire warnings, and calls to action for a broad array of society's institutions. The intense attention directed at growing costs that accompany this demographic trend has resulted in a focus on the network of health care institutions (Estes et al., 1993) and on troubling ethical issues around suggestions of withholding or rationing services (Moody, 1992).

In 1990, almost 13% of the population was 65 years of age and over, having increased 22% from 1980. The proportion of this population who were the oldest old (85 and over) grew at an unprecedented rate of 38% between 1980 and 1990. There were almost 36,000 centenarians (100 and over) in 1990, and this represented a doubling of the 1980 count among the older population (U.S. Bureau of the Census, 1992).

This chapter will discuss the implications of this "imperative," with a focus first on chronic disease, an accompaniment of the aging of the population, and then on prevention and its relevance as a strategy in light of the prevalence and incidence of chronic disease.

In an introduction to a report on prevention and older people, the Institute of Medicine (IOM) panel (IOM, 1990) summarized the issues around prevention and health reflecting an emerging point of view: "The implications of an aging population for health care are being widely discussed but seldom

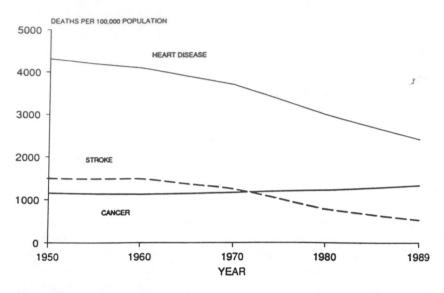

Figure 5.1. Death Rates for Leading Causes of Death for People Aged 75 to 84: 1950-1989

SOURCE: National Center for Health Statistics, 1990a, 1990b, 1990d.

with the understanding that health promotion and disability prevention are workable concepts for people in the 'second 50' years of life" (p. 2). This observation is cogent when we consider the nature of our older population and the relevance of prevention for a group with these specific characteristics.

Chronic Disease: Prevalence, Incidence, Distribution, and Implications

Chronic diseases are both the major cause of death in elders and the most prevalent health problems encountered by this group (Fried & Bush, 1988; U.S. Bureau of the Census, 1992). Any focus on control of symptoms and avoidance of severe sequelae along with the prevention of disease and delay of death demands an understanding of chronic disease—first, because chronic disease is closely associated with mortality and morbidity, and second, because of the intimate connection to disability and hence quality of life. Finally, all of these outcomes of chronic disease have direct bearing on the cost of care, a continuing concern in the current health care enterprise and the upcoming reform.

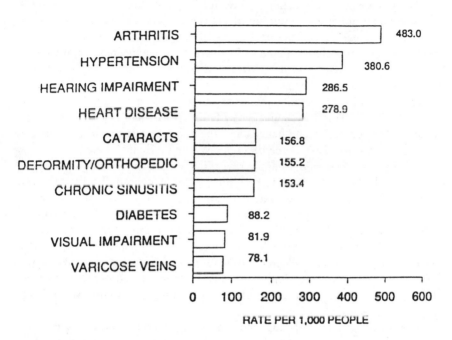

THE TOP TEN CHRONIC CONDITIONS FOR PEOPLE 65+: 1989

Condition	Rate
ARTHRITIS	483.0
HYPERTENSION	380.6
HEARING IMPAIRMENT	286.5
HEART DISEASE	278.9
CATARACTS	156.8
DEFORMITY/ORTHOPEDIC	155.2
CHRONIC SINUSITIS	153.4
DIABETES	88.2
VISUAL IMPAIRMENT	81.9
VARICOSE VEINS	78.1

RATE PER 1,000 PEOPLE

Figure 5.2. The Top 10 Chronic Conditions for People Aged 65+: 1989
SOURCE. National Center for Health Statistics, 1990c.

Figure 5.1 gives the death rates from the three leading causes of death: heart disease, cancer, and stroke. These causes of death, as well as conditions that are prevalent in the older population (see Figure 5.2), have shown changes in patterns that have been noted in national vital statistics and commented on consistently by epidemiologists who study these patterns (Fried & Wallace, 1992; U.S. Special Committee on Aging, 1991). The role of infectious disease has given way as the major cause of death to chronic conditions, and this shift is true for morbidity also. Chronicities are associated with disability and dysfunction and with high use of services, often inpatient and high tech interventions, both of which are very costly. In addition, it can be anticipated that individuals will live with these diseases for longer periods of time because of the nature of the conditions, but also because there has been a degree of success in controlling aspects of chronic disease and hence a reduction and/or delay in mortality.

This increased skill in management of chronic disease is one of the factors in the increase of life expectancy. Average length of life is increasing more slowly than it did at the beginning of the century, but the increase has been continuous nonetheless. Table 5.1 gives life expectancy at birth and at age 65 by age groups and race. Females have greater life expectancy at birth and at age 65, and there is also a difference between whites and nonwhites. Nonwhite males have the lowest life expectancy, and nonwhite females have fewer years of life expectancy than white females (Van Nostrand, Turner, & Suzman, 1993). This last group, white females, has the greatest life expectancy in the population and hence can expect the longest period of dysfunction and disability (Task Force on Older Women's Health, 1993).

Additional data on older people reveal decrements in certain physiologic functions that are considered to be indicators of an overall "frailty." Decrements in these functions are considered signals, in most cases, of early onset of disease and evidence of dependence and decline (Hadley, Ory, Suzman, Weindruch, & Fried, 1993). Some of the more important of these signals are noted in pulmonary function, muscle strength, exercise tolerance, blood values, and memory. An added complication deserving mention and consideration is that because of longer expected years with chronic conditions, there is increased risk of developing other associated conditions and the attendant disabilities of comorbidity.

For many reasons, defining and measuring overall health of the older population present serious problems to clinicians and researchers. Frailty, comorbidities, and conditions that are not specific diagnoses of disease are challenges that complicate the development of a rigorous typology of health status for older individuals. These challenges present problems that are the focus of much conceptual and empirical work in the field. Problems include defining and measuring of "normal" physiological measures for older people that differ from those established for younger individuals; establishing when these measures are within normal range for older people and when they represent pathology; recognizing differences in presentation of symptoms of diseases—for example, less pain or changing lab values; separating the effects of diseases in a population with a high degree of comorbidity; and developing more rigorous measures of function to establish appropriate markers. All of this imprecision contributes to the widely held belief that prevalence and incidence of data on disease in the older population may not be accurate due to both under- and overestimation of specific diseases. Several of the concepts mentioned above require further elaboration.

TABLE 5.1 Projected Life Expectancy (in Years) at Birth and Age 65, by Sex: 1990-2050

	At Birth			At Age 65		
Year	*Men*	*Women*	*Difference*	*Men*	*Women*	*Difference*
1990	72.1	79.0	6.9	15.0	19.4	4.4
2000	73.5	80.4	6.9	15.7	20.3	4.6
2010	74.4	81.3	6.9	16.2	21.0	4.8
2020	74.9	81.8	6.9	16.6	21.4	4.8
2030	75.4	82.3	6.9	17.0	21.8	4.8
2040	75.9	82.8	6.9	17.3	22.3	5.0
2050	76.4	83.8	7.4	17.7	22.7	5.0

SOURCE: U.S. Bureau of the Census, 1992.

Comorbidity

The importance of this dimension of the health of people 65 years of age and over—namely, the coexistence of more than one chronic condition—is seen in both assessment and treatment of such conditions. Eighty percent of people who are 65 and over have at least one chronic condition, and the majority of this 80% has two or more such diseases (U.S. Bureau of the Census, 1992). The prevalence of comorbidity increases with age; for those 80 and over, 70% of women and 53% of men suffer from two or more chronic conditions (Fried & Wallace, 1992). The presence of comorbid conditions confounds outcomes, particularly those of functional capacity, and makes examining the natural history of specific diseases more difficult. From a practical point of view, treatment for one condition can cause complications for another. Comorbidity represents a challenge to epidemiologists who examine the patterns of diseases and their etiologies, to the health care systems concerned with delivery of care, and to the general development of intervention strategies.

Functional Capacity

The epidemiology of disease, especially chronic disease, and demographic trends are essential background information to the issue of prevention for the 65-and-over population. There remains one other dimension to be considered before the case for prevention can be made and the discussion of its relevance enjoined. This concerns definitions and measures of "success" with populations in their later years when the goal can no longer be a "cure" for conditions and diseases that exist. In addition to assessing out-comes, some measure is important as a basis for both designing and evalu-ating interventions. Because of these varied problems and also because of the crucial role of independence in daily life, the concept of "function," its definition and measurement, has been and continues to be an area of attention for gerontological research, observation, and conceptual development. Func-tion and its assessment have been an integral part of experimental demon-stration and evaluation, and the construct of this concept is tied inextricably to independence and hence to quality of life and to cost.

Varying definitions and conceptual frameworks fuel the epistemologic debate over the meaning of function. One model that has been useful operationally and that has become the basis for other more complex models is the World Health Organization [WHO] construct of impairment/disability/handicap (World Health Organization, 1980) shown in Table 5.2. This con-struct has been a tool for organizing measures of physical, social, psycho-logical, and cognitive tasks and interactions that make up the day-to-day activities of individuals. There is an implicit pathway for depicting both improvement as well as decline, and this framework can help organize discrete items that make up the overall concept of function.

Measures of activity that make up function continue to be redefined, adapted, and examined. Although this refinement continues, there are nu-merous purposes for which this concept has proven extremely useful. Some of those are to diagnose overall health status in order to prescribe health care interventions; to monitor changes so that prescribed regimens can be modi-fied over time; to evaluate the overall effect of interventions; and to estimate the prevalence of dependence within specific populations.

Although increasingly sophisticated methods to measure function in its many dimensions and over various levels of severity have been developed (Guralnik & Lacroix, 1992), this area continues to evolve, and conceptual and operational differences continue to exist. There is, however, general agreement that standardized definition and measurement of function are essential to investigations into the health and health care of older people.

Prevention

Background

The demography and epidemiology that delineate the older population, including disease, conditions, comorbidities, and functioning, provide the background against which to consider the relevance of preventive care and programs for this population. This requires defining and examining the range of preventive strategies when considering the potential that preventive ser-

TABLE 5.2 The World Health Organization Model of Impairment, Disability, and Handicap

---

DISEASE → IMPAIRMENT → DISABILITY → HANDICAP

Impairment
In the context of health experience, an impairment is any loss or abnormality of psychological, physiological, or anatomical structure or function.

Disability
In the context of health experience, a disability is any restriction or lack (resulting from an impairment) of ability to perform an activity in the manner or within the range considered normal for a human being.

Handicap
In the context of health experience, a handicap is a disadvantage for a given individual, resulting from an impairment or a disability, that limits or prevents the fulfillment of a role that is normal (depending on age, sex, and social and cultural factors) for that individual.

---

vices may have for the older population. It is essential to understand the types of preventive services and the overall characteristics of the population if we are to target goals appropriate to this population.

Prevention and health promotion are not new developments. Historically, public health interventions aimed at different populations that make use of differing degrees of active participation have ranged from clean water, requiring no consumer participation, to garbage collection and immunization, requiring greater degrees of action on the part of the consumer. An interesting case is that of fluoridated water for dental health, for which the action on the part of the population tends to be political in mandating the establishing of such services locally. However, once fluoridation has been established, all individuals receive these services automatically. Preventive services have been developed to include a more specific focus on screening for specific diseases, lifestyle, and structured regimens believed to influence development of these diseases. Sometimes these programs are aimed at very particular groups of people, although the large public health campaigns aimed at the broad population continue.

Over the past decade or so, the potential for prevention to increase quality of life and to control cost of care has increasingly been the focus of policy debate. The relevance of this area for long-term care has become apparent only recently. A landmark national document on prevention and particularly on "wellness" was the 1980 report on promoting health (U.S. Department of Health and Human Services, 1980). This publication represented one of the early shifts in the concept of appropriate target groups in that objectives for older individuals were included. This trend paralleled WHO's contention that prevention should be an accepted part of "wellness" (WHO, 1980). An important aspect of the WHO report was the reemphasis on a typology suggesting that prevention should parallel various points on a continuum of health status and that it is related specifically to the conditions of older individuals. This typology, discussed earlier, has a relationship to stages of health status and includes the epidemiologic definition of various levels of prevention. Table 5.3 outlines types of prevention.

The second and third levels of prevention are exceedingly important to older populations and can be considered to be the prevention of disability. Kaplan, Haan, and Cohen (1992) develop this thesis in work that examines the viability of prevention, keeping in mind the existing patterns of diseases and conditions among older people. The work concludes that prevention can be an important tool in slowing the rate of progress of disease, thereby influencing transition from preclinical to full-blown disease. There are, in addition, other ways in which preventive services can have a positive effect, and these will be discussed below.

The latest national efforts to summarize the area of prevention and set priorities and goals can be found in *Healthy People 2000* (U.S. Department of Health and Human Services, 1990). This volume drew attention to a steady accretion of consensus and goal setting for preventive services. Though recognizing preventive needs of older people, the report tended to fold long-term care needs into overall goals. This approach, in the view of many gerontologists, was counterproductive and omitted the crucial emphasis of prevention as services and concepts that vary by nature of the population and by objectives that differ for different groups. For the older population, it is essential to take into account the unique epidemiology of this group. Primary prevention will have the greatest impact on a younger population with higher proportions of disease/condition-free individuals but will have less relevance for older populations who have already a moderate to high level of existing chronic disease. This is not to say that for many in the 65-and-over population, primary prevention is not appropriate where diseases have not yet developed. At issue is the sole emphasis on such interventions and the neglect of a broad arena of opportunity to influence the course of existing disease.

Issues in Prevention and Long-Term Care

The foregoing reflects the tendency toward a narrow definition of health promotion goals that unwittingly encourage neglect of an approach to the older population that is related to the needs of this population. The past neglect of prevention in long-term care in both conceptional and empirical work is due to the at times exclusive concentration on primary prevention

TABLE 5.3 Types of Prevention

PRIMARY PREVENTION
Primary Prevention is any intervention that prevents a pathological process from occurring. Examples are immunization against infectious agents or controlling risk factors in health individuals, thereby preventing the development of specific diseases.

SECONDARY PREVENTION
Secondary Prevention occurs after a pathological process has been initiated but before symptoms occur or very early in their occurrence. This makes for early treatment, which can reduce morbidity and mortality.

TERTIARY PREVENTION
Tertiary Prevention refers to prevention of progressive disability, prevention of complications of chronic diseases, and rehabilitation of affected function. It includes control of pain and maintenance of the highest levels of activity.

SOURCE: From "Preventive Medicine in Ambulatory Practice," by D. Kern and L. R. Barker, in *Principles of Ambulatory Medicine* (2nd ed.), edited by L. Barker, J. Burton, and P. Zieve, 1986, Baltimore: Williams & Wilkins. Copyright 1986 by Williams & Wilkins. Adapted with permission.

(German & Fried, 1989), although this has been changing and there have been efforts to consider ways of using prevention in long-term care. Such considerations include development of concepts of patient behaviors (Leventhal, Leventhal, & Schaefer, 1992; Rakowski, 1992) and how care can be delivered (Levizzo-Mourey, Day, Diserens, & Grisso, 1989). These efforts are based on the assumption that the preventive services must consider the presence of existing chronic conditions and diseases in high proportions among older people, but that prevention can nevertheless be important in helping to improve the health status and quality of life for older people. The objectives change from those of primary prevention—namely, preventing a disease from occurring or delaying its occurrence for a significant period of time—to avoiding or limiting functional disability, achieving a slower progress in chronic diseases that are now considered incurable, and maintaining independent living for as long as possible. These goals are associated with increased quality of life and are held to be related to lower costs, or at least to have this potential. This is particularly important if, as in the case of acute episodes of chronic conditions, hospitalization can be avoided. Avoidance of inpatient care, the most costly benefit under Medicare (U.S. Bureau of Census, 1992), could result in significant cost savings.

German and Fried (1989) presented a schematic approach to all types of prevention for older people. This is shown in Table 5.4 and gives selected examples of the range of primary, secondary, and tertiary prevention. This framework assumes identification of illness. It should be emphasized that many of the preventive regimens listed under primary prevention, that is,

TABLE 5.4 Range of Preventive Services by Type of Prevention

Primary	Secondary	Tertiary
Health Habits	*Screening for:*	*Rehabilitation*
Smoking	Hypertension	Physical deficits
Alcohol abuse	Diabetes	Cognitive deficits
Obesity	Periodontal disease	Functional deficits
Nutrition	Dental caries	
Physical activity	Sensory impairment	
Sleep	Medication side effects	*Caretaker Support*
	Colorectal cancer	Introduction of support
	Breast cancer	necessary to prevent
	Cervical cancer	loss of autonomy
	Prostatic cancer	
	Nutritionally induced	*Pain Control*
	amnesias	
Immunization		
Influenza	Depression, stress	
Pneumovax	Urinary incontinence	
Tetanus	Podiatric problems	
Injury Prevention	Fall risk	
Iatrogenesis Prevention	Tuberculosis (high risk)	
Osteoporosis Prevention	Syphilis (high risk)	
	Control of Hypertension to	
	Prevent Stroke	

SOURCE: Adapted, with permission, from the Annual Review of Public Health, Volume 10. © 1989 by Annual Reviews, Inc.

conceived of as helping prevent the occurrence of disease, also are effective in controlling the sequelae of existing diseases, and the development of other conditions associated with a specific disease, as well as preventing the disease from worsening or moving into a more serious stage.

Although there are many indications that progress is being made in including prevention as appropriate in the health care of older people, there remains of course, the crucial question of the effectiveness of preventive strategies in achieving identified outcomes—that is, the "so what" questions. There have been efforts to examine the question of the effectiveness of prevention on the quality of the prolonged life we are providing our elders and on the overall cost of the long-term care. It is, however, not possible to say that the ultimate "cost saving" in such services has been established. Most recently, new ideas are emerging for a better structure with which to assess preventive services (Fries et al., 1993), and these are promising directions for evaluative research. There continue to be many questions about cost-effectiveness of prevention (Russell, 1993), and repeated reference is made to the lack of hard data to substantiate positive results. It is important to note that the examination of the effectiveness of prevention most often uses a population undifferentiated by age group as the basis for examination, and that the effects of more specified types of prevention on older people have not been thoroughly assessed.

Type of prevention and its relevance for an older population are connected to another basic issue in application of preventive strategies, particularly those requiring response and activity on the part of the patient. There is some evidence that response to preventive programs has not been enthusiastic on the part of the older population. This may be attributed, in part, to the emphasis on primary prevention and the heavy stress on secondary prevention aimed at screening for early diagnosis of potential disease not yet identified. The presence of existing disease in the older population and the overall presentation and philosophy surrounding prevention programs make for a perception among older individuals, as well as among their primary caregivers, that these programs are not intended for them. This group, in which large proportions of the population have one or more prevalent diseases and conditions, perceives the focus of primary prevention as intended for younger populations and therefore has a weak response to these programs.

It could be argued, then, that the first step basic to any evaluation of the effect of preventive services is the crucial one of their initial acceptance. This means that a broader interpretation of prevention is necessary not only when programs are being developed but also when and how they are presented. No program will be accepted by all members of a target group, with the exception of universal programs requiring no action, such as water purification. The aim rather is to have sufficient numbers involved to demonstrate an effect of the program for the aggregate group: for example, outcomes of lower annual acute care bed days among the group exposed. This requires a moderate acceptance of programs by a target group. At issue is whether preventive services can be "sold" to the long-term care population and, equally important, accepted as realistic by those giving care to this population.

Summary

It can be argued that prevention of disease and promotion of health have not been utilized appropriately nor their potential exploited in considering problems of the overall health and quality of life of the older population. This chapter has described the demographic trend that will continue and will ensure larger numbers and proportions of older people. I have argued that these factors motivate reconsideration of the role of prevention for this population. The increasing numbers and proportions of individuals aged 65 and over in the population, combined with an increasing life expectancy, will continue the highest population increases in the oldest age groups. Because of these factors, coupled with the presence of chronic disease, conditions, and general frailty associated with old age, it is certain that people will continue to live longer with diseases that are not curable and that this will require a different outlook in how we deal with this older population.

The history of disease prevention is a long one, and only recently have we begun to examine the relevance of disease strategies for the aging population. The past emphasis, and indeed, the continuing one, stresses the importance of preventing disease, a laudable and indisputably important goal. However, given the demographics and epidemiology of our most rapidly increasing population, the impetus to consider secondary and tertiary prevention becomes a crucial step in health care. Secondary prevention not only seeks to screen so as to diagnose disease early when it is more treatable and when maintenance against worsening is more possible, but also can be utilized to approach existing diseases so as to avoid secondary conditions and to control the progress of diseases to a more serious stage. Combined with tertiary prevention, which is focused on rehabilitation, maintenance of function, and control of pain, such interventions can decrease the risk of dependence, thereby increasing quality of life.

The potential for control of the costs of care for the older population needs further investigation. A more targeted approach that matches appropriate prevention to this population may change the nature of the effect on overall cost.

The change in the concept of prevention so as to include secondary and tertiary prevention requires reeducation of both the population of elders and their primary care providers. Elders have more often than not responded to the emphasis on primary care by assuming that the message is not intended for them. We need to work hard to change this perception and to test the power of preventive services specific to the population for the effect they can have in increasing quality and lowering cost.

References

Estes, C. L., Swan, J., and Associates. (1993). *The long term care crisis.* Newbury Park, CA: Sage.

Fried, L., & Bush, T. (1988). Morbidity as a focus of preventive health care in the elderly. *Epidemiology Reviews, 10,* 48-63.

Fried, L., & Wallace, R. (1992). The complexity of chronic illness in the elderly. In R. Wallace & R. Woolson (Eds.), *The epidemiologic study of the elderly* (pp. 10-19). New York: Oxford University Press.

Fries, J. F., Koop, C. E., Beadle, C. E., Cooper, P., England, M. J., Greaves, R. F., Sokolov, J. J., Wright, D., & the Health Project Consortium. (1993). Reducing health care costs by reducing the need and demand for medical services. *New England Journal of Medicine, 329*(5), 321-325.

German, P. S., & Fried, L. P. (1989). Prevention and the elderly. *Annual Review of Public Health, 10,* 319-332.

Guralnik, J., & Lacroix, A. (1992). Assessing physical function in older populations. In R. Wallace & R. Woolson (Eds.), *The epidemiologic study of the elderly* (pp. 159-181). New York: Oxford University Press.

Hadley, E., Ory, M., Suzman, R., Weindruch, R., & Fried, L. (Eds.). (1993). Physical frailty: A treatable cause of dependence in old age. *Journal of Gerontology, 48* (Special Issue), vii-viii.

Institute of Medicine. (1990). *The second fifty years: Promoting health and preventing disability.* Washington, DC: National Academy Press.

Kaplan, G., Haan, M., & Cohen, R. (1992). Risk factors and the study of prevention in the elderly: Methodologic issues. In R. Wallace & R. Woolson (Eds.), *The epidemiologic study of the elderly* (pp. 20-45). New York: Oxford University Press.

Kern, D., & Barker, L. R. (1986). Preventive medicine in ambulatory practice. In L. Barker, J. Burton, & P. Ziero (Eds.), *Principles of ambulatory medicine* (2nd ed., pp. 16-39). Baltimore: Williams & Wilkens.

Leventhal, H., Leventhal, E. A., & Schaefer, P. M. (1992). Vigilant coping and health behavior. In M. G. Ory, R. A. Abeles, & P. D. Lipman (Eds.), *Aging, health, and behavior* (pp. 109-140). London: Sage.

Levizzo-Mourey, R., Day, S., Diserens, D., & Grisso, J. (1989). *Practicing prevention for the elderly.* Philadelphia: Hanley & Belfus.

Moody, H. R. (1992). *Ethics for an aging society.* Baltimore: Johns Hopkins University Press.

National Center for Health Statistics. (1990a, November 28). *Advance report of final mortality statistics, 1988* (Monthly Vital Statistics Report, Vol. 39, No. 7, Supplement). Hyattsville, MD: Author.

National Center for Health Statistics. (1990b, August 30). *Annual summary of births, marriages, divorces, and deaths: United States, 1989* (Monthly Vital Statistics Report, Vol. 38, No. 13). Hyattsville, MD: Author.

National Center for Health Statistics. (1990c, October). *Current estimates from the National Health Interview Survey, 1989* (Vital and Health Statistics, Series 10, No. 176). Hyattsville, MD: Author.

National Center for Health Statistics. (1990d, March). *Health. United States. 1989* (DHHS Pub. No. [PHS] 90-1232). Washington, DC: Department of Health and Human Services.

Rakowski, W. (1992). Disease prevention and health promotion with older adults. In M. G. Ory, R. A. Abeles, & P. D. Lipman (Eds.), *Aging, health and behavior* (pp. 239-275). London: Sage.

Russell, L. B. (1993). The role of prevention in health reform. *New England Journal of Medicine, 329*(5), 352-354.

Task Force on Older Women's Health. (1993). Position paper: Older women's health. *Journal of the American Geriatrics Society, 41,* 680-683.

U.S. Bureau of the Census. (1992). *Sixty-five plus in America* (Current Population Reports, Special Studies, P23 178). Washington, DC: Government Printing Office.

U.S. Department of Health and Human Services. (1980). *Promoting health, preventing disease: Objectives for the nation.* Washington, DC: Government Printing Office.

U.S. Department of Health and Human Services, Public Health Service. (1990). *Healthy people 2000* (DHHS Publication No. [PHS] 91-50212). Washington, DC: Government Printing Office.

U.S. Special Committee on Aging. (1991). *Aging America: Trends and projections* (DHHS No. [FCoA] 91-28001). Washington, DC: U.S. Dept. of Health and Human Services.

Van Nostrand, J., Turner, S., & Suzman, R. (Eds). (1993). *Data on older Americans, 1992* (Vital Health Statistics, Vol. 3, No. 27). Hyattsville, MD: National Center for Health Statistics.

World Health Organization. (1980). *International classification of impairment, disabilities and handicaps.* Geneva: Author.

6

Effects of Age on Resting Energy Expenditure

Eric T. Poehlman

My overall objective is to review information regarding the adaptive response to endurance exercise in aging humans with specific regard to changes in energy metabolism. More specifically, I review studies that have examined biological and environmental factors involved in the regulation of energy requirements, energy expenditure, and body composition in older men and women.

My first objective in this chapter is to review the effects of age on the components of energy balance in humans. Specifically, I have considered age-associated changes in (a) resting metabolic rate, (b) the thermic effect of a meal, (c) physical activity, and (d) total energy expenditure. My second objective is to examine the effects of endurance exercise on the aforementioned components. The reader is referred to earlier reviews that examined the effects of age on energy metabolism (Poehlman, 1992, 1993; Poehlman, Gardner, & Goran, 1990; Poehlman & Horton, 1990).

Resting Metabolic Rate (RMR) and Aging

Resting metabolic rate (RMR) represents the largest component (50-80%) of total daily energy expenditure in older adults (Poehlman, 1989, 1992) and therefore is quantitatively very important in the understanding of the mechanism by which humans regulate body weight and body composition with advancing age. RMR represents the energy consumption (e.g., calories) in the basal state that serves to maintain basic physiological processes. These processes include resting cardiovascular and pulmonary functions, energy

AUTHOR'S NOTE: Gratitude is expressed to all the volunteers who made this study possible. Dr. Eric T. Poehlman is supported by a grant from National Institute of Aging (AG-07857), a Research Career and Development Award from the National Institute of Aging (K04 AG00564), and the American Association of Retired Persons (AARP) Andrus Foundation.

109

consumption by the central nervous system, and other chemical (e.g., enzymatic) reactions. The major scientific concepts to be gained from this first section are: (a) The decline in RMR with advancing age results in a "conservation of energy" that may contribute to the accumulation of body fat; (b) the decline in RMR is primarily related to the loss of fat-free mass, the body composition component that is made up of the visceral organs and muscle tissue; (c) the decline in RMR appears to begin earlier in males (40 years) than females (50 years); (d) the fall in RMR appears to be accelerated in the postmenopausal years in women who are not on estrogen replacement; (e) regular physical activity that preserves fat-free mass and increases aerobic fitness will partially offset the decline in RMR with advancing age; and (f) I offer new equations to predict RMR in older men and women.

One of the most consistent physiologic changes that occurs with age is the decline in resting metabolic rate (RMR). Cross-sectional (Calloway & Zanni, 1980; Robertson & Reid, 1952; Shock, 1955; Shock & Yiengst, 1955; Tzankoff & Norris, 1977; Webb & Heistand, 1975) and longitudinal investigations (Keys, Taylor, & Grande, 1973; Robinson, Dill, Tzankoff, Wagner, & Robinson, 1975; Tzankoff & Norris, 1978) have reported a decline in RMR with age that coincides with the decline in fat-free mass (Forbes, 1976; Forbes & Reina, 1970; Novak, 1972). Since these earlier studies, more recent investigations have confirmed these findings (Flynn, Nolph, Baker, Martin, & Krause, 1989; Fukagawa, Bandini, & Young, 1990; Poehlman, Berke, et al., 1992; Poehlman, Goran, et al., 1993; Poehlman, McAuliffe, Van Houten, & Danforth, 1990; Poehlman, Melby, & Badylak, 1991; Vaughan, Zurlo, & Ravussin, 1991). More recent studies, however (Poehlman, Berke, et al., 1992; Poehlman, Goran, et al., 1993), have suggested a curvilinear decline in RMR with advancing age, in which the decline is accelerated beyond the middle-age and postmenopausal years.

Determinants of the Decline in Resting Metabolic Rate in Aging Humans

Several studies have attributed the age-related decline in RMR primarily to the loss of fat-free mass (Keys et al., 1973; Poehlman, McAuliffe, et al., 1990; Tzankoff & Norris, 1977, 1978), whereas others have suggested that other physiological variables may contribute to the lower RMR in elders (Fukagawa et al., 1990; Poehlman, Berke, et al., 1992; Vaughan et al., 1991). In the Baltimore Longitudinal Study (Tzankoff & Norris, 1977, 1978), cross-sectional and longitudinal designs showed that the loss of muscle mass in healthy men accounted for the age-related decline in RMR. It has been postulated that the rate of decline in RMR with age approximates the rate of loss of fat-free mass. For example, both Forbes and Reina (1970) and Novak (1972) reported a 3% decline in fat-free mass per decade, a value similar to the absolute decline in RMR found by Keys et al. (1973) and Tzankoff and Norris (1978) (3.22% and 3.7% respectively). This rate of decline is somewhat higher, however, than the 1.2% decline in RMR per decade reported in a group of 115 men studied five times during a 17-year period between the ages of 50 and 67 years (Keys et al., 1973).

There is uncertainty as to whether other physiological factors may also contribute to the age-related reduction of RMR. Recently, Fukagawa et al. (1990) examined the relationship between fat-free mass and RMR in young men (18 to 33 years), older men (69 to 89 years), and older women (67 to 75 years). They found that measured RMR was significantly lower in older men (1.04 kcal/min) and older women (0.84 kcal/min) than younger men (1.24 kcal/min), and that the lower RMR persisted even after adjusting for differences in fat-free mass. The authors concluded that differences in fat-free mass between younger and older individuals cannot fully account for the lower RMR in older individuals, thus suggesting that aging is associated with an alteration in the "metabolic activity" of lean tissue contained in the fat-free mass component. Vaughn et al. (1991) recently measured RMR in younger and older individuals in a room calorimeter. They found that RMR was lower in both groups of older subjects compared to younger subjects and persisted after adjustment for differences in fat-free mass, fat mass, and gender.

We have performed a series of experiments to examine other possible modulators of the fall in RMR in older men and women. In the first of these studies, Poehlman, Berke, et al. (1992) examined whether differences in maximal aerobic capacity (VO_2max), daily energy intake, and plasma concentrations of thyroid hormones in a group of 300 healthy males (17 to 78 years) could explain the reduction in RMR with age independent of changes in fat-free mass. Our results showed a curvilinear decline in RMR with age, in which the reduction in RMR was accelerated in males after 40 years. Furthermore, fat-free mass could not fully account for the lower RMR in the men over 40 years. It was only after controlling for differences in fat-free mass, fat mass, and maximal aerobic capacity that the association between RMR and age became nonsignificant. Variations in antecedent dietary practices and plasma thyroid hormones were not independent predictors of the decline in RMR. The results from this study suggested an influence of VO_2max, independent of the decline in fat-free mass to the decline in RMR in healthy males.

In a subsequent study, Poehlman, Toth, and Webb (1993) examined whether a decrease in erythrocyte Na-K pump activity contributes to a portion of the decline in RMR after adjusting for the loss of fat-free mass with advancing age. Erythrocyte Na-K pump rate and the rate constant were determined from plasma and erythrocyte Na and K concentrations using flame photometry after incubation with and without ouabain in 27 younger

(17 to 39 years) and 25 older (56-76 years) males. We found that a lower RMR persisted in older (1.14 ± 0.12 kcal/min) compared to the younger men (1.21 ± 0.12 kcal/min; $p < 0.05$) after controlling for differences in fat-free mass. No age differences were found, however, between older (1.17 ± 0.13 kcal/min) and younger men (1.20 ± 0.13 kcal/min) after adjusting for both fat-free mass and erythrocyte Na-K pump rate constant. These results suggest an independent, but small contribution of changes in Na-K pump activity to the age-related decline in RMR.

In a related study in females, Poehlman, Goran, et al. (1993) considered the association of several metabolic and lifestyle variables as modulators of the decline in resting metabolic rate and fat-free mass in 183 healthy females (18 to 81 years). We found no change (0.6% per decade) in RMR in females 18 to 50 years, whereas a significant decline (4.0% per decade) was observed in females 51 to 81 years (Figure 6.1). These rates of decline in RMR compared favorably with others (Flynn et al., 1989). However, in contrast to our previous male study (Poehlman, Berke, et al., 1992), no age effect on RMR was found after controlling for the effects of fat-free mass.

When the decline in RMR was compared in males and females, we found that the decline in RMR in males occurred at an earlier time point (40 years) than females (50 years), and that the decline beyond the middle-age years was steeper in males (−11 kcal/d/yr) than females (−5.5 kcal/d/yr). In conclusion, these findings suggested that gender is an important parameter to consider when examining the pattern as well as the rate of decline in RMR with advancing age. Taken together, available data suggest that changes in body composition are the most important predictors of the decline in RMR with advancing age. Furthermore, VO_2max and Na-K pump activity also appear to be small independent determinants of the fall in RMR with age in men. In women, however, we were only able to identify the decline in fat-free mass as the single determinant of the decline in RMR with age.

Resting Metabolic Rate, Menopausal Status, and Body Composition

It is well known that menopausal status influences RMR and thus must be taken into account or controlled in experimental studies that examine the influence of environmental factors regulating RMR. For example, it is well known that RMR is higher in premenopausal females during the luteal phase of the menstrual cycle compared to the follicular phase (Bisdee, James, & Shaw, 1989; Ferraro et al., 1992; Webb, 1986). It has been suggested that the decrement in RMR experienced from the pre- to postmenopausal years may result in an energy conservation that approaches 15,000 to 20,000 kcal/yr (Ferraro et al., 1992). It is also known that the transition from the

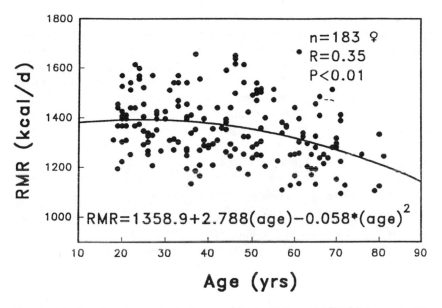

Figure 6.1. Curvilinear Decline in Resting Metabolic Rate (RMR) With Age in 183 Females

SOURCE: Poehlman, Goran, et al., 1993, p. E451.

pre- to postmenopausal years has been associated with increased body weight gain (Wing, Matthews, Kuller, Meilahn, & Plantinga, 1991) and deleterious changes in body composition (Poehlman, Goran, et al., 1993). The suggestion is that the estrogen-deficient state may partially contribute to deleterious changes in energy expenditure and body composition. In our laboratory, Arciero et al. (1993a) showed that postmenopausal status was a significant and independent factor contributing to a lower RMR among older women (> 50 years old). Recently, Gardner and Poehlman (1993) showed a significant decline in leisure-time physical activity and fat-free mass in post-menopausal women relative to premenopausal women. From their data, Gardner and Poehlman (1993) predicted that the percent body fat of healthy older women can be lowered by 0.16 to 0.35% for every 100 kcal/d increase in physical activity, independent of age, mass, body mass index, and subcutaneous fat. The implication is that physical activity may play an important role, particularly in postmenopausal women, in offsetting a gain in body fat and in preserving fat-free mass.

Kohrt, Malley, Dalsky, and Holloszy (1992) examined the association of age and physical activity on body composition and fat distribution in endurance-trained and sedentary younger and older women. These investigators showed that the average difference in fat mass between younger and older sedentary women was 12.2 kg, but only 5.5 kg between younger and older trained women. Moreover, differences in skinfold thicknesses at several central upper body sites between the sedentary younger and older women averaged 86%, compared to only 39% between the trained younger and older women. These findings suggest that chronic participation in endurance exercise during menopause may reduce the accumulation of body fat, especially in the upper truncal regions, thus lowering the risk of developing cardiovascular and metabolic disorders (Després et al., 1990; Wing et al., 1991).

Prediction of Resting Metabolic Rate in Older Individuals

Because of the limitations involved in accurately measuring food intake in older individuals (Goran & Poehlman, 1992b; James, Ralph, & Ferro-Luzzi, 1989; Poehlman, 1992), it has been recommended that energy needs be estimated by measuring daily energy expenditure in healthy individuals (Goran & Poehlman, 1992b; James et al., 1989; Poehlman, 1992, 1993; World Health Organization [WHO], 1985). The determination of resting metabolic rate (RMR) has served as the basis upon which estimates of total caloric needs have been developed (WHO, 1985). However, many of the prediction equations of RMR in older individuals have been derived from data extrapolated from younger individuals (Harris & Benedict, 1919; Owen et al., 1986) or are based on smaller sample sizes in the older age ranges (Fredrix et al., 1990; Harris & Benedict, 1919; Mifflin et al., 1990; Owen et al., 1986; WHO, 1985) and have not been tested for accuracy using cross-validation procedures.

These issues have recently been addressed in our laboratory (Arciero et al., 1993a, 1993b), in which age- and gender-specific equations to predict RMR in clinical and field-testing settings using easily measured variables were developed. We showed that a measure of body weight, leisure-time activity (Taylor et al., 1978), age, and the chest skinfold predicted RMR in older males within a standard error of estimate of ±42 kcal/d. These four variables yielded the following equation:

RMR (kcal/d) = 9.7 (weight, kg) – 6.1 (chest skinfold, mm) –
1.8 (age, years) + 0.1 (activity questionnaire, kcal/d) + 1060)

In older women, a measure of body weight, height, and menopausal status (1, premenopausal; 2, perimenopausal; 3, postmenopausal) were found to best predict RMR within a standard error of estimate of ±66 kcal/d, yielding a prediction equation of

RMR (kcal/d) = 7.8 (weight, kg) + 4.7 (height, cm) −
39.5 (menopausal status; 1-3) + 143.5)

It should be noted, however, that these equations were derived from a population of healthy Caucasian men and women ≤ 81 years and thus may not be applicable to other racial groups or the "oldest old" (> 85 years) population. However, these studies represented an initial attempt to predict more accurately RMR in older individuals from data specifically obtained from the older age groups.

Resting Metabolic Rate, Aging, and Physical Activity

Physical activity, especially in the form of endurance exercise, exerts a significant influence on energy intake (Goran & Poehlman, 1992b; Poehlman, Gardner, & Goran, 1992) and energy expenditure, and is thus an important regulatory component of body composition. Both cross-sectional and exercise intervention studies have examined the influence of chronic physical training on RMR in younger individuals and report that RMR is increased following endurance training (Lawson, Webster, Pacy, & Garrow, 1987; Lennon, Nagle, Stratman, Shrago, & Dennis, 1985; Poehlman, Melby, & Badylak, 1988; Poehlman, Melby, Badylak, & Calles, 1989; Tremblay et al., 1986; Wilson, 1966), although not universally found by others (Bingham, Goldberg, Coward, Prentice, & Cummings, 1989; Broeder, Burrhus, Svanevik, & Wilmore, 1992; Hill, Heymsfield, McManus, & DiGirolamo, 1984; LeBlanc, Diamond, Cote, & Lebrie, 1984; Meredith et al., 1989). The reader is referred to earlier reviews that have addressed the influence of exercise training on younger individuals and methodological considerations that may help explain discrepant results among studies (Poehlman, 1989; Poehlman, Gardner, & Goran, 1990; Poehlman & Horton, 1990; Poehlman, Melby, & Goran, 1991). Less information is available regarding the effects of physical activity and/or endurance training on RMR in elderly individuals. It is interesting to note that nearly 40 years ago Shock (1955) first alluded to the possibility that physical activity may influence RMR in older individuals. At the time, he observed that RMR declined at a slower rate in older individuals who were more physically active in community life than in those who were institutionalized and leading a more sedentary lifestyle.

In one of the earliest longitudinal studies involving 16 elite runners followed up 20 or more years later, Dill, Robinson, and Ross (1967) showed that the average decline in fat-free mass was estimated to be only 1% per decade and that RMR expressed per body surface area declined only 7.8% from the fifth to the eighth decade of life. These results should be interpreted in light of the fact that fat-free mass and body fat were not directly measured but estimated on the basis of observations of runners at a later time period with similar exercise training habits.

Previous cross-sectional investigations have shown that endurance-trained older men have a higher RMR than sedentary older men, independent of differences in fat-free mass and percent body fat. For example, Lundholm et al. (1986) observed a higher RMR in 10 well-conditioned older men than in 10 sedentary older men. More recently, Poehlman, McAuliffe, et al. (1990) showed that a group of older men (≥ 59 years) who had been running an average of 55.5 ± 5.5 km per week for 15.4 ± 4.2 years had a 6% greater RMR (measured at least 36 hours after the last exercise bout) than a group of sedentary older men. In a subsequent study, Poehlman and Danforth (1991) endurance trained 19 older individuals (13 males and 6 females) on a cycle ergometer three times per week for 8 weeks. These investigators reported that RMR increased by 10% following endurance training in the absence of changes in fat-free mass. Furthermore, the increase in RMR was associated with a higher level of sympathetic nervous system activity (as measured by the rate of norepinephrine appearance into the circulation) and with increased food intake. These findings suggest that an increase in RMR is found when an increase in energy expenditure is matched with a proportionate increase in food intake to maintain energy balance. Moreover, the increased RMR may be mediated by enhanced sympathetic nervous system activity.

Recently, Poehlman, Gardner, and Goran (1992) examined the effects of two levels of endurance training (light and moderate intensity) on RMR in six healthy older men and one older woman under controlled inpatient clinical conditions. In this study, RMR was measured after (a) a 10-day inpatient control period (no exercise); (b) a 10-day light exercise period (150 kcal/session, 3 times/week); and (c) a 10-day moderate exercise period (300 kcal/session, 3 times/week). No significant change in RMR was found after the control (1.03 ± 0.12 kcal/min) and light exercise periods (1.04 ± 0.12 kcal/min); however, RMR increased 9% (1.13 ± 0.14 kcal/min) after moderate endurance training, despite no measurable changes in body composition. These results suggest that a threshold of energy expenditure generated by endurance exercise may be necessary to enhance RMR and food intake in elderly persons.

Thermic Effect of a Meal, Physical Activity, and Aging

The thermic effect of a meal is the increase in energy expenditure following food ingestion that is due to the energy cost of digestion, transportation, and storage of nutrients. To date, only a few studies have examined the influence of age and physical activity on the thermic effect of a meal (TEM), and all of these are cross-sectional in design. The limited number of studies may be due to methodological considerations involving the length of the measurement (1 to 6 hours) and the limited contribution of TEM (10%) to total daily energy expenditure. The major scientific concepts to be gained from this section are: (a) The energy expended after meal consumption is a small component of daily caloric output, (b) several investigations show that older individuals expend fewer calories following meal ingestion than younger individuals, and (c) physically active older individuals appear to expend a greater number of calories after meal ingestion than their age-matched inactive counterparts.

In the 1950s, Tuttle, Horvath, Presson, and Daum (1953) examined the thermic response to a protein meal in eight younger men (20 to 30 years) and six older men (72 to 84 years) during a 4.5-hour postprandial period. Postprandial oxygen consumption levels were similar in the younger (9.7%) and older (11.9%) men, even though the older men experienced a blunted initial thermic response to the meal in the first 2 hours. This earlier study demonstrated that older men do not have a decrease in the thermic effect of a protein meal challenge when compared to younger men.

It was not again until the 1980s that the influence of age on TEM was considered. Morgan and York (1983) measured the thermic response for 3 hours following administration of two mixed meals containing 480 kcal and 950 kcal in a group of younger (24 ± 0.7 years) and older (71 ± 1.4 years) men. The older men showed a lower caloric output in response to the meals, and the authors hypothesized that the blunted thermogenic response in the older individuals was due to a chronic adaptation to a lower food intake in an attempt to maintain body energy stores. Golay et al. (1983) observed a 25% lower thermic response to glucose ingestion in older (38 to 68 years) than in younger (18-39 years) volunteers. Bloesch, Schutz, Breitenstein, Jequier, and Felber (1988) measured TEM for 3 hours following a 75-g oral glucose load in 12 older (61 ± 3 years) and 12 younger (25 ± 1 year) men and showed a 15% lower thermogenic response in the older compared to the younger. These findings were recently corroborated and extended by Schwartz, Jaeger, and Veith (1990), who showed that a lower thermic response to a meal in elders was associated with reduced sympathetic nervous system activity. These preliminary findings favor the interpretation that the lower TEM in older individuals may represent an energy conservation mechanism that contributes to their lower energy needs and propensity to accumulate body fat. In contrast, Fukagawa et al. (1991) found no difference among younger men, older men, and older women in their thermic response to a protein meal challenge measured during a 6-hour postprandial period.

Because it is common for food to be consumed in close proximity to physical exercise, it is of interest to examine the relationship between acute and chronic exercise and meal ingestion. Schutz, Bray, and Margen (1987) measured TEM in seven older men (68.8 ± 3 years) at rest and during acute exercise following meals containing varying amounts of protein. The authors noted a dose-dependent response in which higher protein content of the meals was associated with a greater thermic response. These authors, however, did not find a potentiating effect of exercise on TEM when exercise was performed in close proximity to food ingestion in older individuals.

Two lines of evidence have recently shown that the level of physical activity may be an important modulator of TEM in older individuals. Lundholm et al. (1986) examined TEM for 3 hours in 10 endurance-trained and 10 sedentary older men after ingestion of a 500-kcal liquid meal of mixed dietary composition. They found a greater TEM in the trained older men than the untrained, but no differences in plasma catecholamines between the groups. These findings suggested that the enhanced thermic response to a meal in older trained men was mediated not by circulating catecholamines but by some other energy-consuming processes that are yet to be identified. We have recently measured TEM for 3 hours in four separate groups of healthy men: 10 sedentary younger, 10 active younger, 7 sedentary older, and 9 active older men (Poehlman, Melby, & Badylak, 1991). A mixed liquid meal with an energy content of 10 kcal/kg FFM was administered to each volunteer. The results showed no age-related differences in the thermic response to a meal challenge, although the physically active older and younger men had a significantly greater thermic effect of a meal than their age-matched sedentary counterparts. Collectively, these studies provide preliminary evidence for a potentiating effect of a physically active lifestyle on TEM in older individuals.

Total Energy Expenditure in Elders

The purpose of this section is to review data on age-related changes in total daily caloric expenditure and the associated implications for the determination of caloric requirements in elders. The important scientific concepts to be gained in this section are: (a) It is now possible to measure accurately daily caloric output in humans using room calorimeters or the doubly labeled water technique, and (b) knowledge of daily caloric output in older individuals using these methods will assist in the establishment of appropriate guidelines to predict caloric needs.

Vaughan et al. (1991) examined age-related differences in 24-hour caloric expenditure by comparing data collected in 38 elderly men and women (71 ± 6 years; 71.2 ± 13.5 kg) and 64 younger men and women (24 ± 4 years; 84.5 ± 23.1 kg) living in a room calorimeter. On an absolute basis, 24-hour sedentary energy expenditure was lower by 13% in the older individuals (younger, 2,155 ± 352 kcal/min, vs. older, 1,870 ± 285 kcal/min), a difference that was primarily attributed to the lower amount of fat-free mass in older individuals.

Studies in room calorimeters (Vaughan et al., 1991) offer the opportunity to quantify total caloric expenditure under controlled but somewhat artificial sedentary living conditions. The recent availability of the doubly labeled water technique allows accurate quantification of total caloric expenditure over extended time periods (typically 7-14 days) under free-living conditions in an unobtrusive and noninvasive manner. Because doubly labeled water is a relatively new technique for use in humans, there have only been three published studies in elderly humans to date (Goran & Poehlman, 1992a, 1992b; Roberts et al., 1992).

The doubly labeled water technique was first introduced by Lifson, Gordon, and McClintock in the 1950s (1955) as an isotopic technique for measuring carbon dioxide production rate in small animals, and was originally validated in adult humans by Schoeller and colleagues (Schoeller et al., 1986; Schoeller & Webb, 1984) and subsequently by others (Coward et al., 1984; Ravussin, Harper, Rising, & Bogardus, 1991; Seale, Rumpler, Conway, & Miles, 1990; Westerterp, Brouns, Saris, & Hoor, 1988). As reviewed elsewhere (Prentice, 1988; Roberts, 1989; Schoeller, 1988; Schoeller & Fjeld, 1991; Schoeller & Racette, 1990), the technique has an accuracy of 5 to 10% when compared to indirect calorimetry techniques. Speakman, Nair, and Goran (1993) recently provided revised equations for doubly labeled water that improved the accuracy of previously performed validation studies to approximately 3%. The theoretical precision of the doubly labeled water technique is 3 to 5% (Cole & Coward, 1992; Goran, Beer, Poehlman, Wolfe, & Young, 1993; Schoeller & Taylor, 1987). However, the experimental reliability in young, free-living males is ±12%, due to fluctuations in physical activity levels within individuals over time (Goran et al., 1993). Under more controlled sedentary living conditions the experimental reproducibility of the technique is ±8%, closer to theoretical estimates (Goran, Poehlman, & Danforth, 1994).

Briefly, the doubly labeled water technique is based on the fact that deuterium-labeled water is lost from the body in the usual routes of water loss (urine, sweat, evaporative losses), whereas oxygen-18-labeled water is lost from the body in the usual routes of water loss and also via carbon dioxide production, through the carbonic anhydrase equilibrium (Lifson et al., 1955). The difference in the rate of loss in these two isotopes is therefore a function of the rate at which the body produces carbon dioxide. The assumptions of the doubly labeled water technique (Lifson et al., 1955; Lifson & McClintock, 1966; Nagy, 1980) and the equations (Prentice, 1990; Speakman et al., 1993) for calculating CO_2 production are reviewed elsewhere.

There are advantages and disadvantages of the doubly labeled water technique. One of the major advantages is that it can be used to estimate the cost of energy expenditure during nonexercising time when used in combination with the measurement of RMR by indirect calorimetry (Goran & Poehlman, 1992b). This is of particular importance because accurate quantification of this component of daily energy expenditure has traditionally proven difficult, especially under free-living conditions. Other methods that have previously been used to estimate the daily energy cost of physical activity (e.g., activity diaries, motion sensors, heart rate monitoring) have been difficult to apply because they require a high degree of dependence on the research subject, they are too inaccurate, and/or the invasive nature of the technique applied does not exclude the possibility of behavioral change in usual activity during the measurement period.

The disadvantages of the doubly labeled water technique make it unsuitable for large-scale epidemiologic studies. Because the technique is a direct measure of CO_2 production, additional information on macronutrient oxidation during the study period is required to convert CO_2 production to O_2 consumption before energy expenditure can be calculated. Unfortunately, this issue is mistakenly considered to be a major limitation of the doubly labeled water technique. During a period of energy balance, the food quotient of the diet, obtained from published population-specific data (Elia, 1991; Wright, Guthrie, Wang, & Bernardo, 1991) or calculated from dietary information (Black, Prentice, & Coward, 1986), is used to derive O_2 consumption from CO_2 production. Even with the complete absence of information on the food quotient, the maximum error in deriving energy expenditure from carbon dioxide production rate is only 3 to 5% (Elia, 1991).

In our preliminary studies (Goran & Poehlman, 1992b) of free-living total energy expenditure in healthy older subjects (seven men, 68 ± 6 years; six women, 64 ± 5 years), we found a high degree of interindividual variation in total energy expenditure (range, 1,856 to 3,200 kcal/min). This was due primarily to the wide variation in physical activity (range, 187 kcal/d to 1,235 kcal/d), which contributed 10% to 43% of total caloric output. Variation in daily caloric expenditure was most significantly related to VO_2max (r^2 = 0.79). That is, individuals who showed the highest level of aerobic fitness also displayed the higher levels of daily caloric expenditure. The practical implication of this finding is that VO$_2$max should be considered a useful physiological marker for total caloric expenditure and therefore a useful variable for the determination of energy needs in healthy elderly persons.

Despite wide interindividual variation, the energy expenditure associated with physical activity could be accurately predicted from the leisure-time activity as estimated by a questionnaire (Goran & Poehlman, 1992b). This was a surprising finding, given the relatively simple task of estimating leisure-time activity from a structured interview (Taylor et al., 1978). These results essentially validated this questionnaire as an estimate of the calories expended in leisure time, although these findings need to be replicated using a larger number of subjects.

Roberts et al. (1992) have also used the doubly labeled water technique to measure daily caloric expenditure in elderly men. Total energy expenditure in 15 subjects (69 ± 2 years; 75.5 ± 2.5 kg) was 2,498 ± 100 kcal/d. The authors found that daily energy expenditure values for these elders were significantly higher than the RDAs for energy. They concluded that current RDAs for energy may significantly underestimate usual energy requirements in older men.

Energy Requirements in Elders

Ideally, energy requirements are defined as the energy intake required to support optimal physiological function and physical activity. According to the WHO (1985) report on protein and caloric requirements, caloric needs in nonpregnant, nonlactating, and nongrowing persons are defined as the caloric intake needed to match caloric expenditure, and should be based on measurements of caloric expenditure rather than from determination of energy intake. Clearly, there is a need to provide well-founded recommendations for dietary energy, not only in developing countries, but in developed countries where overnourishment (i.e., obesity) is a growing concern.

The establishment of guidelines, however, for individual energy requirements has been a problematic issue, primarily due to (a) reliance on the questionable nature of food intake data, and (b) the failure to recognize the heterogeneity of the population with respect to age, body composition, and physical activity, which are important modulators of daily caloric needs.

How caloric intake data relate to energy requirements remains unclear, mainly due to the difficulty in measuring food intake under free-living conditions. The technique of self-recording energy intake is too dependent on the motivation level and cooperation of subjects. In addition, the very act of recording energy intake may actually alter ingestive behavior, even in compliant volunteers. These methodological weaknesses have been highlighted by several studies that suggest that self-reporting food intake is consistently underestimated when compared to measures of total energy expenditure (Bandini, Schoeller, Cyr, & Dietz, 1990; Goran & Poehlman, 1992b; Lichtman et al., 1992; Prentice et al., 1986; Schoeller, 1990). Our studies show that healthy older subjects underreported energy intake by 20% (Goran & Poehlman, 1992b), and this effect was more pronounced in females (30% underreporting) than in males (12% underreporting). Reliance on existing energy intake data for determining requirements is of further concern because preexisting databases on energy intake may not be relevant to the modified lifestyle of the 1990s, particularly due to changes in physical activity patterns over the last few decades and to increased reliance by adults on labor saving devices (e.g., central heating, cars) (Prentice et al., 1985).

An alternative means to estimate caloric needs has been to rely on estimating total daily energy expenditure using a factorial approach, which uses multiples of resting energy expenditure. James et al. (1989) defined the energy requirements of elders at approximately 1.51 times the basal metabolic rate, based on subjective assessment of the activity pattern of an individual and a factorial type of calculation based on the energy costs of the various activities performed. The factorial approach, however, does not take into account two components of daily energy expenditure that contribute to individual variation: (a) the thermic effect of feeding, which contributes approximately 10 to 15% of daily energy expenditure (Poehlman, 1989; Poehlman, Melby, & Badylak, 1991), and (b) the caloric cost of nonspecific, spontaneous activity (fidgeting), which is highly variable between subjects and contributes as much as 500 to 700 kcal/d in young adults, even when they are confined to a room calorimeter (Ravussin, Lillioja, Anderson, Christin, & Bogardus, 1986; Schutz, Ravussin, Diethelm, & Jequier, 1980). Thus the factorial approach in which RMR is multiplied by a constant activity factor is based on an inappropriate mathematical model for total daily caloric expenditure, because daily caloric expenditure has at least three compartments (resting, physical activity, and thermic response to feeding). We have recently reviewed data from our laboratory and others to show that resting metabolic rate explains less than 50% of individual variation in total energy expenditure (Carpenter, Poehlman, O'Connell, & Goran, in press). Stated another way, the ratio of total energy expenditure to resting energy expenditure (the activity factor) is highly variable even in the healthy elderly population (Goran & Poehlman, 1992a) among whom activity energy expenditure is not confounded by occupationally related energy expenditure (range of activity factor, 1.25 to 2.11; mean 1.51 ± 0.27). These data suggest that factors in addition to RMR need to be identified to further explain individual variation in total energy expenditure and thus more accurately predict individual caloric requirements.

cal activity. This heterogeneity in physical activity makes estimation of energy requirements for individuals a difficult task. However, preliminary studies have identified that VO_2max and other activity indices may be useful markers for estimating energy requirements on an individual basis. Furthermore, attempts to increase total caloric expenditure in elders by prescribing physical activity are not as straightforward as they seem, due to exercise-induced compensatory reductions in physical activity during the remainder of the day. Thus optimal exercise interventions need to be identified for elders that maximize increase in daily caloric expenditure.

References

Arciero, P. J., Goran, M. I., Gardner, A. W., Ades, P. A., Tyzbir, R. S., & Poehlman, E. T. (1993a). A practical equation to predict resting metabolic rate in older females. *Journal of the American Geriatrics Society, 41,* 389-395.

Arciero, P. J., Goran, M. I., Gardner, A. W., Ades, P., Tyzbir, R. S., & Poehlman, E. T. (1993b). A practical equation to predict resting metabolic rate in older men. *Metabolism, 42,* 950-957.

Bandini, L. G., Schoeller, D. A., Cyr, H. N., & Dietz, W. H. (1990). Validity of reported energy intake in obese and nonobese adolescents. *American Journal of Clinical Nutrition, 52,* 421-425.

Bingham, S. A., Goldberg, G. R., Coward, W. A., Prentice, A. M., & Cummings, J. H. (1989). The effect of exercise and improved fitness on basal metabolic rate. *British Journal of Nutrition, 61,* 155-173.

Bisdee, J. T., James, W. P. T., & Shaw, M. A. (1989). Changes in energy expenditure during the menstrual cycle. *British Journal of Nutrition, 61,* 187-199.

Black, A. E., Prentice, A. M., & Coward, W. A. (1986). Use of food quotients to predict respiratory quotients for the doubly-labelled water method of measuring energy expenditure. *Human Nutrition: Clinical Nutrition, 40C,* 381-391.

Bloesch, D., Schutz, Y., Breitenstein, E., Jequier, E., & Felber, J. P. (1988). Thermogenic response to an oral glucose load in man: Comparison between young and elderly subjects. *Journal of the American College of Nutrition, 7,* 471-483.

Broeder, C. E., Burrhus, K. A., Svanevik, L. S., & Wilmore, J. H. (1992). The effects of aerobic fitness on resting metabolic rate. *American Journal of Clinical Nutrition, 55,* 795-801.

Calloway, D. H., & Zanni, E. (1980). Energy requirements and energy expenditure of elderly men. *American Journal of Clinical Nutrition, 33,* 2088-2092.

Carpenter, W. H., Poehlman, E. T., O'Connell, M., & Goran, M. I. (in press). A proposal for normalizing total energy expenditure data based upon a meta-analysis. *American Journal of Clinical Nutrition.*

Cole, T. J., & Coward, W. A. (1992). Precision and accuracy of doubly labeled water energy expenditure by multipoint and two-point methods. *American Journal of Physiology, 263,* E965-E973.

Coward, W. A., Prentice, A. M., Murgatroyd, P. R., Davies, H. L., Cole, T. J., Sawyer, M., Goldberg, G. R., Halliday, D., & MacNamara, J. P. (1984). Measurement of CO_2 and water production rates in man using ^{2}H, ^{18}O-labelled H_2O; comparisons between calorimeter and isotope values. In A. J. H. van Es (Ed.), *Human energy metabolism: Physical activity and energy expenditure measurements in epidemiological research based upon direct and indirect calorimetry* (Euro Nutrition Report 5, pp. 126-128). Wageningen: Koninklijke Bibliotheek, Den Haag.

Després, J.-P., Moorjani, S., Lupien, P. J., Tremblay, A., Nadeau, A., & Bouchard, C. (1990). Regional distribution of body fat, plasma lipoproteins, and cardiovascular disease. *Arteriosclerosis, 10,* 497-511.

Dill, D. B., Robinson, S., & Ross, J. C. (1967). A longitudinal study of 16 champion runners. *Journal of Sports Medicine, 7,* 4-27.

Elia, M. (1991). Energy equivalents of CO_2 and their importance in assessing energy expenditure when using tracer techniques. *American Journal of Physiology, 260,* E75-E88.

Ferraro, R. S., Lillioja, A. M., Fontvieille, A.-M., Rising, R., Bogardus, C., & Ravussin, E. (1992). Lower sedentary metabolic rate in women compared to men. *Journal of Clinical Investigation, 90,* 1-5.

Flynn, M. A., Nolph, G. B., Baker, A. S., Martin, W. M., & Krause, G. (1989). Total body potassium in aging humans: A longitudinal study. *American Journal of Clinical Nutrition, 50,* 713-717.

Forbes, G. B. (1976). The adult decline in lean body mass. *Human Biology, 48,* 162-173.

Forbes, G. B., & Reina, J. C. (1970). Adult lean body mass declines with age: Some longitudinal observations. *Metabolism, 19,* 653-663.

Fredrix, E. W. H. M., Soeters, P. B., Deerenberg, I. M., Kester, A. D. M., Von Meyenfeldt, M. F., & Saris, W. H. M. (1990). Resting and sleeping energy expenditure in the elderly. *European Journal of Clinical Nutrition, 44,* 741-747.

Fukagawa, N. K., Bandini, L. G., Lim, P. H., Roingeard, F., Lee, M. A., & Young, J. B. (1991). Protein-induced changes in energy expenditure in young and older individuals. *American Journal of Physiology, 260,* E345-E352.

Fukagawa, N. A., Bandini, L. G., & Young, J. B. (1990). Effect of age on body composition and resting metabolic rate. *American Journal of Physiology, 259,* E233-E238.

Gardner, A. W., & Poehlman, E. T. (1993). Physical activity is a significant predictor of body density in women. *American Journal of Clinical Nutrition, 57,* 8-14.

Golay, A., Schutz, Y., Broquet, C., Moreri, R., Felber, J. P., & Jequier, E. (1983). Decreased thermogenic response to an oral glucose load in older subjects. *Journal of the American Geriatrics Society, 31,* 144-148.

Goran, M. I., Beer, W. H., Poehlman, E. T., Wolfe, R. R., & Young, V. R. (1993). Variation in total energy expenditure in young, healthy free living men. *Metabolism, 42,* 487-496.

Goran, M. I., & Poehlman, E. T. (1992a). Endurance training does not enhance total energy expenditure in healthy elderly persons. *American Journal of Physiology, 263,* E950-E957.

Goran, M. I., & Poehlman, E. T. (1992b). Total energy expenditure and energy requirements in healthy elderly persons. *Metabolism, 41,* 744-753.

Goran, M. I., Poehlman, E. T., & Danforth, E., Jr. (1994). Experimental reliability of the doubly labeled water technique. *American Journal of Physiology, 266,* E510-E515.

Harris, J. A., & Benedict, F. G. (1919). *A biometric study of basal metabolism in man* (Carnegie Institute of Washington publication 279). Washington, DC: Carnegie Institute of Washington.

Hill, J. O., Heymsfield, S. B., McManus, C. B., & DiGirolamo, M. (1984). Meal size and the thermic response to food in male subjects as a function of maximum aerobic capacity. *Metabolism, 33,* 743-749.

James, W. P. T., Ralph, A., & Ferro-Luzzi, A. (1989). Energy needs of the elderly: A new approach. In H. N. Munro & D. E. Danford (Eds.), *Human nutrition. A comprehensive treatise, Vol. 6: Nutrition, aging, and the elderly* (pp. 129-151). New York: Plenum.

Keys, A. H., Taylor, H. L., & Grande, F. (1973). Basal metabolism and age of adult man. *Metabolism, 22,* 579-587.

Kohrt, W. M., Malley, M. T., Dalsky, G. P., & Holloszy, J. O. (1992). Body composition of healthy sedentary and trained, young and old men and women. *Medicine and Science in Sports and Exercise, 24,* 832-837.

Lawson, S., Webster, J. D., Pacy, P. J., & Garrow, J. S. (1987). Effect of a 10-week aerobic exercise programme on metabolic rate, body composition and fitness in lean sedentary females. *British Journal of Clinical Practice, 41,* 684-688.

LeBlanc, J., Diamond, P., Cote, J., & Labrie, A. (1984). Hormonal factors in reduced postprandial heat production of exercise trained subjects. *Journal of Applied Physiology, 56,* 772-776.

Lennon, D., Nagle, F., Stratman, F., Shrago, E., & Dennis, S. (1985). Diet and exercise training effects on resting metabolic rate. *International Journal of Obesity, 9,* 39-47.

Lichtman, S. W., Pisarska, K., Berman, E. R., Pestore, M., Dowling, H., Offenbacher, E., Weisel, H., Heshka, S., Matthews, S. E., & Heymsfield, S. B. (1992). Discrepancy between self-reported and actual caloric intake and exercise in obese subjects. *New England Journal of Medicine, 327,* 1893-1898.

Lifson, N., Gordon, G. B., & McClintock, R. (1955). Measurement of total carbon dioxide production by means of $D_2{}^{18}O$. *Journal of Applied Physiology, 7,* 704-710.

Lifson, N., & McClintock, R. (1966). Theory of use of the turnover rates of body water for measuring energy and material balance. *Journal of Theoretical Biology, 12,* 46-74.

Lundholm, K., Holm, G., Lindmark, L., Larsson, B., Sjostrom, L., & Bjontorp, P. (1986). Thermogenic effect of food in physically well-trained elderly men. *European Journal of Applied Physiology, 55,* 486-492.

Meredith, C. N., Frontera, W. R., Fisher, E. C., Hughes, V. A., Herland, J. C., Edwards, J., & Evans, W. J. (1989). Peripheral effects of endurance training in young and older subjects. *Journal of Applied Physiology, 66,* 2844-2849.

Mifflin, M. D., St. Jeor, S. T., Hill, L. A., Scott, B. J., Daugherty, S. A., & Koh, Y. O. (1990). A new predictive equation for resting energy expenditure in healthy individuals. *American Journal of Clinical Nutrition, 51,* 241-247.

Morgan, J. B., & York, D. A. (1983). Thermic effect of feeding in relation to energy balance in elderly men. *Annals of Nutrition and Metabolism, 27,* 71-77.

Nagy, K. A. (1980). CO_2 production in animals: Analysis of potential errors in the doubly labeled water method. *American Journal of Physiology, 238,* R466-R473.

Novak, L. P. (1972). Aging, total body potassium, fat-free mass, and cell mass in males and females between ages and 18 and 85 years. *Journal of Gerontology, 27,* 438-443.

Owen, O. E., Kavle, E., Owen, R. S., Polansky, M., Capiro, S., Mozzoli, M. A., Kendrick, Z. V., Bushman, M. C., & Boden, G. (1986). A reappraisal of the caloric requirements of women. *American Journal of Clinical Nutrition, 44,* 1-19.

Poehlman, E. T. (1989). A review: Exercise and its influence on resting energy metabolism in man. *Medicine and Science in Sports and Exercise, 21,* 515-525.

Poehlman, E. T. (1992). Energy expenditure and requirements in aging humans. *Journal of Nutrition, 122,* 2057-2065.

Poehlman, E. T. (1993). Regulation of energy expenditure in aging humans. *Journal of the American Geriatrics Society, 41,* 552-559.

Poehlman, E. T., Berke, E. M., Joseph, J. R., Gardner, A. W., Katzman-Rooks, S. M., & Goran, M. I. (1992). Influence of aerobic capacity, body composition and thyroid hormones on the age-related decline in resting metabolic rate. *Metabolism, 41,* 915-921.

Poehlman, E. T., & Danforth, E., Jr. (1991). Endurance training increases metabolic rate and norepinephrine appearance rate in older individuals. *American Journal of Physiology, 261,* E233-E239.

Poehlman, E. T., Gardner, A. W., & Goran, M. I. (1990). The impact of physical activity and cold exposure on food intake and energy expenditure in man. *Journal of Wilderness Medicine, 1,* 265-278.

Poehlman, E. T., Gardner, A. W., & Goran, M. I. (1992). Influence of endurance training on energy intake, norepinephrine kinetics, and metabolic rate in older individuals. *Metabolism, 41,* 941-948.

Poehlman, E. T., Goran, M. I., Gardner, A. W., Ades, P. A., Arciero, P. J., Katzman-Rooks, S. M., Montgomery, S. M., Toth, M. J., & Sutherland, P. T. (1993). Determinants of decline in resting metabolic rate in aging females. *American Journal of Physiology, 264,* E450-E455.

Poehlman, E. T., & Horton, E. S. (1990). Regulation of energy expenditure in aging humans. *Annual Review of Nutrition, 10,* 255-275.

Poehlman, E. T., McAuliffe, T., Van Houten, D. R., & Danforth, E., Jr. (1990). Influence of age and endurance training on metabolic rate and hormones in healthy men. *American Journal of Physiology, 259,* E66-E72.

Poehlman, E. T., Melby, C. L., & Badylak, S. F. (1988). Resting metabolic rate and postprandial thermogenesis in highly trained and untrained males. *American Journal of Clinical Nutrition, 47,* 793-798.

Poehlman, E. T., Melby, C. L., & Badylak, S. F. (1991). Relation of age and physical exercise status on metabolic rate in younger and older healthy men. *Journal of Gerontology: Biological Sciences, 46,* B54-B58.

Poehlman, E. T., Melby, C. L., Badylak, S. F., & Calles, J. (1989). Aerobic fitness and resting energy expenditure in young adult males. *Metabolism, 38,* 85-90.

Poehlman, E. T., Melby, C. L., & Goran, M. I. (1991). The impact of exercise and diet restriction on daily energy expenditure. *Sports Medicine, 11,* 78-101.

Poehlman, E. T., Toth, M. J., & Webb, G. D. (1993). Sodium-Potassium pump activity contributes to the age-related decline in resting metabolic rate. *Journal of Clinical Endocrinology and Metabolism, 76,* 1054-1059.

Prentice, A. M. (1988). Applications of the $^2H_2^{18}O$ method in free-living humans. *Proceedings of the Nutrition Society, 47,* 258-269.

Prentice, A. M. (Ed.), (1990). *The doubly-labelled water method for measuring energy expenditure: Technical recommendations for use in humans. A consensus report by the IDECG Working group.* Vienna: International Atomic Energy Agency.

Prentice, A. M., Black, A. E., Coward, W. A., Davies, H. L., Goldberg, G. R., Murgatroyd, P. R., Asford, J., Sawyer, M., & Whitehead, R. G. (1986). High levels of energy expenditure in obese women. *British Medical Journal, 292,* 983-987.

Prentice, A. M., Coward, W. A., Davies, H. L., Murgatroyd, P. R., Black, A. E., Goldberg, G. R., Ashford, J., Sawyer, M., & Whitehead, R. G. (1985). Unexpectedly low levels of energy expenditure in healthy women. *Lancet, 1,* 1419-1422.

Ravussin, E., Harper, I., Rising, R., & Bogardus, C. (1991). Energy expenditure by doubly labeled water: Validation in lean and obese subjects. *American Journal of Physiology, 261,* E402-E409.

Ravussin, E., Lillioja, S., Anderson, T. E., Christin, L., & Bogardus, C. (1986). Determinants of 24-hour energy expenditure in man. Methods and results using a respiratory chamber. *Journal of Clinical Investigation, 78,* 1568-1578.

Roberts, S. B. (1989). Use of the doubly labeled water method for measurement of energy expenditure, total body water, water intake, and metabolizable energy intake in humans and small animals. *Canadian Journal of Physiology and Pharmacology, 67,* 1190-1198.

Roberts, S. B., Young, V. R., Fuss, P., Heyman, M. B., Fiatarone, M., Dallal, G. E., Cortiella, J., & Evans, W. J. (1992). What are the dietary energy needs of elderly adults? *International Journal of Obesity, 16,* 969-976.

Robertson, J. D., & Reid, D. D. (1952). Standards for the basal metabolism of normal people in Britain. *Lancet, 1,* 940-943.

Robinson, S., Dill, D. B., Tzankoff, S. P., Wagner, J. A., & Robinson, R. D. (1975). Longitudinal studies of aging in 37 men. *Journal of Applied Physiology, 38,* 263-267.

Schoeller, D. A. (1988). Measurement of energy expenditure in free-living humans by using doubly labeled water. *Journal of Nutrition, 118,* 1278-1289.

Schoeller, D. A. (1990). How accurate is self-reported dietary energy intake?. *Nutrition Reviews, 48,* 373-379.

Schoeller, D. A., & Fjeld, C. R. (1991). Human energy metabolism: What have we learned from the doubly labeled water method. *Annual Review of Nutrition, 11,* 355-373.

Schoeller, D. A., & Racette, S. B. (1990). A review of field techniques for the assessment of energy expenditure. *Journal of Nutrition, 120* (Suppl.), 1492-1495.

Schoeller, D. A., Ravussin, E., Schutz, Y., Acheson, K. J., Baertschi, P., & Jequier, E. (1986). Energy expenditure by doubly labeled water: Validation in humans and proposed calculation. *American Journal of Physiology, 250,* R823-R830.

Schoeller, D. A., & Taylor, P. B. (1987). Precision of the doubly labelled water method using the two-point calculation. *Human Nutrition. Clinical Nutrition, 41C,* 215-223.

Schoeller, D. A., & Webb, P. (1984). Five-day comparison of the doubly labeled water method with respiratory gas exchange. *American Journal of Clinical Nutrition, 40,* 153-158.

Schutz, Y., Bray, G., & Margen, S. (1987). Postprandial thermogenesis at rest and during exercise in elderly men ingesting two levels of protein. *Journal of the American College of Nutrition, 6,* 497-506.

Schutz, Y., Ravussin, E., Diethelm, R., & Jequier, E. (1980). Spontaneous physical activity measured by radar in obese and control subjects studied in a respiration chamber. *International Journal of Obesity, 6,* 23-28.

Schwartz, R. S., Jaeger, L. F., & Veith, R. C. (1990). The thermic effect of feeding in older men: The importance of the sympathetic nervous system. *Metabolism, 39,* 733-737.

Seale, J. L., Rumpler, W. V., Conway, J. M., & Miles, C. W. (1990). Comparison of doubly labeled water, intake-balance, and direct- and indirect-calorimetry methods for measuring energy expenditure in adult men. *American Journal of Clinical Nutrition, 52,* 66-71.

Shock, N. W. (1955). Metabolism and age. *Journal of Chronic Diseases, 2,* 687-703.

Shock, N. W., & Yiengst, M. J. (1955). Age changes in basal respiratory measurements and metabolism in males. *Journal of Gerontology, 10,* 31-50.

Speakman, J. R., Nair, K. S., & Goran, M. I. (1993). Revised equations for calculating CO_2 production from doubly labeled water in humans. *American Journal of Physiology, 264,* E912-E917.

Stevenson, J. A. F., Box, B. M., Feleki, V., & Beaton, J. R. (1966). Bouts of exercise and food intake in the rat. *Journal of Applied Physiology, 21,* 118-122.

Taylor, H. L., Jacobs, D. R., Schucker, B., Knudsen, J., Leon, A. S., & Debacker, G. (1978). Questionnaire for the assessment of leisure time physical activities. *Journal of Chronic Diseases, 31,* 741-755.

Thomas, B. M., & Miller, A. T., Jr. (1958). Adaptation to forced exercise in the rat. *American Journal of Physiology, 193,* 350-354.

Tremblay, A., Fontaine, E., Poehlman, E. T., Mitchell, D., Perron, L., & Bouchard, C. (1986). The effect of exercise-training on resting metabolic rate in lean and moderately obese individuals. *International Journal of Obesity, 10,* 511-517.

Tuttle, W. W., Horvath, S. M., Presson, L. F., & Daum, K. (1953). Specific dynamic action of protein in men past 60 years of age. *Journal of Applied Physiology, 5,* 631-634.

Tzankoff, S. P., & Norris, A. H. (1977). Effect of muscle mass decrease on age-related BMR changes. *Journal of Applied Physiology, 43,* 1001-1006.

Tzankoff, S. P., & Norris, A. H. (1978). Longitudinal changes in basal metabolism in man. *Journal of Applied Physiology, 45,* 536-539.

Vaughan, L., Zurlo, F., & Ravussin, E. (1991). Aging and energy expenditure. *American Journal of Clinical Nutrition, 53,* 821-825.

Webb, P. (1986). 24-hour energy expenditure and the menstrual cycle. *American Journal of Clinical Nutrition, 44,* 614-619.

Webb, P., & Heistand, M. (1975). Sleep metabolism and age. *Journal of Applied Physiology, 38,* 257-262.

Westerterp, K. R., Brouns, F., Saris, W. H., & Hoor, F. T. (1988). Comparison of doubly labeled water with respirometry at low- and high-activity levels. *Journal of Applied Physiology, 65,* 53-56.

Wilson, O. (1966). Field study of the effect of cold exposure and increased muscular activity upon metabolic rate and thyroid function in man. *Federation Proceedings of the Federation of American Societies of Experimental Biology (FASEB), 25,* 1357-1362.

Wing, R. R., Matthews, K. A., Kuller, L. H., Meilahn, E. N., & Plantinga, P. L. (1991). Weight gain at the time of menopause. *Archives of Internal Medicine, 151,* 97-102.

World Health Organization. (1985). *Energy and protein requirements* (Technical Report Series, No. 724). Geneva: Author.

Wright, H., Guthrie, H., Wang, M., & Bernardo, V. (1991). The 1987-88 nationwide food consumption survey: An update of the nutrient intake of respondents. *Nutrition Today, 26,* 21-27.

7

Prospects for Prevention of Dementia and Associated Impairments

James A. Mortimer

Alzheimer's disease has been described as "an epidemic" (Clark, 1979, p. 95) and "the disease of the century, the worst of all diseases" (Thomas, 1981, p. 34). Estimates of its growing prevalence include the prediction that the number of cases in the United States will increase by a factor of 5 from 1980 to 2040 (U.S. Congress, Office of Technology Assessment, 1987). Most of these new cases will come from elders 85 years and above, the fastest growing segment of the U.S. population, who are at very high risk of being affected by this illness (Evans et al., 1989).

Figure 7.1 shows the predicted numbers of cases of Alzheimer's disease under the assumption that the age- and sex-specific prevalence of this disease will remain stable over the next several decades. Projections like this are alarming in the context of a society increasingly aware of the health care demands placed on it by its aging population and its finite resources to deal with those demands. Although the publication of ominous projections of societal cost and impact has been important in raising interest in dementia treatment and prevention, it also may encourage age-based rationing of medical care in response to the perceived hopelessness of the situation.

There has been a pervasive belief that little can be done about dementia and, in particular, Alzheimer's disease. People with this disease are frequently labeled as victims. Alzheimer's disease is referred to as a "slow death of the mind" or, in more graphic terms, "a nightmare that never ends" or "a never-ending funeral." The implication of these statements is that we are dealing with a disease that cannot be prevented, slowed, or effectively treated. In this chapter it will be argued that this view is unnecessarily

AUTHOR'S NOTE: This chapter was supported in part by NIH grants R01-AG09238, R01-AG08539, and R01-AG09769.

131

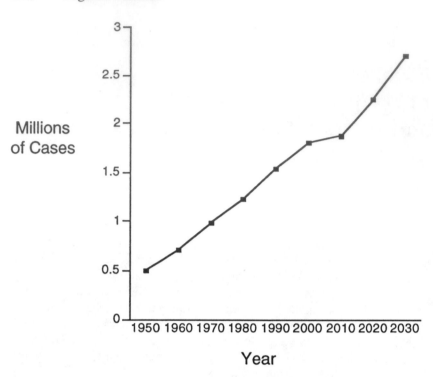

Figure 7.1. Predicted Total Number of Cases of Alzheimer's Disease in the United States, 1950-2030, Based on Stable Age- and Sex-Specific Prevalence Rates

pessimistic—that primary and secondary as well as tertiary prevention may well be possible for dementing illnesses. In fact, demographic changes that have already occurred in the composition of future elderly populations may markedly reduce the impact of Alzheimer's disease and related disorders over the next 50 years.

A Threshold Model for Dementia

To understand how dementia may be prevented, we need to understand why some people become demented, whereas others do not. The common belief is that dementia reflects an increased incidence of particular diseases and conditions in old age that specifically compromise brain function. In this view, individuals remain cognitively intact until a specific disease process is initiated, after which they undergo a rapid decline. An alternative view is that dementia is the net result of a lifetime of growth and degeneration of the brain—that the sum of brain development during childhood and damage resulting from a variety of insults over the life course determines whether and when a critical threshold of functioning brain tissue is reached at which an individual is no longer capable of normal intellectual performance and fulfills criteria for the diagnosis of dementia.

To understand why a threshold model of brain function may be applicable to understanding the etiology of dementia, it is useful to review some basic facts about the human brain. The development of neurons is virtually complete by the age of 6. The inability to replace lost cells after this age represents an important source of vulnerability. Given the fixed number of neurons, it is remarkable that the human brain functions adequately for up to 100 years without a high incidence of failure.

The principal reason for preservation of brain function appears to be the high redundancy of its components. We know from human autopsy studies as well as from animal experiments that approximately 80% of the neurons in the substantia nigra pars compacta must be lost before the clinical signs of parkinsonism become evident (Mortimer & Webster, 1982). A similar proportion (80%) of lower motor neurons must be lost before weakness or muscle atrophy becomes clinically discernable in poliomyelitis (McComas, Sica, Campbell, & Upton, 1971). The brain is not unlike a spaceship that is designed to be sent to Mars. Because there is little possibility of replacement or repair, there are multiple backup systems. It is capable of operating fairly normally even when most neurons are absent or malfunctioning. This capability provides benefits as well as deficits. The principal benefit is that the system is capable of adequate functioning when there has been a remarkable amount of damage. The main deficit is that we do not get early warning of brain diseases. These diseases may progress behind the scenes for years and in some cases decades. By the time Parkinson's disease or Alzheimer's disease is diagnosable, a great deal of damage has already occurred and the possibility of effective treatment is certainly reduced.

The effects of redundancy can be interpreted in the context of a threshold for clinical dementia. As shown in Figure 7.2, dementia could result from several scenarios. If one begins with a well-developed complement of neurons at birth (high brain reserve capacity), loss of neurons over the life course may lead to a crossing of the dementia threshold after age 100, an age to which very few individuals live (A). Given the same rate of loss of neurons, an individual who begins with fewer neurons in critical regions of the nervous system may cross the threshold at an earlier age (B). The dementia threshold also can be crossed early if the rate of loss of neurons over the life course is greater (C). Curves D and E correspond to the effects of a sudden loss of functioning neurons, as would occur following a stroke (D), and an acceleration in the rate of neuronal loss following the onset of a clinical brain disease (E).

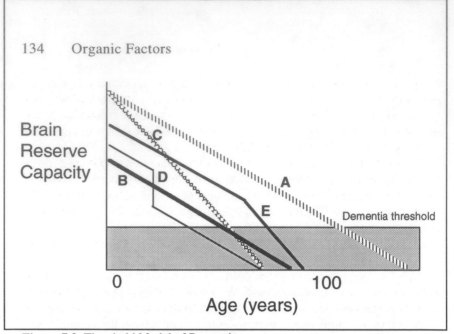

Figure 7.2. Threshold Model of Dementia
Critical value of brain reserve capacity is attained when decline enters shaded area corresponding to dementia. Five scenarios are shown. See text for description.

Dementia as a Multifactorial Condition

The most common diagnosis of dementing illness in the United States and in most of the world is Alzheimer's disease. We know from recent epidemiologic, clinical, and neuropathologic studies that approximately two thirds of cases of dementia are probably attributable to this illness (Evans et al., 1989; Jellinger, Danielczyk, Fischer, & Gabriel, 1990; Kokmen, Beard, Offord, & Kurland, 1989). Although Alzheimer brain lesions appear to be the principal pathology underlying dementia in elders, a very large number of diseases and conditions can produce dementia (Cummings & Benson, 1983; Haase, 1977). Other quantitatively important causes include vascular lesions (multiple strokes), Parkinson's disease, and alcohol abuse. Although each of these causes is sufficient by itself to cause dementia, attribution of a case of dementia to a single cause, such as Alzheimer's disease, vascular lesions, or alcohol abuse, is probably too simplistic. Dementia probably is better regarded as a multifactorial condition, resulting from a variety of brain insults. In any single case, one etiology may be predominant. However, multiple factors are likely to determine when and whether a clinical threshold is crossed.

The latter point is illustrated well by the relationship between alcohol abuse and dementia. Although alcoholic dementia has been described in virtually all clinical series of cases (Cummings & Benson, 1983), its neuro-pathological basis is unclear (Victor & Adams, 1985). Recent studies suggest that alcohol abuse may be more important as a risk factor for Alzheimer's disease than for a primary alcoholic dementia. For example, a large community-based case-control study of Alzheimer's disease in Sweden (Fratiglioni, Ahlbom, Viitanen, & Winblad, 1993) found that people who were judged to have abused alcohol were approximately 4.4 times as likely to have Alzheimer's disease as individuals of the same age, sex, and education who were not heavy drinkers. This increase in risk is almost identical to that reported in an earlier study in Liverpool, England (Saunders et al., 1991). These findings, combined with the proportion of cases of dementia attributed to alcohol consumption, imply that avoidance of heavy alcohol consumption could result in a 10% reduction in the number of dementia cases. In addition to the possibility of primary prevention of dementia through the reduction of alcohol abuse, the severity of Alzheimer's disease could be reduced through this means as well (secondary prevention). Alzheimer patients with a history of alcohol abuse have been reported to exhibit a more aggressive disease course in comparison to those without this risk factor (Teri, Hughes, & Larson, 1990).

Additional support for a multicausal etiology for dementia comes from the classic clinicopathologic study of dementia by Tomlinson, Blessed, and Roth (1970). These investigators clinically evaluated 50 cases of dementia and following death obtained the brains for neuropathologic study. They found that approximately 50% of the cases had dementia on the basis of Alzheimer lesions alone, 20% from an accumulation of small strokes (vascular dementia), and 15% from a combination of the two. In the 15% of cases resulting from a combination of Alzheimer and vascular lesions, there were insufficient numbers of Alzheimer lesions or volumes of infarcted tissue to make either diagnosis. Presumably, the dementia in these cases resulted from summation of subclinical vascular and Alzheimer lesions.

As with alcohol abuse, the overlap between Alzheimer's disease and vascular dementia has implications for both primary and secondary prevention. With regard to primary prevention, modifiable risk factors for stroke have been identified, including hypertension, smoking, poorly controlled diabetes, and atrial fibrillation. Treatment of hypertension by antihypertensive medications, treatment of atrial fibrillation by anticoagulants, and the use of aspirin in persons at high risk of ischemic stroke can prevent initial or subsequent strokes. If the risk of stroke is reduced, it may be possible to postpone the onset of Alzheimer dementia in individuals who have not yet reached the threshold for this condition to occur.

The rate of decline of individuals with Alzheimer's disease may also be modified by risk factors for vascular dementia. In a recent study of 79 patients with clinically diagnosed probable Alzheimer's disease followed for a period of up to 4 years, patients with a history of hypertension were found to exhibit faster rates of functional decline when age, education, and gender were controlled (Mortimer, unpublished).

Improvements in Status
by Symptomatic Treatment

Because dementia is probably the result of multiple conditions, it may be possible to improve the status of a patient, even dramatically, by means of certain interventions (for example, abstinence from alcohol or treatment of B12 deficiency or depression) without curing the primary dementing process. Many putative etiologies of dementia may not cause dementia by themselves but may rather require susceptibility, usually in the form of Alzheimer's disease or some other degenerative process. For example, it is rare to encounter a case of dementia due solely to depression (Reifler, 1982). In most cases of cognitive impairment with depression, patients improve transiently with depression treatment, but then continue to progress secondary to an underlying degenerative disease (Larson, Reifler, Sumi, Canfield, & Chinn, 1985; Reding, Haycox, & Blass, 1985). Another example of susceptibility is dementia pugilistica, seen in some boxers. Epidemiologic studies suggest that this outcome is a rare sequela to boxing and may not be expressed until fairly late in life when other processes, such as Alzheimer's disease, contribute (Mortimer & Pirozzolo, 1985). Similarly, hypothyroidism and drug toxicity, though capable of producing dementia by themselves, are frequently seen in association with Alzheimer's disease, where they can increase the severity of cognitive impairment (Larson et al., 1985). Treatment of any of these potential dementing etiologies, particularly in very mild or preclinical cases, could conceivably reduce the prevalence of dementia by moving individuals away from the critical threshold for dementia symptoms. In established cases of dementia, such treatments may reduce severity of the cognitive impairment.

Other Causes of Excess Disability
in Dementia and Alzheimer's Disease

Demented patients are likely to be at the same or higher risk of medical illnesses and conditions as nondemented individuals of similar age and sex. However, because of difficulties in communicating symptoms, attribution of the symptoms to the dementing illness, and the burden of care resulting from the dementia, these illnesses and conditions may not be recognized and treated, resulting in excess disability (Peters, Reifler, & Larson, 1989). Excess disability is reflected in decreased ability to perform activities of daily living and an increased frequency of certain behavioral problems. Treatment of comorbid conditions, therefore, can lead to a reduction in disabilities as well as reductions in the need for care. It also is important for physicians to recognize the presence of dementia in persons presenting with medical illnesses, because it places individuals at greater risk of morbidity from potentially preventable problems, such as falls and fractures, adverse drug reactions, and delirium.

Risk Factors for Alzheimer's Disease

Table 7.1 summarizes known risk factors for Alzheimer's disease. Some of these, such as chronological age, can be neither modified nor prevented. However, others may be susceptible to change, enabling primary prevention of Alzheimer's disease.

Most of the information we have on risk factors comes from case-control studies, in which informants for cases and controls provide exposure histories. In 1991, the results of a pooled reanalysis of 11 case-control studies were published (van Duijn, Stijnen, & Hofman, 1991). Risk factors investigated in this analysis included family history of dementia, Down's syndrome, and Parkinson's disease; mother's age at the time of birth; head injury; smoking; alcohol consumption; exposures to solvents and lead; history of depression; and a number of medical conditions. As shown in Table 7.2, significant associations were found for a number of risk factors. However, with the exception of family history of dementia, Down's syndrome, and Parkinson's disease, the adjusted relative risks were quite modest. Head injury represents the only exposure for which prevention is straightforward. The recent demonstration that the e4 allele of the apolipoprotein gene greatly increases the susceptibility to Alzheimer's disease (Corder et al., 1993) offers significant hope that many cases of this disease can be prevented by modifying the protein coded by this allele. The inverse association with smoking (Graves et al., 1991) suggests that some element of cigarette smoke, perhaps nicotine, may provide protection against Alzheimer's disease. However, the serious health consequences of smoking imply that if the element could be identified, some other form of administration would be preferable.

The role of aluminum in causing Alzheimer's disease remains controversial (Doll, 1993). Recent studies (Jacobs, Duong, Jones, Trapp, & Scheibel, 1989; Lovell, Ehmann, & Markesbery, 1993) have called into question initial findings showing an accumulation of aluminum in association with the brain

TABLE 7.1 Risk Factors for Alzheimer's Disease (AD)

Definite
  Chronological age
  Family history of AD
  Down's syndrome

Possible
  High maternal age
  History of depression
  History of hypothyroidism
  Aluminum, other toxins
  Smoking (protective)

Probable
  Head trauma
  Low education, socioeconomic status, and intelligence

lesions of Alzheimer's disease, including senile plaques (Candy et al., 1984) and neurofibrillary tangles (Perl & Brody, 1980; Perl, Munoz-Garcia, Good, & Pendlebury, 1985). Although several ecologic investigations have suggested a possible association between aluminum concentrations in the drinking water and the prevalence of this condition (Flaten, 1990; Leventhal, 1987; Martyn et al., 1989; Michel et al., 1991; Neri & Hewitt, 1991), these studies have suffered from a number of weaknesses, including incomplete or biased ascertainment of cases (e.g., based on death certificate data or medical records), reliance on residence at time of death rather than residential history (allowing for the possibility of migration from a region of low aluminum to a region of high aluminum exposure), and limited retrospective information on aluminum concentrations for the years during which most exposure would have occurred. If elevated aluminum in the drinking water increases the risk of Alzheimer's disease, then fluoridation should reduce the risk because fluoride competes with aluminum for absorption in the gut. Indeed, it has been suggested that fluoridation may represent a relatively inexpensive and effective preventative strategy for this illness (Rifat, 1992).

Low Education as a Risk Factor for Dementia

It has been shown repeatedly that less educated people perform worse on mental status tests and on psychometric tests in general than those with more education (Mortimer & Graves, 1993). Similar associations have been found for other indices of low socioeconomic status, including low income and occupational status. The poorer performance of individuals with low education and socioeconomic status could be explained by impaired test-taking ability, a higher frequency of mental impairment, or both.

TABLE 7.2 Risk Factors Found to Be Significantly Associated With Alzheimer's Disease in the Pooled Analysis

Risk Factor	Adjusted Odds Ratio[a]
Family history of dementia	3.5
Family history of Down's syndrome	2.7
Family history of Parkinson's disease	2.4
Maternal age at birth > 40 yrs.	1.7
Head injury with loss of consciousness	1.8
Hypothyroidism	2.3
Depression prior to AD onset	1.8
Ever having smoked cigarettes	0.8

a. Adjusted for age, education, gender, and number of siblings (for family history risk factors).

A number of recent population-based studies have demonstrated significant associations between the lower educational attainment and the prevalence of either Alzheimer's disease or dementia (Bonaiuto, Rocca, & Lippi, 1990; Dartigues et al., 1991; Fratiglioni et al., 1991; Zhang et al., 1990). In a community-based survey of 2,790 persons aged 65 and above, Dartigues et al. (1991) reported a strong dose-response effect of the level of education on the prevalence of probable Alzheimer's disease, with prevalence rates decreasing progressively from illiterates (5.4%) to those with a university education (0%). A remarkable finding in this study was that of 151 individuals surveyed with a university education, none suffered from any form of dementia. Surveys of incident Alzheimer's disease and dementia have been less numerous, but preliminary findings indicate a similar increase in dementia incidence with lower education (Mortimer & Graves, 1993).

Four explanations can be given for the association between low education and socioeconomic status and increased risk of dementia:

1. Low socioeconomic status and education are associated with increased exposure during adult life to a wide variety of factors that augment the risk of dementia, including infectious diseases, chronic illnesses, and high-risk behaviors and health practices.

2. Differences in fetal and childhood exposures and nutrition associated with the socioeconomic status of the family of origin may lead to differential brain development. Inadequate brain development at an early age associated with low socioeconomic status may place one at greater risk of becoming demented later in life.

3. Higher education and its correlates (higher occupational status, higher income) may provide a richer intellectual environment during adult life, leading to growth and preservation of the neural substrate ("use it or lose it").

4. Finally, more well-educated individuals may be able to cover up their dementing illnesses at an early stage by utilizing learned strategies to increase
their level of performance on cognitive screening examinations.

Low Education and Intelligence
as Risk Factors for Dementia

To assess the association between childhood exposures and cognitive
impairment in late life, we have been following 700 elderly Catholic sisters
(nuns). The sisters selected for study come from a teaching congregation, the
School Sisters of Notre Dame. Although the majority of these sisters completed at least a bachelor's degree, a substantial percentage finished only
high school or had less education. Initial studies with this congregation
indicated that nuns with lower attained education (less than a bachelor's
degree) who survived to participate in the study (age > 75) were about twice
as likely to be severely cognitively impaired as sisters who had higher
educational attainment (Snowdon, Ostwald, Kane, & Keenan, 1989).

Because nuns lead very similar adult lives (nonsmoking, low alcohol
consumption, no children, same access to medical care, eating out of the
same kitchens), the risk factors for cognitive impairment in late life associated with low attained education may already have been present when they
joined the congregation at around age 21. Alternatively, the increased intellectual stimulation engendered by higher education may have been crucial
in keeping the well-educated nuns from deteriorating cognitively in old
age. To assess whether there were already substantial differences between
those nuns who would go on to attain higher degrees after entering the
congregation and those whose education would be limited, we analyzed
autobiographical essays written by the nuns at the time they took their vows
around age 21. These essays, handwritten by the sisters, were entered into a
computerized database and analyzed for the complexity of vocabulary employed. We chose as a measure the percentage of words four or more
syllables in length that were used by only one sister in the sample (examples: *ingratitude, mortification, transitory*). To validate this measure, we
selected 20 elderly sisters (average age = 79.3 years) with a score of 28 or
higher on the Mini-Mental State Examination, indicating that they were not
mentally impaired. These sisters were administered the Vocabulary subtest
of the Wechsler Adult Intelligence Scale-Revised (WAIS-R) and the National Adult Reading Test-Revised (NART-R). Both of these measures are
used extensively to estimate premorbid intelligence. Spearman correlations between the autobiographic vocabulary index and both the WAIS-R
Vocabulary subtest and the NART-R were 0.53 ($p = 0.02$), suggesting

that the autobiographic vocabulary index in youth is a valid measure of intelligence.

Associations between severe cognitive impairment in old age and the autobiographic vocabulary index were then assessed using a case-control design, comparing 10 sisters who were alive and severely cognitively impaired (MMSE scores 4-17, M = 5.4) in 1992 with 10 sisters who were alive and cognitively intact (MMSE > 26, M = 29.3) at this time. The two groups were matched on current age (81). Logistic regression analyses, with the autobiographic vocabulary index categorized as a dichotomous variable (above and below the median) and attained education as a continuous variable, showed that those sisters with low autobiographic vocabulary scores at the time they joined the congregation were 20 times more likely to be cognitively impaired in old age than those with higher vocabulary scores (95% CI = 1.4, 276.0, p = 0.03). Attained education failed to predict cognitive performance in late life when it was simultaneously entered into the model with the autobiographic vocabulary score. These preliminary findings suggest that attained education may be a surrogate for intelligence, and that individuals with higher intelligence in youth may be less likely to suffer from severe cognitive impairment in old age.

Brain Development and the Risk of Dementia

The finding that sisters who were more intelligent at age 21 have a lower risk of cognitive impairment in old age may be related to differences in brain development. Individuals from low socioeconomic status backgrounds have been shown on average to have reduced physical development (Nystrom Peck & Vagero, 1987). Given the very strong correlation between brain size and body size, it is likely that such individuals also have diminished brain size. Furthermore, recent studies suggest that brain volume is strongly associated with intelligence (Andreason et al., 1993; Willerman, Schultz, Rutledge, & Bigler, 1991).

To assess the possible role of brain size in determining cognitive function in late life, data were analyzed from an ongoing epidemiologic study of all Japanese Americans over the age of 65 living in King County, Washington (Graves et al., 1993). Data from the first 521 individuals in this cohort to be screened were used to assess the relationship of brain size, determined indirectly by measuring head circumference, to scores on a cognitive screening test, the Cognitive Abilities Screening Instrument (CASI). Adjusting for age, gender, and years of education in multiple regression models, smaller head circumference was found to be significantly related to lower CASI scores in both men and women. This effect was most pronounced in individuals with a positive family history of memory problems in late life and was amplified by both low education and older age. The findings are consistent with a threshold hypothesis of dementia, in which initial brain size (as estimated by head circumference) is most important in individuals who are vulnerable because of family history, low education, or old age.

Public Health Significance

The public health significance of a risk factor in the causation of disease depends not only on the strength of association between the risk factor and the disease (assessed by the relative risk or odds ratio), but also on the population frequency of exposure to the risk factor. Risk factors that occur rarely in populations can explain relatively few cases of a disease, even when the association between the risk factor and the outcome is strong. To assess the public health significance of a risk factor, epidemiologists utilize a measure called the etiologic fraction. The etiologic fraction, defined as the proportion of all cases of a given disease that is attributable to a specific risk factor, describes the relative importance of an exposure in the population.

Table 7.3 gives etiologic fractions for three risk factors for Alzheimer's disease: low education, family history of dementia, and head trauma with unconsciousness. The etiologic fraction for low education represents the mean etiologic fraction for two population-based community studies (Bonaiuto et al., 1990; Dartigues et al., 1991), and those for family history of dementia and head trauma are derived from the pooled reanalysis of case-control data (Mortimer et al., 1991; van Duijn, Clayton, et al., 1991). The mean etiologic fraction for low education (.77) far exceeds that for family history of dementia (.26), one of the most well-established risk factors for Alzheimer's disease, whereas that for head trauma, another putative risk factor for Alzheimer's disease (Mortimer et al., 1991) is only .04.

The interpretation of the large etiologic fraction for low education is not straightforward. If low education is causally related to Alzheimer's disease, then increasing the level of education of the population should theoretically lead to the elimination of approximately 80% of the cases. This would certainly be an economical way to prevent the disease. However, chances are that education is a surrogate for something else, perhaps intelligence related to early brain development. If this turns out to be true, the most effective primary prevention for Alzheimer's disease might be improvements in perinatal care and childhood nutrition that would facilitate brain growth.

TABLE 7.3 Etiologic Fractions for Selected Risk Factors

Risk Factor	Probability of Exposure	Etiologic Fraction
Low education	0.70	0.77
Family history of dementia	0.16	0.26
Head trauma with loss of consciousness	0.05	0.04

Will We Be Deluged by Cases of Dementia in the First Half of the 21st Century?

Predictions based on present age- and sex-specific rates of dementia have been used to suggest an approaching epidemic of this condition (Figure 7.1). However, these predictions neglect several important changes in the elderly population. If a threshold model of dementia is appropriate, then loss of functioning brain tissue secondary to stroke will facilitate the development of dementia in individuals with subclinical Alzheimer lesions. The decline in stroke incidence experienced during the past 40 years (Garraway, Whisnant, & Drury, 1983), if it were to continue, would lead to lower rates of vascular dementia as well as Alzheimer's disease. However, more important is the change that is occurring in educational attainment of elders. Over the past 30 years, the median educational level of the U.S. population among individuals 65 years and older increased by almost 4 years (U.S. Department of Health and Human Services, 1991). This increase is still occurring, and in fact the biggest change for those 80 and over will take place in the next 20 years. Furthermore, the increase in educational attainment among elders has paralleled improvements in the nutrition of pregnant women, in childhood and adult nutrition, and in the control of infectious diseases.

Figure 7.3 compares the predicted number of cases of Alzheimer's disease among individuals aged 85 to 89 years in the United States under two assumptions: (a) that age- and sex-specific rates of Alzheimer's disease will be unchanged from 1985 onward (solid line) and (b) that these rates will be modified by the increasing level of education of these individuals since 1985 (broken line). As can be seen, these two models have very different implications. If higher education translates into lower rates of Alzheimer's disease, we may actually experience a decrease rather than an increase in the number of cases at the beginning of the next century. Clearly, given the remarkably different predictions of these models, it is essential that the age-specific incidence of Alzheimer's disease be monitored closely over the next 10 years.

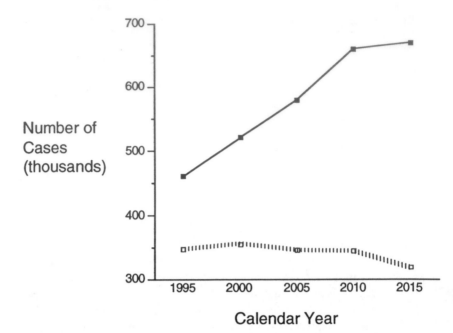

Figure 7.3. Predicted number of cases of Alzheimer's disease among individuals aged 85 to 89 in the United States under two assumptions: that age- and sex-specific prevalence rates of Alzheimer's disease are unchanged from 1995 onward (solid line), and that these prevalence rates are modified in accord with changes in educational attainment of the elderly population (broken line). The two curves converge in 1995 (not shown).

Conclusions

The prevention of dementia is both necessary and possible. Besides the potential benefit of reduction in exposures that we know are related to dementia, research in molecular genetics offers hope that the pathogenesis of Alzheimer's disease may soon be modifiable. Overly pessimistic projections serve little purpose in the present debate concerning allocation of health care resources.

References

Andreason, N. C., Flaum, M., Swaze, V., O'Leary, D. S., Alliger, R., Cohen, G., Ehrhardt, J., & Yuh, W. T. C. (1993). Intelligence and brain structure in normal individuals. *American Journal of Psychiatry, 150,* 130-134.

Bonaiuto, S., Rocca, W. A., & Lippi, A. (1990). Impact of education and occupation on the prevalence of Alzheimer's disease (AD) and multi-infarct dementia (MID) in Appignano, Macerata Province, Italy. *Neurology, 40*(Suppl. 1), 346.

Candy, J. M., Oakley, A. E., Atack, J., Perry, R. H., Perry, E. K., & Edwardson, J. A. (1984). New observations on the nature of senile plaque cores. In E. S. Vizi & K. Magyar (Eds.), *Regulation of transmitter function: Basic and clinical aspects* (pp. 301-306). Amsterdam: Elsevier.

Clark, M. (1979, November 5). Epidemic of senility. *Newsweek*, p. 95.

Corder, E. H., Saunders, A. M., Strittmatter, W. J., Schmechel, D. E., Gaskell, P. C., Small, G. W., Roses, A. D., Haines, J. L., & Pericak-Vance, M. A. (1993). Gene dose of apolipoprotein E type 4 allele and the risk of Alzheimer's disease in late onset families. *Science, 261,* 921-923.

Cummings, J. L., & Benson, D. F. (1983). *Dementia: A clinical approach.* Boston: Butterworths.

Dartigues, J. F., Gagnon, M., Michel, P., Letenneur, L., Commenges, D., Barberger-Gateau, P., Auriacombe, S., Rigal, B., Bedry, R., Alperovitch, A., Orgogozo, J. M., Henry, P., Loiseau, P., & Salamon, R. (1991). Le programme de recherche PAQUID sur l'epidemiologie de la demence: Methodes et resultats initiaux. *Revue Neurologique, 3,* 225-230.

Doll, R. (1993). Review: Alzheimer's disease and environmental aluminum. *Age and Ageing, 22,* 138-153.

Evans, D. S., Funkenstein, H. H., Albert, M. S., Scheer, P. A., Cook, N. R., Chown, M. J., Hebert, L. E., Hennekens, C. H., & Taylor, J. O. (1989). Prevalence of Alzheimer's disease in a community population of older persons. Higher than previously reported. *Journal of the American Medical Association, 262,* 2551-2558.

Flaten, T. P. (1990). Geographic associations between aluminum in drinking water and dementia, Parkinson's disease and amyotrophic lateral sclerosis in Norway. *Environmental Geochemistry and Health, 12,* 152-167.

Fratiglioni, L., Ahlbom, A., Viitanen, M., & Winblad, B. (1993). Risk factors for late-onset Alzheimer's disease: A population-based case-control study. *Annals of Neurology, 33,* 258-266.

Fratiglioni, L., Grut, M., Forsell, Y., Viitanen, M., Grafstrom, M., Holmen, K., Ericsson, K., Backman, L., Ahlbom, A., & Winblad, B. (1991). Prevalence of Alzheimer's disease and other dementias in an elderly urban population: Relationship with age, sex and education. *Neurology, 41,* 1886-1892.

Garraway, W. M., Whisnant, J. P., & Drury, I. (1983). The continuing decline in the incidence of stroke. *Mayo Clinic Proceedings, 58,* 520-523.

Graves, A. B., Larson, E. B., Mortimer, J. A., Kramer, J., Rice, M., & Chinn, N. (1993). Migrant status and performance on cognitive screening and reaction time tests in a population-based study of older Japanese-Americans in King County, WA. In International Psychogeriatric Association (Ed.), *Sixth Congress of the International Psychogeriatric Association Abstract Book* (p. 83). Berlin: International Psychogeriatric Association.

Graves, A. B., van Duijn, C. M., Chandra, V., Fratiglioni, L., Heyman, A., Jorm, A. F., Kokmen, E., Kondo, K., Mortimer, J. A., Rocca, W. A., Shalat, S., Soininen, H., & Hofman, A. (1991). Alcohol and tobacco consumption as risk factors for Alzheimer's disease: A collaborative re-analysis of case-control studies. *International Journal of Epidemiology, 20*(Suppl. 2), S48-S57.

Haase, G. R. (1977). Diseases presenting as dementia. In C. E. Wells (Ed.), *Dementia* (2nd ed., pp. 27-67). Philadelphia: F. A. Davis.

Jacobs, R. W., Duong, T., Jones, R. W., Trapp, G. A., & Scheibel, A. B. (1989). Re-examination of aluminum in Alzheimer's disease, analysis by energy dispersive X-ray microprobe and flameless atomic absorption spectrophotometry. *Canadian Journal of Neurological Sciences, 16,* 498-503.

Jellinger, K., Danielczyk, W., Fischer, P., & Gabriel, E. (1990). Clinicopathological analysis of dementia disorders in the elderly. *Journal of the Neurological Sciences, 95,* 239-258.

Kokmen, E., Beard, C. M., Offord, K. P., & Kurland, L. T. (1989). Prevalence of medically diagnosed dementia in a defined United States population: Rochester, Minnesota, January 1, 1975. *Neurology, 39,* 773-776.

Larson, E. B., Reifler, B. V., Sumi, S. M., Canfield, C. G., & Chinn, N. M. (1985). Diagnostic evaluation of 200 elderly outpatients with suspected dementia. *Journal of Gerontology, 40,* 536-543.

Leventhal, G. H. (1987). *Alzheimer's disease and environmental aluminum in Maryville and Morristown, Tennessee.* Unpublished doctoral dissertation, University of Tennessee.

Lovell, M. A., Ehmann, W. D., & Markesbery, W. R. (1993). Laser microprobe analysis of brain aluminum in Alzheimer's disease. *Annals of Neurology, 33,* 36-42.

Martyn, C. N., Osmond, C., Edwardson, J. A., Barker, D. J. P., Harris, E. C., & Lacey, R. F. (1989). Geographical relation between Alzheimer's disease and aluminum in drinking water. *Lancet, 1,* 59-62.

McComas, A. J., Sica, R. P., Campbell, M. J., & Upton, A. R. M. (1971). Functional compensation in partially denervated muscles. *Journal of Neurology, Neurosurgery and Psychiatry, 34,* 453-460.

Michel, P., Commenges, D., Dartigues, J. F., Gagnon, M., Barberger-Gateau, P., & Letenneur, L. (1991). Study of the relationship between aluminum concentrations in drinking water and risk of Alzheimer's disease. In K. Iqbal, D. R. C. McLachlan, B. Winblad, & H. M. Wisniewski (Eds.), *Alzheimer's disease: Basic mechanisms, diagnosis and therapeutic strategies* (pp. 387-391). Chichester, UK: John Wiley.

Mortimer, J. A., & Graves, A. B. (1993). Education and other socioeconomic determinants of dementia and Alzheimer's disease. *Neurology, 43*(Suppl. 4), S39-S44.

Mortimer, J. A., & Pirozzolo, F. J. (1985). Remote effects of head trauma. *Developmental Neuropsychology, 1,* 215-229.

Mortimer, J. A., van Duijn, C. M., Chandra, V., Fratiglioni, L., Graves, A. B., Heyman, A., Jorm, A. F., Kokmen, E., Kondo, K., Rocca, W. A., Shalat, S., Soininen, H., & Hofman, A. (1991). Head trauma as a risk factor for Alzheimer's disease: A collaborative re-analysis of case-control studies. *International Journal of Epidemiology, 20*(Suppl. 2), S28-S35.

Mortimer, J. A., & Webster, D. D. (1982). Comparison of extrapyramidal motor function in normal aging and Parkinson's disease. In J. A. Mortimer, F. J. Pirozzolo, & G. J. Maletta (Eds.), *The aging motor system* (pp. 217-241). New York: Praeger.

Neri, L. C., & Hewitt, D. (1991). Aluminum, Alzheimer's disease, and drinking water. *Lancet, 338,* 390.

Nystrom Peck, A. M., & Vagero, D. H. (1987). Adult body height and childhood socioeconomic group in the Swedish population. *Journal of Epidemiology and Community Health, 41,* 333-337.

Perl, D. P., & Brody, A. R. (1980). Alzheimer's disease: X-ray spectrometric evidence of aluminum accumulation in neurofibrillary tangles. *Science, 208,* 297-299.

Perl, D. P., Munoz-Garcia, D., Good, P., & Pendlebury, W. W. (1985). Intracytoplasmic aluminum accumulation in neurofibrillary tangle bearing neurons: Detection by laser microprobe mass analyser (LAMMA). *Annals of Neurology, 18,* 143.

Peters, D. W., Reifler, B. V., & Larson, E. B. (1989). Excess disability in dementia. In N. Billig & P. V. Rabins (Eds.), *Issues in geriatric psychiatry* (pp. 17-30). Basel: Karger.

Reding, M. J., Haycox, J., & Blass, J. P. (1985). Depression in patients referred to a dementia clinic: A three-year prospective study. *Archives of Neurology, 42,* 894-896.

Reifler, B. V. (1982). Arguments for abandoning the term pseudodementia. *Journal of the American Geriatrics Society, 30,* 665-668.

Rifat, S. (1992). Fluoridation: A prophylaxis program for dental caries and dementia? *Canadian Journal of Public Health, 83,* 93-94.

Saunders, P. A., Copeland, J. R. M., Dewey, M. E., Davidson, I. A., McWilliam, C., Sharma, V., & Sullivan, C. (1991). Heavy drinking as a risk factor for depression and dementia in elderly men. Findings from the Liverpool Longitudinal Community Study. *British Journal of Psychiatry, 159,* 213-216.

Snowdon, D. A., Ostwald, S. K., Kane, R. L., & Keenan, N. K. (1989). Years of life with good and poor mental and physical function in the elderly. *Journal of Clinical Epidemiology, 42,* 1055-1066.

Teri, L., Hughes, J. P., & Larson, E. B. (1990). Cognitive deterioration in Alzheimer's disease: Behavioral and health factors. *Journal of Gerontology: Psychological Sciences, 45,* P58-P63.

Thomas, L. (1981). On the problem of dementia. *Discover, 2,* 34-36.

Tomlinson, B. E., Blessed, G., & Roth, M. (1970). Observations on the brains of demented old people. *Journal of the Neurological Sciences, 11,* 205-242.

U.S. Congress, Office of Technology Assessment. (1987). *Losing a million minds: Confronting the tragedy of Alzheimer's disease and other dementias* (OTA-BA-323). Washington, DC: U.S. Government Printing Office.

U.S. Department of Health and Human Services. (1991). *Aging America. Trends and projections.* Washington: Author.

van Duijn, C. M., Clayton, D.,Chandra, V., Fratiglioni, L., Graves, A. B., Heyman, A., Jorm, A. F., Kokmen, E., Kondo, K., Mortimer, J. A., Rocca, W. A., Shalat, S., Soininen, H., & Hofman, A. (1991). Familial aggregation of Alzheimer's disease and related disorders: A collaborative re-analysis of case-control studies. *International Journal of Epidemiology, 20*(Suppl. 2), S13-S20.

van Duijn, C. M., Stijnen, T., & Hofman, A. (1991). Risk factors for Alzheimer's disease: Overview of the EURODEM collaborative re-analysis of case-control studies. *International Journal of Epidemiology, 20*(Suppl. 2), S4-S12.

Victor, M., & Adams, R. D. (1985). The alcoholic dementias. In J. A. M. Frederiks (Ed.), *Handbook of clinical neurology* (Series 2, Vol. 46, pp. 335-352). Amsterdam: Elsevier.

Willerman, L., Schultz, R., Rutledge, J. N., & Bigler, E. D. (1991). In vivo brain size and intelligence. *Intelligence, 15,* 223-228.

Zhang, M., Katzman, R., Jin, H., Cai, G., Wang, Z., Qu, G., Grant, I., Yu, E., Levy, P., & Liu, W. T. (1990). The prevalence of dementia and Alzheimer's disease (AD) in Shanghai, China: Impact of age, gender, and education. *Annals of Neurology, 27,* 428-437.

PART III

PSYCHOSOCIAL PERSPECTIVES ON COMPETENCE AND COPING THROUGH AGING

A large proportion of the efforts to promote successful and productive development through early periods of the life span have emerged from psychosocial perspectives. Although strategies for promoting successful aging have placed somewhat less emphasis upon this domain, psychosocial perspectives have played a central role not only in understanding development through the later years but also in guiding the design of effective prevention and promotion strategies to foster successful aging.

The chapters in this section are varied, drawing from sociology, psychology, human development, and public health, among other backgrounds. Moreover, their diverse emphases range from the intrapsychic to interpersonal and sociocultural levels of analysis. Each chapter considers ways in which human functioning within society can be better understood and can inform us in developing strategies for supporting successful aging. This section attends to issues that are common to daily concerns and discussions throughout the life span—experiencing autonomy and control, providing and receiving social support, dealing with stress, maintaining competence, and examining our role options. In fact, these notions have been used widely and perhaps loosely through varied channels of lay and professional media and publication, leading to overgeneralizations regarding their nature, value, and role through the life span. Fortunately, the chapters in this section of the book examine these issues with a care and scrutiny that both call us to question a number of prevailing assumptions and guide us in crafting more effective strategies for supporting successful and productive aging.

We begin with Chapter 8, by Alex Zautra, John Riech, and Jason Newsom, examining the effects of autonomy and sense of control among older adults on their mental health. Working beyond simplistic cultural assumptions regarding the importance of self reliance for well being, the authors systematically address the ways in which a sense of control is related to the psychological adjustment of older adults.

Drawing from data of a nearly 5-year longitudinal study of 269 older adults, the authors discuss findings related to older adults' perceptions of control and autonomy, relations between these perceptions and mental health, and the effects of an intervention designed to enhance sense of control through cognitive and behavioral manipulations of perceived control over daily experiences. Zautra and colleagues add a distinctive twist to this work by examining, as well, the role of social network in promoting a sense of control and autonomy and in preserving mental health for older adults. Although their overall findings support the notion that mental health benefits are associated with beliefs in personal control, they reveal more complex and differentiated views of the meaning and value of control beliefs. Their data suggest, as well, that the timing of support from social networks may be critical. Their findings are important not only in their content but in their reminder that what is frequently perceived as "noise" in experimental findings may actually reflect relationships that are central to the design and implementation of effective prevention and promotion strategies.

Moving from these findings of a complex relationship between autonomy, well-being, and social support, Chapter 9 calls for a rigorous examination of our assumptions and applications regarding social support concepts and strategies. Author Neena Chappell highlights both the scope and the limitations of the knowledge that has emerged from the voluminous research on social support over the past several decades. She places particular focus on the question of the relation between social support and well-being in later life.

Chappell notes that recent health care reforms in Canada and much of the industrialized world are focusing upon community care with informal support as a "major cornerstone." She encourages continued examination of such possibilities. Meanwhile, Chappell cautions us to tread with care and outlines a number of unanswered questions that must be addressed if we are effectively to incorporate social support strategies into the development and implementation of social policies and programming.

On a related note, Chapter 10, by Michael Smyer, focuses upon formal social supports for older adults, although emphasizing that the distinction between formal and informal supports is often difficult to make and that the ideal is a "seamless web of support" from formal and informal sources. Smyer notes that just as there are diverse aging experiences, formal support for older adults may take diverse forms reflecting the intersection of social policy, economic well-being, physical health, mental health, and other domains. In this chapter, Smyer examines supports within a wide range of residential contexts for elders—nursing homes, community settings, and continuing care communities—as he discusses the relevance of preventive approaches within each of these contexts.

Smyer has been engaged in a variety of studies of the development, implementation, and evaluation of health-related interventions for older adults and their families. Throughout this chapter, he offers a number of "lessons learned" and "opportunities for action" that may guide future primary prevention efforts to support older adults. Of particular note is his current research on continuing care retirement communities (CCRCs), or life care communities, an increasingly popular residential structure in recent times that is designed around the inclusion of diverse formal (as well as informal) supports for older adults. In fact, Smyer argues that "the development and implementation of a CCRC can be viewed as a preventive intervention, aimed at providing a context for successful aging," although residency in such a context in no way guarantees "successful aging" (any more than participation in other preventive interventions does).

Chapter 11, by Neal Krause, brings together a broad range of research on stress in order to pose a framework for conceptualizing effective preventive interventions for older adults. Referring specifically to financial stress as an illustration, Krause carefully takes us through a step-by-step analysis to reveal how shortcomings in aggregate or cumulative measures of stress lead to difficulties in (a) identifying the genesis or origins of stressful experiences, (b) discerning the natural history of events through time, (c) understanding the relationship between stress and coping resources, and (d) delineating the effects of stress on mental health outcomes. His analysis illustrates the sort of detailed information that is crucial to gather if we are to understand who is at risk and implement preventive interventions that are effective in supporting these persons.

In Chapter 12, Roger Dixon considers the promotion of competence through compensation. Within the context of cognition, Dixon examines the changing course of competence with age, distinguishing between competence and ability, with competence involving the utilization of varied abilities. He notes that through expertise and compensatory techniques, performance in specific domains can be maintained or enhanced despite declines in components of cognitive and psychomotor skills with advancing age.

Dixon raises questions regarding the decline, improvement, and maintenance of competence through the older years and factors that contribute to varied performance outcomes. With an emphasis upon the role of compensation in maintaining competence, he argues that practitioners should place greater focus upon developing intervention efforts that improve the match between contextual demands and individuals' resources.

The final chapter in this section, by Phyllis Moen, uses a life course perspective to examine role options—in particular, paid and volunteer work—for persons in their postretirement years.

After addressing the importance of a life course view of aging, health, and productive activity, Moen considers our knowledge base regarding gender differences, volunteering, and the potential for interventions to enhance productivity following retirement. She draws upon theoretical and research evidence that suggests links between multiple roles and well-being in the later years of life and calls upon us to consider why some individuals remain or become involved in paid or volunteer work, two forms of "productive activity." This line of questioning, in turn, is used to stimulate recommendations regarding the design and evaluation of interventions for promoting such productive engagement in the later years.

8

Autonomy and Sense of Control Among Older Adults: An Examination of Their Effects on Mental Health

Alex J. Zautra
John W. Reich
Jason T. Newsom

Theory and research on prevention of mental health problems pose many paradoxes and a host of blind alleys. Only a few results thus far provide practical guidance without equivocation. Nowhere are the tensions in theory and research felt more acutely than in the examination of the value of a sense of control to the mental health of the older adult. At the center of the controversy is how to understand the meaning of sense of control for a group that is often faced with loss of autonomy due to a chronic disabling illness. Real personal and contextual constraints on choice and control often accompany functional limitation. How do beliefs about control affect the mental health of those older adults with such constraints on their autonomy? For those who are healthy, do control beliefs function as a resistance resource aiding in the prevention of future mental health problems if they become disabled? In this chapter, we focus on these and related issues in examining the contribution of sense of control to the psychological adjustment for older adults. We present data from our longitudinal study of older adults as a means of illustrating our points.

We begin our inquiry with brief reviews of concepts underlying autonomy and sense of control, and the meanings and operationalizations that we prefer

AUTHORS' NOTE: This research was supported in part by a grant from the National Institute on Aging, AG4924-06, to the first and second authors.

for them in our work. The utility of our framework is examined through the analysis of interviews of older adults conducted over a 4.6-year period. We ask how perceptions of control and autonomy are related, how each relates to the mental health of older adults, and whether interventions designed to enhance a sense of control increase well-being. We then address central questions in the prevention of mental health problems. Do individual differences in control perceptions play a role in the preservation of autonomy and in the prevention of adjustment difficulties over time? We take these questions one step further than most studies of control and autonomy by investigating the role of the person's social network in promoting a sense of control and autonomy and preserving mental health for older adults. As we will attempt to show, the encouragement, by the social network, of self-reliance versus reliance on others affects how well the person is able to cope with a loss of autonomy in ways unanticipated by most models of control.

Autonomy and Sense of Control

The Meaning of Autonomy

Autonomy is often mistakenly equated with independence of the influence of others. A more precise definition would be freedom to act, to make choices on how to live. Constraints on this freedom may come from within as well as from without. The development of autonomy may depend upon personal disposition and may be strengthened or weakened by the nature of social relationships. Gruen (1986) defined autonomy wholly in terms of the person's relationship with him or herself when he wrote that autonomy is "the freedom to experience the self" (p. 1) and "harmony with one's feelings and needs" (p. 1). By losing one's awareness of inner needs, including needs for relating, Gruen reminded us that we lose our freedom to act in accordance with our own needs, and in doing so lose autonomy. Haworth (1986) saw competence and the effectance motivation that underlies competence (White, 1959) as the basis for autonomy. Free choice in how we learn is less important than the knowledge gained because it is knowledge that allows us choices on how to act. Relying on others to support needs for competence also affords us autonomy even if we are depending upon the assistance of others, because we are making the choices that shape the direction of our lives. These are important themes that we shall return to in understanding the meaning of autonomy for older adults.

The principal challenge for older adults is the preservation of quality of life in the face of threats of constraints on autonomy from deterioration in health and impoverishment of social life. Activity limitation due to arthritis, stroke, diabetes, and heart disease places dramatic limitations on older people's abilities; their choices in life can be severely limited by these chronic diseases. Changes like retirement and conjugal bereavement can also constrain autonomy by removing social contexts that were central to the person's means of self-expression. But those changes are sometimes a blessing in disguise, and lead to an enhanced sense of autonomy when the change removes the person from dystonic circumstances. In contrast, health problems are viewed almost universally as threats to autonomy. For that reason, we focus on health problems in this chapter as a means of identifying a major threat to autonomy among the older adults we have studied.

Multiple Meanings of Sense of Control

There are two aspects of control with relevance to older adults about which most social scientists would agree: Control is good for adjustment because it allows the person maximum flexibility in adaptation to changing environmental demands and because loss of control and the feelings of helplessness that result have a profound negative impact on mental health (Fry, 1989; Seligman, 1975). But control is a fuzzy set of many related and some unrelated concepts, and it is unlikely that we will ever arrive at a single consensual definition on what constitutes sense of control. Averill (1963) was among the first to identify dimensions by which to judge degree of control. Fry (1989) and Baltes and Baltes (1986) provided recent reviews of the domain of theories of control relevant to older adults. We do not even attempt to be exhaustive in our treatment of these many approaches in the limited space available in this chapter.

In our work, we have found it useful to distinguish among the various models of control perceptions in two ways: models of control that seek to identify a person's general beliefs about control, and control perceptions that arise out of the person's specific transactions with his or her social and physical environment. Rotter's (1966) IE Scale is an example of the former global measure; it seeks to assess generalized expectancies for locus of control over reinforcement. Pearlin and Schooler's (1978) Mastery Scale is another example of a global scale because it asks the person to generalize across situations when rating his or her own mastery. Although these beliefs derive from interpretations of life experience, they are clearly properties of the person, not the environment. These measures have been shown to be useful in identifying individual differences in control beliefs related to mental health and well-being of older adults as well as younger groups (e.g., Thompson & Spacapan, 1991).

Another form of control is transactional, rooted in the everyday life of the person-in-environment. Transactional control is a set of ratings of perceived control over specific events, aggregated across occasions. These perceptions are different from beliefs because they are ratings of actual experience. They are also different in meaning: The control is vested in the ongoing relationship between the person and the environment rather than being solely a property of the individual. Past research has shown that ratings of efficacy over specific events (Aldwin & Revenson, 1987; Bandura & Adams, 1977; Zautra & Wrabetz, 1991) capture aspects of control perceptions that are not accounted for in assessments of global perceptions of control or mastery.

Another distinction in control perceptions that we have found useful has been in control over positive versus negative outcomes. At the basis of human experience are needs to avoid pain and to seek sources of pleasure, and these two motives define very different sequences of action. People may differ in level of control over each. That is, someone may be able to control aversive circumstances well but feel unable to make positive events happen with any confidence. Alternatively, certain people may feel that they are able to find sources of pleasure in their lives but that they can neither predict nor control the experience of negative affects. Gregory, Steiner, Brennan, and Detrick (1978) found that locus-of-control beliefs for positive outcomes were independent of those for negative outcomes among young adults. Crandall, Katkovsky, and Crandall (1965) found similar results for children's locus-of-control beliefs. We report here on analyses of differences in ratings of control over positive and negative affective experiences for older adults, starting with factor analytic studies we have conducted (see Reich & Zautra, 1991). We extend that work to examine how control perceptions affect autonomy and mental health over time.

Differences Between Control and Autonomy

In this chapter we use the term *control* to refer to perceptions of one's chances to shape the course of life events. We assess general control beliefs and transactional control through ratings of specific events. By *autonomy* we mean the capacity to perform functions of everyday life; *loss of autonomy* refers to activity limitation. In a very broad sense, one could think of loss of autonomy as loss of control of another sort, and some investigators may prefer that label. In our experience, functional limitation is the foundation for a loss of autonomy among older adults. Loss of a sense of control that elders feel in their lives often accompanies loss in autonomy, but not always. Elders make distinctions between these two conditions, and we find it useful to do so as well.

Autonomy and control beliefs do not take shape in a vacuum; they depend upon the contours of response from the social and physical environment. Whether a wheelchair-bound person can travel into the city depends not only on his or her own physical capacities but also upon the availability of social supports and whether the local transit system has retrofitted its buses to provide wheelchair access. How functional impairment affects sense of control and feelings of helplessness and hopelessness may depend upon these types of contextual supports as much as on "inner strengths" such as optimism and hardiness.

Person-Environment Fit

We have also begun to examine and find evidence, consistent with the work of Kahana, Kahana, and Riley (1989), that the meaning and value of control beliefs depend greatly on whether those beliefs are congruent with the needs of the person at the time (Reich & Zautra, 1990; Reich, Zautra, & Manne, 1993). In the best of all worlds, the older adult has high levels of personal control and autonomy. Would beliefs in personal control be detrimental, though, for those who have lost autonomy? Affleck, Tennen, Pfeiffer, and Fifield (1987) found that arthritis patients who held beliefs of personal control over their symptoms reported good adjustment if their symptoms were mild, but poor psychological adjustment if their physical symptoms were severe. Similarly, Burish et al. (1984) reported evidence that maintaining beliefs in personal control in the face of negative evidence increases feelings of personal defeat.

Yet others have suggested that even for people with a life-threatening disease, beliefs in the "illusion of control" can aid in adjustment (Taylor, Helgeson, Reed, & Skokan, 1991). A number of intervention studies have found that increasing a sense of control and feelings of personal efficacy can enhance the quality of life of disabled populations (e.g., Langer & Rodin, 1976; Lorig, Chastain, Ung, Shoor, & Holman, 1989). It may be important to distinguish among these various forms of control, however, when evaluating their utility. The timing of the intervention may also be critical. Encouragement to identify ways of increasing personal control for those who have lost a sense of their own abilities and who feel helpless due to a functional loss may provide a person with new options for regaining feelings of personal mastery. Social networks that continue to encourage (or preach) self-reliant forms of control for those facing new impairments may be less advantageous to mental health. We explore evidence on these issues presently with empirical data from our study of older adults. We divert attention away from those issues briefly, however, in order to introduce that study: the Life Events and Aging Project (LEAP).

The Life Events and Aging Project

Sample

LEAP assessed the mental health of 269 older adults over a period of nearly 5 years. The project involved 10 consecutive monthly interviews, an 11th interview 6 months after the 10th, and a final 12th follow-up interview approximately 3.5 years later. The original focus of this project was to study reactions to, and recovery from, two major life stressors of older adults: loss of autonomy through physical disability and recent conjugal bereavement (Ns = 61 and 62, respectively, in each of the groups).

The participants were selected from extensive canvassing of a range of contacts such as senior centers, home health care organizations, retirement villages, and hospices. No one was in extended care or nursing home environments at the start of the study; all participants lived either in their own homes or in an apartment. Elders evidencing signs of dementia were excluded from participation.

Sixty people who suffered conjugal bereavement within the past 6 months, as identified though vital statistics records, and 61 who had moderate to severe activity limitation from continuing health problems (but not both) were selected and matched with control subjects without functional impairment or conjugal bereavement. A 26-item instrumental activities of daily living scale (Teresi, Golden, Gurland, Wilder, & Bennett, 1983) was used to estimate degree of impaired functioning. It was administered during initial screening, after 10 months, and again at the end of the study. Control subjects were matched on the basis of age (within 5 years), sex, and income. Mean age of the total sample at the start of the study was 70 years; 78% were female, and 1.6% were of minority status.

Measurements of Control

The global measure of control employed in our research program was the Pearlin and Schooler Personal Mastery Scale (1978). The personal mastery measure was administered with the mental health measures in questionnaire form, filled out, and mailed back each of 10 months. Transactional control assessments were tied specifically to event occurrences that were assessed in each of the 10 monthly interviews. Participants were asked to select up to three most desirable and up to three most undesirable events that had occurred in the past month and to respond to a series of questions about those events. For desirable events, ratings were obtained on the degree to which the person felt he or she was a cause of the event and the degree to which the person felt he or she could cause the event to occur again in the future. For undesirable events, the probe questions asked for a rating of the degree of satisfaction the person felt with his or her own efforts in coping with the event, and the degree of confidence the person had in being able to cope successfully with a similar undesirable event should one occur in the future. Scores were obtained by aggregating across event ratings over 10 months for each item. By aggregating across months, we were able to obtain a thorough sampling of the efficacy perceptions that the older adults made to a wide range of positive and negative life experiences.

Factor Analysis Results

Confirmatory factor analyses of the personal mastery scale and the two event mastery ratings revealed a multidimensional structure. The fit of a four-factor model was good: The χ^2/df ratio was 38.54/44; the GFI was .968; the AGFI was .905. Control over positive events was distinct from control over negative events, and global ratings of personal mastery were independent of transactional or event-based sense of control.

One factor, labeled Fatalism, consisted of five of the personal mastery items relating to lack of mastery over negative life events: for example, "Sometimes I feel that I'm being pushed around in life," and "There is really no way I can solve some of the problems I have." The remaining two items on the scale formed a Control Over Positive Outcomes factor, with the items stating: "I can do just about anything I really set my mind to," and "What happens to me in the future mostly depends on me." The event-based scales resulted in two uncorrelated factors: Positive Event Efficacy assessed perceived ability to create or to bring about positive events in life, and Coping Efficacy assessed satisfaction with past efforts and confidence in coping with future stressors.

These results provided support for our multidimensional view of control perceptions: People had different conceptualizations of their control over positive versus negative life experiences, and they had generalized beliefs (Fatalism and Personal Control) that were independent of their perceptions of control over their transactions with everyday events. Transactional control itself is composed of two distinct, uncorrelated factors—Positive Event Efficacy and Coping Efficacy. In the analyses relating control to mental health, we relied on these four scales to tap dimensions of control in the LEAP Study.

Control Perceptions and Loss of Autonomy

We first examined whether these control dimensions would detect differences between those elders who entered the study with less autonomy, as determined by moderate to severe activity limitation, and the other groups. This involved testing for differences between the disabled and the rest of the sample on the four control dimensions outlined above. The disabled rated themselves higher in Fatalism and lower in Personal Control than the rest of the sample (F values respectively were $F(1,252) = 7.856$, $p < .005$, and $F(1,252) = 30.252$, $p < .001$). The disabled also were significantly different from controls on Positive Event Efficacy, $F(1,252) = 8.55$, $p < .004$, but analyses showed only marginal effects on Coping Efficacy, $F(1,252) = 2.997$, $p < .10$, respectively. We note in passing that the bereaved group did not differ from their matched comparison group, so the data indicate that the death of a spouse does not per se reduce either global control beliefs or coping efficacy.

Loss of Autonomy and Mental Health

We employed a comprehensive assessment of mental health employing items from the Veit and Ware (1983) Mental Health Inventory and the PERI-Demoralization Composite (Dohrenwend, Shrout, Egri, & Mendelsohn, 1980). Our prior factor analyses (Zautra, Guarnaccia, & Reich, 1988) yielded two inversely correlated superordinate factors: Psychological Distress and Psychological Well-Being. The subscales assessed depression, anxiety, helplessness/hopelessness, suicidal ideation, and confused thinking for distress, and positive affects, self-esteem, and emotional ties for well-being. For the purposes of this chapter, these two scales are combined, with Psychological Well-Being minus Psychological Distress used as the indicator of overall mental health.

In every direct test of differences between disabled participants and controls made on mental health ratings over the first 10 months of the study, the disabled were worse off. These analyses are reported in depth elsewhere (see Reich, Zautra, & Guarnaccia, 1989). In brief, it is important to note that those disabled at the start of the study showed poorer mental health on each subscale and did not improve in mental health as a group through the course of the study. The bereaved showed decrements only in subscales of distress such as depression and helplessness/hopelessness, and their scores as a group did increase, so that by the 10th interview there were no differences between them and controls in mental health.

Control Intervention Enhances Mental Health

To address whether control perceptions could play a role in recovery from the mental health problems of those with functional limitations, we examined data from an intervention designed to enhance sense of control. Randomly selected halves of each of the four groups of participants in the main LEAP project were offered a separate honorarium if they would participate in a special four-session, 10-week program. Because the details of the intervention are presented in detail in other publications (Reich & Zautra, 1990, 1991), only the design features important to this discussion follow.

Halves of the participant groups were randomly assigned to one of two cells of the design: a control-enhancing intervention or a placebo contact condition to control for the social contact inherent in the main manipulation (as indicated by Krantz & Schulz, 1980). The remaining halves of the participant groups were assigned to a no-contact control condition to control for the passage of time over the 10 weeks of the experiment; these participants were never informed of the intervention, although they also responded to the mental health instrument (the dependent measure) administered during the main LEAP assessments.

The intervention, conducted by trained older adult women LEAP staff members, involved cognitive and behavioral manipulations of perceived control over positive and negative daily experiences. The technique engaged the participant in inventorying his or her pattern of daily living and finding examples of controllable and uncontrollable positive and negative events with an aim toward increasing perceptions of personal control and accommodating better to uncontrollable events. Suggestions and daily tasks to enhance both aspects of control were given to the participant to perform between intervention sessions.

The intervention worked, short-term. There were increases in the mental health of those receiving control enhancement compared with placebo and no-contact groups. Further, the disabled group benefited most from the intervention. Their scores on mental health showed the greatest improvement. But the effect was short-lived. As soon as the intervention was completed, the group differences became nonsignificant. Nevertheless, the data are consistent with findings of studies; other programs designed to enhance sense of control are useful as a means of rehabilitation for those who have become demoralized by functional limitations.

Preservation of Autonomy and
Mental Health Among the Initially Healthy

Thus far our analyses of control and autonomy relationships with mental health have focused on those participants who had functional limitation at the time of their selection into the study. We turn next to the long-term prospects for preservation of well-being for those who were healthy at the start of the study. We ask two critical questions relevant to prevention in older adult populations:

1. To what extent do control beliefs and ratings of transactional control predict who suffers loss of autonomy through increases in activity limitation by the end of the 4.6-year study?

2. Do control perceptions recorded during the first 10 months of study serve as a protective resource in the prevention of mental health problems in the years that follow?

To examine these relationships, we correlated the measures with criteria and also conducted two regression analyses, one predicting residualized change in activity limitation using our four control measures, and a second predicting residualized changes in mental health from scores at baseline to those obtained 4.6 years later. To ensure that the control measurements were taken while the elders were still relatively unconstrained by health problems, we excluded anyone who had moderate or higher levels of activity limitation at baseline or who showed loss in function by the 10th month. This last criterion turned out to be important because there were 40 older adults who became functionally impaired over the first 10 months of the study. We return to a discussion of those older adults later in the chapter; they provided us a special circumstance with which to evaluate the meaning of support for control beliefs during a time of crisis in autonomy.

The simple correlations with mental health and control beliefs are shown in Table 8.1 for the 96 participants who met criteria and for whom we had scores on all variables through the entire course of the study.

We have drawn the results of the two regression analyses in Figure 8.1. The figure shows important differences in the way control perceptions predict changes in autonomy and mental health. First, the best predictors of preservation of autonomy were measures of positive control, most notably ratings of positive event efficacy. Second, the best predictors of changes in mental health were loss of autonomy, as expected, and sense of control over negative events. Coping efficacy, in particular, which characterizes the person's belief in his or her ability to cope with future negative events, built up from numerous experiences with everyday life events, was the single best resistance resource in the prevention of mental health downturns for this population.

These findings support our contention that control over real-life transactions is of considerable value to the quality of life of older adults. These effects were independent of those found for dispositional measures of control beliefs. Also, control over positive events appears to have a distinctive effect in the preservation of health and well-being among older adults, not accounted for by assessments of control over negative life experience.

Why would control over positive events be important to the preservation of a sense of autonomy? These ratings had little direct effect on the mental health of the healthy elders. The answer may reside in the role of motivation on activity limitation. People with the same levels of physical impairments

TABLE 8.1 Correlations Between Control Perceptions and Mental Health for Initially Healthy Sample ($N = 96$)

	Initial Mental Health	Final Mental Health
Control over positive experiences		
Personal control	.47**	.45**
Positive event efficacy	.01	.05
Control over negative experiences		
Fatalism	−.60**	−.56**
Coping efficacy	.21**	.33**
Support: Self-reliant versus other-reliant	.19*	.30**

can differ markedly in their performance of everyday life tasks. Differences in what White (1959) referred to as "effectance motivation" may explain why some older adults continue to try when others have given up. Perceptions of control over the occurrence of desirable events resulting from actual experiences may enhance motivation to overcome physical limitations through what Nuttin (1973) called "causality pleasure." In short, "nothing succeeds like success."

This study is not the first to report findings in support of the importance of coping efficacy to the mental health of older adults. They are striking in their consistency with the results we found in other studies (e.g., Zautra & Wrabetz, 1991). Sense of efficacy for present and future stressors is the single best predictor of the preservation of mental health for older adults. These perceptions are grounded in experiences of control with a differentiated set of real-life events. Such experiences may be less resistant to erosion in the face of a single negative life experience than those control beliefs about coping that are not grounded in active control.

The global measure of fatalism obtained in the mastery scale showed strong inverse correlations with mental health, but after initial mental health status was controlled for, fatalism contributed only slightly to the prediction of change in mental health. It may be most useful to think of this measure as overlapping to some degree with modern conceptions of low mental health. Items assessing helplessness/hopelessness and depressive symptoms are nearly synonymous with fatalism. Thus, when we control for initial mental health scores, we remove variance that the fatalistic beliefs share with mental health outcomes. Such confounding explains why the simple correlations are high, even though the relationship between fatalistic beliefs and change in mental health is only marginally significant.

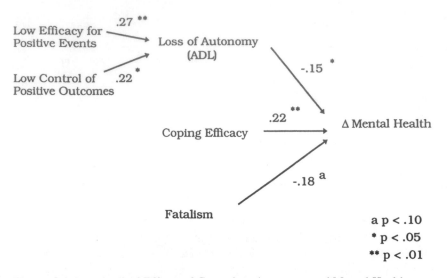

Figure 8.1. Longitudinal Effects of Control on Autonomy and Mental Health

Control Perceptions When Autonomy Is Lost:
Are They Risk Factors or Resistance Resources?

We examined potential interaction effects between the four types of control perceptions and loss of autonomy in the prediction of mental health changes for those in our sample who were healthy throughout the first 10 months of the study. If control beliefs lessened the mental health impact of loss of autonomy, then those measures could be thought of as resistance resources: ways of inoculating the person against mental health problems that might arise as a consequence of loss of autonomy. For one of the variables, Personal Control, we did find those types of interaction effects. Loss of autonomy was associated with changes for the worse in mental health except for those who avowed strong beliefs in personal control. The interaction effect is plotted in Figure 8.2 below.

Thus personal control appears to have two primary preventative benefits: It appears to lower the risk of physical impairment, and it inoculates against the sense of despair for those faced with a loss of autonomy. Why would this particular control belief and not the other dimensions of control have these effects? One explanation is that this feature of control focuses most on personal agency and a self-reliant attitude toward future events. These beliefs in one's own efficacy in the planning and execution of actions may be what provides the greatest source of strength when autonomy is compromised.

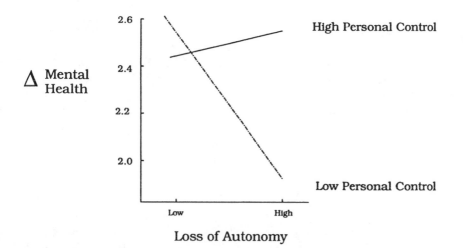

Figure 8.2. Personal Control × Autonomy Interaction (*N* = 96)

The Social Encouragement of Self-Reliance

A critical issue in the prevention of mental health problems among older adults is when to intervene, and with what message. If control is essential to well-being, one message that might be beneficial is the encouragement of control beliefs. For persons with established disabilities, an intervention targeted to enhance a sense of control had a positive effect on mental health in our work as well as in that of others. Do control-relevant social supports protect those healthy from future harm in the same manner as control beliefs? We addressed this question with our sample of initially healthy elders. Would social support networks that encouraged self-reliance, what will be referred to here as the "own bootstraps" approach, prove to be a resistance resource over time more than those support networks that were inclined to encourage other-reliance, what we refer to as the "lean on me" approach to social support?

The LEAP assessment battery included measures of the extent to which participants perceived that important members of their social support networks encouraged them to be self-reliant and/or to rely on others. These items were developed and tested extensively in a doctoral dissertation by Grossman (1986). Participants first provided a detailed list of members in their social support network (see Finch, Okun, Barrera, Zautra, & Reich, 1989). From the list of names they provided, the participants identified up to five "most important" members and then rated each of the members of their network with three items on degree of self-reliance encouragement and

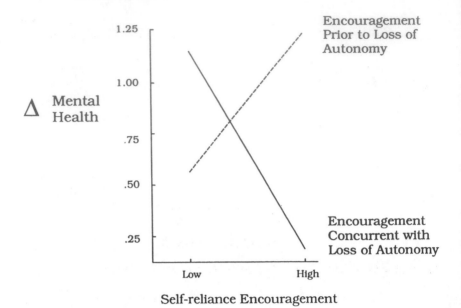

Figure 8.3. Self-Reliance Encouragement × Time of Disability Interaction ($N = 51$)

three items on degree of encouragement to rely on others as a source of strength. The other-reliance items were: (This person) "Encouraged me to let others take more responsibility for solving my problems," "Made me feel like others know what's best for me," and "Encouraged me to be more dependent on others." The self-reliance items were: (This person) "Encouraged me to make my own decisions," "Made me feel like I am in control of my future," and "Encouraged me to work on my problems in my own way." We constructed a composite scale from these items that consisted of self-reliance encouragement minus other-reliance encouragement to see what we could learn about the consequences of natural reinforcement of control versus dependency within the changing lives of our sample of elders.

We examined the effects of self-reliant encouragement on autonomy and mental health. First, there was no evidence that the type of encouragement affected activity limitations. However, there were significant findings for mental health. The message of support imbued with a call for self-reliance, or "own bootstraps," was positively related to mental health for those who remained healthy. In addition, those who had greater "own bootstraps" encouragement and later acquired physical limitations reported fewer mental health problems. Thus self-reliant encouragement appears to be a good primary prevention strategy. However, this form of support was inversely related to mental health for those who had significant increases in activity limitation at the time they were receiving those messages of support. Those respondents who increased in functional limitations within the first 10 months and who reported having a network over the same time period that encouraged self-reliance had the lowest mental health scores at the first follow-up, an effect that persisted to the end of the study 3 years later. Those who had a social network that gave the "lean on me" message during their crisis over loss of function were better off emotionally. In secondary prevention efforts, other-reliant encouragement appears to be indicated, not self-reliant support. Figure 8.3 graphs the significant interaction changes in mental health from initial status to the final assessment 4.6 years later.

Autonomy, Control, and Support: Implications for Prevention

The belief that control is the key factor in the mental health of older adults has reached mythic proportions in our society. Images of active, healthy aging abound in the popular media. The myth is perhaps a consequence of the magnetism of individualism. Self-reliance and personal agency beliefs are embedded deeply within our culture. Our results are not inconsistent with those beliefs either. Personal control was highly correlated with good mental health; fatalism was associated with significantly poorer mental health. Indeed, holding such beliefs in control over future positive events reduces the likelihood of loss of autonomy. For those who eventually face such losses due to illness or injury, such control beliefs also protect their mental health. Our findings add a more differentiated view of the meaning and value of control beliefs among those older adults who are threatened with loss of autonomy due to physical health limitations. They support the use of transactional measures and urge further development of concepts of control over positive outcomes.

The value of the messages that friends, family, and mental health professionals send to older adults about control needs to be evaluated separately from the importance of control beliefs themselves. Our examination of the usefulness of social reinforcement of control beliefs lead us to the conclusion that the timing of the support vis-à-vis the person's loss of autonomy is critical. It comes as no surprise that healthy individuals gain in mental health with a social network that encourages self-reliance. For those with an established impairment, these types of messages may also ease feelings of helplessness. It is during the time of loss that the social network messages of self-reliance are incongruent with the person's experience and his or her needs. During this period of crisis, receiving messages that you can rely on others, the "lean on me" message, appears to play a valuable part in limiting the damage caused by the crisis events, perhaps by providing ways of maintaining a sense of control under the helpful guidance of close confidants.

Why does self-reliant encouragement not always work to preserve mental health during a crisis in autonomy? Encouragement of self-reliance may constrain the openness of the person to experience his or her needs for care, and keep him or her from recognizing that action of a different kind from self-as-agent is needed at times to allow the person to be fully "present" in the world (Gruen, 1986). Under the circumstances of loss of physical abilities, the person may need to maintain an "inner autonomy" through self-expression of dependency needs. These results serve as a reminder that the condition of the person is the most important context from which to judge the efficacy of our models of control. Humane responsiveness to need is still a most powerful and effective means of preventing mental health problems.

References

Affleck, G., Tennen, H., Pfeiffer, C., & Fifield, H. (1987). Appraisals of control and predictability in adapting to a chronic stress. *Journal of Personality and Social Psychology, 53,* 273-279.

Aldwin, C. M., & Revenson, T. A. (1987). Does coping help? A reexamination of the relation between coping and mental health. *Journal of Personality and Social Psychology, 53,* 337-348.

Averill, J. R. (1963). Personal control over aversive stimuli and its relationship to stress. *Psychological Bulletin, 80,* 286-303.

Baltes, M. M., & Baltes, P. B. (1986). *The psychology of control and aging.* Hillsdale, NJ: Lawrence Erlbaum.

Bandura, A., & Adams, N. (1977). Analysis of self-efficacy theory of behavioral change. *Cognitive Therapy and Research, 1,* 387-310.

Burish, T., Carey, M., Wallston, K., Stein, M., Jamison, P., & Lyles, J. (1984). Health locus of control and chronic disease: An external orientation may be advantageous. *Journal of Social and Clinical Psychology, 2,* 326-333.

Crandall, V. J., Katkovsky, W., & Crandall, V. C. (1965). Children's belief in their own control of reinforcement in intellectual-academic situations. *Child Development, 36,* 91-109.

Dohrenwend, B. P., Shrout, P. E., Egri, G., & Mendelsohn, F. S. (1980). Nonspecific psychological distress and other dimensions of psychopathology. *Archives of General Psychiatry, 37,* 1229-1236.

Finch, J. R., Okun, M. A., Barrera, M., Zautra, A. J., & Reich, J. W. (1989). Positive and negative social ties among older adults: Measurement models and the prediction of psychological distress and well-being. *American Journal of Community Psychology, 17,* 585-605.

Fry, P. S. (1989). Perceptions of vulnerability and controls in old age: A critical reconstruction. In P. S. Fry (Ed.), *Psychological perspectives of helplessness and control in the elderly* (pp. 1-39). Amsterdam: North Holland.

Gregory, W. L., Steiner, I. D., Brennan, G. T., & Detrick, A. (1978). A scale to measure benevolent versus malevolent perceptions of the environment. *JSAS Catalog of Selected Documents in Psychology, 8,* 36. (Ms. No. 1679)

Grossman, R. M. (1986). *Attributions of responsibility and social support.* Unpublished doctoral dissertation, Arizona State University, Tempe.

Gruen, A. (1986). *The betrayal of the self.* New York: Grove.

Haworth, L. (1986). *Autonomy.* New Haven: Yale University Press.

Kahana, E., Kahana, B., & Riley, K. (1989). Person-environment transactions relevant to control and helplessness in institutional settings. In P. S. Fry (Ed.), *Psychological perspectives of helplessness and control in the elderly* (pp. 121-153). Amsterdam: North Holland.

Krantz, D. S., & Schulz, R. (1980). A model of life crisis, control, and health outcomes: Cardiac rehabilitation and relocation of the elderly. In A. Baum & J. E. Singer (Eds.), *Advances in environmental psychology* (Vol. 2, pp. 23-57). Hillsdale, NJ: Lawrence Erlbaum.

Langer, E. J., & Rodin, J. (1976). The effects of choice and enhanced personal responsibility for the aged: A field experiment in an institutional setting. *Journal of Personality and Social Psychology, 34,* 191-198.

Lorig, K., Chastain, R. L., Ung, E., Shoor, S., & Holman, H. R. (1989). Development and evaluation of a scale to measure perceived self-efficacy in people with arthritis. *Arthritis and Rheumatism, 32*(1), 37-44.

Nuttin, J. (1973). Pleasure and reward in human motivation and learning. In D. E. Berlyne & K. B. Madsen (Eds.), *Pleasure, reward, and preference* (pp. 243-274). New York: Academic Press.

Pearlin, L., & Schooler, C. (1978). The structure of coping. *Journal of Health and Social Behavior, 19,* 2-21.

Reich, J. W., & Zautra, A. J. (1990). Dispositional control beliefs and the consequences of a control-enhancing intervention. *Journal of Gerontology: Psychological Sciences, 45,* P46-P51.

Reich, J. W., & Zautra, A. J. (1991). Experimental and measurement approaches to internal control in at-risk older adults. *Journal of Social Issues, 47*(4), 143-158.

Reich, J. W., Zautra, A. J., & Guarnaccia, C. A. (1989). Effects of disability and bereavement on the mental health and recovery of older adults. *Psychology and Aging, 4*(1), 57-65.

Reich, J. W., Zautra, A. J., & Manne, S. (1993). How perceived control and congruent spouse support affect rheumatoid arthritis patients. *Journal of Social and Clinical Psychology, 12,* 148-163.

Rotter, J. B. (1966). Generalized expectancies for internal versus external control of reinforcement. *Psychological Monographs, 80*(1) (Whole No. 609).

Seligman, M. E. P. (1975). *Helplessness: On depression, development, and death.* San Francisco: W. H. Freeman.

Taylor, S. E., Helgeson, V. S., Reed, G. M., & Skokan, L. A. (1991). Self-generated feelings of control and adjustment to physical illness. *Journal of Social Issues, 47,* 91-109.

Teresi, J. A., Golden, R. R., Gurland, B. J., Wilder, D. E., & Bennett, R. G. (1983). *Construct validity of indicator scales development from the comprehensive assessment and interview schedule.* Unpublished manuscript.

Thompson, S. C., & Spacapan, S. (1991). Perceptions of control in vulnerable populations. *Journal of Social Issues, 47,* 1-23.

Veit, C. T., & Ware, E. E. (1983). The structure of psychological distress and well being in general populations. *Journal of Consulting and Clinical Psychology, 51,* 730-742.

White, R. W. (1959). Motivation reconsidered: The concept of competence. *Psychological Review, 66,* 297-333.

Zautra, A. J., Guarnaccia, C. A., & Reich, J. W. (1988). Factor structure of mental health measures for older adults. *Journal of Consulting and Clinical Psychology, 56,* 514-519.

Zautra, A. J., & Wrabetz, A. B. (1991). Coping success and its relationship to psychological distress for older adults. *Journal of Personality and Social Psychology, 61*(5), 801-810.

9

Informal Social Support

Neena L. Chappell

Since the early 1970s, the interest in and research published on social support in the later years has burgeoned. Cohen and Syme (1985) attributed this increased attention at least in part to its potential relationship with health and well-being—specifically, its potential role both in the etiology of illness and disease and in treatment and rehabilitation programs following the onset of illness. Because of its relationship with health and well-being, social support is an appropriate topic in a volume that focuses on promoting successful and productive aging.

In this chapter I discuss some of what we have learned from this voluminous research and some of what remains unknown. I relate this knowledge to the current health care reforms that claim community care (and therefore, necessarily, informal support) as a cornerstone of the new vision. In assessing the role of social support in new policy directions, I discuss both what we know about social support and well-being in old age and what we do not know. I include a research agenda of some critical questions that require answers, especially given the new directions in health reform, and discuss the issue of whether we know enough about informal support to proceed with policy and program implementation.

New Directions in Health Care

Canada's health care system is much more similar to those found in European countries than to that of the United States. Indeed, as is now well documented, the United States is the only major industrialized country in the world that does not have universal health care. The health care system found in most industrialized countries, and evident in Canada and the European countries, offers universal access to physician and acute care hospital services. Long-term institutional care and community care tend not to be included within the national schemes.

Canada is somewhat distinctive in that it delivers both health and community services through its departments of health. Most countries keep these two areas distinct in terms of allocations of money and the administrative structure through which they flow. In Canada however, 6 of the 10 provinces deliver community social services through their departments of health, with the remaining provinces and territories delivering some of their community services through their departments of health, frequently jointly with a department of community and social services. This structural uniqueness is important because it facilitates a redistribution of funds between the two sectors, at least to the extent that there are fewer structural barriers.

Of particular relevance for the topic under discussion are the directions for reform within health care. In Canada and Europe, informal caregiving as the predominant form of care to seniors has increasingly been recognized by governments and policy makers. Indeed, it has become a cornerstone in the rhetoric for health reform in virtually all provinces in Canada and throughout the European community. With concerns over increasing costs and possible overmedicalization of the health care system, the new-found recognition of informal caregivers is embraced as a key element of community care for seniors. The recognition of informal caregiving follows from over two decades of gerontological research (Antonucci, 1990; Chappell, 1992; Kane, 1990) establishing:

1. The widespread involvement of seniors in social networks
2. Informal caregiving as the predominant source of care provided to seniors
3. Family and friends as the first resort of care to elders
4. Lack of informal support, not ill health, as the main predictor of long-term institutional care

Despite changes taking place in society such as increased divorce rates and women working in paid labor, the informal network remains the mainstay of care for most older persons who require it. Furthermore, although the research is not abundant, that which exists suggests that the establishment of formal home care programs does not discourage informal care provision but can prolong it, especially among those providing heavy care (Horowitz, Dono, & Brill, 1983; Noelker & Poulshock, 1982). Families, by and large, want to and do provide care to their older members.

Documenting the predominance of informal care and of social interaction in the lives of elders was an important function of gerontological research during the 1970s. During this period, it was commonplace to stereotype old people as ignored by their families and, where possible, dumped into long-term institutional care. Gerontological research documented the falsity of these assumptions. The recognition by government of the role of informal support networks in later life comes after it has become a well-established fact among gerontologists. However, it also comes at a time when a perceived cost crisis is taking place in the health care systems of virtually all countries. The recognition of informal caregivers is being used as part of the argument for reshaping universal health insurance. It offers the promise of a new vision that appeals to governments as less expensive than high-tech medical care in hospitals and to the populace as a more appropriate health care system focused on health rather than illness.

The reforms have begun in Canada, and they promise profound change within the health care system. One of the implications of the new rhetoric is a shift from institutional services to community home care (social support) services. A recent federal committee (Porter, 1991) explicitly recommended that this shift take place. Bed closures in acute care hospitals are occurring in virtually all provinces, with the announcement of entire hospitals being closed in rural Saskatchewan and in urban Vancouver, British Columbia. Slight decreases in hospital budgets and the removal of some medical procedures that used to be eligible under Medicare are now standard (for example, cosmetic surgery is no longer covered in Manitoba). At the same time we see movement toward funding of more home care, albeit relatively small. For example, Ontario is transferring 1% of its acute care hospital budget (totaling $67 million) to community care. British Columbia recently announced a 4% increase in hospital budgets but an 8% increase in continuing care budgets. At the same time, user fees are being imposed where none were before (such as for medical equipment in Manitoba), and both increased room and board charges for long-term care institutions and means testing for such charges have now been introduced in British Columbia and Manitoba.

There is also movement to ensure broader perspectives on health and broader representation of decision makers in the distribution of health care dollars. For example, in British Columbia regionalization of health care has begun, and each community will make appointments to a regional health board that ultimately will allocate health dollars for that region. These regional health boards will replace hospital boards. We do not yet know if we are going to end up with a more appropriate holistic health care system or simply a less adequate medical care system. Concerns are widespread, especially given memories of the deinstitutionalization of the mentally ill that took place several years ago. In that instance, institutions were closed, but adequate community support was never put in place.

The questions I would like to address are: Does our knowledge about social support tell us how to have a healthier population? Can we implement what we know into practice? Will the initiatives in health care reform result in greater burden on informal caregivers and therefore on women (mainly wives and daughters)?

Social Support and Well-Being

In addition to documenting the prevalence of social ties in later life, the last two and a half decades of research have also documented the importance of social support for well-being. Despite inconsistencies, many studies report a relationship between these concepts. Cohen and Syme (1985) concluded, after their review, that there is fairly strong evidence for an association between support and mental health and between support and mortality, but that the evidence is less convincing regarding the relationship between social support and physical illness. The mortality studies include some that are prospective and have demonstrated that people with low levels of social relationships have at least twice the risk of mortality, from all causes, that people with moderate to high levels of relationships have (Berkman & Syme, 1979; Blazer, 1982; House & Kahn, 1985; House, Robbins, & Metzner, 1982). It appears that individuals with virtually no social relationships are especially at risk. In Berkman and Syme's longitudinal study, larger networks and greater frequency of contact are related to decreased mortality for both men and women of all ages when socioeconomic status, initial health status, and health practices are controlled for.

In studies of social support and mortality, there may be questions about the mechanism by which social support operates to affect mortality (more will be said about this later), but the issue of direction of causation is not raised (that is, mortality cannot affect one's social relationships). In studies of the relationship between support and mental health and social support and physical health, however, direction of causality is important. Mental illness, for example, can operate to reduce access to support. Others have argued that social competence might be the key factor for both support and emotional functioning (Gottlieb, 1985; Kessler & MacLeod, 1985). Studies relating to social support and physical health are even less consistent. Nevertheless, there is some evidence that a positive relationship between the two exists. Studies showing that social psychological factors such as control and decision making at work are related to less heart disease (Marmot & Theorell, 1988) and to dramatic rises in life expectancy in Japan (Canadian Institute for Advanced Research, 1991; Marmot & Smith, 1989), and studies showing the importance of enrichment programs for children's health (Berrueta-Clement, 1989) all support the notion of the important effects of social and environmental factors on our physical health. Lubben, Weiler, and Chi (1989) reported an association between social networks and less hospitalization, with a stronger relationship than that which led to the warning on cigarette packages many years ago.

In any event, despite inconsistent findings and the vast array of different measures of social support, there is much evidence for both a direct and indirect relationship between social support and well-being in later life. One could argue that the repeated emergence of this finding, despite different samples and the diversity of indicators of both social support and well-being, adds to the strength of the argument that there is indeed a relationship between these two variables. But there is much that we do not know, and I proceed here to some of the complexities in the area of social support that we are only beginning to address. Then I turn to the question of whether any of our knowledge can be used in policy and programming in order to promote successful and productive aging.

Social Support—What We Do Not Know

Although there is now well-documented evidence of a correlation between social support and well-being, we still do not have a good understanding of the mechanisms through which this is operative. Gottlieb (1985) noted that the process of social comparison lies at the heart of the social support stress-mediating role. It is through social comparison that validation for old and new social identities emerges. It is through interactions with others that we evolve and confirm our sense of self and our own identities. But as noted elsewhere (Antonucci, 1985; Berkman, 1985; Chappell, 1992), we do not know how much the association of social support with well-being is a function of a personality or skill factor (such as social competence), the information provided through this support network, or the services that an individual ultimately receives because of this information.

In addition, there are negative aspects of social interaction, although little research focuses on this area. Wortman and Conway (1985) cited dramatic examples of negative support, describing how healthy persons went out of their way to cheer up individuals with cancer but how the majority of cancer patients reported the "unrelenting optimism" of others as unauthentic and disturbing, and found it unhelpful when others minimized their problems. Similarly, women who have undergone a mastectomy find that others think their major concern is the loss of their breast. However, such women are much more concerned about recurrences, death, and treatment side effects. Antonucci (1990) argued that negative relations may have a much more powerful effect on well-being than positive support. We know far too little about these areas. There is much we do not know about what types of interaction have more negative than beneficial effects. No doubt this varies by personality of the individual. Those with a high internal locus of control may find authoritative interactions more negative than individuals with a high external locus of control, for example.

There is also the very serious question of causation, raised earlier. Most of the surveys on social support and well-being are cross-sectional. Mental health problems may be related to a lower ability to build social networks; individuals who are socially competent may be better able to negotiate the health care system and receive health care services that are more appropriate to their needs. Even if social support does affect our health, it is not yet clear how this takes place. There is accumulating evidence of a physiological link.

As Berkman (1985) noted, social support seems to be related to health generally rather than to susceptibility to specific diseases. There may be biological mechanisms that increase an individual's vulnerability to a host of conditions. If there is a direct physiological pathway, it may operate such that individuals who are stressed have a changed psychological state, such as being depressed or fatalistic, and the psychological state leads to alterations in physiological functioning, or the stress acts directly on physiological states. In this instance, one would see social networks as influencing a generalized susceptibility to illness, as Cassel hypothesized in 1976. Cassel (1974, 1976) expanded the work of Selye (1956), who argued that the physiological influence is through an alteration of the neuroendocrine system, thereby increasing susceptibility to disease agents.

There is now growing evidence that emotions and mental function affect the nervous system, in turn influencing host defense mechanisms that directly affect our physiology, including our neuroendocrine and immune systems. The research suggests that all of our physiological systems communicate with one another (Stead, Bienenstock, & Stantsz, 1987). Current research follows from Selye's (1956) work showing that stress in rats caused peptic ulcers, atrophy of the immune system tissues, and enlargement of the adrenal glands. Later work showed that part of this effect was mediated through secretion of some hormones and inhibition of others. Work in the 1960s demonstrated a link between emotional conflict and the onset in the course of rheumatoid arthritis (Levine, Collier, Busbaum, Moskowitz, & Helms, 1985). More of this current work refers to animal studies than to human studies.

Research that suggests direct links between social support and the physiological functioning of the human anatomy is consistent with the growing amount of research demonstrating the importance of social psychological and environmental factors for overall health. This literature raises the possibility of a general host response within the individual. In this instance, one would argue that stress diminishes a general host defense, which could explain greater overall vulnerability of individuals to a variety of illnesses rather than simply to a specific illness.

This concept of a general host response is explored in some detail in a paper by the Canadian Institute for Advanced Research (CIAR, 1991). That paper noted evidence from several studies around the world, pointing to a relationship between health and socioeconomic class that is a continuous gradient and not a threshold function. In other words, people in the top stratum appear to be healthier than those on the second rung even when those on the second rung are well above population averages for socioeconomic status. The import of this continuous gradient, if confirmed in the future, is that the burden of ill health is not restricted to the most marginalized and disadvantaged segments of society. Rather, large numbers of persons who are only somewhat deprived, and not only the much smaller numbers of people who are relatively severely deprived, suffer the consequences of ill health.

The notion of a generalized host response is important for several reasons. Most epidemiological research into the causes of illness examines risk factors for only one disease, such as Parkinson's, liver or kidney dysfunctions, or cancer. Few funding resources are available for examining the broad determinants of overall health. If it is true that a large population is susceptible to a whole host of illnesses rather than to one particular illness, the single-disease route for seeking cures is going to be inadequate. As a cure for any specific disease is found, another disease will arise to take its place. Moreover, with regard to work in gerontology, this research calls for much greater funding for truly multidisciplinary research that examines, in detail, factors such as social support together with physiological measures of health. That is, this work calls for general-disease, multidisciplinary research.

Another area that is becoming popular and has great promise for future research on social support is a feminist perspective. Over the last few years, the feminist perspective has become evident within the gerontological literature and is inevitably relevant on at least two counts to the area of social support. On the one hand, much has been written about women's greater expressive and kin-keeping function compared with men's, and women's greater role as caregivers is now well documented.

The caregiving literature has, to date, focused primarily on functional tasks, that is, on activities of daily living. This is true whether the focus has been on informal caregivers or on formal caregivers whose job descriptions are oriented primarily toward functional tasks. Nevertheless, a growing body of literature suggests that the salient aspects of the caregiving role for caregivers and elders alike are not functional tasks but emotional and identity-maintaining aspects of the relationship.

Hasselkus (1988) argued that informal caregivers are not particularly task oriented, in contrast to many paid workers, and herein lies the discrepancy in understanding caregivers' needs. The invisible work of caregiving, that is, decision making and protecting the elder's self-image and sense of identity and autonomy, is more important for caregivers than particular tasks and skills. Experience in small group homes with demented elders in Sweden (Jackson & Gallagher, 1992) suggests that caregivers can maintain peace with residents provided they relate on an emotional level. Similarly, Bowers (1987) found that a task-based definition of caregiving was inconsistent with the experiential world of caregiving. Emotional issues, include, for example, feelings of trust, empathy, and control. Much more work needs to be done on the emotional aspects of caregiving.

We also know that the vast majority of caregivers are women, primarily wives and daughters. In the United States (Stone, Cafferata, & Sangl, 1987), 72% of caregivers are women; of these, 52% are wives or daughters. Women are more likely to be involved in kin keeping than are men and are more likely to be involved in expressive relationships, whereas men are more likely to be involved in instrumental relationships and are much more likely to have only their wives as confidantes. Women are more likely to expand this close circle of intimates to include friends and children (Chappell, 1992). In fact, because women predominate as caregivers, relatively little is known about male caregivers, particularly husbands providing care to an ailing spouse. Husbands who find themselves in this role are such a minority that studies of caregivers frequently cannot attain sufficient numbers to provide in-depth analyses. Kaye and Applegate (1990) reported that men are better at "getting the job done" than are women, an approach that helps men maintain a great emotional distance within the role and shield themselves more from feelings of burden. Alternatively, men may mask their feelings more effectively. We also know that men can provide care and do step in if there is no female alternative available (either because of distance or because there is no daughter). Furthermore, we know that women are more likely to provide hands-on assistance and emotional support, whereas men are more likely to provide supervision, money, and transportation.

Bringing a feminist perspective to caregiving, Hooyman (1990) noted two underlying trends that have made female caregivers hidden victims:

1. Historically, an ideology of separate spheres between men's and women's work has perpetuated the expectation that women's major role is to provide uncompensated care to dependents.
2. The welfare of family caregivers has not been a goal of public policy.

Within current social structures, women are largely isolated. At the present time, informal caregiving is a low-cost alternative to public responsibility—one that relies primarily on women's invisible and unpaid labor. Indeed, women, unlike men, are socialized to give priority to the needs of others. This has been an explanation for why women find caregiving more stressful than do men (Horowitz & Dobrof, 1982). Women caregivers have been characterized as "caring about" in addition to "caring for" (Lewis & Meredith, 1988).

As Fischer, Rogne, and Eustis (1990) expressed it, women are now caught between conservative criticism that blames women for not having traditional caring values and feminist criticism that women's caring work is oppressive and exploitative. The new feminist critique has highlighted the cultural and structural circumstances that create caring as an element of female identity. But women who accept caregiving as their "natural" role can find their access blocked to socially valued marketplace resources such as equitable paid employment, and so have their powerlessness in society perpetuated. This is not necessarily a critique of caregiving values per se, but it is a critique of the lack of reward and recognition within the societal power structure that women receive for undertaking these tasks.

In this section I have tried to point out directions for our future research by highlighting some of the intriguing questions that remain unanswered in the area of social support. These include the mechanism through which social support operates, the negative aspects of social support, the causal direction of the relationship between social support and well-being, the physiological link, and feminist issues in caregiving. I have only scratched the surface, but all the issues I have raised are relevant to the next section. I now discuss whether we know enough, and whether what we know in the area of social support allows us to mount programs that can indeed promote and enhance well-being in later life.

Policies and Programming in Social Support

Sauer and Coward (1985) argued that although the concept of social support networks has been around for a long time, its practical applicability to the field of gerontology is only just beginning to be recognized fully. Certainly, it is not clear that we should be rushing to implement programs to encourage social support. There is so much we do not know and there are so many pitfalls that we could be in dangerous territory indeed: We could encourage the negative rather than the positive aspects of interaction; we could accomplish little if social competence or some other factor explains the association between social support and well-being; we could further exploit women in the caregiving role. If informal care is given unwillingly, it loses its special qualities—its emotional warmth and affection (Walker, 1991). In this instance, few would argue that it is superior to formal care.

Some researchers, such as Kessler and McLeod (1985), offer a qualified "no" to the question of whether we can generalize knowledge to interventions. They argue that we can make general inferences about general exposure to stress but that we need studies of support that provide an in-depth look into a particular life crisis before we begin programming in the area. We do not know where social networks have the greatest impact along a spectrum of disease. Is it in incidence? Is it in recovery, and if so, which aspect? Does it affect case fatality? And does this differ for different diseases? Even the research that does suggest that social support may be important in promoting recovery from illness does little to tell us the mechanisms through which support influences recovery. Intervention studies vary in terms of who provides the support, sometimes including different informal members and other times including different types of formal health care workers. In no instance do we gain a clear understanding of how social support operates to affect the desired relationship (Wortman & Conway, 1985).

With suitable caution, it nevertheless would appear that we can use some of our knowledge about social support during old age in devising our social policies and make explicit those assumptions that exist in current policies. In terms of the latter, there is a growing recognition of the centrality of the family to the political agenda. Canadian policies, for the most part, assume that family care and support are givens—that is, formal caregiving starts where family care ends. Existing social policies reinforce traditional family structures, values, and authorities in both the family and the state and make women vulnerable to policies that define them as essentially familial. Policies that support caregivers do not question why women are doing the job and/or whether the job is organized in a just and equitable manner. Rather, most formal care is provided as crisis intervention, short-term support, or long-term residential care when there is no informal support available (McDaniel & Gee, 1993; Neysmith, 1991; Walker, 1991). The ideology of familism assumes that the family is necessarily the correct location for the care of older relatives and that within it female kin are the most appropriate caregivers. One can argue that this is not necessarily just, appropriate, or the way it should or must be.

As others have noted (see, e.g., Walker, 1991), to change the ideology is not easy. If women are to be truly free to choose, then there must be alternatives to their support and to family support. There will have to be a change in professional attitudes and values in the formal sector for a true partnership between informal and formal caregivers. And there will have to be a change, some might call it a revolution, in the attitudes of men and in the division of caregiving work by gender. There is no indication that primary group values of belonging, emotional support, and love are waning in their importance to human society. It is equally clear, however, that the structural arrangements in which we conduct our lives are steadily evolving. The nuclear family of two parents and children has changed drastically and is no longer the dominant form. Given life expectancy increases, individuals can now assume they will spend more time in parent care than they did in child care. One-parent families are common, as are new family arrangements resulting from increasing divorce and remarriage rates. Increase in the recognition of gay and lesbian relationships is but another form through which we see the need for love and companionship manifested. One last example of our evolving society would include the groups of RVers (those who spend much time in recreational vehicles) in old age. These individuals find a new family among other RVers rather than among blood ties.

The important distinction here is between the content and the form. Presumably we want to support the values, but if we devise policies that support only certain structural forms and discriminate against others, they will fall short of supporting the values that manifest themselves in a diversity of structural forms. Flexibility is critical. We need policies sufficiently flexible and open that needs can be met rather than bureaucratic criteria simply fulfilled. For example, a policy should first determine an individual's need and then the services or group of services that can meet this need, rather than simply assessing individuals in terms of whether they may be eligible for a particular service.

At a general level, the direction of social policy can reflect the importance of social support in the lives of elders. Much research documents the desires of elders to maintain their relationships with family and friends. Yet when we examine government policies, we see that programs that aim to enhance interaction with others tend to be viewed as "fun and games" or "soft" programs that receive little or no funding. For example, transportation programs for the mobility impaired will transport an elder to an appointment with a physician but not to a friend's house. In addition, programs that promote social support tend to be among the first to be cut when dollars are scarce. In Canada, the New Horizons program has been an example throughout the years. Its major goals include socialization. Although it continues to this day, it is not, by monetary standards, a rich program.

Although social support and informal caregivers have been recognized within the new rhetoric of health care reform, it is not yet clear whether this is simply a means to shift the burden of care to this sector. If we are to have a health care system rather than an illness care system, and a community care rather than an institutional care system, we must shift resources to caregivers and to the community. This inevitably means, particularly in this climate of economic restraints, that many of the current vested interests (physicians, acute care hospitals, pharmaceutical companies, etc.) must lose some of their current power within the system. Decision making and also resources have to be shared. It is too early to determine what the results of reform are going to be within Canada. The current atmosphere of reform does provide opportunity for qualitative shifts and real improvement within the health care system. Meanwhile, it holds very real dangers that we will end up with a less adequate Medicare system and no better community care system.

Although we may wish to be hesitant and cautious in designing specific programs to enhance social support, there is nevertheless much to be learned from the now many years of experience in the health promotion area. Programs that provide opportunities for and assist elders to become involved in their own communities appear to be workable without taking us into the quagmire of encouraging relationships that may actually be destructive for the elders. A framework that promotes empowerment and emphasizes a multifactorial concept of health and the importance of community involvement sees social support as critical without being prescriptive. Professionals can help promote healthy initiatives by advocating on behalf of self-health groups, establishing more active and reciprocal referral relations, and lending their expertise when invited to do so. At the same time, as Gottlieb (1985) cautioned, formal health care workers must refrain from both dictating to others their own values or standards of practice and attempting to control natural helping networks or impose their system of credentials upon those networks.

Summary and Conclusions

This chapter discusses what we know about social support in old age in terms of its relevance for new directions in health care reform, particularly in Canada but also throughout the industrialized world. It began with a discussion of new directions in health care currently evident within Canada. These include embracing a rhetoric of community care with informal support as a major cornerstone. Much specific reform is demonstrating a determination by provincial governments to ensure spending limits on medical care and acute care hospital services. Although some movements suggest a redistribution of resources and decision-making power to community care, it is too early in the redistribution process to conclude that there will be major transfers of resources to the community sector. Meanwhile, it does appear that the allocation of resources and decision making to medical and short-term institutional sectors is being reduced.

A key question that remains is whether we actually know enough about social support to shift our policy in this direction. There is now a voluminous literature on social support in old age that includes many literature reviews as well. The general conclusion is that social support is alive and well in old age and, furthermore, that it has general positive relationships with health and well-being in old age. However, there is much that we do not know about social support, and these areas raise policy and program implementation concerns. If social support does enhance well-being, we still do not understand the mechanism through which it operates. Indeed, there is a strong suggestion that its relationship to well-being may be spurious, with something like social competence actually accounting for the relationship. In addition, we know little about the negative aspects of social interaction that may outweigh positive effects or about the circumstances in which the negative effects outweigh the positive. There is also a serious question about the direction of causation (other than in the relationship between social support and mortality) In the areas of both mental and physical health, it could be that mental competence and physical well-being lead the individual to greater involvement with others.

There is mounting evidence that social support has an ultimate effect on our physiological functioning. This has profound implications in terms of how we conduct research into health and in terms of how we conceptualize this aspect of our lives. It calls for truly multidisciplinary research. Finally, there is the importance of a feminist perspective on social support in terms of the importance of understanding both the emotional and identity-maintaining aspects of the care relationship and the dominance of women as caregivers and their necessary continuation in this role for a community health strategy under current circumstances.

Despite necessary cautions against rushing to implement strategies that encourage or force individuals into various modes of interaction, there does seem to be sufficient evidence both for making explicit the social support assumptions that underlie our existing policies and for policies that encourage general social support. I have chosen to support a general health promotion strategy that facilitates, provides opportunities for, and generally encourages empowerment of individuals in old age (as well as in younger years) and that sees community development encouraged and strengthened. Such a strategy allows us to incorporate what we do know about social support while avoiding some of the dangers of specific intervention strategies that focus upon social support. If we can foster an environment where elders build their own social support networks and avoid our past policies that fail to recognize families or significant others in their lives, we may be taking a first step toward a healthy society where we can all age successfully.

References

Antonucci, T. C. (1985). Personal characteristics, social support, and social behavior. In R. H. Binstock & E. Shanas (Eds.), *Handbook of aging and the social sciences* (2nd ed., pp. 94-128). New York: Van Nostrand Reinhold.

Antonucci, T. C. (1990). Social supports and social relationships. In R. H. Binstock & L. K. George (Eds.), *Handbook of aging and the social sciences* (3rd ed., pp. 205-226). San Diego: Academic Press.

Berkman, L. F. (1985). The relationship of social networks and social support to morbidity and mortality. In S. Cohen & S. L. Syme (Eds.), *Social support and health* (pp. 241-262). Orlando, FL: Academic Press.

Berkman, L. F., & Syme, S. L. (1979). Social networks, host resistance, and mortality: A nine-year follow-up study of Alameda County residents. *American Journal of Epidemiology, 109*(2), 186-204.

Berrueta-Clement, J. (1989). *Changed lives, the effects of the Perry Preschool Program on youths through age 19.* Ypsilanti, MI: High/Scope.

Blazer, D. G. (1982). Social support and mortality in an elderly community population. *American Journal of Epidemiology, 115*(5), 684-694.

Bowers, B. J. (1987). Intergenerational caregiving: Adult caregivers and their aging parents. *Advanced Nursing Science, 9,* 20-31.

Canadian Institute for Advanced Research. (1991). *The determinants of health* (CIAR Publication No. 5). Toronto: Author.

Cassel, J. (1974). Psychosocial processes and stress: Theoretical formulations. *International Journal of Health Services, 4,* 471-482.

Cassel, J. (1976). The contribution of the social environment to host resistance. *American Journal of Epidemiology, 104,* 107-123.

Chappell, N. L. (Ed.). (1992). *Social support and aging.* Toronto: Butterworths.

Cohen, S., & Syme, S. L. (1985). Issues in the study and application of social support. In S. Cohen & S. L. Syme (Eds.), *Social support and health* (pp. 3-22). Orlando, FL: Academic Press.

Fischer, L. R., Rogne, L., & Eustis, N. N. (1990). Support systems for the familyless elderly: Care without commitment. In J. F. Gubrium & A. Sankar (Eds.), *The home care experience: Ethnography and policy* (pp. 129-143). Newbury Park, CA: Sage.

Gottlieb, B. H. (1985). Social support and community mental health. In S. Cohen & S. L. Syme (Eds.), *Social support and health* (pp. 303-326). Orlando, FL: Academic Press.

Hasselkus, B. R. (1988). Meaning in family caregiving: Perspectives on caregiver/professional relationships. *The Gerontologist, 28*(5), 686-691.

Hooyman, N. R. (1990). Women as caregivers of the elderly: Implications for social welfare policy and practice. In D. E. Biegel & A. Blum (Eds.), *Aging and caregiving: Theory, research, and policy* (pp. 221-241). Newbury Park, CA: Sage.

Horowitz, A., & Dobrof, R. (1982). *The role of families in providing long-term care to the frail and chronically ill elderly living in the community. Final report to the Health Care Financing Administration.* Washington, DC: Department of Health and Human Resources.

Horowitz, A., Dono, J. E., & Brill, R. (1983, November). *Continuity or changes in informal support? The impact of an extended home care program.* Paper presented at the annual meeting of the Gerontological Society of America, San Francisco.

House, J. S., & Kahn, R. L. (1985). Measures and concepts of social support. In S. Cohen & S. L. Syme (Eds.), *Social support and health* (pp. 83-108). Orlando, FL: Academic Press.

House, J. S., Robbins, C., & Metzner, H. L. (1982). The association of social relationships and activities with mortality: Prospective evidence from the Tecumseh Community Health Study. *American Journal of Epidemiology, 116,* 123-140.

Jackson, M. F., & Gallagher, E. (1992, September). *Expanding the options: Scandinavian approaches to care of persons with Alzheimer's disease.* Paper presented at a symposium of the Centre of Aging, University of Victoria, British Columbia.

Kane, R. L. (1990). Introduction. In R. L. Kane, J. G. Evans, & D. MacFadyen (Eds.), *Improving the health of older people: A world view* (pp. 15-18). New York: Oxford University Press.

Kaye, L. W., & Applegate, J. S. (1990). *Men as caregivers to the elderly.* Lexington, MA: Lexington.

Kessler, R. C., & McLeod, J. D. (1985). Social support and mental health in community samples. In S. Cohen & S. L. Syme (Eds.), *Social support and health* (pp. 219-240). Orlando, FL: Academic Press.

Levine, J. D., Collier, D. H., Busbaum, A. I., Moskowitz, M. A., & Helms, C. A. (1985). The nervous system may contribute to the pathophysiology of rheumatoid arthritis. *Journal of Rheumatology, 12,* 406-411.

Lewis, J., & Meredith, B. (1988). *Daughters who care: Daughters caring for mothers at home.* London: Routledge & Kegan Paul

Lubben, J. E., Weiler, P. G., & Chi, I. (1989). Health practices of the elderly poor. *American Journal of Public Health, 79,* 731-734.

Marmot, M. G., & Smith, G. D. (1989). Why are the Japanese living longer? *British Medical Journal, 299,* 1547-1551.

Marmot, M. G., & Theorell, T. (1988). Social class and cardiovascular disease: The contribution of work. *International Journal of Health Sciences, 18*(4), 659-674.

McDaniel, S. A., & Gee, E. M. (1993). Social policies regarding caregiving to elders: Canadian contradictions. *Journal of Aging and Social Policy, 5*(1/2), 57-72.

Neysmith, S. M. (1991). Closing the gap between health policy and the home care need of tomorrow's elderly. *Canadian Journal of Community Mental Health, 8*(2), 141-150.

Noelker, L. S., & Poulshock, S. W. (1982). *The effects on families of caring for impaired elderly in residence: Final report.* Washington, DC: Department of Health and Human Services, Administration on Aging.

Porter, B. (1991). *The health care system in Canada and its funding: No easy solutions.* Ottawa, Ontario: Canada Communication Group, Supply and Services.

Sauer, W. J., & Coward, R. T. (1985). The role of social support networks in the care of the elderly. In W. J. Sauer & R. T. Coward (Eds.), *Social support networks and the care of the elderly* (pp. 3-20). New York: Springer.

Selye, H. (1956). *The stress of life.* New York: McGraw-Hill.

Stead, R. H., Bienenstock, J., & Stantsz, A. M. (1987). Neuropeptide regulation of mucosal immunity. *Immunological Reviews, 100,* 333-359.

Stone, R., Cafferata, G. L., & Sangl, J. (1987). Caregivers of the frail elderly: A national profile. *The Gerontologist, 27,* 616-626.

Walker, A. (1991). The relationship between the family and the state in the care of older people. *Canadian Journal on Aging, 10*(2), 94-110.

Wortman, C. B., & Conway, T. L. (1985). The role of social support in adaptation and recovery from physical illness. In S. Cohen & S. L. Syme (Eds.), *Social support and health* (pp. 281-302). Orlando, FL: Academic Press.

10

Formal Support in Later Life: Lessons for Prevention

Michael A. Smyer

This chapter is designed to be a thought-provoking essay rather than an exhaustive review. If successful, I will stimulate your curiosity about the applicability and limits of preventive approaches to the provision of formal social supports for older adults across a wide range of functioning.

At the outset, it is important to define what is encompassed by formal social support. Cantor (1992) offered a useful distinction between social network analysis and social support research. Her discussion helps focus our attention:

> Social support research . . . covers a broader canvas. Although it may begin by describing an older person's network, its main focus is on those elements, informal as well as formal, that operate to assist an older person in maintaining independence, primarily in the community, by providing instrumental, emotional, informational, or financial assistance. Thus, the main focus is on support rather than integration, and the interest is in the identification of those social ties which provide support to the elderly, the conditions which maximize the provision of support, and the effect of supportive ties on social and health interventions. (p. 4)

Several elements of Cantor's discussion are important. First, it alerts us to the inevitable links between formal and informal sources of support. Although the two are divided for discussion purposes here, in the lives of older adults, when it is effective, there is a seamless web of support. Cohler

AUTHOR'S NOTE: This work was supported in part by a grant from the Retirement Research Foundation and Grant # IT32-MH-18904 from the National Institute of Mental Health. I appreciate the helpful suggestions of Murna Downs and Lori Frank on an earlier version of this chapter.

(1992), for example, reminded us that for most older adults later life is spent in interdependence at home and in the community:

> The reality of aging in our society is that most older adults remain as healthy through their mid-seventies as they were at younger ages, equally active and often still working. Even those who retire during their sixties may expect to spend as much as one-third of their lives after retirement, living within a modified-extended multi-generational family system often encompassing five generations. Finally, at least until their mid-seventies, most older adults enjoy the same continued good health as had characterized their earlier adult life. Less than ten percent of adults over age sixty-five live in residential care, and most older adults enjoy independent living through oldest age. (p. 19)

Second, the focus of Cantor's definition is on maintaining independence. Some have argued, however, that this perspective inevitably leads to an overemphasis on vulnerability and weakness, what Tornstam (1992) called a "misery perspective" (p. 318). In contrast, many clinicians and researchers have called for a balanced view of older adults, emphasizing both their strengths and their weaknesses (e.g., Cohen, 1993; Finkel & Cohen, 1982; Kivnick, 1993; Sherman, 1993). For service providers and for many researchers, however, an emphasis on maintaining independence is consistent with both research traditions and public policy (e.g., Gelfand, 1988; Hudson, 1993, in press).

Third, Cantor's definition alerts us to the variability and diversity that characterize older adults and their formal support. The diversity of the aging experience encompasses the full range of aging from physical frailty and disability to what some would call "successful aging." At any age, and for any individual, inter- and intraindividual variability among older adults cannot be overlooked (Hultsch & Dixon, 1990; Jackson, Antonucci, & Gibson, 1990; Morse, 1993). Similarly, formal support may take diverse forms. It may include instrumental, economic, and/or emotional assistance. The development and provision of formal support reflect the intersection of several domains—social policy, economic well-being, physical health, mental health—as they affect the personal trajectory of aging.

This chapter is designed to illustrate the relevance of preventive perspectives on formal support across a range of functioning and settings for older adults. The first section focuses on nursing homes and nursing home residents. The second section emphasizes community settings and community-dwelling elders. The final section considers highly functioning elders who seek out continuing care communities. In each section, the relevance of preventive approaches will be highlighted.

Nursing Homes: The Forgotten 5%

Prevalence

Some of my colleagues often ask me: Why worry about nursing home care? They accurately point out that if one takes a cross-sectional perspective, at any one point in time 5% of older adults in the United States are using institutional settings, primarily nursing homes, as their formal source of support (Kastenbaum & Candy, 1973). In 1987, for example, there were slightly more than 1.5 million older adults in nursing homes (Lair & Lefkowitz, 1990). This cross-sectional view belies individuals' lifetime risks of nursing home use, however. Kemper and Murtaugh (1991), for example, used data from the National Long Term Care Survey to simulate the risks of nursing home care for members of a cohort turning 65 in 1990. They estimated that almost a third of men and just over half of women who turned 65 in 1990 could be expected to spend some time in a nursing home before death—substantially higher lifetime rates than the 5% cross-sectional view.

The interdependence of lives in later life makes family rates of risk for nursing home use also important to consider. Again, Kemper and Murtaugh (1991) provided useful information. For couples with both members turning 65 in 1990, about 7 out of 10 can expect that at least one member of the dyad will spend time in a nursing home.

Offspring also are likely to encounter nursing home issues. In a simulated family with four parents (parents and in-laws) turning 65 in 1990, 9 out of 10 children can expect to have at least one parent enter a nursing home (Kemper & Murtaugh, 1991).

Thus the lifetime risks of nursing home use are substantially higher than the cross-sectional 5% rates. The lifetime view suggests that nursing homes might have more personal and professional relevance than is apparent at first glance.

Who Are the Nursing Home Residents?

Nursing home residents have a combination of physical and mental health problems. For example, Strahan and Burns (1991) summarizing information from the 1985 National Nursing Home Survey, found that 65% of nursing home residents had at least one mental disorder. Lair and Lefkowitz (1990), drawing on the 1987 National Medical Expenditure Survey (NMES), estimated that a similar proportion had a mental disorder. In addition, they found that a majority of nursing home residents needed help with self-care activities (such as bathing and dressing)—a common proxy for physical disability. In short, nursing home residents are both mentally and physically ill, with nursing homes now playing a major role in mental health care for older adults (Smyer, Cohn, & Brannon, 1988).

Who Provides Care?

A central question of people for whom nursing home care becomes either a personal or a professional concern is necessarily: Who will provide care? Who will be the support in this "formal support"?

Given the residents' mixture of mental and physical health problems, one might expect to find high rates of mental health service providers. Not so! Burns et al. (1993), drawing on data from the National Nursing Home Survey, reported that only 4.5% of those with mental disorders received any mental health treatment in a month; half of that treatment was provided by primary care physicians. Similarly, Smyer, Shea, and Streit (1994), drawing on the NMES, reported that 80% of residents with a mental disorder were in a facility that reported providing mental health services. Unfortunately, only 19% of those residents received mental health services any time during their stay.

Rather than mental health professionals, the primary caregivers in nursing homes are nursing assistants who are, on average, high school graduates working for minimum wage. They provide the majority of the full-time (72%) and part-time (57%) staff, according to the 1977 National Nursing Home Survey (National Nursing Home Survey, 1985). They also have the most direct daily contact with nursing home residents and are a major source of support and treatment for mentally and physically ill nursing home residents. Because of their central role, nursing assistants can be involved in preventive interventions both to avoid excess disability and to improve the functioning of residents.

A Sample Intervention

The Penn State Nursing Home Intervention Project illustrates a preventive intervention designed to improve the functioning of residents by improving the skills and motivation of nursing assistants. (See Smyer & Walls, 1994, and Smyer, Brannon, & Cohn, 1992, for a more complete discussion of the project.)

This intervention project assumed that nursing assistants' job performance directly affects their residents' quality of life. Therefore, to improve job performance, we implemented a short-term longitudinal study designed to assess the single and combined effects of two components: a skills training intervention to increase knowledge and skills (Cohn, Horgas, & Marsiske, 1990) and a job redesign intervention to change the nature of the work itself and, consequently, the nursing assistants' motivation (Brannon & Streit, 1990).

The project's outcomes provide important lessons for prevention programming in nursing homes. We found that we could significantly improve the knowledge of nursing assistants, as reflected in a paper-and-pencil measure (Smyer et al., 1992; Spore, Smyer, & Cohn, 1991). But we also found that the knowledge change did not lead to a change in performance in the nursing unit, as reflected in supervisors' ratings. Not surprisingly, there were also no changes in resident outcomes related to our efforts.

A major lesson to be learned from our experience is the importance of the organizational culture and structure in enhancing or opposing preventive interventions (Bowers & Becker, 1992; Brannon, 1992; Kruzich, Clinton, & Kelber, 1992). We had underestimated the crucial role of supervisors in the diffusion of innovation in the setting. They were critical in facilitating or blocking the transfer of training skills from the classroom to the nursing unit. Our current efforts are focused on improving both nursing assistants' skills and supervisors' skills to enhance the functioning of impaired nursing home residents.

Implications for Prevention

Nursing homes suggest three important lessons for prevention specialists. First, prevention efforts may usefully focus on transition points for older adults and their families. For example, recent policy efforts (e.g., the Nursing Home Reform Act of 1987) have sought to identify potential nursing home residents who need solely mental health treatment (Lair & Smyer, 1993; Smyer, 1989), with mandated assessment and referral efforts at the time of nursing home placement.

Second, even within the nursing home setting, prevention efforts can focus on identifying risk factors for mental illness or excess disability. For example, Foster and Cataldo (1993) identified predictors of onset of clinical depression in a long-term care facility, using physical health, mental health, and social functioning indicators. Once such predictors have been identified with psychometric reliability and validity, they can be used to develop programmatic preventive interventions to avoid excess disability for nursing home residents.

Third, preventive efforts must focus attention on the contexts of functioning for older adults. In nursing homes, preventive efforts can usefully engage the primary caregivers, nursing aides, as key elements in prevention (Smyer et al., 1992). The key here is to leverage professional efforts—to extend the impact of the small number of prevention professionals who are available to work in long-term care settings.

Community-Dwelling Elders:
The Role of Formal Services

The Need for Formal Services

The majority of older adults are enjoying the rewards and facing the challenges of aging in the community, not in institutional settings. A number of national estimates have focused specific attention on two challenges: chronic illness and functional impairment. For example, 85% of older adults have one or more chronic conditions, with patterns of morbidity varying by age (65-74 vs. 75+) and gender (Cassel, Rudberg, & Olshansky, 1992). The four most common chronic conditions, for example, are arthritis, hypertension, hearing impairment, and heart disease (Cassel et al., 1992).

The second dimension used in focusing on older adults' use of formal services is functional impairment as reflected in activities of daily living (ADLs) and instrumental activities of daily living (IADLs). ADLs and IADLs are important because they are often proxies for underlying abilities (Kemp & Mitchell, 1992). ADLs and IADLs are a basic index of the individual's ability to live independently in the community and a reflection of everyday decision-making capacity (Willis & Schaie, 1993). For these reasons, ADLs are relied upon in policy-making and regulatory settings to establish eligibility for services or to depict populations who are in need of services (Wiener & Hanley, 1992).

The link between these two indices—chronic conditions and functional capacity—is illustrated by work by Stewart et al. (1989). They analyzed data from the Medical Outcomes Study (MOS) (Tarlov et al., 1989), using a cross-sectional sample of 9,385 respondents who ranged in age from 18 to 103 (average age = 46). Stewart et al. were interested in the relationship between chronic conditions and six areas of functioning: physical functioning (comparable to ADLs and IADLs), role performance; social functioning; mental health; health perceptions; and bodily pain. Their conclusion is a powerful summary statement: "The impact of chronic conditions on health is substantial, varies according to condition, and, for most conditions, involves all aspects of functioning and well-being" (p. 911).

Linking Functioning and Formal Services

Short and Leon (1990) analyzed the 1987 NMES data to depict patterns of community service use by functionally impaired older adults. Because NMES used a national probability sample, these data provide the best available estimates of current patterns of functioning and service use by community-dwelling elders.

Short and Leon pointed out that 5.6 million older adults have difficulty with at least one ADL or IADL or have a problem that affects their ability to walk. This estimate is consistent with Wiener and Hanley's (1992) estimate drawn from the 1982 National Long Term Care Survey. Of these 5.6 million individuals with functional impairment, 20% are using formal services only; another 35% are using only informal services; 16% are using both formal and informal services; and 29% are using neither formal nor informal services.

For the minority of functionally impaired elders using formal services, the following six services were the most frequently used: home care (19.7%); senior center (7.3%); congregate meals (6.1%); transportation (5.3%); and phone check (4.2%). For those interested in linking preventive services to the use of formal services, these use patterns should be a cause for some concern. They suggest that even the most frequently used services are reaching a very small portion of the at-risk population.

The majority of services used by the functionally impaired older adults were provided at home (62%), whereas 27% of the services were community based. As in the nursing home, the paraprofessional providers (homemakers and home health aides) were the most common home care providers, followed by nurses, other medical personnel, and physicians. Again, these patterns suggest that paraprofessional training may have an important role to play in community-based long-term care, as in nursing homes.

Not surprisingly, these use patterns were moderated by the personal characteristics of the care recipients. For example, there were higher rates of use in the 85+ group (40%) compared to the 65- to 74-year-olds (32%). Similarly, there were higher rates of use by women (41%) than men (25%), higher rates for those living alone (49%) than those living with others (26%), and higher rates for those with three or more ADL difficulties (47%) than those with only IADL problems (30%). These use patterns suggest that preventive interventions must be targeted and directed to reflect the diversity of older adult consumers and the varying risk patterns associated with different patterns of aging (Rodeheaver & Datan, 1988).

Whereas Short and Leon (1990) focused on a wide range of community services, George (1992) recently reviewed community and home care specifically for mentally ill older adults. She noted that despite research and treatment advances, our "mental health delivery system is underfunded and underutilized" (p. 793). The general medical sector (e.g., primary care physicians), rather than mental health specialists, provides a large portion of diagnostic and treatment services for older adults who seek outpatient mental health care (George, Blazer, Winfield-Laird, Leaf, & Fishbach, 1988; Leaf et al., 1988). General physicians often do not recognize psychological symptoms in older adults and are less likely to refer them for treatment, compared with younger adults, even with equivalent mental symptoms (e.g., Kucharski, White, & Schratz, 1979; Rapp, Parisi, Walsh, & Wallace, 1988). In short, primary care physicians play a central role in treating mental disorders of older adults, even though they are not skilled at detection and appropriate treatment of older adults' mental disorders (Waxman & Carner, 1984).

Implications for Prevention

Several lessons for prevention emerge from these patterns of formal community service provision. First, the current service array reaches a minority of older adults in need of services. Second, the majority of the services received are provided in the older adult's home. Both of these elements suggest that traditional models of service delivery (i.e., the professional in an office, waiting for clients to seek service) are inadequate for effectively providing community services to older adults. We must develop, implement, and evaluate alternative models better suited to the opportunities and constraints of older adults' lives.

A third lesson is clear from these service patterns: The majority of community services for older adults are provided by paraprofessionals or by professionals without specialized training in geriatrics or gerontology. Again, this suggests the importance of "leveraging" gerontological expertise by providing consultation and training to those direct-service providers and their immediate supervisors. In this way, gerontologists can collaborate with those on the front line to avoid inappropriate treatment and excess disability.

We also have much to learn from those impaired older adults who do not use formal services. We must understand the individual resilience of older adults and the contexts of their lives that allow them to face the challenges of later life without formal service use. We can learn much from these individuals that can help shape effective and supportive contexts for their age-peers.

Closely linked to assessing the strengths and weaknesses of those who do not use formal services is the important task of assessing the optimal combination of formal and informal services for community-dwelling older adults. We need to know more about the dynamic and interactive roles of formal and informal sources of support and care for older adults. This knowledge can then be used more effectively to provide a range of preventive services for the range of difficulties that some older adults and their families encounter.

Continuing Care Retirement Communities: Successful Aging?

What Is Successful Aging?

For more than a decade, gerontological researchers have called for a shift in emphasis from "normal" or "usual" aging to "successful" aging (e.g., Baltes, 1987; Baltes & Baltes, 1990b; Baltes & Schaie, 1973; Kahn, 1983; Rowe & Kahn, 1987). Rowe and Kahn (1987) summarized the distinction between these two emphases: "Within the category of normal aging, a distinction can be made between usual aging, in which extrinsic factors heighten the effects of aging alone, and successful aging, in which extrinsic factors play a neutral or positive role" (p. 143). Rowe and Kahn argued that the earlier emphasis on usual aging neglected the substantial heterogeneity of older adults and stressed the average age-related losses of capacity and functioning found in the elderly. In contrast, they suggested that a focus on successful aging redirects attention to the limits of functioning in later life and the conditions that allow for continued maintenance of capacity and functioning.

The emphasis on successful aging has generated both critical debate (e.g., Cohler, 1992; Cole, 1991) and empirical inquiry (e.g., Roos & Havens, 1991). At the same time, there has been a lack of consensus regarding the criteria for gauging "success."

On one hand, theorists like Baltes and Baltes (1990a) suggest a multi-criteria approach that includes basic biological functioning (e.g., length of life and biological health) and psychological functioning (mental health), and positive aspects of personal agency (e.g., cognitive efficacy, social competence and productivity, personal control, and life satisfaction). In contrast, others (e.g., Roos & Havens, 1991) have defined successful aging as the absence of service receipt, ADL dependencies, or cognitive impairment.

Baltes and Baltes (1990b) suggested that successful aging can most usefully be viewed as a process of selective optimization with compensation. This view emphasizes both the individual's role in selectively optimizing functioning and the role of the social environment that exacerbates the deficits of aging or compensates for losses, while allowing the individual to continue to maximize functioning.

CCRCs: One Setting for Successful Aging

Continuing care retirement communities (CCRCs), or life care communities, offer an excellent example of the process of successful aging through selective optimization with compensation. CCRCs offer housing and essential supportive services, including a wide spectrum of health care services.

The basic feature of a life care community is the life care contract, which requires the payment of an entry fee (ranging from $35,000 to more than $100,000, depending upon the location and size of the living unit) and a monthly service charge. In exchange, the community's services are available to the resident for life, including inpatient and outpatient medical services, as well as nursing home services. In many cases, those who enter CCRCs exchange home equity for long-term care equity.

Retirement communities based on the life care concept have existed in various forms throughout history, but they have grown in popularity since the 1960s. Currently, there are over 300 communities in the United States providing variations on the basic life care concept.

Recent studies (e.g., Tell, Cohen, Larson, & Batten, 1987) suggest that older adults choose CCRCs for two major reasons: economic and social. The economic benefit is that by paying the one-time entry fee and assuming a predictable monthly fee, the older adult who chooses a life care community ensures that, if needed, high-quality long-term care will be available at an affordable price and in predictable circumstances. The social benefit of a CCRC is that it offers a convenient pool of other old people as potential friends and confidantes, in addition to those already developed.

Recent surveys have documented that older adults who live in CCRCs are a select group, both economically and socially (e.g., Cohen, Tell, Greenberg, & Wallack, 1987; Tell et al., 1987). Cohen et al., for example, suggested that a little less than 10% of elders could afford to dedicate both the entry fee and monthly fees to health care costs. Although these characteristics may make CCRC residents inappropriate for studying issues of "usual" aging, the same characteristics make them particularly appropriate for investigating processes of successful aging.

The Penn State Study of Life Transition to a CCRC

Rowe and Kahn (1987) suggested that research on successful aging should pursue three steps: Concentrate on understanding transitions in later life; assess the single and combined influence of "extrinsic factors" (e.g., personal autonomy and social support) on successful aging; and explore links between and among psychological and physiological levels of functioning.

The process of entering a CCRC offers an opportunity to study successful aging on both an individual and an aggregate level. CCRCs attract well-educated, relatively healthy, economically advantaged elders who are concerned with finding a setting that will be socially supportive while providing a range of supportive health and social services. In short, entrance to a CCRC is a case example of selective optimization with compensation. As such, it offers a good opportunity to study the process of successful aging. That opportunity is enhanced by the likelihood that not all residents in CCRCs will age successfully.

Our research group at Penn State has been carrying out a short-term longitudinal study of physiological reactivity and psychological adjustment among a sample of older adults who are experiencing the major life transition of moving into a CCRC (Reid, Smyer, Susman, & Zarit, 1993; Susman, Smyer, Reid, & Zarit, 1992). We are interested in assessing older adults' response to the stress of relocation, as well as their reaction to a proximal stressor within the interview.

Our sample was recruited during the opening of a CCRC. Residents were interviewed four times over 21 months. The first assessment took place within 2 weeks of moving into the CCRC, and the second interview was 3 months later. In all interviews, participants' current mental health functioning and life satisfaction were assessed with standardized measures: the Center for Epidemiological Studies Depression Scale (CES-D) (Radloff, 1977); the Brief Symptom Inventory (BSI) (Derogatis & Spencer, 1982); and the Affect Balance Scale (Bradburn, 1969). Salivary cortisol levels were used to assess participant's physiological reactivity because the reliability and validity of salivary cortisol as a measure of the hypothalamic-pituitary-adrenal (HPA) axis reactivity in older adults have been established (Reid, Intrieri, Susman, & Beard, 1992).

The interviews lasted 90 minutes, on average. As part of the interview process, saliva samples were collected five times, starting at the beginning of the interview and following at 20-minute intervals. Thirty minutes into the interview, each participant was presented with 70 number addition problems from the Schaie-Thurstone Primary Mental Abilities Test (Schaie & Thurstone, 1985). This served as a proximal stressor.

Several important results have emerged from our analysis of the first two times of measurement (see Reid et al., 1993, for more details). First, our participants exhibited low levels of distress, even at the initial interview, indicating that they were coping well with the transition. Second, our respondents did react both to the stress of the interview and to the stress of the mental arithmetic. Cortisol levels changed within each interview in response to the cognitive challenge. In addition, cortisol levels were consistently lower at the 3-month follow-up assessment, indicating perhaps adjustment to both the CCRC and the interview itself. Third, there were significant relationships among physiological reactivity, as measured by salivary cortisol and indices of mental health. These findings extend earlier work that linked hypercortisolism and depression, particularly melancholia (Gold, Goodwin, & Chrousos, 1988); however, in our sample adjustment scores were well below levels associated with a clinical diagnosis of depression. These results suggest, therefore, an extension of physiological processes across the continuum of depression among relatively healthy elders. Fourth, although cortisol levels were contemporaneously related to mental health and life satisfaction, HPA reactivity at the initial interview failed to predict mental health and life satisfaction at the 3-month follow-up. This suggests, perhaps, that cortisol reactivity reflects a state (instead of a trait-like) characteristic among older adults.

Finally, when our sample was divided between those who were consistently reactive to the proximal stressor and those who either were inconsistent or showed no reactivity, the consistently reactive participants showed greater symptoms of emotional distress. These data are consistent with recent suggestions regarding individual differences in HPA axis activation (Berger, Krieg, Bossert, Schreiber, & von Zerssen, 1988) and suggest that failure to regulate HPA axis activity may indicate a risk status for some members of this "successfully aging" sample.

Implications for Prevention

Our research in CCRCs underscores several important themes for prevention work. First, the development and implementation of a CCRC can be viewed as a preventive intervention aimed at providing a context for successful aging. Second, even among these well-educated and healthy older adults, there is an indication of the initial stress of relocation, even to a community they have freely chosen! Third, our data remind us of the importance of individual differences among older adults, even within the somewhat narrow range of functioning represented in CCRCs. Clearly, becoming a resident does not guarantee "successful aging." Risk status in these circumstances may be reflected in self-regulation failures rather than overt pathology. Fourth, the results remind us again of the reciprocal relationship between mental and physical functioning among older adults (Cohen, 1992). Preventive efforts, therefore, must take these relationships into account when defining the target populations and when defining the measures of success. Finally, these preliminary results suggest that we should explore more fully what it is about CCRCs, the older adults who live in them, and the staff who work in them that produces "successful" outcomes for older adults. Lessons from this "end" of the aging distribution may have important relevance for prevention programming across the distribution of aging populations.

Discussion and Conclusions

This chapter is intended to be illustrative of the range of issues that emerge in a consideration of the role of formal supports for older adults. It is designed to reflect the range of functioning exhibited by older adults (from significant mental and physical impairment among nursing home residents to the functioning of CCRC residents). It is also designed to reflect the range of preventive strategies that can be linked to formal services (from tertiary prevention in nursing homes to primary prevention in the creation of CCRCs).

A major theme underlying this discussion is the partial success of formal services in reaching older adults. For example, we know that for every institutionalized older adult, there are another two equally impaired older adults in the community. Similarly, we know that a sizable minority of impaired elders is receiving neither formal nor informal services.

Another counterpoint to this discussion is the link between formal and informal services. Although my focus has been on formal services, clearly the two are linked in the lives of older adults. For example, family members are often centrally involved in the decision to institutionalize an older relative, and they continue to be involved in the daily life of nursing home residents (Smyer et al., 1988). Similarly, community-dwelling elders rely more heavily upon informal sources of support than upon formal services (Short & Leon, 1990).

Finally, what is offered here is a cross-sectional view, representing current service arrays and service realities in the United States. Some have argued that demographic changes and changing rates of mortality and morbidity may very well change the availability of services for older adults (e.g., Olshansky, Rudberg, Carnes, Cassel, & Brody, 1991; Schneider & Guralnik, 1990) and affect our ability to pay for them (e.g., Mendelson & Schwartz, 1993). Projections of individual inability to pay for long-term care (e.g., Zedlewski & McBride, 1992), linked with projections of substantial increases in public expenditures for both community and institutional care (e.g., Wiener & Hanley, 1992), have led to discussions of rationing or greater flexibility in the use of benefits (e.g., Callahan, 1987, 1993). We can anticipate that the shape and scope of formal services for older adults will change along with the changing cohorts of elders. Presumably, however, the challenge for prevention professionals will remain constant—to specify conditions under which preventive interventions can have their optimal effects for older adults and their families.

Note

1. Dr. Lawrence Myers has correctly pointed out that the Gaussian curve is used to reflect the continuous distribution of random variables. In this discussion, the shape of the distribution is used for discussion purposes, without the assumption of underlying random variation. In fact, much of the chapter focuses on the nonrandom pattern of service provision for older adults.

References

Baltes, P. B. (1987). Theoretical propositions of life-span developmental psychology: On the dynamics of growth and decline. *Developmental Psychology, 23,* 611-626.

Baltes, P. B., & Baltes, M. M. (1990a). Psychological perspectives on successful aging: The model of selective optimization with compensation. In P. B. Baltes & M. M. Baltes (Eds.), *Successful aging: Perspectives from the behavioral sciences* (pp. 1-34). Cambridge, UK: Cambridge University Press.

Baltes, P. B., & Baltes, M. M. (Eds.). (1990b). *Successful aging: Perspectives from the behavioral sciences.* Cambridge, UK: Cambridge University Press.

Baltes, P. B., & Schaie, K. W. (Eds.). (1973). *Life-span developmental psychology: Personality and socialization.* New York: Academic Press.

Berger, M., Krieg, C., Bossert, S., Schreiber, W., & von Zerssen, D. (1988). Past and present strategies of research on the HPA-axis in psychiatry. *Acta Psychiatrica Scandinavica, 341*(Suppl.), 112-125.

Bowers, B., & Becker, M. (1992). Nurse's aides in nursing homes: The relationship between organization and quality. *The Gerontologist, 32,* 360-366.

Bradburn, N. M. (1969). *The structure of psychological well-being.* Chicago: Aldine.

Brannon, D. (1992). Toward second-generation nursing home research. *The Gerontologist, 32,* 293-294.

Brannon, D., & Streit, A. (1990). *Job redesign manual for nursing homes.* University Park: Pennsylvania State University, College of Health and Human Development.

Burns, B. J., Wagner, R., Taube, J. E., Magaziner, J., Permutt, T., & Landerman, L. R. (1993). Mental health service use by the elderly in nursing homes. *American Journal of Public Health, 83*(3), 331-337.

Callahan, D. (1987). *Setting limits.* New York: Simon & Schuster.

Callahan, D. (1993). Caring and curing: A Medicare proposal. *Hastings Center Report, 23*(3), 18-19.

Cantor, M. H. (1992, November). *Some thoughts on measuring social supports.* Paper presented at the Workshop of the Minority Task Force on Aging, 45th Annual Scientific Meeting of the Gerontological Society of America, Washington, DC.

Cassel, C. K., Rudberg, M. A., & Olshansky, S. J. (1992). The price of success: Health care in an aging society. *Health Affairs, 11*(2), 87-99.

Cohen, G. (1993). Comprehensive assessment: Capturing strengths, not just weaknesses. *Generations, 17*(1), 47-50.

Cohen, G. D. (1992). The future of mental health and aging. In J. E. Birren, R. B. Sloane, & G. D. Cohen (Eds.), *Handbook of mental health and aging* (pp. 893-914). San Diego: Academic Press.

Cohen, M. A., Tell, E. J., Greenberg, J. N., & Wallack, S. S. (1987). The financial capacity of the elderly to insure for long-term care. *The Gerontologist, 27,* 494-501.

Cohler, B. J. (1992, December). The myth of successful aging. *Readings: A Journal of Reviews and Commentary in Mental Health,* pp. 18-22.

Cohn, M. D., Horgas, A. L., & Marsiske, M. (1990). Evaluation of a behavior management training program for nursing home caregivers. *Journal of Gerontological Nursing, 16*(11), 21-25.

Cole, T. R. (1991). *The journey of life: A cultural history of aging in America.* New York: Cambridge University Press.

Derogatis, L. R., & Spencer, P. N. (1982). *The Brief Symptom Inventory (BSI): Administration and procedures manual—I.* Baltimore: The Johns Hopkins University School of Medicine, Clinical Psychometric Research Unit.

Finkel, S. I., & Cohen, G. (1982). The mental health of the aging. *The Gerontologist, 22,* 227-228.

Foster, J. R., & Cataldo, J. K. (1993). Prediction of first episode of clinical depression in patients newly admitted to a medical long-term care facility: Findings from a prospective study. *International Journal of Geriatric Psychiatry, 8,* 297-304.

Gelfand, D. E. (1988). *The aging network: Programs and services* (3rd ed.). New York: Springer.

George, L. (1992). Community and home care for mentally ill older adults. In J. E. Birren, R. B. Sloane, & G. D. Cohen (Eds.), *Handbook of mental health and aging* (pp. 793-813). San Diego: Academic Press.

George, L. K., Blazer, D. G., Winfield-Laird, I., Leaf, P. J., & Fishbach, R. L. (1988). Psychiatric disorders and mental health service use in later life. In J. A. Brody & G. L. Maddox (Eds.), *Epidemiology and aging* (pp. 189-221). New York: Springer.

Gold, P. W., Goodwin, F. K., & Chrousos, G. P. (1988). Clinical and biochemical manifestations of depression. *New England Journal of Medicine, 319,* 413-420.

Hudson, R. B. (1993). Social contingencies, the aged, and public policy. *Milbank Quarterly, 71*(2), 252-277.

Hudson, R. B. (in press). The Older Americans Act and the defederalization of community-based care. In P. K. H. Kim (Ed.), *Services to the aged: Public policies and programs.* New York: Garland.

Hultsch, D. F., & Dixon, R. A. (1990). Learning and memory in aging. In J. E. Birren & K. W. Schaie (Eds.), *Handbook of the psychology of aging* (3rd. ed., pp. 258-274). San Diego: Academic Press.

Jackson, J. S., Antonucci, T. C., & Gibson, R. C. (1990). Cultural, racial, and ethnic minority influences on aging. In J. E. Birren & K. W. Schaie (Eds.), *Handbook of the psychology of aging* (3rd ed., pp. 103-123). San Diego: Academic Press.

Kahn, R. L. (1983). Productive behavior: Assessment, determinants, and effects. *Journal of the American Geriatrics Society, 3*(12), 750-757.

Kastenbaum, R., & Candy, S. E. (1973). The 4% fallacy: A methodological and empirical critique of extended care facility population statistics. *International Journal of Aging and Human Development, 4,* 15-21.

Kemp, B. J., & Mitchell, J. M. (1992). Functional impairment in geriatric mental health. In J. E. Birren, R. B. Sloane, & G. D. Cohen (Eds.), *Handbook of mental health and aging* (pp. 671-697). San Diego: Academic Press.

Kemper, P., & Murtaugh, C. M. (1991). Lifetime use of nursing home care. *New England Journal of Medicine, 324,* 595-600.

Kivnick, H. Q. (1993). Everyday mental health: A guide to assessing life strengths. *Generations, 17*(1), 13-20.

Kruzich, J. M., Clinton, J. F., & Kelber, S. T. (1992). Personal and environmental influences on nursing home satisfaction. *The Gerontologist, 32,* 342-350.

Kucharski, L. T., White, R. M., & Schratz, M. (1979). Age bias, referral for psychological assistance, and the private physician. *Journal of Gerontology, 34,* 423-428.

Lair, T., & Lefkowitz, D. (1990). *Mental health and functional status of residents of nursing and personal care homes* (DHHS Publication No. PHS 90-3470, National Medical Expenditure Survey Research Findings 7). Rockville, MD: Public Health Service, Agency for Health Care Policy and Research.

Lair, T., & Smyer, M. A. (1993). *The impact of OBRA 1987 preadmission screening: A simulation from the National Medical Expenditure Survey.* Manuscript submitted for publication.

Leaf, P. J., Berkman, C. S., Weissman, M. M., Holzer, C. E., Tischler, G. L., & Myers, J. K. (1988). The epidemiology of late-life depression. In J. A. Brody & G. L. Maddox (Eds.), *Epidemiology and aging* (pp. 117-133). New York: Springer.

Mendelson, D. N., & Schwartz, W. B. (1993). The effects of aging and population growth on health care costs. *Health Affairs, 12*(1), 119-125.

Morse, C. K. (1993). Does variability increase with age? An archival study of cognitive measures. *Psychology and Aging, 8*(2), 156-164.

National Nursing Home Survey. (1985). *Vital and health statistics* (DHHS Publication No. PHS 89-1758, National Health Survey Series 13, No. 97). Washington, DC: Government Printing Office.

Olshansky, S. J., Rudberg, M. A., Carnes, B. A., Cassel, C. K., & Brody, J. A. (1991). Trading off longer life for worsening health: The expansion of morbidity hypothesis. *Journal of Aging and Health, 3*(2), 194-216.

Radloff, L. S. (1977). A self-report depression scale for research in the general population. *Applied Psychological Measurement, 1,* 385-401.

Rapp, S. R., Parisi, S. A., Walsh, D. A., & Wallace, C. E. (1988). Detecting depression in elderly medical inpatients. *Journal of Consulting and Clinical Psychology, 56,* 509-513.

Reid, J. D., Intrieri, R. C., Susman, E. J., & Beard, J. (1992). The relationship of serum and salivary cortisol levels in a sample of healthy elderly. *Journal of Gerontology: Psychological Sciences, 47,* P176-P179.

Reid, J. D., Smyer, M. A., Susman, E. J., & Zarit, S. H. (1993). *Physiological reactivity, mental health, and successful aging: Longitudinal predictors of adjustment to life transitions.* Manuscript submitted for publication.

Rodeheaver, D., & Datan, N. (1988). The challenge of double jeopardy: Toward a mental health agenda for aging women. *American Psychologist, 43*(8), 648-654.

Roos, N. P., & Havens, B. (1991). Predictors of successful aging: A twelve-year study of Manitoba elderly. *American Journal of Public Health, 81*(1), 63-68.

Rowe, J. N., & Kahn, R. L. (1987). Human aging: Usual and successful. *Science, 237,* 143-149.

Schaie, K. W., & Thurstone, L. L. (1985). *Adult mental abilities test: Form OA.* Palo Alto, CA: Consulting Psychologists Press.

Schneider, E. L., & Guralnik, J. M. (1990). The aging of America: Impact on health care costs. *Journal of the American Medical Association, 263,* 2335-2340.

Sherman, E. (1993). Mental health and successful adaptation in later life. *Generations, 17*(1), 43-46.

Short, P. F., & Leon, J. (1990). *Use of home and community services by persons ages 65 and older with functional difficulties* (DHHS Publication No. PHS 90-3466, National Medical Expenditure Survey Research Findings 5). Rockville, MD: Public Health Service, Agency for Health Care Policy and Research.

Smyer, M. A. (1989). Nursing homes as a setting for psychological practice: Public policy perspectives. *American Psychologist, 44,* 1307-1314.

Smyer, M. A., Brannon, D., & Cohn, M. D. (1992). Improving nursing home care through training and job redesign. *The Gerontologist, 33,* 327-333.

Smyer, M. A., Cohn, M. D., & Brannon, D. (1988). *Mental health consultation in nursing homes.* New York: New York University Press.

Smyer, M. A., Shea, D., & Streit, A. (1994). The provision and use of mental health services in nursing homes: Results from the National Medical Expenditure Survey. *American Journal of Public Health, 84*(2), 284-287.

Smyer, M. A., & Walls, C. T. (1994). Design and evaluation of interventions in nursing homes. In C. B. Fisher & R. M. Lerner (Eds.), *Applied developmental psychology* (pp. 475-501). Cambridge, MA: McGraw-Hill.

Spore, D. L., Smyer, M. A., & Cohn, M. D. (1991). Assessing nursing assistants' knowledge of behavioral approaches to mental health problems. *The Gerontologist, 31,* 309-317.

Stewart, A. L., Greenfield, S., Hays, R. D., Wells, K., Rogers, W. H., Berry, S. D., McGlynn, E. A., & Ware, J. E. (1989). Functional status and well-being of patients with chronic conditions: Results from the Medical Outcomes Study. *Journal of the American Medical Association, 262,* 907-913.

Strahan, G. W., & Burns, B. J. (1991). *Mental illness in nursing homes: United States, 1985* (Vital Health Statistics, Vol. 13, No. 105). Washington, DC: Government Printing Office.

Susman, E. J., Smyer, M. A., Reid, J. D., & Zarit, S. H. (1992, August). *Successful aging: Emotional and hormonal processes in adaptation.* Paper presented at the annual meeting of the American Psychological Association, Washington, DC.

Tarlov, A., Ware, J. E., Jr., Greenfield, S., Nelson, E. C., Perrin, E., & Zubkoff, M. (1989). The Medical Outcomes Study: An application of methods for monitoring the results of medical care. *Journal of the American Medical Association, 262,* 925-930.

Tell, E. J., Cohen, M. A., Larson, M. J., & Batten, H. L. (1987). Assessing the elderly's preferences for life care retirement options. *The Gerontologist, 27,* 503-509.

Tornstam, L. (1992). The quo vadis of gerontology: On the scientific paradigm of gerontology. *The Gerontologist, 32,* 318-326.

Waxman, H. M., & Carner, E. A. (1984). Physicians' recognition, diagnosis, and treatment of mental disorders in elderly medical patients. *The Gerontologist, 24,* 593-597.

Wiener, J. M., & Hanley, R. J. (1992). Caring for the disabled elderly: There's no place like home. In S. M. Shortell & U. E. Reinhardt (Eds.), *Improving health policy and management: Nine critical research issues for the 1990s* (pp. 75-110). Ann Arbor, MI: Health Administration Press.

Willis, S. L., & Schaie, K. W. (1993). Everyday cognition: Taxonomic and methodological considerations. In J. M. Puckett & H. W. Reese (Eds.), *Life-span developmental psychology: Mechanisms of everyday cognition* (pp. 33-53). Hillsdale, NJ: Lawrence Erlbaum.

Zedlewski, S. R., & McBride, T. D. (1992). The changing profile of the elderly: Effects on future long-term care needs and financing. *Milbank Quarterly, 70*(2), 247-275.

11

Stress and Well-Being in Later Life: Using Research Findings to Inform Intervention Design

Neal Krause

This chapter reviews selected findings from the stress literature to show how our understanding of the stress process may be used to guide preventive mental health interventions for older adults. Perhaps more important, an effort will be made to identify weak points or gaps that must be addressed in the knowledge base so that more focused and more effective intervention programs may be developed.

Given the allotted space, it will not be possible to review all of the ways in which stress research can inform intervention design. As a result, an emphasis will be placed on one fundamental area, whereas others will be examined only briefly. In particular, this chapter will focus on a necessary first step in developing any intervention program—determining who is at risk. As Sandler and his associates point out, there are two reasons why this emphasis may be especially important (Sandler, Gersten, Reynolds, Kallgran, & Ramirez, 1988). First, when the target group is not defined clearly, the intervention will be ineffective because services will be offered to those who are not in need. This problem has obvious cost implications as well. Second, the more imprecise the target group, the more difficult it is to make pragmatic program decisions, such as defining the requirements for staff.

The discussion that follows begins with a brief overview of problems in stress measurement. The main theme is that standard ways of assessing life events will not yield the type of precise information needed for improving intervention design; we need to know much more about the behavior of individual stressors for this purpose. Next, research on chronic financial strain is used as a vehicle for identifying the type of detailed knowledge that can be used to better serve the mental health needs of our aging population.

Problems in Stress Measurement

The inclusion of a chapter on stress and well-being in this volume indicates that many feel that there is an important relationship between these constructs, and that a preventive intervention based on stress research will provide an effective way of improving the mental health status of older adults. This assumption places a heavy burden on those who work in the stress field. Even casual readers of the stress literature realize that not every person who is confronted by a stressful experience subsequently suffers from psychological distress or some other mental health problem; in fact, most do not. This means that we are looking at a complex process and that basing an intervention simply on the notion that stress causes mental health problems is not likely to be fruitful. Knowing that there is a simple bivariate relationship between stress and well-being provides little guidance for defining the target group. Stress is ubiquitous: There is not a single elderly person who has not experienced the loss of a loved one or been confronted by some other significant life event. Stress is simply a fundamental part of life. If stress is everywhere and all people encounter a diverse array of stressful experiences, then we must begin to develop a rational basis for identifying those who are at greatest risk. One way to approach this problem is to reconsider carefully how stress has been measured in most studies.

Historically, there has been a major emphasis in survey research on measuring stressful life events with checklists of varying lengths that contain a wide array of experiences ranging from the death of a spouse to getting a traffic ticket. These events are either added together or differentially weighted in some fashion in order to arrive at a summary score reflecting cumulative exposure to stress (see Sandler & Guenther, 1985, for a detailed discussion of these weighting schemes). As George (1989) pointed out, this is good and useful information. However, we pay a certain price for relying on this aggregate approach.

The intent of this chapter is to show that the aggregate approach to assessing stressful life events produces a loss of precision or specificity in our knowledge of how stress operates, and that this in turn limits our ability to identify what people are at risk and how we might develop effective intervention strategies to help them. In particular, the remainder of this chapter is devoted to showing how aggregate or cumulative measures of stress limit our knowledge in four key ways. First, they make it difficult to identify the genesis or origins of stressful experiences. Second, they make it difficult to discern the course or natural history of events through time. Third, they tend to obscure the relationship between stress and key coping resources—especially social support. Finally, they make it difficult to delineate clearly the effects of stress on mental health outcomes.

In order to demonstrate the need for a more focused approach, the discussion below will be devoted entirely to one particular type of stressful experience—chronic financial strain. The intent is to use research on this stressor as a forum for pinpointing the type of detailed knowledge that will be helpful in narrowing down the task of defining groups at risk and in developing intervention strategies that are focused more specifically on their needs.

Financial Strain in Later Life

There are two reasons that financial strain was selected to illustrate the need for more focused knowledge on the stress process. First, research indicates that financial strain may have an especially noxious impact on older adults. In addition, there is some evidence that many elderly people are exposed to significant financial problems.

Before a discussion of research on the impact and prevalence of financial problems in later life, it may be helpful to define this key stressor and briefly review how it has been measured. Generally speaking, researchers tend to work with one of three types of stressful experiences. These stressors are referred to as stressful life events, chronic strains, and daily hassles. Essentially, these types of stress are thought to vary in intensity and duration.

Following the definition devised by George (1989), *stressful life events* are identifiable discrete changes that disrupt usual behavioral patterns and threaten well-being. They can be clearly dated in terms of onset, and they tend to have a fixed duration. The death of a loved one would be a good example of this type of stressful experience.

In contrast, *chronic strains* are thought to be persistent and ongoing, and it is assumed that they exert a more deleterious impact on well-being than stressful life events. Chronic financial strain—the example used in this chapter—would fit in here. Finally, *daily hassles* are defined as ordinary and generally less stressful experiences that are encountered in the normal course of daily living. Hassles checklists typically include things like getting caught in traffic jams (see, for example, Zautra, Guarnaccia, Reich, & Dohrenwend, 1988).

Unfortunately, a standardized measure of chronic financial strain has not been developed or accepted by all investigators. Nevertheless, it may be helpful to examine one widely used index of financial strain so that the fundamental nature of this ongoing problem may be illustrated more clearly. This measure, which was developed by Ilfeld (1976), is contained in Table 11.1.

Two points should be emphasized about these indicators. First, the items deal with subjective evaluations of one's own financial state—as is evident in the phrase, "How much difficulty do you have . . . ?" This has led some

TABLE 11.1 An Example of How Financial Strain Is Measured

1. How much difficulty do you have in meeting the monthly payments on your bills?
2. In general, how do your finances work out at the end of the month? Do you find that you usually end up with some money left over, just enough money to make ends meet, or not enough money to make ends meet?
3. At the present time, are you able to afford a home or apartment that is large enough and comfortable enough for you?
4. How often does it happen that you do not have enough money to afford:

   A. the kind of food you need?

   B. the kind of medical care you need?

   C. the kind of clothing you need?

SOURCE: Reproduced with permission of author and publisher from: Ilfeld, F. W., Jr. Characteristics of current social stressors. *Psychological Reports*, 1976, 39, 1231-1247. © *Psychological Reports* 1976.

investigators to argue that these measures are confounded with psychological distress. However, research by Krause (1987) and others suggests that this may not be the case.

Second, nothing is contained in the wording of these questions to determine whether financial problems are actually continuous and ongoing. Even though it is possible to address the issue of chronicity by asking the same questions repeatedly over long periods of time, this has rarely been done in the literature. The issue of subjectivity and chronicity will be examined in greater detail at a later point in this chapter.

There is now fairly substantial evidence that financial strain tends to exert a much more negative impact on symptoms of psychological distress than many other types of life events. For example, data from a recent nationwide survey suggest that the impact of financial strain on depressive symptoms is four times stronger than the corresponding effect of the death of a family member (Krause, 1991). In fact, the only stressor that appears to exert a greater impact on well-being is a physical health problem. Unfortunately, there are clear concerns about the direction of causality between measures of health and measures of depressive symptoms (e.g., Lurie, 1987).

It is also important to emphasize that the noxious effects of financial strain have been observed with remarkable consistency in a wide range of diverse ethnic and cultural groups, including older white Americans (Krause, 1991), elderly black Americans (Krause, 1993b), older adults of Hispanic heritage (Krause & Goldenhar, 1992), elderly people in Japan (Krause, Jay, & Liang, 1991), and older adults in the People's Republic of China (Krause & Liang, 1993). This brief overview suggests that if we are going to invest scarce resources in stress interventions and if all stressors do not affect well-being equally, then it makes sense to focus on those types of events that are likely to do the most damage. Financial strain appears to be one such stressor.

Although evidence of the impact of chronic financial strain is relatively straightforward, it is more difficult to discuss the prevalence of this stressor in later life. This problem arises because measures of financial strain are inherently subjective and have not been standardized or normed in the elderly population. Nevertheless, it is important to examine this issue because if a stressor is not encountered by a significant number of older adults, then it is more difficult to justify investing scarce resources in its eradication or treatment.

In order to get a handle on the prevalence of financial strain in later life, it may be helpful to assume that financial strain is somehow linked to income so that those elderly people with less money are more likely to report experiencing chronic financial problems than older adults who enjoy a better income. If this is true, those elderly people who live below the poverty level should be more likely to be exposed to ongoing financial difficulties. Fortunately, there are plenty of data on the objective financial status of older adults in this country. For example, Chen (1991) reported that in 1989, approximately 11.4% of all persons aged 65 and over lived below the poverty level. However, the poverty level is a somewhat arbitrary cut-off point, and one could easily argue that those just above the poverty level are in many ways no better off than those below the poverty level. Chen (1991) provided some useful information on these "near poor." He defined this group as those people making between 100% and 125% of the poverty-level income. Chen (1991) indicated that in 1989 an additional 7.7% of the elderly were near-poor. Taken together, these data suggest that 19.1% of the aged population (fully 5.6 million people) live in or near poverty. Although these data would appear to suggest that financial strain is fairly widespread in later life, the validity of this conclusion rests on the assumption that financial strain and income are correlated highly. It is important to examine this assumption carefully because in the process of addressing the issue, it will be possible to explore the genesis of financial problems among the elderly.

The Genesis of Financial Strain

On the surface, the argument that financial strain is related to income appears to be intuitively pleasing. However, it is surprising to find that the relationship between these measures is often overlooked in the gerontological literature. One study by Krause and Baker (1992) indicated that the correlation between yearly family income and financial strain is statistically significant, but not as strong as might be expected. In particular, this study revealed that the correlation between these measures is −.386, which suggests that approximately 85% of the variance in perceptions of financial strain is left unexplained after the effects of yearly family income have been removed statistically. These findings reveal that perceptions of financial difficulty are clearly more than just a simple function of income and that merely focusing on those older adults with the lowest income may not necessarily be the only, or even the best, way to target an intervention. It is important to pursue this issue further because the resolution may help to identify those older adults who are at greatest risk.

The literature provides very little guidance on the genesis of financial strain, but it is possible to identify four arguments. The first simply targets income, which has been discussed above. The second focuses on the ratio of income to expenses, and the third suggests that those who are just above the poverty level may subsequently experience the greatest financial strain. The fourth indicates that perceptions of financial strain arise from social psychological processes involving social comparisons.

The financial strain items contained in Table 11.1 ask respondents whether they have enough money for things like a house, food, and clothing. In effect, these measures really ask whether a study participant's income can cover his or her essential expenses. Stated simply, these indicators imply that the ratio of income to expenses is a key component of chronic financial strain. An example may help to clarify why this may be an important factor. The financial situation of a person who earns $20,000 a year and lives alone is probably better than the financial situation of an individual who also has an income of $20,000 but must support five additional people with this revenue. This is why in any given year, the poverty threshold is made up of a range of incomes that take household composition into account.

There do not appear to be any studies in the literature that examine the interface between income, expenses, and perceptions of financial strain among older adults. Nevertheless, the information provided by this perspective may be helpful for identifying high-risk groups. This view suggests that given a limited amount of funding, it would be more beneficial to focus intervention efforts on households with high essential expenses.

Recently, Holden and Smeeding (1990) conducted research on a group of high-risk people they referred to as the "tweeners." This work has been cast specifically in a gerontological context and provides some interesting insights into the genesis of financial strain in later life.

Essentially, the tweeners are those older adults who are making too much money to qualify for means-tested entitlement benefits but who are at the same time making too little to adequately protect themselves from economic misfortune with things like proper medical insurance. In essence, the tweeners are those people positioned between the public and private income security systems. Holden and Smeeding (1990) argued that the key factor is the constant feeling of insecurity created by living with the fear of paying for an extended illness or a prolonged stay in a nursing home. They suggested that up to one fifth of all older adults and as many as one quarter of those over 75 fit into this category.

If we can assume that Holden and Smeeding's (1990) tweener criteria adequately explain the genesis of financial strain in later life, then we arrive at a very different intervention target group. Instead of focusing on those elderly people at the very bottom of the income ladder, it may be more useful to target older adults whose incomes hover just above the poverty level.

The discussion provided up to this point indicates why it is essential to have a thorough understanding of the genesis of stress in later life. Without this type of more focused knowledge, it becomes difficult to identify those who are in greatest need of preventive efforts. This point is further emphasized by reviewing the potential role played by social comparisons in the genesis of financial problems among the elderly.

Although there has been a good deal of research on the social comparison process in later life, some of the better work was done some time ago by Liang (Liang & Fairchild, 1979; Liang, Kahana, & Doherty, 1980). This research indicates that older people arrive at a subjective evaluation of their economic status by comparing their situation to that of their significant others. If they are doing better than their peers, then they tend to evaluate their economic position in a more positive way. If they are not doing as well as their significant others, however, they tend to develop more negative views of their own financial well-being. Two additional points are worth noting about this research. First, it suggests that these feelings of relative deprivation play a larger role than income in shaping perceptions of financial difficulty in later life. Second, it reveals that feelings of relative deprivation are not restricted to those with the lowest dollar income.

Up to this point, only the findings involving comparisons of self with others have been examined; however, Liang et al. (1980) also examined a second point of reference. In particular, they argued that people arrive at a sense of financial well-being by comparing their present situation to their own financial situation at an earlier point in time. In fact, the work of Liang et al. suggests that these intrapersonal comparisons have a greater impact on perceptions of financial well-being than comparisons with others.

Once again, the notion of relative deprivation and social comparison has clear implications for targeting intervention strategies. Assume for the moment that Liang et al. (1980) are correct and that self-comparisons through time are the most important source of financial strain. To the extent that this is true, interventions should be focused on those who have experienced a significant decline in their overall financial standing during some specified time period. Because such losses can occur across the full spectrum of income groups, the implication of this work for targeting interventions is quite different than the direction hinted at by the other sources (e.g., the tweeners).

When viewed from a broader perspective, the evidence presented in this section begins to illustrate how knowledge of the genesis of stressful experiences may be helpful in targeting older adults who are at risk. It is important to emphasize that the potential sources of financial strain examined above need not be mutually exclusive and that changes in the ratio of income to expenses through time can shape the types of social comparisons described by Liang et al. (1980). It should also be evident at this point that the underlying factors that give rise to perceptions of financial strain may not necessarily play a similar role in the genesis of other life events, such as bereavement. If this proves to be the case, then we must turn to other causal factors and other target groups in order to develop interventions for individuals who are exposed to different types of stressful experiences.

The Natural History of Financial Strain

The notion of comparing one's present financial position to one's own financial status at an earlier point in time serves as a convenient segue for raising some additional points about the stress process that are relevant for intervention design. Unlike the other explanations offered in the previous section, this perspective introduces a time element; it makes us realize that we must think in terms of dynamics and change. In addition, the notion of self-comparisons through time raises fundamental issues about stability and change in perceptions of financial strain. As discussed above, few researchers working with financial strain have explicitly examined whether this stressor is in fact chronic and whether it continues unabated for relatively long periods of time. Krause (1987) conducted one of the few studies to examine this issue in a sample of older adults. This study looked at the correlation between identical measures of financial strain that were administered twice—once at baseline and again 18 months later. The two measures were indeed correlated highly, but it is not clear whether 18 months is a sufficient amount of time to evaluate chronicity. Obviously other so-called stressful events (e.g., bereavement) may have effects that last this long.

One way to avoid the problem identified in the work of Krause (1987) is to delay the administration of the second measurement until a later point in time—say, 3 years after the baseline assessment. Unfortunately, there is an inherent weakness in taking this approach. The greater the distance in time between the two measurement points, the greater the likelihood that significant short-term fluctuations may go undetected. Once again, the work of Holden is useful for showing how this can happen in the financial realm (Holden, Burkhauser, & Myers, 1986).

Essentially, Holden et al. (1986) charted income levels for older adults over a 10-year period in order to determine changes in the risk of slipping below the poverty level through time. The findings from this complex study suggest that far from being stable, the older population undergoes substantial movement into and out of poverty through time. In order to illustrate this point more clearly, it may be helpful to focus briefly on the data for married couples only. Holden et al. (1986) reported that standard cross-sectional data reveal that at any one point in time, approximately 9% of all older adults who are married have household incomes below the poverty level. Following income fluctuations over a 10-year period, however, they found that about 21% of the continuously married couples spent at least some time below the poverty level.

The dynamic aspect of the work by Holden et al. (1986) is especially intriguing. They found that of those couples who slipped below the poverty level at some point, fully 88% climbed back out of poverty within the next 6 years. Of all intact couples who exited poverty, however, approximately 20% reentered poverty during the following period. On the basis of these as well as other data, Holden et al. (1986) concluded that poverty is a much less permanent state for either married or widowed older adults than cross-sectional data would suggest.

If financial strain is a function of self-comparisons through time and one's financial status fluctuates or goes through cycles, then we arrive at a very dynamic view of financial strain that has not appeared previously in the gerontological literature. This new perspective suggests that older adults may slip in and out of periods of financial strain through time, and that rather than continuing unabated, financial strain may be cyclical or vacillating.

Two factors, however, must be considered in the interpretation of these data. First, the analyses conducted by Holden et al. (1986) focused solely on whether someone was either above or below the poverty level and never indicated the precise dollar amount of these economic swings. It is possible that those who move above and below the poverty level hover within a fairly restricted income range. Meanwhile, perhaps even minor fluctuations may be sufficient to cause changes in welfare benefits, thereby promoting perceptions of financial strain (see the discussion of the tweeners above). Second, Holden et al.'s findings have implications for the way we conceptualize financial strain. They suggest that it is entirely possible that there is more than one type of financial strain and that although some people may experience truly chronic financial problems that last their entire lifetime (e.g., the very poor), others may be exposed to a more episodic type of financial strain that fluctuates over the life course.

Assume for the moment that financial strain is truly cyclical or episodic in nature. If so, we are faced with a whole host of factors that can have an important bearing on intervention design. At the broadest level, this realization forces us to bring the issue of timing into the foreground during intervention planning. We must know whether a stressor is truly chronic or changing, and if it is episodic, we must know when each period begins and how long each cycle lasts.

Focusing more explicitly on the notion of timing makes it possible to bring in threads of research on the stress process that have rarely been considered by many investigators. A small but growing literature suggests that the adaptation of coping strategies and the utilization of coping resources may change over the natural course of a stressor. Evidence for this comes from two streams of research that have developed largely independently of one another. Although these areas have not been subjected to careful empirical scrutiny, the possibilities they open up represent a major challenge to those interested in primary prevention.

The first line of research may be found in the work of Thomas Ashby Wills (1987), who devoted a considerable amount of attention to the social comparison process. He noted that when people are first confronted by a noxious stressor, they tend to make downward social comparisons. That is, they compare their situation to that of someone who is also experiencing the same problem but who is not doing as well as they are themselves. Wills argued that this serves to restore the bruised egos and bolster the self-esteem that is often depleted by stressful experiences.

Wills (1987) went on to point out, however, that relying on downward social comparisons does not facilitate effective adaptation. Instead, upward social comparisons are needed for this purpose. Essentially, upward social comparisons involve comparing yourself to someone who is confronted by a similar stressor but who is doing better than you are. Wills argued that this type of comparison is necessary because only by studying those who cope more effectively can we begin to figure out what we need to do to improve our own situation.

The key point to emphasize here is that downward social comparisons appear to be more useful during the early stages or phases of a stressor. Once the battered sense of self-esteem has been restored, however, people must make the transition to using upward social comparisons in order to learn how to deal more effectively with the problem that confronts them.

The second stream of research comes from a frequently overlooked paper by Jacobson (1986) on the use of social support over the course of a stressor. He argued that we must think about social support in more dynamic terms because different types of support may be helpful at different points in the natural history of a stressor. In a vein similar to Wills (1987), Jacobson (1986) pointed out that emotional support is usually most helpful during the early stages of a stressor because it helps people deal with the emotional fallout from an event. However, once emotions are under control, other types of assistance, such as tangible or informational support, are needed to provide specific guidance or a more pragmatic strategy for overcoming the stressor and repairing the damage caused by the event.

The same themes seem to emerge from the work of Wills (1987) and Jacobson (1986): People tend to deal with the emotional aspects of a stressor first, and only later do they turn to the more pragmatic confrontation of the problems created by the event and take steps to restore equilibrium. As an important corollary, both investigators noted that the length of time taken to make the transition from one state to the next is at least partially a function of the type of stressor under consideration. For example, Wills (1987) speculated that downward social comparisons are more likely to be used for a longer period of time when the stressor confronting the individual is uncontrollable and relatively enduring.

It is important to take a moment and sketch out how the work of Wills (1987) and Jacobson (1986) can be used to inform intervention design. Interventions must clearly be linked to the needs of the clients. As the research of these investigators indicates, however, the needs of clients may vary depending upon where clients are located temporally in the natural history of an event. Early in the history of a stressor, emotional support may be most useful, but later on tangible assistance may be more helpful as the client becomes more willing to take concrete steps to reconstruct his or her life.

In order to know what to do and when to do it, we must know more about the dynamic nature of the stressors that confront older adults. It is quite likely that the dynamic nature or natural history is not the same for all types of stressors. For example, we have seen some evidence that at least some older adults may experience episodes of financial strain; however, it is unlikely that bereavement follows a similar course through time. Instead, it may be more helpful to use a relatively smooth but steadily declining curve to depict the impact of losing a loved one through time. Unfortunately, outside of research on bereavement, little is known about the dynamic nature of many stressful life events. We clearly need more research that focuses on stressors as dependent variables.

Financial Strain and Social Support

Jacobson's (1986) work on social support is useful because it forces us to think more carefully about the relationship between stress and coping resources.

In particular, his work challenges the static assumptions that most investigators make about the social support process. However, this is only one of many unexamined assumptions that researchers frequently make about the process of exchanging informal social support. An additional assumption that is especially relevant for intervention design is examined below.

When discussing informal assistance that is provided by family and friends, many investigators assume implicitly that social support is stress-responsive. This means that during stressful times, older people are thought to either actively seek out or at least gratefully receive assistance from their significant others. This is sometimes referred to in the literature as the resource mobilization perspective (Alloway & Bebbington, 1987). This assumption frequently forms the basis of support groups that are designed to bolster natural support networks in the community.

The main theme to emerge from the discussion provided below is that we need to gather more specific information about the stressors confronting the target group before we develop interventions based on the assumption that older adults are ready and willing to receive assistance from their informal social support systems. Research will be reviewed briefly that suggests that this may not be true in all stressful situations and that when financial problems arise, some elderly people may even withdraw from their social networks.

Research in the United States (Krause, 1991) and Canada (Krause, 1993a) indicates that higher levels of financial strain tend to be associated with greater isolation from social network members, including family and friends. However, this work further demonstrates that other types of life events, such as bereavement, fail to have a similar effect on social isolation.

It is important to consider carefully why financial strain may erode social support networks. There are at least four possibilities, but it is hard to know which is most accurate because there is little empirical work in this area. First, the members of the current cohort of older adults may find their financial problems to be stigmatizing or embarrassing. Second, some elderly people may withdraw from their significant others when they encounter financial difficulties because they are afraid of becoming overly dependent on them or because they are worried about being able to pay back the assistance they have received.

A third explanation may be found in the work of Deborah Belle (1982). She maintained that people who are poor have social networks that are made up of people who are equally poor. Belle argues that turning to others who are also financially strapped may create feelings of resentment and the perception that older adults are burdensome. Support for Belle's observations may be found in a recent study by Krause and Liang (1993) that was conducted in the People's Republic of China (PRC). These analyses were designed to test the assumption that children in the PRC adhere strongly to the norm of filial piety, which dictates that they must provide for their aging parents if the need arises. Krause and Liang (1993) found, in accordance with this view, that as financial problems intensify, elderly people in the PRC report receiving more economic assistance from their family members. However, the data further revealed that at the same time, greater financial strain was associated with diminished emotional support as well as increased negative interaction. This means that although financial strain increased some types of assistance, it tended to erode other kinds of support at the same time. Taken as a whole, the findings from this study suggest that intergenerational support may be a mixed blessing.

The fourth reason why financial strain may lead to greater isolation from others has to do with distrust. In particular, findings from a nationwide survey by Krause (1991) indicate that those elderly people who are experiencing ongoing financial problems tend to be more distrustful of others than older adults who are not confronted by chronic financial problems. Moreover, these data reveal that other stressful events, such as bereavement, fail to exert a similar effect on distrust (a detailed theoretical rationale for the relationship between financial strain and distrust is provided by Krause, 1993a).

Taken as a whole, the literature reviewed in this section suggests that we may need to reevaluate the assumption that elderly people who are confronted by stressful situations always actively pursue and gratefully receive assistance from others. A resolution of this issue has important implications for the way that interventions are designed and promoted.

Assume for the moment that a program is being developed to help older adults cope with the effects of chronic financial strain. The main thrust of this intervention is to strengthen the natural support systems of these unfortunate elderly people. The literature discussed above indicates that it is important to know beforehand that the stressor confronting these elderly clients may be disrupting the very social networks that the program is now attempting to mobilize. Those in charge of the intervention must be prepared to deal with the feelings of burden and resentment that may be harbored by the social network members. Moreover, a plan must be devised to confront the feelings of dependency and distrust on the part of the elderly clients. Because other stressors may not have a similar effect on social networks, it is imperative that we must learn more about when to expect these kinds of problems. This sort of information cannot come from studies that examine stressors in aggregate form.

The Mental Health Effects of Financial Strain

The major thrust in this chapter has been on identifying older adults who are at risk for developing mental health problems; however, the precise nature of these psychological difficulties has not been specified clearly. The main point made in this section is that we need to know more about how the effects of stress are manifest if we are to devise more effective intervention programs. Within this context, two specific issues will be addressed. First, researchers in the life stress field have not paid sufficient attention to the task of tailoring their mental health outcome measures to the specific samples that are under investigation. Second, most investigators have not reflected carefully on what the relationship between stress and mental health problems may actually represent; most assume that stress causes mental health problems to arise where none had existed previously, but as the discussion provided later in this section will reveal, this is only one of several possibilities.

The vast majority of studies on the stress process has used depressive symptoms or some global measures of psychological distress as an outcome measure. By pursuing this approach, researchers are, in effect, assuming that this is the only way that the effects of stress manifest in older adults. Meanwhile, a study by Aneshensal and her colleagues identifies the kinds of problems that may be created by making this assumption (Aneshensal, Rutter, & Lachenbruch, 1991). Their research included adults from all age groups and focused on the Diagnostic Interview Schedule as a measure of clinical psychiatric syndromes. Financial strain was included among the stressors that were examined. Initially, when affective or anxiety disorders served as the outcome measure, the findings appeared to suggest that financial strain has a more damaging effect on women. However, when substance abuse disorder was used as the dependent variable, the differential vulnerability of women disappeared and both men and women appeared to be affected equally by ongoing financial problems.

The study by Aneshensal et al. (1991) offers at least two lessons for those seeking to design preventive mental health interventions. First, it suggests that in the process of defining who is at risk, it may not be sufficient to assume a single disorder-specific orientation. Instead, when we think about prevention, it may be more helpful to think in terms of multiple disorders that adequately capture how distress may be manifest in the groups and subgroups that will be targeted by the intervention. Second, the findings from the work of Aneshensal et al. have clear implications for the evaluation of intervention programs. Their work suggests, for example, that the effectiveness of an intervention program may be underestimated if depression is used as the sole outcome measure. Instead, it is important to also consider substance abuse if men are included in the target group.

In addition to using the correct outcome measures, it is equally important to specify more clearly how these mental health indicators are related to the stressor under consideration. Merely establishing that there is a relationship between financial strain and specific kinds of mental health problems like depression or alcohol abuse may not tell us all that we need to know in order to develop effective intervention strategies. As Belle (1990) pointed out, a correlation between these constructs may mask at least three different processes, each of which puts a slightly different spin on the kind of intervention program that is called for. First, a relationship between financial strain and depression may mean that financial strain causes depression to emerge in older adults who were previously free of any mental health problem before they encountered their present financial difficulties. Second, a relationship between these constructs may mean that instead of causing depression to arise de novo, financial strain may merely serve to prolong depressive episodes that have arisen from other causes. Finally, a relationship between financial strain and depression may indicate that ongoing economic problems have precipitated a relapse of depression following a recovery from previous bouts of depression.

The design of more effective interventions may clearly be informed by knowing which of the three options identified above most accurately depicts the relationship between stress and mental disorder. In particular, this kind of more focused knowledge can help target the group who will benefit most from a proposed program. For example, if financial strain causes depression to arise among those who were previously free of mental health problems, then the target group will be much larger than the group that we would focus upon if financial strain merely caused a relapse of depression among those who had previously had this kind of mental health problem. In fact, knowing which of the three options identified above is correct may tell us whether stress-related primary prevention is even possible.

Unfortunately, there do not appear to be any studies in the gerontological literature that attempt to determine which of the three options identified above best captures the relationship between stress and mental health problems. It should be emphasized that the three options are not mutually exclusive and that it is possible that stressors such as financial strain operate in all three ways. Meanwhile, researchers must invest the time and effort that are necessary to determine whether this is true.

Conclusions

Throughout this chapter, an effort has been made to show that there is a tremendous amount we do not know about the genesis or origins of stressors, the natural history or course of these events through time, the interface between stressful life events and coping resources, and the way that the effects of stress manifest. At each juncture, it has been argued that the answers to these questions are likely to vary considerably depending upon the stressor that is under consideration. Moreover, as each of these issues was discussed, an attempt was made to show how it related to the first and perhaps most fundamental step in intervention design—determining who is at risk.

Although survey research on the stress process has been going on for well over 30 years, the gaps in our knowledge are substantial. In fact, given the current state of the knowledge base, it is not terribly surprising to find that recently a group of prominent investigators openly questioned whether stress-based interventions are premature and even ill advised. Led by Richard Lazarus (1992), these researchers expressed fears about substituting beliefs for facts and prematurely applying untested interventions.

The position taken by Lazarus (1992) and his colleagues appears to be a bit overstated because some interventions have met with at least some success (see, for example, Toseland, Labrecque, Goebel, & Whitney, 1992). Meanwhile, by becoming more informed users of the stress literature and by striving to illuminate some of the finer points of the stress process, we can move toward developing more focused and even more effective preventive interventions in later life.

References

Alloway, R., & Bebbington, P. (1987). The buffer theory of social support. *Psychological Medicine, 17,* 91-108.

Aneshensal, C. S., Rutter, C. M., & Lachenbruch, P. A. (1991). Social structure, stress, and mental health: Competing conceptual and analytic models. *American Sociological Review, 56,* 166-178.

Belle, D. (1982). The impact of poverty on social networks and supports. *Marriage and Family Review, 5,* 89-103.

Belle, D. (1990). Poverty and women's mental health. *American Psychologist, 45,* 385-389.

Chen, Y. P. (1991). Improving the economic security of minority persons as they enter old age. In J. S. Jackson (Ed.), *Minority elders: Longevity, economics, and health* (pp. 14-23). Washington, DC: Gerontological Society of America.

George, L. K. (1989). Stress, social support, and depression over the life course. In K. S. Markides & C. L. Cooper (Eds.), *Aging, stress, and health* (pp. 241-267). Chichester, UK: John Wiley.

Holden, K. C., Burkhauser, R. V., & Myers, D. A. (1986). Income transitions at older stages of life: The dynamics of poverty. *The Gerontologist, 26,* 292-297.

Holden, K. C., & Smeeding, T. M. (1990). The poor, the rich, and the insecure elderly caught in between. *Milbank Quarterly, 68,* 191-219.

Ilfeld, F. W., Jr. (1976). Characteristics of current social stressors. *Psychological Reports, 39,* 1231-1247.

Jacobson, D. E. (1986). Types and timing of social support. *Journal of Health and Social Behavior, 27,* 250-264.

Krause, N. (1987). Chronic strain, locus of control, and distress in older adults. *Psychology and Aging, 2,* 375-382.

Krause, N. (1991). Stress and isolation from close ties in later life. *Journal of Gerontology: Social Sciences, 46,* S183-S194.

Krause, N. (1993a). Neighborhood deterioration and social isolation in later life. *International Journal of Aging and Human Development, 36,* 9-38.

Krause, N. (1993b). Race differences in life satisfaction among the aged. *Journal of Gerontology: Social Sciences, 48,* S235-S244.

Krause, N., & Baker, E. (1992). Financial strain, economic values, and somatic symptoms in later life. *Psychology and Aging, 7,* 4-14.

Krause, N., & Goldenhar, L. (1992). Acculturation and psychological distress in three groups of elderly Hispanics. *Journal of Gerontology: Social Sciences, 47,* S279-S288.

Krause, N., Jay, G., & Liang, J. (1991). Financial strain and psychological well-being among the American and Japanese elderly. *Psychology and Aging, 6,* 170-181.

Krause, N., & Liang, J. (1993). Stress, social support, and psychological distress among the Chinese elderly. *Journal of Gerontology: Psychological Sciences, 48,* P282-P291.

Lazarus, R. (1992). Four reasons why it is difficult to demonstrate psychosocial influences on health. *Advances: The Journal of Mind-Body Health, 8,* 6-7.

Liang, J., & Fairchild, T. J. (1979). Relative deprivation and perception of financial adequacy among the aged. *Journal of Gerontology, 34,* 746-758.

Liang, J., Kahana, E., & Doherty, E. (1980). Financial well-being among the aged: A further elaboration. *Journal of Gerontology, 35,* 409-420.

Lurie, E. E. (1987). The interrelationship of physical and mental illness in the elderly. In E. E. Lurie & J. H. Swan (Eds.), *Serving the mentally ill elderly: Problems and perspectives* (pp. 39-60). Lexington, MA: Lexington.

Sandler, I. N., Gersten, J. C., Reynolds, K., Kallgran, C. A., & Ramirez, R. (1988). Using theory and data to plan support interventions: Design of a program for bereaved children. In B. H. Gottlieb (Ed.), *Marshalling social support: Formats, processes, and effects* (pp. 53-83). Newbury Park, CA: Sage.

Sandler, I. N., & Guenther, R. T. (1985). Assessment of life stress events. In P. Karoly (Ed.), *Measurement strategies in health psychology* (pp. 555-600). New York: John Wiley.

Toseland, R. W., Labrecque, M. S., Goebel, S. T., & Whitney, M. H. (1992). An evaluation of a group program for spouses of frail elderly veterans. *The Gerontologist, 32,* 382-390.

Wills, T. A. (1987). Downward comparison as a coping mechanism. In C. R. Snyder & C. E. Ford (Eds.), *Coping with negative life events: Clinical and social psychological perspectives* (pp. 243-268). New York: Plenum.

Zautra, A. J., Guarnaccia, C. A., Reich, J. W., & Dohrenwend, B. P. (1988). The contributions of small events to stress and distress. In L. H. Cohen (Ed.), *Life events and psychological functioning: Theoretical and methodological issues* (pp. 123-148). Newbury Park, CA: Sage.

12

Promoting Competence Through Compensation

Roger A. Dixon

A term such as *competence* often strikes concern—if not fear—into the hearts of many middle-aged and older adults. Most vulnerable, perhaps, are those who are employed in a variety of jobs subject to restructuring and downsizing, or who are seeking employment in changing economic conditions. The concern may be that the greater the general economic hardship, the higher the standards for retaining one's position and the more selective the criteria for obtaining one. Anecdotes regarding how such conditions have affected the lives of laborers, professionals, and executives are abundant in the popular press. The concern, of course, is not just about competence, but about competence testing. And competence testing implies some evaluation of abilities or skills that (a) one may not have been actually practicing for some lengthy period, (b) one may never have been too skilled at (or confident of) anyway, (c) one may feel have declined with advancing age, or (d) one may have mastered but that no longer are useful because of changing demands and conditions. The stakes, as we have alluded to them thus far, are certainly high. They include livelihood, prestige, family vitality, and personal sense of achievement and well-being.

The topic of this chapter is competence and aging—and how competence may be preserved through expertise or promoted through compensatory techniques. We explore whether competence declines, improves, or is maintained with advancing age—and whether such changes are inevitable or universal. In doing so, we discuss such issues as differentiating competence from related constructs, the expected life span trajectories of competence and its components, how competence may be maintained through expertise, and

AUTHOR'S NOTE: Preparation of this chapter was supported by grants from the Canadian Aging Research Network and the Natural Sciences and Engineering Research Council of Canada. I appreciate the collaboration of Lars Bäckman in developing the ideas about compensation.

220

how compensatory techniques may play a role in promoting successful adaptation to the demands of one's personal and professional careers.

Cognition, Competence, and Aging

The field of research that informs many of my comments in this chapter is often referred to as "cognitive aging." In brief, cognitive aging is the study of aging-related changes that occur in such processes as remembering, problem solving, attention, and decision making. Such changes are often based on or related to corollary changes occurring in the brain or neurological substrate and reflected in psychomotor performance. Cognitive processes are involved in nearly all everyday activities involving some degree of competence. Conversing, learning, teaching, writing, thinking, making decisions, performing tasks, helping others, selecting activities, planning—all of these involve cognition. The level at which they are performed is one global indicator of competence.

A variety of research programs are being pursued in the field of cognitive aging. One scheme that includes five lines of research questions for categorizing these programs is as follows (Baltes, 1987; Dixon & Baltes, 1986):

1. *Directionality:* Do the many processes or aspects of cognition "age" alike or differently? Are there differential gains and losses?

2. *Interindividual Differences:* How similar (or different) is cognitive aging between individuals within a given cohort and across cohorts?

3. *Plasticity:* How much reserve capacity or plasticity can older individuals display in cognitive skills? Can older individuals learn new skills, or does the capacity for acquiring new information and skills decline?

4. *Maintenance:* For given cognitive processes, what are the conditions under which older adults develop or maintain competent or skilled levels of performance? What are the skills or components of skills that are associated with or supporting such maintenance?

5. *Compensation:* Can older adults attain, maintain, or surpass normal levels of performance in some skills by using alternative mechanisms?

Numerous reviews have noted how, with regard to the first and second research lines, there is wide variability in how cognitive processes change with aging and in how individuals develop in given processes (Baltes, 1987). Normal neurological slowing is responsible for much decline in some basic cognitive functioning, especially speeded performance (Salthouse, 1985). Nevertheless, the rate and magnitude of decline may vary across processes and individuals. In addition, research on plasticity and maintenance suggests that older adults can learn new skills, relearn old skills, and through training and practice maintain adequate or higher levels of performance in selected domains of skill (Charness, 1989). Furthermore, compensatory mechanisms may be useful in overcoming given deficits and thereby maintaining skilled performance (Bäckman & Dixon, 1992).

The Conundrum of Competence and Aging

In order to evaluate the competence of aging adults, one should consider performance in a variety of domains. Many seniors report that they perform such everyday activities as housework, exercising, traveling, visiting public places, conversing with others, reading, working accurately (if not as swiftly as before), and practicing hobbies or skills. There is neurological, physical, and cognitive decline with aging—there can be no doubt about that—but the overall picture is not as depressing as one might expect given some stereotypes of aging and old age. Yet there is a conundrum that must be addressed by interested scholars and practitioners. This riddle has three components. First, much mainstream neurological, psychomotor, and cognitive research indicates decline with advancing age. Second, there are indeed stereotypes of aging that suggest a shared belief in the inevitability and universality of aging-related losses. Nevertheless, and third, a growing number of self-reports, anecdotes, and research suggest that there may also be continued competence in selected areas. As Salthouse (1990) described the situation, "One of the greatest challenges in the field of psychology and aging is to account for the discrepancy between the inferred status of older adults based on their performance in psychometric testing situations and cognitive laboratories and that derived from observations of their successful functioning in everyday functioning" (p. 310). How can we address—and resolve—the challenge represented in this quotation? Equally important, how can we begin to conduct more research into competence and aging, and communicate more broadly what we already know and what we learn about this topic?

We must take four main steps to begin to address adequately this challenge. First, it is critical to maintain a distinction between ability and competence. This distinction has been made in various ways on numerous occasions. Salthouse's (1990) differentiation is typical and appropriate: Whereas *ability* refers to the level of performance one attains in standardized or conventional tests of cognitive or physical performance, *competence* refers to how well one's abilities are used in performing activities demanded in particular situations. Abilities are the basic tools one brings to particular situations, including conventional tests, performance evaluations, leisure pursuits, and interpersonal communication and interactions. In contrast, competence is how well one uses whatever level of abilities one has to adapt to new or demanding situations.

The second way of beginning to address Salthouse's (1990) challenge is to extend the range of domains and indicators of competence. Thus evaluation efforts would attend not just to (a) school-like competence (or abilities, such as rote episodic memory), (b) quantitative work-related competence (such as sheer speed or quantity of production), or (c) quantitative leisure-activity competence (such as wins/losses or points scored), but also to (d) qualitative indicators of competent performance. The latter, often over-looked, set of indicators includes accuracy, punctuality, knowledge, mentoring, advice giving, interest and motivation, and willingness to work or train. Whereas evaluation efforts directed at (a), (b), and (c) might reveal substantial decline with advancing age, those attending also to (d) may result in a different profile in some cases. This is not to say that competence in (a), (b), and (c) is irrelevant or to be devalued in assessing competence; rather, the point is that additional or alternative avenues of developing and evaluating competence should be encouraged.

The third step in addressing the discrepancy noted by Salthouse (1990) is to consider more completely the roles of (a) experience in maintaining competence in a variety of skills and (b) compensation in overcoming the effects of declining abilities (Salthouse, 1987). Gains in experience can be achieved through very large amounts of practice or simulated through training (Charness, 1989). With enough practice, some degree of expertise may be developed. Such expertise is specific to a particular domain and, with continued practice, may be resistant to aging-related declines. One reason expertise may be resistant to decline—in addition to continued practice and effort—is that mechanisms for compensating for decrements in constituent elements may be used. We return to this important point later.

The fourth step in addressing the discrepancy between observations from the lab and real life is to turn more attention in research and theory to the study of successful aging. The investigation of successful aging implies both attending to aspects of individual development that show growth-like functions throughout adulthood (e.g., possibly mentoring, and/or wisdom) and focusing on adults who continue to be productive into late life. Both of these research directions are just beginning, but both hold promise. For example, the study of wisdom has received considerable attention in recent years (Baltes & Smith, 1990). In addition, it is a simple matter to come up with a long list of people who have demonstrated a high degree of vitality or competence in particular domains into late life (Utall & Perlmutter, 1989). Pablo Casals, Golda Meir, Agatha Christie, and George Burns are among the frequently mentioned examples. The major point is that many older adults can and do maintain a high level of functioning despite the fact that they have—almost undoubtedly—experienced substantial and typical losses in critical abilities.

Conclusion

The guiding questions for research and practice in the psychology of aging can now be further refined. Two are of particular importance for current purposes. First, does competence, as defined here, decline inevitably with advancing age? Research on the "natural life course" of competence would follow. Second, are there underexplored and underutilized domains of competence? Whereas *underexplored* refers to domains of competence that merit further research, *underutilized* refers to domains of competence that may not be assessed and used by scholars and practitioners in the development of theories and the evaluation of the need for (and directions of) interventions. Research on the expected life course of competence in particular domains would follow. In the next section, we address what researchers currently understand about how this process of balancing gains, maintenance, and losses might work in everyday life skills.

The Aging of Competence

Consider any set of professional, work, or leisure activities that could be considered skills. These could include activities from such categories as handiwork (e.g., home maintenance, gardening, sewing, cooking), hobbies and games (e.g., fishing, singing, card games, chess), sports and physical activities (e.g., swimming, golf, lawn bowling, dancing), life management (e.g., investment decisions, giving or seeking advice, solving family problems), or social (e.g., shopping, correspondence, conversations, planning events). Each of these skills can be considered as "molar" in the sense that each is constituted by two or more "components." One becomes an expert gardener, bridge player, dancer, family problem solver, or conversationalist by mastering (and often automatizing) components to each of these skills. Each molar skill is performed with a different constellation of components. Expert gardening requires considerable knowledge, but also some physical work capacity. Playing expert bridge may require some physical endurance, but also a great deal of memory and reasoning. Of course, to become an expert in any domain requires considerable motivation, effort, and practice (Charness, 1989).

By considering now two general clusters of components of skills—and, for the moment, limiting our consideration to just these two—we can appreciate further why performance on some skills may decline or be maintained into late life. The first cluster of components may be termed *motor perform-*

ance, which implies that some skills require the execution of coordinated muscle activity. Examples include muscular strength, muscular endurance, physical work capacity, dexterity, and speed (Spirduso & MacRae, 1990). Skills that are executed with the assistance of one or more of these may be said, therefore, to have a motor performance component. The second cluster of components may be termed *cognitive performance,* which implies that some coordinated mental activity is required for successful performance of the skill. All of the major processes of cognition—such as memory, reasoning, attention, perception, and social cognition—are included. Skills that are executed with the assistance of one or more of these may be said to have a cognitive component. Indeed, it is the rare leisure or work skill that does not involve one component from these two general categories.

On the basis of much research, the typical expectation for the development of motor performance across the life span is one of increasing ability (speed, strength, endurance, capacity, dexterity) until early adulthood and then decline throughout the remainder of life (Spirduso & MacRae, 1990). Also on the basis of much research, the typical expectation for the life span development of much of laboratory and psychometric cognitive performance is one of increasing ability through early adulthood and then gradual decline (Hultsch & Dixon, 1990; Schaie, 1990). (Notable exceptions to both rules are addressed selectively later.) Putting these two typical patterns together, one may generate a general expectation for the life span development of competence or skills. In the absence of some other mechanism or process, the expectation would be for an increase in competent performance early and then, because of declining cognitive and motor abilities, a decline in performance with aging. There is, however, increasing anecdotal and scientific evidence that this may not be the predominant way that competence "ages." In the next section I explore one mechanism that may be responsible for a different trajectory for the development of competence.

Experience and Expertise

I have suggested that in order to understand the aging of competence, researchers should both broaden the range of skills to be tested and improve the match between the testing instrument and target domain of competence. There is no single, general, cognitive test with which one can evaluate competence in the wide variety of domains in which adults may demonstrate competent behavior. It would be peculiar to expect that performance on a general intelligence test would indicate anything about how good one was in sailing, sewing, or auto mechanics. In contrast, tests tailored to reflect cognitive skills related to sailing, sewing, or auto mechanics should be related to performance on those skills. A great deal of knowledge—represented in both declarative and procedural forms—is involved in the performance of each of these skills. Two expert sailors can converse at great length and detail about the intricacies of sailing, using a vocabulary to which an expert in sewing or auto mechanics may not have access. If placed in vivo and tested on response to typical challenges of sailing (measuring, e.g., accuracy of diagnosis, speed of response, effectiveness of remedy), expert sailors should perform quite well and predictably. This does not necessarily make sailors intellectual or athletic giants. Similar well-constructed tests tailored to the domains of sewing and auto mechanics would yield similar results, with experts performing relatively well and novices relatively poorly.

Principles of Expertise

After examining research on expertise in several well-structured domains, Glaser and Chi (1988) summarized the main principles of expertise. Several of these generalizations are pertinent to the study of the aging of competence. First, Glaser and Chi noted that expertise is domain-specific. Being an expert in sailing gives one a definite advantage when one is asked to skipper a racing yacht, but is of no direct value when one is asked to pilot a Beechcraft 99, repair an errant stitch, or tune up a Citroen. Second, Glaser noted that competence in a given domain continues to develop as long as domain-relevant experience accumulates. This implies that experience is one of the keys to the maintenance (and growth) of a given skill. As Charness (1989) noted, the practice required to achieve expertise is enormous. The practice and experience required to maintain it may be similarly demanding. This generalization carries no attendant or implied expectation about when (in the life course) experience ceases to contribute to continued high levels of performance.

A third principle of expertise is related to the first: Experts display high domain-specific cognitive or intellectual performance, but they do not necessarily produce top performances on more general cognitive or intellectual abilities (Glaser & Chi, 1988). Auto mechanics may readily solve complex reasoning problems pertaining to diagnosing and repairing automobile engines, but perform quite differently on more general reasoning tests. This may not be surprising to most observers, but are other examples equally unsurprising? To wit, the chess master, though exhibiting prodigious analyses and comparisons of possible moves, may be able to keep no more unrelated nouns in working memory than the average adult. Although a chess master's "Chess IQ" is, by definition, extremely high, his or her "Sailing IQ" or "Automobile IQ" may be considerably lower. Indeed, because of the investment of practice (and time) required to develop high levels of competence in a given domain, it is unlikely that a given expert in one domain will be equally adept at other domains, although some generalized problem-solving skills may be developed (Glaser & Chi, 1988).

These principles help to clarify the role of experience in cognitive aging, as well as the function of cognitive testing. Standardized cognitive testing is often conducted with tasks that relate perhaps most closely to educational experience. This correspondence is quite important when the goal is to assess either (a) adaptation to academic environments or (b) level of functioning in a normative sense. If, however, cognitive adaptation to nonacademic environments is investigated, then nonacademic (even specialized) experience may play a critical role in predicting performance (e.g., Ceci & Liker, 1986; Dixon, 1992). Whereas most standardized cognitive batteries or intelligence tests are somewhat academic in nature, most cognitively demanding activities in which mature adults engage are not oriented to formal or speeded educational demands. For this reason, researchers have increasingly turned their attention to the roles of experience, practice, and expertise in the assessment of competence in later life (e.g., Charness, 1989; Salthouse, 1987; Willis, 1985). When experience is considered—for example, domains of cognitive functioning in which adults of many ages have considerable practice or expertise—older adults are not necessarily inferior performers. Hence a critical issue is the extent to which observed individual differences reflect (a) aging effects, (b) experience effects, or (c) some combination of the two (Salthouse, 1987). If they reflect to a significant extent experience effects, then the exceptions to the stereotype of inevitable decline—and the exceptions to the expectation of molar decline—may be more numerous and, more important, theoretically coherent (Dixon, 1992).

Plasticity

Thus extensive experience in a particular domain may mitigate basic aging-related changes in fundamental cognitive hardware, not overall but with respect to performance in tasks related to the domain of expertise. To what extent, then, is it possible to simulate experience in a given molar domain and thereby remediate aging-related changes that might have occurred? This is the issue of plasticity, one of the key research directions identified at the outset of this chapter. If differences in experience play a role in observed age differences in cognitive performance, then experimentally manipulating pertinent experience could result in attenuated age differences or even improvements for older adults on tasks for which older adults have had little if any recent experience. Indeed, providing "educational" experiences—such as training in specific abilities or sheer practice—to older adults has resulted in improved performance for some abilities thought to be closely related to neurological (Baltes & Willis, 1982; Willis, 1985) and psychomotor (Dixon, Kurzman, & Friesen, 1993) decline. Although these improvements for older adults may not be to the same level or with the same robustness as for younger adults (Kliegl, Smith, & Baltes, 1990), the demonstration of plasticity in cognitive abilities thought for decades to decline inevitably and universally is intriguing.

Let us consider an example of the "engineering" of a cognitive skill that is particularly impressive. Although the task is a simple one, constructing the skill is far more complex. The task is serial recall, which is remembering a list of items (e.g., digits, common words) in the exact order in which they are presented. Typically, one might remember five to nine such items in a row, and younger adults may perform better than older adults. In a ground-breaking study, Ericsson and Chase (1982) found that a young man with extensive practice was able to remember almost 80 digits in consecutive order. He was able to accomplish this feat by using a mnemonic technique. One feature of the young man's technique was an extensive preexisting knowledge base of track-running times, which he used to help incorporate the to-be-remembered digits into storage. Kliegl and Baltes (1987) devised a procedure to engineer such a knowledge system in older adults and to teach them a mnemonic technique, the method of loci. Briefly, their procedure involved teaching the adults (a) a sequence of geographic locations (the loci), (b) a knowledge base (historical dates) to use in encoding the digits, and (c) the method of mentally pegging sets of digits in particular locations and then generating a bizarre image to link the location to a particular date. For recall, then, the adult would simply cycle through the sequence of locations, retrieving the bizarre image and with it the set of digits stored in each. By following the sequence assiduously, the adult could maintain the proper sequence of digits and extend serial recall.

The results of this and similar studies showed that indeed experience in a novel and complex task could be engineered successfully for older adults. Two normal older women (one 69 years old and the other 72 years old), who could recall only about 7 digits prior to their training, remembered over 100 digits in consecutive order. There is, of course, very little functional utility to remembering long strings of digits (and the rewards of a professional mnemonist are skimpy and unpredictable). This research by Kliegl and Baltes (1987), however, firmly demonstrates an important theoretical lesson. Specifically, normal older adults, despite experiencing substantial aging-related declines in numerous areas, have enough potential for plasticity that, with experience simulated through training, they are capable of enormous cognitive feats.

Conclusion

Experience is necessary for the development of high levels of competence in a variety of domains. Such experience may be gained "naturally" through skill training or practice in everyday life, or through a carefully designed regimen of training. Although many constituent components of cognitive and psychomotor skills decline with advancing age, performance in specific domains may be maintained. One reason for this maintenance is continued experience and practice in related tasks. All things being equal, then, one might expect experts in a given domain to simply continue to get better and better throughout their active careers. What would cause expertise, even with the support of experience and motivation, to decline? For the answer to this question, we must revisit and refine our earlier comments on molar skills and components. This will allow us to explicate another mechanism through which competence may be maintained.

Maintaining Competence Through Compensation

There is an interactive relationship between aging skills and changing contextual demands. Deficits may occur both (a) when a person's skill declines as a function of advancing age and (b) when a person's skill is actually maintained but the demands of the context are increased substantially. As a potentially adaptive response, compensation may occur in either case. In principle, some aspects of skilled performance may decline while other spared aspects may serve to compensate for this decline. One expectation is that experience and practice in particular skill domains are often (but not necessarily) associated with the tendency to compensate (Salthouse, 1987). Thus the aging chess master is more likely to have developed compensatory techniques for chess than an older novice player who must learn to play the game with his or her available cognitive resources, and who lacks the experience and skill to even be aware of a need for compensation.

One condition under which cognitive decline with advancing age may not occur inevitably (or may be slowed and diminished in magnitude) is when the participant is managing a skill that matches the requirements of the cognitive task. An older chess master may do well (as compared to unskilled older and younger controls, and perhaps as well as skilled younger adults) on tasks that are related to cognitive activities undertaken in a chess match (Charness, 1989). The same chess master will probably perform no better than other older adults (and worse than younger adults) on similar tasks presented out of context of the skill. For example, an episodic memory task containing neutral words would be remembered worse than one containing esoteric chess vocabulary. The notion of compensation extends this principle of domain specificity. The question becomes: To what extent may preserved molecular cognitive components operate as cognitive support for molar skills (Charness, 1989; Dixon & Bäckman, 1993; Salthouse, 1987)? That is, if the molar skill is maintained into late adulthood, but the molecular components of that skill are declining with advancing age, then the molar skill must be supported by an alternative component.

A good example of this process is recent research conducted on transcription typing (Bosman, 1993; Salthouse, 1987). This research began with the observation that young and old professional typists perform well at a cognitively and motorically demanding task. They do so despite the expectation that the molecular components of the task may decline with advancing age. To identify the molecular components of a molar skill one must conceptually analyze that skill, attending to its constituent aspects: If one were to decompose a skill or, alternatively, train it from scratch, what aspects would be identified as critical? For speeded typing, being able to tap one's fingers quickly is clearly an asset, as is the ability to react quickly and selectively to stimuli. These two components, as indexed by tapping rate and choice reaction time, were assessed in these studies, along with speed of typing. Salthouse (1987) observed that, as expected, the two components were correlated with the molar skill and that younger typists were better on them (but not on the molar skill) than older typists. How, then, did older typists maintain their molar competence? Salthouse discovered that they had developed an alternative way of performing the skill, an alternative component on which to rely. This component was a larger eye-hand span: Essentially, older typists look further ahead in the text when typing so that they have more opportunity to prepare their fingers to strike the to-be-typed characters.

Definition and Forms

A pause to offer a proper definition of compensation is in order. In a recent review of several conceptual treatments of compensation, Bäckman and Dixon (1992) offered a deliberately general working definition:

> Compensation can be inferred when an objective or perceived mismatch between accessible skills and environmental demands is counterbalanced . . . by investment of more time or effort, . . . utilization of latent (but normally inactive) skills, or acquisition of new skills so that a change in the behavioral profile occurs, [typically] in the direction of adaptive attainment, maintenance, or surpassing of "normal" levels of proficiency. (p. 272)

Our review supported the notion that compensation can occur through more than one form.

Substitution

Perhaps the prototypic form is that of substitution. In the definition, substitution is implied when an individual begins to use an already existing, but not typically involved, component of a skill. Substitution is also implied when an individual develops a new component that both contributes to the performance of the skill and has not previously been involved in supporting that performance. These are forms of substitution in that new components of a molar skill substitute for declining typical molecular components.

A methodologically sophisticated strategy for conducting research on compensation as substitution was developed by Charness (1981, 1989) and Salthouse (1987). Termed the molar equivalence-molecular decomposition (ME-MD) strategy, it has been used to examine empirically the aging of such experience-related, cognitively complex skills as chess, bridge, and typing. It begins with the assumption that the successful performance of a cognitive skill is accomplished through a finite set of molecular components. We have seen how this applies to the skill of typing. *Molar equivalence* refers to the requirement that the correlation between age and the molar skill performance be close to zero. Thus a skilled sample (sailors, chess masters, typists) should show no age differences in performance of the molar skill. As was the case with the earlier typing example, the next task is to conceptually analyze the molar skill such that molecular components are evident. Given the absence of age differences on the molar task, the research task is one of identifying age-related differences in the molecular components of the molar skill. Some molecular components of complex cognitive skills—for example, those associated with transcription typing—typically decline with advancing age. If the molar skill is being maintained into late life at a high level even though some molecular components of that skill are declining, then there may be alternative molecular components supporting the molar performance. *Molecular decomposition* refers to the identification of specific molecular components of the molar skill. Overall, the ME-MD strategy allows the researcher to identify the extent to which the individuals are relying on the same (or different) molecular components.

Compensation as substitution occurs when there is an age-related decline in the components typically used to perform a molar skill and a counterbalancing increase in at least one substitutable component. This interaction allows the molar competency to be maintained into late life. The ME-MD strategy is a valuable addition to research on compensation and to the promotion of compensation in older adults. In terms of research, it provides us with one way of unambiguously distinguishing between maintenance of competence via continued expertise (in the molecular components) and via compensation as substitution. The theoretical importance of this model is evident as well. The debate about the potential role of experience in cognitive aging can now be sharpened. There is a conceptual difference between experience contributing (a) to the maintenance of typical molecular components and (b) to the emergence of new compensatory mechanisms (Dixon & Bäckman, 1993). In terms of application, the unambiguous identification of mechanisms through which some older adults maintain high levels of productivity in a given domain may suggest that others who have endured declines could be trained in substitutable components with perhaps similar encouraging results. At both the individual and societal levels, such specific means to enhance the productivity and performance of older adults are potentially useful.

Selection

Substitution is an important form of compensation, but successful efforts at compensation may occur through other mechanisms as well. For example, Baltes and colleagues (Baltes, 1987; Baltes, Dittmann-Kohli, & Dixon, 1984; Dixon & Baltes, 1986) used the expression *selective optimization with compensation* to refer to the process whereby adult age-related decrements in basic cognitive processes are compensated by age-related gains in the ability to select alternative expressions or forms of skills. Compensation occurs by channeling one's efforts into a select number and set of domains. The increased selection and reduction of domains of activity are referred to as *selective optimization*. As reserve capacity declines with aging, so does the ability to cope with increasing demands. When an older adult's threshold of capacity is exceeded, it is arguably more adaptive to reduce the number of domains that must be managed—and manage the remaining ones well—than to do the full complement at a mediocre level, or even give up entirely. Of course, there is a loss associated with this apparent gain, and that is that compensatory efforts in a select set of domains are, by definition, carried out at the expense of the domains that have been excluded. The applied implications of this model are clear. Older adults need not invest excessive effort in managing all of the skills they have developed. Indeed, they should be content to tailor their professional and leisure pursuits—with no necessary loss in zeal or ambition—to a subset thereof.

We have illustrated a similar compensatory process of selection in Figure 12.1 (Bäckman & Dixon, 1992). Let us assume that Goal A in the figure is the most valued goal, perhaps one associated with a career (e.g., becoming editor of a newspaper, senior partner in a prestigious law firm, or university

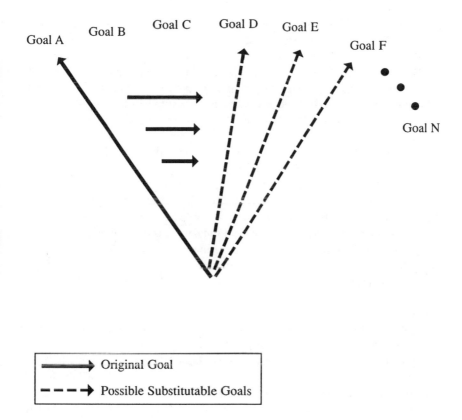

Figure 12.1. Representation of the process of selecting substitutable goals (Goals B through N) when the initial goal (Goal A) cannot be achieved because of a mismatch between accessible skills and environmental demands.

SOURCE: Bäckman & Dixon, 1992, p. 274. Copyright 1992 by the American Psychological Association. Reprinted by permission.

president, or making the baseball or rock music hall of fame) or a favorite hobby (e.g., becoming a national champion bridge player or horseback rider, skippering a winning yacht in a classic regatta, having one's needlework displayed or collected, completing a marathon). If, because of aging-related changes, individuals realize that their preferred goal is unattainable, they may compensate by selecting and pursuing an alternative goal. This alternative goal (e.g., Goal B in the figure) would have the characteristics of being both presumably attainable and desirable. Because of continued mismatches between the requirements of attaining a specific goal and the resources one has (or is able to devote to the pursuit of the goal), further adjustments in goals may occur. Throughout this process, original goals—

and the fact that they have changed, perhaps even dramatically—may even be forgotten.

The selection of goals can be horizontal or vertical. An example of a horizontal shift could be when one changes one's goal from being a research scientist to being an applied scientist upon realizing that one prefers to work with people or that one's temperament is not suited to the laboratory. An example of a vertical shift could be when one raises one's goal (e.g., from being a top car salesperson to being the manager or owner of a dealership) upon discovering that one is better at the activity than expected. A vertical selection can also occur when one lowers one's goal (e.g., from becoming state amateur master's tennis champion to competing successfully at the city level) upon discovering the improbability of achieving the former goal. Compensatory selections such as these are important means of adjusting to mismatches between one's resources and the demands of the context. Changes in goals include adjustments in expectations for one's own performance. Indeed, an important form of such compensation is to relax the criteria of what constitutes success (Baltes, 1987; Dixon & Bäckman, 1993).

External Aids

Although the results of training older adults in specific internal mnemonic skills are startling and theoretically important, perhaps the simplest form of compensation for cognitive problems in later life is the use of external memory aids. Whereas internal mnemonic skills increase the efficiency of memory performance for particular materials, learning to use external memory aids relieves the adult of some memory demands with no expense to performance. External memory aids include writing notes in a calendar or leaving something in an obvious place. Some research has even suggested that middle-aged or older adults may use external aids in everyday life (Dixon & Hultsch, 1983; Dobbs & Rule, 1987; Loewen, Shaw, & Craik, 1990). They have the advantage of being concrete, practical, easy to learn and use, and efficient. One form of frequently used external aid has only recently received research attention. This form is simply other people: Teachers, colleagues, friends, spouses, and strangers are often asked to help solve a perplexing cognitive problem (Dixon, 1992).

Examples of this form illustrate the reason that it is often referred to as *collaborative cognition* (Dixon, 1992):

1. Asking teachers for assistance in understanding the logic behind a complicated problem
2. Asking colleagues to demonstrate how they solved an analogous problem
3. Asking friends for advice about child rearing or gardening

4. Asking a spouse to help you remember to make a phone call in the morning

5. Asking a stranger for assistance in finding a location or reading a road map

Recent research in collaborative cognition and aging has demonstrated the extent to which adults of all ages make use of collaborators in solving everyday and laboratory cognitive tasks (Dixon, 1992). Research has focused both on the quantity or level of performance by collaborating older adults (as compared to individuals and younger adults) and on the quality or style of performance (e.g., Gould & Dixon, 1993). Older married couples, for example, perform some complex cognitive tasks by allocating aspects of the task in ways that reflect their knowledge of each other's skills.

Compensation through other individuals—such as caregivers and spouses— is a natural way of overcoming individual aging-related decline. This is theoretically important, for it reveals the extent to which older adults may maintain competence in a variety of practical domains despite fundamental aging-related changes. It is practically important, as well, for it suggests alternative and often available means of maintaining functional levels of performance.

Summary:
Promoting Competence Through Compensation

The study of competence and aging provokes several challenges for researchers and practitioners alike. First, researchers (and consumers of the research literature) can benefit from further awareness of the distinction between ability and competence. In this distinction, competence is the utilization of abilities—including cognitive, physical, and interpersonal—in adapting to particular situations. For researchers, the concept of competence is valuable in that it provides a potential theoretical explanation for the often observed discrepancy between how older adults perform on standardized tests (poorly) and how they perform on well-practiced professional tasks and leisure activities (relatively well), with the latter being no less cognitively demanding than the former. For practitioners, it is important in that it encourages pluralistic evaluations of individuals' skills. Adaptation to everyday life is not necessarily indicated by performance on standardized tests; modified, perhaps even in vivo, assessments would be valuable.

Second, there are two connected theoretical explanations for the discrepancy that is being resolved. On the one hand, experience plays a major role in performance on complex cognitive and motor tasks. Indeed, experience (to the level of expertise) is one of the principal reasons that competence in select domains can be maintained through late life. Again, the challenge to researchers seeking to understand the life course of competence is to evaluate performance at least in part on the basis of areas to which the individual is seeking to adapt. And the challenge to practitioners is to focus intervention efforts, as much as possible, on improving the match between contextual demands and an individual's resources. This could include simulating experience—through training or practice—so that an individual recovers enough skill to meet the demands in select areas.

On the other hand, improving the match between contextual demands and an individual's resources can also be accomplished by changing the demands (e.g., selecting alternative goals) or by relaxing the criteria of success (whereby a lower level of performance is understood to be acceptable). Such strategies are also examples of compensation. The role of compensation in the maintenance of competence is likely to be substantial, especially if a broader definition of *compensation,* such as the one proposed here, is accepted. Substitution is indeed a powerful form of compensation, not only because it is effective but because it is attached to a research design that provides for relatively unambiguous conclusions. Where skills are well defined, compensation research using the ME-MD model may identify substitutable mechanisms. An interesting question for practitioners is whether these mechanisms can then be taught to others practicing the same skill and perhaps experiencing a similar profile of aging-related losses.

A major goal of this chapter has been to describe some ways in which successful cognitive aging may be promoted. Partly by focusing on issues of compensation, practitioners can identify ways of encouraging (a) the continued utilization of the abilities of older adults in appropriate contexts, (b) continued productivity in old or alternative domains of competence, and (c) the emergence of new domains of competence. Such worthy goals of benefitting individual development raise a host of social policy issues. Not the least of these urgent policy issues is what we should do with generations of older adults who have (a) energy and interest in continuing to be productive citizens, (b) maintained competence and skills into late life through extensive practice, and (c) newly found means of overcoming their declining abilities. Demographic changes in our society could produce large groups of undervalued or out-of-work skilled and competent individuals, and yet a compelling need to hire, retrain, and perhaps redefine the careers and obligations of older workers. There is no answer yet as to how to reconcile such trends as problematic allocation of limited resources (jobs, training programs), increasingly high-tech work environments (requiring substantial retraining for many older adults), and mandatory retirement with what increasingly appears to be a population of competent and trainable older adults.

References

Bäckman, L., & Dixon, R. A. (1992). Psychological compensation: A theoretical framework. *Psychological Bulletin, 112*, 259-283.

Baltes, P. B. (1987). Theoretical propositions of life-span developmental psychology: On the dynamics between growth and decline. *Developmental Psychology, 23*, 611-626.

Baltes, P. B., Dittmann-Kohli, F., & Dixon, R. A. (1984). New perspectives on the development of intelligence in adulthood: Toward a dual-process conception and a model of selective optimization with compensation. In P. B. Baltes & O. G. Brim (Eds.), *Life-span development and behavior* (Vol. 6, pp. 33-76). San Diego: Academic Press.

Baltes, P. B., & Smith, J. (1990). Toward a psychology of wisdom and its ontogenesis. In R. J. Sternberg (Ed.), *Wisdom: Its nature, origins, and development* (pp. 87-120). Cambridge, UK: Cambridge University Press.

Baltes, P. B., & Willis, S. (1982). Plasticity and enhancement of intellectual functioning in adulthood: Penn State's Adult Development and Enhancement Project (ADEPT). In F. I. M. Craik & S. E. Trehub (Eds.), *Aging and cognitive processes* (pp. 353-389). New York: Plenum.

Bosman, E. A. (1993). Age-related differences in the motoric aspects of transcription typing skill. *Psychology and Aging, 8*, 87-102.

Ceci, S. J., & Liker, J. (1986). Academic and nonacademic intelligence: An experimental separation. In R. J. Sternberg & R. K. Wagner (Eds.), *Practical intelligence: Nature and origins of competence in the everyday world* (pp. 119-142). Cambridge, UK: Cambridge University Press.

Charness, N. (1981). Search in chess: Age and skill differences. *Journal of Experimental Psychology: Human Perception and Performance, 7*, 467-476.

Charness, N. (1989). Age and expertise: Responding to Talland's challenge. In L. W. Poon, D. C. Rubin, & B. A. Wilson (Eds.), *Everyday cognition in adulthood and late life* (pp. 437-456). Cambridge, UK: Cambridge University Press.

Dixon, R. A. (1992). Contextual approaches to adult intellectual development. In R. J. Sternberg & C. A. Berg (Eds.), *Intellectual development* (pp. 350-380). Cambridge, UK: Cambridge University Press.

Dixon, R. A., & Bäckman, L. (1993). The concept of compensation in cognitive aging: The case of prose processing in adulthood. *International Journal of Aging and Human Development, 36*, 199-217.

Dixon, R. A., & Baltes, P. B. (1986). Toward life-span research on the functions and pragmatics of intelligence. In R. J. Sternberg & R. K. Wagner (Eds.), *Practical intelligence: Nature and origins of competence in the everyday world* (pp. 203-235). Cambridge, UK: Cambridge University Press.

Dixon, R. A., & Hultsch, D. F. (1983). Structure and development of metamemory in adulthood. *Journal of Gerontology, 38*, 682-688.

Dixon, R. A., Kurzman, D., & Friesen, I. C. (1993). Handwriting performance in younger and older adults: Age, familiarity, and practice effects. *Psychology and Aging, 8*, 360-370.

Dobbs, A. R., & Rule, B. G. (1987). Prospective memory and self-report of memory abilities in older adults. *Canadian Journal of Psychology, 41*, 209-222.

Ericsson, K. A., & Chase, W. G. (1982). Exceptional memory. *American Scientist, 70*, 607-615.

Glaser, R., & Chi, M. T. H. (1988). Overview. In M. T. H. Chi, R. Glaser, & M. J. Farr (Eds.), *The nature of expertise* (pp. xv-xxviii). Hillsdale, NJ: Lawrence Erlbaum.

Gould, O. N., & Dixon, R. A. (1993). How we spent our vacation: Collaborative storytelling by young and old adults. *Psychology and Aging, 8,* 10-17.

Hultsch, D. F., & Dixon, R. A. (1990). Learning and memory in aging. In J. E. Birren & K. W. Schaie (Eds.), *Handbook of the psychology of aging* (3rd ed., pp. 258-274). San Diego: Academic Press.

Kliegl, R., & Baltes, P. B. (1987). Theory-guided analysis of mechanisms of development and aging through testing-the-limits and research on expertise. In C. Schooler & K. W. Schaie (Eds.), *Cognitive functioning and social structure over the life course* (pp. 95-119). Norwood, NJ: Ablex.

Kliegl, R., Smith, J., & Baltes, P. B. (1990). On the locus and process of magnification of age differences during mnemonic training. *Developmental Psychology, 26,* 894-904.

Loewen, E. R., Shaw, R. J., & Craik, F. I. M. (1990). Age differences in components of metamemory. *Experimental Aging Research, 16,* 43-48.

Salthouse, T. A. (1985). *A theory of cognitive aging.* Amsterdam: North Holland.

Salthouse, T. A. (1987). Age, experience, and compensation. In C. Schooler & K. W. Schaie (Eds.), *Cognitive functioning and social structure over the life course* (pp. 142-150). Norwood, NJ: Ablex.

Salthouse, T. A. (1990). Cognitive competence and expertise in aging. In J. E. Birren & K. W. Schaie (Eds.), *Handbook of the psychology of aging* (3rd ed., pp. 310-319). San Diego: Academic Press.

Schaie, K. W. (1990). Intellectual development in adulthood. In J. E. Birren & K. W. Schaie (Eds.), *Handbook of the psychology of aging* (3rd ed., pp. 291-309). San Diego: Academic Press.

Spirduso, W. W., & MacRae, P. G. (1990). Motor performance and aging. In J. E. Birren & K. W. Schaie (Eds.), *Handbook of the psychology of aging* (3rd ed., pp. 183-200). San Diego: Academic Press.

Utall, D. H., & Perlmutter, M. (1989). Toward a broader conceptualization of development: The role of gains and losses across the life span. *Developmental Review, 9,* 101-132.

Willis, S. L. (1985). Towards an educational psychology of the adult learner: Cognitive and intellectual bases. In J. E. Birren & K. W. Schaie (Eds.), *Handbook of the psychology of aging* (2nd ed., pp. 818-847). New York: Van Nostrand Reinhold.

13

A Life Course
Approach to Postretirement
Roles and Well-Being

Phyllis Moen

Trends

Two trends have enormous import for the social integration of the aged and for American society more generally:

1. We have extended the average length of life to an impressive degree, such that Americans now live—and live healthier—much longer than ever before (Berg & Cassells, 1990; Gilford, 1988; Lonergan, 1991). The proportion of the population 65 years and older was 12.5% in 1989, compared to 9.8% in 1970 (U.S. Bureau of the Census, 1991).

2. Public and private sector retirement policies encourage early exit from the workforce, such that American workers are retiring from full-time involvement in the labor force at progressively earlier ages (Burkhauser & Quinn, 1990; Fields & Mitchell, 1984; Quinn, Burkhauser, & Myers, 1990). In 1950, almost one in two American men aged 65 and over was in the labor force; by 1989 only one in six men in this age group was employed (Burkhauser & Quinn, 1989).

These two trends are producing an expanding "third age" of life (Laslett, 1991) after retirement and prior to the onset of serious health problems or disability, but a stage for which our age-stratified society provides few socially defined roles. Age grades or strata, such as childhood or early adulthood, are defined by shared norms, roles, and behavioral expectations (Elder, 1975; Riley, Johnson, & Foner, 1972). However, there are few normatively prescribed productive roles for the elderly in contemporary American society. In fact, the postretirement years are too often cast as postproductive years, a period when adults with few family obligations have discharged their "work" obligations along with departure from their

239

career jobs. It is in this period of comparative "rolelessness" that individuals can be especially at risk in experiencing social isolation (Rosow, 1974, 1985) and the onset of poor health.

The expanding retired segment of the American population represents a body of untapped human potential that governments, communities, and organizations can no longer afford to ignore. The challenge we now face is to invent new roles or refashion old ones that accommodate to the reality of this third stage of life in order both to draw on the potential of a large and growing human resource pool and to enhance the quality of life for those who risk being marginalized and isolated from their communities.

For many adults, paid work is a major, if not the principal, source of purposive activity, social relations, independence, identity, and self-respect. It is the way that we become integrated and acknowledged as members of the larger community. Given the centrality of paid employment in American society, what can be said about the social value, as well as the lives, lifestyles, and prospects, of individuals who retire early from their full-time career jobs or the growing number of those in the postretirement "third age?"

Strategies

One possible option is to embark on a second or third career—whether by starting an entirely different type of job or continuing one's previous work, but at a reduced level. A second possibility is unpaid work—as a volunteer or as an active participant in a voluntary association. The first, labor force participation, is an extension of the productive activity typically representative of adulthood in our society. The second, volunteer participation, may be either a continuation of activities begun in earlier and middle adulthood or a qualitative shift in relative emphasis from paid work to unpaid volunteer labor. Both options afford opportunities for productive activity, social interaction, and identity-defining status within society. But neither has been institutionalized as a means of drawing on the talents and integrating members of the third age into the larger society in a meaningful way. Although an expanded definition of *productive activity* can incorporate housework, child care, and help to family and friends (Fischer, Mueller, & Cooper, 1991; Fischer & Schaffer, 1993; Herzog, Kahn, Morgan, Jackson, & Antonucci, 1989; Morgan, 1986), I focus here on two nonfamily activities promoting sustained social integration: paid work and volunteer work.

Neugarten (1974, p. 46) described those in the 55 to 75 age range as the "young old," relatively healthy and vigorous individuals who have fulfilled the traditional responsibilities of employment and parenthood. A significant portion of this group goes on to seek self-fulfillment through either paid work or unpaid community service. But we know little about the circumstances leading to this sustained productive activity, or about the life paths of those who contemplate and go on to early retirement. As individuals make the transition to retirement they also make productivity-related decisions as to whether to engage in paid work or voluntary activities, decisions that in turn may be tied to the timing of their retirement.

In this chapter I highlight four themes I consider especially relevant to this topic. I then discuss the theoretical and research evidence suggesting the links between multiple roles and well-being in the later years of life, constructing a conceptual model in light of this evidence. Finally, I turn to the implications both for future research and for social change.

Aging, Roles, and Well-Being: Four Themes

In considering both role occupancy in the later years of life and the implications of role occupancy for well-being, I argue for the importance of

1. providing a life course view of aging, health, and productive activity, including the dynamics of entry into or continued involvement in paid or volunteer work and the salutary effects of employment and volunteering on health and well-being,
2. examining possible gender differences in postretirement life paths, considering the interplay and multiple pathways between family and nonfamily role involvements for both men and women in different occupations,
3. describing the incidence and implications of volunteering in men's and women's lives in later midlife and beyond, focusing especially on the possible interplay between paid work and unpaid volunteer work, as well as timing and context, and
4. assessing potential practical interventions in enhancing engagement in productive activity following retirement.

A Life Course Approach to Aging, Health, and Productive Activity

A life course and age stratification perspective highlights the importance of the environmental context as well as the processes of development and change over the life span (Elder, 1985, 1992; Riley, Foner, & Waring, 1988). This perspective on aging challenges traditional ways of investigating roles in late midlife and old age. Most studies of older people focus exclusively on the later years, ignoring their life history of role involvements and relationships throughout adulthood. The tacit assumption is that older people are a specific subpopulation group for whom past experiences matter little.

But recent theoretical advances view the developmental course of later adulthood within a life course and continuity theory framework, recognizing that older individuals are embedded in a changing social, cultural, and economic environment, as well as being products of a life history of events, relationships, and behavior (e.g., Atchley, 1989; Morgan, 1986; O'Rand, Henretta, & Krecker, 1992; Rosow, 1985; Sorenson, Weinert, & Sherrod, 1986).

In establishing a personal identity, most adults primarily define themselves by their jobs, and this is increasingly true of women as well as men (Moen, 1992). But how do past employment and volunteering, in addition to past and current health, affect the self-definitions and decisions of those in the third stage, the postretirement years? Drawing on life course and continuity theory perspectives, I submit that the pattern and type of roles throughout adulthood are critical to an understanding of the lives and choices of those in the third age of life. However, situational demands, opportunities, and barriers, including current and anticipated health problems, may also shape paid and unpaid participation. These reality imperatives suggest the opportunity to develop interventions in the form of institutional arrangements that promote the social integration and productivity of older adults. An understanding of how past experiences affect subsequent rates and forms of participation can help identify those at greatest risk of social disengagement and isolation. Although clearly a number of satisfying social roles and activities are potentially available to older individuals—such as grandparenting, neighboring, socializing with friends, and pursuing hobbies—I see paid work and unpaid volunteer work as particularly integrative in that they provide culturally sanctioned ways of participating in the broader community as well as access to various components of society (see discussion of social integration in Stryker, 1980).

Gender Differences

We have little understanding of the role choices and life paths of those in the third age of life, how these differ for men and women, and how they relate to education, race, ethnicity, and specific experiences throughout adulthood in both paid and unpaid work. And as Bronfenbrenner (1979) proposed, location in these different ecologies may render the same experience—moving into the postretirement years—individually distinctive and may produce quite different effects.

Historically, gender has had a profound influence on the role options of men and women. The fact that women have been allocated the principal responsibility for the care of children and of families has traditionally limited their participation in the nonfamilial sectors of society. However, a number of social changes in both attitudes and behavior have substantially increased the labor force participation of American women (Moen, 1992). The significance of these changes is enormous, yet we have little knowledge of the manner in which they have touched individual women's lives in the postretirement phase of their life course.

The whole process of retirement may well be a different experience for women than men, in part because of the historical difference in their attachment to the labor force. When men leave their jobs, they are exiting from a role that has typically dominated their adult years. Women, on the other hand, typically experience greater discontinuity, moving in and out of the labor force and in and out of part-time jobs in tandem with shifting family responsibilities. Consequently they are less likely to have the same duration of employment or accumulation of work experience as men (DeViney & O'Rand, 1988). Given occupational segregation by gender and their less stable employment histories, women are also less likely to be covered by a pension than are men, and those with pensions have incomes far lower than men's.

The differential experiences of men and women approaching retirement are only beginning to be documented (Hayward & Liu, 1992; Herzog et al., 1989; Matthews & Brown, 1988; O'Rand, 1988), even though more women than men reach retirement age every year. Women in the third age are more likely both to be caregivers to other family members and to be poor than are men. How do these considerations affect their options and choices regarding work and volunteering? There has been, to date, no study of the life course dynamics of women in late midlife, their shifting lifestyles, health, and psychosocial well-being. In fact, this age category of women has been conspicuously ignored in studies of women's changing roles (e.g., reviews by Matthews & Rodin, 1989; Repetti, Matthews, & Waldron, 1989).

The challenge of research on women, as Janet Giele (1982) pointed out, is not only to map out their various life patterns but also to ascertain which of these patterns are the most psychologically and physiologically adaptive. Research on the significance of women's employment for health and well-being remains ambiguous as to whether paid work has salutary or negative effects (see review in Moen, 1992). Neither do these studies consider the role of paid work at different stages in a woman's life course, and few studies consider the effects of retirement on women (Quinn & Burkhauser, 1990). Even less research has investigated the consequences of women's (or men's) involvement in unpaid volunteer activities (but see Chambré, 1987; Fischer & Schaffer, 1993).

The Role of Volunteering

Volunteering can be defined as unpaid work, as "the giving freely of an individual's time, talents, and energy" (Anderson, 1991, p. 74). Volunteer activity represents a pervasive but typically overlooked and underrated experience in women's and men's lives (Luks & Payne, 1991). It is estimated that 89 million Americans were engaged in volunteer activities in 1985 (Anderson, 1991), and that in 1981 nearly one fourth of Americans 65 and older engaged in formal (organizational) volunteering and almost two in five (37%) were volunteering either formally or informally (Gallup, 1981). Yet despite its prevalence, we have little reliable knowledge about the enduring influence of volunteering on lives or the pathways leading men and women into and out of volunteering coterminous with aging and retirement. Neither do we understand the processes by which volunteering or participation in voluntary associations may serve to promote health and well-being.

Participation in voluntary associations is an important form of social integration, but, with the exception of church membership, it may decline following retirement (Riley & Foner, 1968), and postretirement involvement (Wilensky, 1961) may well be a function of lifelong patterns of participation. Herzog et al. (1989) pointed out that volunteer work in community organizations is similar to paid employment, with volunteers engaging in work with "clear market value" (p. S134).

A history of previous volunteering should also be related to current volunteering (Chambré, 1984, 1987; Cohen-Mansfield, 1989; Fischer & Schaffer, 1993; Moen & Dempster-McClain, 1993). However, 70% of retirees who volunteer through the Retiree Volunteer Program report never having volunteered before (Cleveland, 1992). And a study of middle-aged women found that fewer than 15% who were currently volunteering did so year after year (Romero, 1986).

Part of the difficulty in recruiting and retaining older volunteers is the absence of anticipatory socialization for the postretirement years. Our society typically prepares individuals for moving into new roles, whether it is kindergarten or employment, but we do not prepare individuals for role disengagement, such as that involved in leaving the world of work (Ebaugh, 1988).

Theoretical and empirical work on factors affecting the likelihood of volunteering suggests that personal gain, not merely pure altruism, is frequently an important motivator (Romero, 1986), although helping others and wanting to do something useful are the principal reasons volunteers give for volunteering (Gallup, 1981). Research looking at volunteering rates of older Americans by employment status has found that full-time employment is negatively related to volunteering (Herzog & Morgan, 1992), but what is required is consideration of the dynamics of the decision-making process concerning volunteering around the time of and after the retirement transition. For example, Barfield and Morgan (1968) found in the 1960s that more men expected to increase their volunteer activity following retirement than actually did so. It is estimated that about 40% of Americans aged 55 to 74 engage in some form of volunteer work (Herzog & Morgan, 1992). Moreover, there appear to be significant numbers of latent volunteers who would be willing to volunteer if someone asked them, and of conditional volunteers who would be willing to volunteer under certain conditions (Okun, 1992). A study of those 60 and older found that conditional volunteers tended on average to be somewhat older, whereas latent volunteers were in their 60s (Okun, 1992).

It is not clear whether voluntary participation is responsive to the same motivators and constraints as paid labor force participation. For example, poor health promotes the transition to retirement (Parnes & Nestel, 1974) and may be an important consideration, but less of an impediment, to volunteer work (Chambré, 1987). The fact that volunteer work apparently does not become a substitute for paid work following retirement suggests the possible lack of motivation and/or perceived opportunities (Chambré, 1987; Romero, 1986). However, only longitudinal research can capture the activity patterns and choices of the postretirement years.

Practical Applications

The issue of postretirement productivity has practical as well as theoretical implications in applied social gerontology and provides the opportunity for translating knowledge into action. The trends in longevity and retirement are extremely consequential for American society generally and for the quality of individual lives. Given the age stratification system, roles and resources are unequally distributed, offering limited options for older people in our society. Research has shown that chronological age is a poor predictor of ability, competence, and performance (e.g., Sorenson et al., 1986), but societal norms and institutional practices nevertheless effectively limit the opportunities for productive activity for those in the postretirement third age. This suggests a potential for intervention strategies that offer opportunities for productive roles following retirement.

What is the value of various organizational and community-level interventions aimed at optimizing the social integration of those making the retirement transition, or already retired, in terms of participation in work and volunteer roles? Consider, for example, interventions to attract or retain the semiretired or fully retired to volunteer work.

To the degree that social integration, in the form of such role involvements, promotes health and well-being, postretirement participation in paid jobs and unpaid volunteer activities may extend the third stage of healthy aging, reducing demands on the health care system and enhancing quality of life. An understanding of how different subgroups of workers manage their transition into retirement is necessary to identify those at greatest risk of social disengagement and isolation and, consequently, poor health.

The issue is to design realistic intervention strategies that can effectively involve retired persons in productive volunteer work. In designing these strategies, a key concern is whether there is a greater need to create new opportunities for productive engagement or to improve the utilization of existing opportunities. Opportunities for volunteerism are plentiful; what is required is providing information about and motivation for volunteering.

Another issue concerns the targeting of interventions. Does one focus on the individuals in transition, such as those undergoing retirement, or design community-level interventions broadly providing a base of information? Those with less education and in poor health, as well as the unmarried, have the greatest risk of social isolation. What types of interventions can best promote the participation of those who are least likely to volunteer?

Possible strategies include organizationally based interventions, such as highlighting volunteering as an option in preretirement planning programs (Chambré, 1987), as well as community-based recruitment by voluntary organizations. One plausible intervention, incorporated in corporations throughout the country, is the Corporate Retiree Volunteer Program, aimed at bringing corporate retirees into an organizationally structured program of volunteering (National Retiree Volunteer Center, 1990).

Structural conditions and institutional arrangements may effectively channel men and women eligible for retirement out of paid employment, limiting their opportunities for purposive activity. Thus workplace or community-level interventions may be especially useful in mobilizing individuals to engage in volunteering. Three features of the workplace are particularly important: the package of retirement benefits available and postretirement income; opportunities within the firm for reemployment, either part or full time; and the procedures followed in negotiating and managing the retirement transition. Each of these structural characteristics may affect workers' timing of retirement as well as their behavior following retirement.

Four points from the research literature are important in planning an intervention to promote volunteering. First, perennial nonvolunteers, that is those who are not now volunteering nor have ever volunteered, are likely to be difficult to recruit compared with those who have volunteered in the past (Fischer & Schaffer, 1993). Older nonvolunteers may be particularly problematic. Second, there appears to be little targeted recruitment aimed specifically at the older population (Herzog & Morgan, 1992). Third, personal contact is an important recruitment mechanism (Fischer & Schaffer, 1993; Gallup, 1981). And fourth, some degree of choice in type of volunteering and the matching of skills and interests of the volunteer with the volunteer work may be important recruitment and retention considerations (Romero, 1986).

The Research Evidence

A life course approach to the role trajectories of those in their later years builds on a platform of existing theory and knowledge concerning the importance of multiple roles generally for psychosocial health.

The Women's Roles and Well-Being Study[1]

I, together with colleagues, have undertaken a program of longitudinal research applying a life course perspective to studies of women's labor force participation in midlife (funded by the National Science Foundation) and of women's roles and well-being (funded by the National Institute on Aging). The emphasis of this research program has been on continuities and discontinuities in roles as well as on both the contemporaneous and enduring effects of social integration on health and well-being (Miller, Moen, & Dempster-McClain, 1991; Moen, Dempster-McClain, & Williams, 1989, 1992, 1993). The Women's Roles and Well-Being Project, a study of women in upstate New York, focused on several roles prominent in women's lives in addition to that of paid worker, including volunteer and caregiver. We found that women in late midlife in more recent cohorts are more likely than early cohorts to be in the labor force, as well as in volunteer and caregiving roles. Moreover, these caregiving and volunteering roles remain prominent long after women begin exiting the paid worker role (Moen & Dempster-McClain, 1993; Moen, Robison, & Fields, 1993). Although multiple role involvements may be salutary for health and psychosocial well-being (e.g., Moen, Dempster-McClain, & Williams, 1989, 1992, 1993), excessive role obligations may also interfere with women's ability to care for themselves (e.g., Brody, 1981; Gove & Hughes, 1979).

In this program of work, social integration, in the form of multiple role involvements over the life course, is viewed as an important bridge to women's health and well-being in their later years (Moen, Dempster-McClain, & Williams, 1989, 1992, 1993). Such multiple role occupancy may be especially important in later adulthood, a time when role reduction, rather than role accumulation, becomes increasingly common in our culture (Markides & Cooper, 1989; Morgan, 1988). We found that participation in clubs and organizations, as well as in volunteer activities generally, was particularly salutary to women's health and well-being.

The findings of the Women's Roles and Well-Being Study have introduced a number of provocative questions, and provide both the platform and the motivation for future research in this area. Who, in the postretirement third age, is active in volunteer (or paid) work, and who is not, and why? Are some voluntary activities more beneficial for health and well-being than others? Is volunteer work still beneficial after controlling for enduring personality characteristics? Is it equally beneficial for men as well as women? What are the links between the nature and circumstances of paid and volunteer work prior to retirement and involvement in paid and volunteer work following retirement? The challenge is to understand what it is in the person-environment nexus that promotes social integration and produces its salutary outcomes.

A life course perspective on paid and volunteer work following retirement calls for more research on the mechanisms linking role involvements, lifestyles and acquired risks, and health and well-being. Facile assumptions about positive or negative ties between employment or volunteering and health should not be accepted uncritically (Cutler, 1973). Merely being in or out of the labor force, or in or out of volunteering, is not sufficient to account for changes in psychosocial or other health outcomes.

A motivation for this program of research is to interrelate the various components of the life course, which too often are studied in isolation. Thus we aim to relate aspects of earlier and middle adulthood to experiences in the later years of life. A testable proposition of life course analysis is that an understanding of one life phase requires it to be placed in the larger context of life pathways. Such a focus necessitates the collection of life histories of the men and women confronting and/or living through retirement.

The findings of research linking health with social integration, defined as "the existence or quantity of social ties or relationships," are ambiguous because the causal direction of effects is unclear (House, Landis, & Umberson, 1988, p. 302). As Verbrugge (1983) pointed out, the issue is one of social causation versus social selection. Social causation assumes that social integration (occupying multiple roles) influences health. By contrast, social selection assumes that healthy people are the ones most likely to take on and maintain multiple social roles. But the choice between the social causation versus the social selection argument is less crucial than gaining an understanding of the pathways to health and social integration in later adulthood. Causation and selection probably operate simultaneously and interactively in a dynamic cascade of events over the life course. Successful aging encompasses both social integration (multiple roles) and health in the later years of life. What is required is a dynamic approach to health and social integration, examining the extent to which experiences throughout the life course shape roles, relationships, and well-being later in life (e.g., George, 1989; Moen et al., 1992; Riley & Riley, 1989; Rowe & Kahn, 1987).

An overview paper for the National Institutes of Health (Moen, 1990) concluded that the life course paradigm argues for the simultaneous consideration of many elements in the study of the interplay between health and social roles. Differences in postretirement well-being in relation to current employment or volunteer status may be a composite function of four sets of factors: (a) self-selection—individuals' predispositions and experiences drawing them into or out of roles, (b) conditions and quality of the role, (c) structural options—including the larger opportunity structure within society that pushes or pulls individuals into or out of certain roles, (d) family situation—including the presence of a spouse. The findings of the best research in this area direct attention to the dynamic interplay among these elements in promoting or reducing health and well-being.

Conceptual Model

Figure 13.1 provides a graphic representation of the conceptual model that posits three broad sets of factors affecting the likelihood, duration, and form of productive involvement in paid and volunteer work following retirement: (a) institutional ties (contemporaneous and throughout adulthood), including the content of the career job and life patterns of paid and unpaid work; (b) individual characteristics, including health and motivation (incorporating a sense of personal efficacy, psychological well-being, educational level, and satisfaction with the work role); and (c) situational constraints and opportunities, including financial need, family composition and circumstances, and existing options for paid and volunteer work. These factors operate in a complex and contingent fashion to both shape the timing of retirement and give rise to activities following retirement.

An Agenda for Research

A life course approach offers a distinctive perspective on aging, multiple roles, and well-being. First, it focuses on the mechanisms influencing individuals to stay actively engaged in productive activities beyond retirement, seeking to answer why individuals remain or become involved in paid or volunteer work. Second, a life course focus targets employment and volunteering experiences throughout adulthood as major routes to productive activity in the postretirement years. Third, the life course paradigm highlights the contexts affecting paid and volunteer work choices, especially avenues of opportunity for women, as well as for men, that promote or, conversely, inhibit productive role involvements. Fourth, in addition to

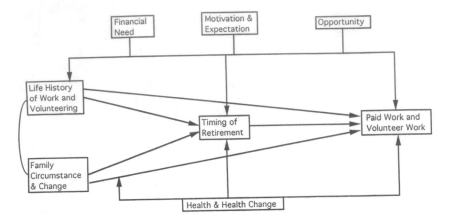

Figure 13.1. A Conceptual (Nonpath) Model of Retired Persons' Paid Work and Volunteer Work

mapping the pathways to productive activity, we can apply this knowledge in designing and testing interventions that can alter the effectiveness of existing opportunity structures for productive engagement in the later years.

A life course approach suggests that the process of retirement and activity in the postretirement life phase are influenced by roles and resources throughout adulthood, as well as by current opportunities and situational constraints, including health. However, these factors may well operate so as to shape distinctive postretirement life pathways by gender and by occupation.

What is required is research to examine how institutional ties (contemporaneous and throughout adulthood), individual characteristics, and situational constraints and opportunities affect the likelihood, duration, and form of productive involvement in paid and unpaid work following retirement. An important research agenda is (a) to formulate and test models of the causes, consequences, and pathways of postretirement productive activity; (b) to elucidate the mechanisms by which circumstances affect choices and opportunities for productive activity for men and women at different locations in the social structure; (c) to test and evaluate the utility of various intervention strategies designed to promote productive involvement in the postretirement years; and (d) to test the validity of findings linking role involvements with health, results that have not systematically addressed the complex interface between the life pathways and health trajectories of men and women in the retirement years.

An Agenda for Social Change

The theoretical and empirical foundation for an understanding of postretirement roles and well-being suggests not only an agenda for research but also an agenda for social change, one that fashions new role options for the growing numbers of educated, healthy, and productive individuals who are moving out of their career jobs at progressively earlier ages.

Examples of possible interventions promoting volunteering include personal recruitment by retired individuals who are already volunteers, programs of retirement education within the workplace, and the establishment of outplacement systems for volunteer activities. Other possible interventions involve institutional supports and community-based activities. (An early study of volunteers found that a trigger for volunteering is often a friend, neighbor, or coworker; see Sills, 1957.) Special efforts are necessary to design interventions that are no less appropriate for women than men (e.g., Matthews & Brown, 1988; Meade & Walker, 1988).

The first step in planning field interventions would be to identify those members of the target population (those already retired or about to retire from their career jobs) who are most at risk of social isolation and to assess the factors promoting productive activities for those not at risk. For example, the continuity of behavior hypothesis suggests that persons who have not developed a pattern of volunteering in earlier years are unlikely to begin doing so following retirement. And research also suggests that the unmarried are less likely than those who are married to volunteer, as are those with less education and in poorer health (Chambré, 1987). What may be important is not only the relative utility of different forms of interventions but the effects of their timing in relation to retirement.

Necessary as well is a rethinking of productive roles for older individuals in our society and a broad restructuring of the social organization of the life course, with greater role flexibility and opportunity. As Riley and Riley (1994) pointed out, "While the 20th century has experienced a revolution in human development and aging, there has been no comparable revolution in the role structures of society to keep pace with the changes in the ways people grow up and grow old" (p. 16). Clearly, structural reorganization of a variety of roles is called for.

I have concentrated in this chapter on volunteering, but paid work, in various forms, should also be a viable option for those in the third age. Certainly greater opportunity and flexibility in paid labor force participation should be available for all age groups (Kahn, 1994; Moen, 1994). Still, participation in voluntary activities remains a neglected and undervalued social role offering avenues of integration that remain open to adults in our society, regardless of age. It also provides a human resource pool available throughout the day, enabling service agencies to assist more clients (Anderson, 1991; Wilder Research Center, 1991). If volunteering is both personally and socially beneficial, how do we promote it in the later years? What types of volunteering produce the greatest benefits? Under what circumstances is volunteering particularly advantageous? The challenge is to design more effective social opportunities and roles for older people in our society. Because Americans are spending almost a third of their lives beyond the time of retirement, the question of social integration, in the form of productive social roles, in these years becomes especially crucial.

Note

1. This is a two-wave panel study of women who were interviewed in 1956 in a medium-sized city in upstate New York and reinterviewed 30 years later, in 1986. A random sample of 427 women aged 23 to 51 who were both wives and mothers were interviewed in 1956 (Dean & Williams, 1956). This same group was located and reinterviewed 30 years later, in 1986. We were able to find 76.3% (326) who were still alive in 1986 and to ascertain that 19.2% (82) had died during the 30-year period (Moen, Dempster-McClain, & Williams, 1989). Only 4.4% (19 women) of the original sample could not be located. This "catch-up" design (Kessler & Greenberg, 1981) of the Women's Roles Study offers the rare opportunity to examine the long-term health effects of multiple roles. Of the 326 women who were alive and contacted in 1986, only 3% (13 women) refused to be interviewed. We draw on information from the initial interview in 1956 as well as the second interview of 313 women in 1986, when extensive life history material was collected, in addition to responses to more structured questions.

References

Anderson, D. (1991). Retirees: Community service resources. *Resourceful aging: Today and tomorrow* (Conference Proceedings, Vol. 2, pp. 73-78). Washington, DC: American Association of Retired Persons.

Atchley, R. C. (1989). A continuity theory of normal aging. *The Gerontologist, 29,* 183-190.

Barfield, R., & Morgan, J. N. (1968). *Early retirement: The decision and the experiences.* Ann Arbor, MI: Institute for Social Research.

Berg, R. L., & Cassells, J. S. (Eds.). (1990). *The second fifty years: Promoting health and preventing disability.* Washington, DC: National Academy Press.

Brody, E. (1981). Women in the middle and family help to older people. *The Gerontologist, 21,* 471-480.

Bronfenbrenner, U. (1979). *The ecology of human development.* Cambridge, MA: Harvard University Press.

Burkhauser, R. V., & Quinn, J. F. (1989). American patterns of work and retirement. In W. Schmall (Ed.), *Redefining the process of retirement: An international perspective* (pp. 91-114). Berlin: Springer-Verlag.

Burkhauser, R. V., & Quinn, J. F. (1990). Economic incentives and the labor force participation of older workers. In L. Bassi & D. Crawford (Eds.), *Research in labor economics* (Vol. 11, pp. 159-179). New York: JAI.

Chambré, S. M. (1984). Is volunteering a substitute for role loss in old age: An empirical test of activity theory. *The Gerontologist, 24,* 294-295.

Chambré, S. M. (1987). *Good deeds in old age: Volunteering by the new leisure class.* Lexington, MA: Lexington.

Cleveland, H. (1992). *A simple and compelling idea: Linking retiree volunteers with people in need.* Minneapolis: National Retiree Volunteer Center.

Cohen-Mansfield, J. (1989). Employment and volunteering roles for the elderly: Characteristics, attributions, and strategies. *Journal of Leisure Research, 21,* 214-227.

Cutler, S. J. (1973). Voluntary association participation and life satisfaction: A cautionary research note. *Journal of Gerontology, 28,* 96-100.

Dean, J., & Williams, R. M. (1956). *Social and cultural factors affecting role-conflict and adjustment among American women: A pilot investigation.* Progress report submitted to the National Institute of Mental Health, Bethesda, MD.

DeViney, S., & O'Rand, A. M. (1988). Age, gender, cohort succession and labor force participation of older workers, 1951-1984. *Sociological Quarterly, 29,* 525-540.

Ebaugh, C. (1988). *Becoming an ex: The process of role exit.* Chicago: University of Chicago Press.

Elder, G. H., Jr. (1975). Age differentiation and the life course. *Annual Review of Sociology, 1,* 165-190.

Elder, G. H., Jr. (1985). *Life course dynamics: Trajectories and transitions, 1968-1980.* Ithaca, NY: Cornell University Press.

Elder, G. H., Jr. (1992). The life course. In E. F. Borgatta & M. L. Borgatta (Eds.), *The encyclopedia of sociology* (pp. 1120-1130). New York: Macmillan.

Fields, G. S., & Mitchell, O. S. (1984). *Retirement, pensions, and Social Security.* Cambridge: MIT Press.

Fischer, L. R., Mueller, D. P., & Cooper, P. W. (1991). Older volunteers: A discussion of the Minnesota Senior Study. *The Gerontologist, 31,* 183-194.

Fischer, L. R., & Schaffer, K. B. (1993). *Older volunteers: A guide to research and practice.* Newbury Park, CA: Sage.

Gallup Organization. (1981). *Americans volunteer—1981.* Princeton, NJ: Author.

George, L. K. (1989). Stress, social support, and depression over the life-course. In K. S. Markides & C. L. Cooper (Eds.), *Aging, stress and health* (pp. 241-268). Manchester, UK: John Wiley.

Giele, J. Z. (1982). Women's work and family roles. In J. Z. Giele (Ed.), *Women in the middle years* (pp. 115-150). New York: Free Press.

Gilford, D. M. (Ed.). (1988). *The aging population in the twenty-first century: Statistics for health policy.* Washington, DC: National Academy Press.

Gove, W. R., & Hughes, M. (1979). Possible causes of the apparent sex differences in physical health: An empirical investigation. *American Sociological Review, 44,* 126-146.

Hayward, M. D., & Liu, M. (1992). Men and women in their retirement years: A demographic profile. In M. Szinovacz, D. J. Ekerdt, & B. H. Vinick (Eds.), *Families and retirement* (pp. 23-50). Newbury Park, CA: Sage.

Herzog, A. R., Kahn, R. L., Morgan, J. N., Jackson, J. S., & Antonucci, T. C. (1989). Age differences in productive activities. *Journal of Gerontology: Social Sciences, 44,* S129-S138.

Herzog, A. R., & Morgan, J. N. (1992). Formal volunteering among older Americans. In S. Bass, F. Caro, & Y. P. Chen (Eds.), *Achieving a productive aging society* (pp. 119-142). Westport, CT: Auburn House.

House, J. S., Landis, K. R., & Umberson, D. (1988). Social relationships and health. *Science, 241,* 540-545.

Kahn, R. L. (1994). Opportunities and aspirations of older men and women: A social-psychological approach to structural lag. In M. W. Riley, R. L. Kahn, & A. Foner (Eds.), *Age and structural lag: Society's failure to provide meaningful opportunities in work, family, and leisure* (pp. 37-53). New York: John Wiley.

Kessler, R. C., & Greenberg, D. F. (1981). *Linear panel analysis: Models of quantitative change.* New York: Academic Press.

Laslett, P. (1991). *A fresh map of life: The emergence of the third age.* Cambridge, MA: Harvard University Press.

Lonergan, E. T. (Ed.). (1991). *Extending life, enhancing life: A national research agenda on aging.* Washington, DC: National Academy Press.

Luks, A., & Payne, P. (1991). *The healing power of doing good.* New York: Fawcett Columbine.

Markides, K. S., & Cooper, C. L. (1989). Aging, stress, social support and health: An overview. In K. S. Markides & C. L. Cooper (Eds.), *Aging, stress and health* (pp. 1-12). Manchester, UK: John Wiley.

Matthews, A. M., & Brown, K. H. (1988). Retirement as a critical life event: The differential experiences of women and men. *Research on Aging, 9,* 548-557.

Matthews, K. A., & Rodin, J. (1989). Women's changing work roles: Impact on health, family, and public policy. *American Psychologist, 44,* 1389-1393.

Meade, K., & Walker, J. (1988). Gender equality: Issues and challenges for retirement education. *Educational Gerontology, 15,* 171-186.

Miller, M., Moen, P., & Dempster-McClain, D. (1991). Motherhood, multiple roles and maternal well-being: Women of the 1950s. *Gender and Society, 5,* 565-582.

Moen, P. (1990, October). *Multiple roles and women's well-being: A life course perspective.* Paper presented at NIH sponsored seminar on Women, Health and Behavior, National Institutes of Health, Bethesda, MD.

Moen, P. (1992). *Women's two roles: A contemporary dilemma.* Westport, CT: Auburn House.

Moen, P. (1994). Women, work and family: A sociological perspective on changing roles. In M. W. Riley, R. L. Kahn, & A. Foner (Eds.), *Age and structural lag: Society's failure to provide meaningful opportunities in work, family, and leisure* (pp. 151-170). New York: John Wiley.

Moen, P., & Dempster-McClain, D. (1993). *The structure of women's paid and unpaid non-family work roles.* Unpublished draft.

Moen, P., Dempster-McClain, D., & Williams, R. M., Jr. (1989). Social integration and longevity: An event history analysis of women's roles and resilience. *American Sociological Review, 54,* 635-647.

Moen, P., Dempster-McClain, D., & Williams, R. M., Jr. (1992). Successful aging: A life course perspective on women's multiple roles and health. *American Journal of Sociology, 97,* 1612-1638.

Moen, P., Dempster-McClain, D., & Williams, R. M., Jr. (1993). *Multiple roles and women's psychological well-being in the later years: A life course perspective.* Revised version of a paper presented at the Gerontological Society of America, November 1991, San Francisco.

Moen, P., Robison, J., & Fields, V. (1993). *Women's employment and caregiving roles: A life course perspective.* Unpublished draft.

Morgan, D. L. (1988). Age differences in social network participation. *Journal of Gerontology: Social Sciences, 43,* S129-S137.

Morgan, J. N. (1986). Unpaid productive activity over the life course. In Committee on Aging Society (Eds.), *Productive roles in an older society* (pp. 73-109). Washington, DC: National Academy Press.

National Retiree Volunteer Center. (1990). Annual report. Minneapolis: Author.

Neugarten, B. L. (1974). Age groups in American society and the rise of the young-old. *Annals of the American Academy of Political and Social Science, 415,* 187-198.

Okun, M. A. (1992, November). *Interest in organizational volunteering among elders.* Paper presented at the annual meeting of the Gerontological Society of America, Washington, DC.

O'Rand, A. M. (1988). Convergence, institutionalization, and bifurcation: Gender and the pension acquisition process. In G. Maddox & M. P. Lawton (Eds.), *Annual review of gerontology and geriatrics* (Vol. 8, pp. 132-155). New York: Springer.

O'Rand, A. M., Henretta, J. C., & Krecker, M. L. (1992). Family pathways to retirement. In M. Szinovacz, D. J. Ekerdt, & B. H. Vinick (Eds.), *Families and retirement* (pp. 81-98). Newbury Park, CA: Sage.

Parnes, H. S., & Nestel, G. (1974). Early retirement. In H. S. Parnes, G. Nestel, A. V. Adams, P. Andrisani, & A. I. Kohen (Eds.), *The retirement years: Five years in the work lives of middle aged men* (Vol. 4, pp. 153-196). Columbus: Ohio University, Center for Human Resource Research.

Quinn, J. F., & Burkhauser, R. V. (1990). Work and retirement. In R. H. Binstock & L. K. George (Eds.), *Handbook of aging and the social sciences* (3rd ed., pp. 307-327). San Diego: Academic Press.

Quinn, J. F., Burkhauser, R. V., & Myers, D. A. (1990). *Passing the torch: The influence of economic incentives on work and retirement.* Kalamazoo, MI: Upjohn Institute for Employment Research.

Repetti, R., Matthews, K. A., & Waldron, I. (1989). Effects of paid employment on women's mental and physical health. *American Psychologist, 44,* 1394-1401.

Riley, M. W., & Foner, A. (1968). *Aging and society: An inventory of research findings* (Vol. 1). New York: Russell Sage.

Riley, M. W., Foner, A., & Waring, J. (1988). Sociology of age. In N. J. Smelser (Ed.), *Handbook of sociology* (pp. 243-290). Newbury Park, CA: Sage.

Riley, M. W., Johnson, M. E., & Foner, A. (Eds.). (1972). *Aging and society: A sociology of age stratification* (Vol. 3). New York: Russell Sage.

Riley, M. W., & Riley, J. W., Jr. (1989). The lives of old people and changing social roles. *Annals of the American Academy of Political and Social Science, 503,* 14-28.

Riley, M. W., & Riley, J. W., Jr. (1994). Structural lag: Past and future. In M. W. Riley, R. L. Kahn, & A. Foner (Eds.), *Age and structural lag: Society's failure to provide meaningful opportunities in work, family, and leisure* (pp. 15-36). New York: John Wiley.

Romero, C. J. (1986). The economics of volunteerism: A review. In Committee on Aging Society (Ed.), *Productive roles in an older society* (pp. 23-50). Washington, DC: National Academy Press.

Rosow, I. (1974). *Socialization to old age.* Berkeley: University of California Press.

Rosow, I. (1985). Status and role change through the life cycle. In R. H. Binstock, & E. Shanas (Eds.), *Handbook of aging and the social sciences* (2nd ed., pp. 62-93). New York: Van Nostrand Reinhold.

Rowe, J. W., & Kahn, R. L. (1987). Human aging: Usual and successful. *Science, 237,* 143-149.

Sills, D. (1957). *The volunteers.* Glencoe, IL: Free Press.

Sorenson, A. B., Weinert, F. E., & Sherrod, L. R. (Eds.). (1986). *Human development and the life course: Multidisciplinary perspectives.* Hillsdale, NJ: Lawrence Erlbaum.

Stryker, S. (1980). *Symbolic interaction: A social-structural version.* Menlo Park, CA: Benjamin/Cummings.

U.S. Bureau of the Census. (1991). *Population profile of the United States: 1991* (Current Population Reports, Series P-23, No. 173). Washington, DC: Government Printing Office.

Verbrugge, L. M. (1983). Multiple roles and physical health of women and men. *Journal of Health and Social Behavior, 24,* 16-30.

Wilder Research Center. (1991). *Retiree volunteers and the agencies they serve: A national survey* (Final Report). St. Paul, MN: Author.

Wilensky, H. (1961). Life cycle, work situation, and participation in formal associations. In R. W. Kleemier (Ed.), *Aging and leisure: A research perspective into the meaningful use of time* (pp. 213-242). New York: Oxford University Press.

PART IV

COMPARATIVE ISSUES AND PERSPECTIVES

Policies and programmatic interventions intended to promote successful and productive aging must recognize that considerable variability exists among the older population. Age itself, for example, represents an important dimension of diversity. Just as we would be loath to attempt to aggregate the experience of persons in the first three decades of life into global statements about "the young," it is equally simplistic to try to encapsulate the situations of persons in the last three decades of life into modal statements about "the aged" or "the elderly." Categorical depictions of this sort surely fail to take into account the heterogeneity of older people. Recognizing that the life experiences and situations of older persons differ greatly by cohort and by age, gerontological research has thus begun to distinguish routinely among subgroups such as the "young-old" (i.e., those 65-74), the "old-old" (those 75-84), and the "oldest-old" (those 85 and over).

Age, however, represents only one among a number of dimensions of diversity that need to be taken into consideration when one is formulating intervention programs. The experience of aging differs, additively and interactively, by gender, by race and ethnicity, by residence in urban or in rural areas, and by personal resources (e.g., economic, health, etc.) available to the individual, to name just a few important variables. Not only do aging and the life conditions of older people vary within societies along these and other dimensions, but they also vary between societies as a function of factors such as historical circumstances, cultural differences, and levels of socioeconomic development.

The chapters in this section of the book deal explicitly with issues of diversity within the older population and with variation in the aging experience as it occurs within and between societies. Collectively, these chapters illustrate the need to target prevention programs, and they point to lessons for primary prevention that may be learned by adopting a comparative perspective on aging.

The section begins with Chapter 14, by Elizabeth Markson, which focuses on issues affecting older women. Markson notes how the combination of ageism and sexism has led to the denigration of older women and to the dominance of male models in developmental and gerontological research. Yet older women confront a variety of problems to a far greater extent than older men. Women are considerably more likely to be widowed and to live alone; their economic status is more precarious, with implications for sense of control and psychological distress; women are much more likely than men to be caregivers, with the attendant stresses; and they are more likely to be disabled. Of particular relevance to public policy is Markson's contention that women in general, but especially older women, would bear the brunt of proposed responses to concerns about intergenerational equity.

Racial and ethnic differences represent another critically important dimension of diversity, a theme that is the focus of Chapter 15, by Rose Gibson, on older minority populations. Gibson cautions us about accepting "romanticized" notions of minority elders and points to the need for an accurate knowledge base on which to base interventions designed to promote successful and productive aging. For example, it is widely thought that the greater prevalence of extended families among blacks provides assurance that support will be available to frail and needy elders. Gibson notes, however, that the capacity of black families to provide support for elders is often strained by a variety of factors: social problems besetting youth, poverty, unemployment, and multiple generations of older women within the household. With a number of dependents and scarce resources to care for them, it is incorrect to assume that minority elders and their families are not in need of supportive interventions.

Similarly, it is often assumed that minority elders are uniformly beset by poorer health and higher mortality. Drawing on her own research and that of others, Gibson presents evidence of a health and mortality crossover: Beyond age 75, blacks appear to enjoy better health than whites. If the factors associated with an advantage in health status among blacks over the age of 75 could be identified, such knowledge might provide the basis for health promotion programs, with the ultimate effect of enhancing the personal resources brought to old age. Thus Gibson pleads for new knowledge that points to the unique problems confronted by minority elders as well as to lessons that can be learned from them about successful aging.

In Chapter 16, Douglas Kimmel considers commonalities and differences that follow from sexual orientation. Like older people in general, older gays and lesbians have faced a history of stigma, prejudice, and discrimination. And along with older people more generally, they have been pioneers in the establishment of new social roles and statuses. Kimmel also points to similarities and differences between older people in general and older gays and lesbians in pathways to successful aging. On the one hand, research he reviews suggests several universal correlates of psychological well-being in old age: good health, the availability of social support, financial security, independence, dignity and self-respect, and the freedom to live one's life as one chooses. On the other hand, certain aspects of the lifestyles of older gays and lesbians may be better suited to the promotion of successful aging: freedom from gender role expectations, living arrangements and relationships that may be more conducive to the receipt of caregiving, involvement in social networks, and competence in dealing with crises. Importantly, Kimmel suggests that the dimension of "community" is one that is more prevalent among older gays, thus facilitating successful aging.

The final chapter in this section presents results from Project AGE, a two-phase, comparative cross-cultural analysis of successful aging conducted in seven sites in four countries (Botswana, Ireland, Hong Kong, and the United States). After noting some of the major methodological problems that arise in conducting cross-cultural research and discussing ways in which descriptions of the life course vary by culture, Charlotte Ikels and her colleagues review data on age group preferences and on correlates of life satisfaction. Perhaps as a reflection of the status of older people, old age does not fare well as a preferred group. Although there is a clear tendency for persons to prefer their own group, overall few respondents select old age as the group they would most want to belong to; rather, most identify this age group as that least preferred. Across the several sites, gender is not a major predictor of life satisfaction, and age differences in life satisfaction exhibit both positive and negative correlations, but health is found to be a clear and consistent predictor of this dimension of psychological well-being.

More generally, these cross-cultural data indicate that material needs and health issues predominate in respondents' perceptions of what constitutes successful aging and a good old age. Further, older people rank themselves highest in those societies in which material needs are met by a reliable source of income. Ikels and her colleagues caution that what constitutes an acceptable standard of living varies widely across societies and as a product of cohort factors within societies, but their comparative analysis points clearly to the importance of programs to raise the standard of living of older persons and of the families that provide support to them.

14

Issues Affecting Older Women

Elizabeth W. Markson

The dramatic increase in the number of women over 65 and 85, both in the United States and elsewhere, poses critical issues both for psychologists and for all of us. Their situations inform us of the quality of life for contemporary older women and issues affecting their aging and that of women in the future. This chapter reviews the social construction of older women, their current life situations, and social policy issues and directions affecting their lives—three relevant topics for primary prevention.

Why focus on older women? There are two major reasons. First, females live longer than males. American women 65 and over now outnumber their male age peers 3:2—a dramatic increase from 30 years ago, when the ratio was 6:5. Clearly, old age is a territory pioneered and inhabited by women for longer periods of time, and, given present patterns of life expectancy, women will make up the majority of U.S. elders in the future. Second, until relatively recently, few gerontologists or others paid attention either to primary prevention or to gender in old age. Both men and women were lumped together as "elderly"—implying that gender becomes irrelevant in old age—and male models of aging were defined as "normal aging." Women undergo more exams, lab tests, and blood pressure checks than men but, for reasons that are unclear, receive fewer major diagnostic or therapeutic interventions, even for gender-sensitive testing such as breast exams, Pap tests, and mammograms (Clancy & Franks, 1993). And most medical and pharmaceutical research is based on males, their problems and issues, with little attention to women's unique problems (Culpepper, 1993).

The women's movement, too, has largely ignored older women, reflecting the ambivalence that many founders felt to old age in general and their own mothers in particular. As one older woman activist commented:

> From the beginning of this wave of the women's movement . . . the message has gone out to those of us over sixty that your sisterhood does not include us. . . . You do not see us in our present lives, you do not identify with our

issues, you exploit us, you patronize us, you stereotype us. Mainly you ignore us. (MacDonald, 1989, p. 6)

Yet, as Reinherz (1986) noted, there are unrecognized links between feminist and gerontological theories. Just as feminists reject models of gender-based division of labor as the right and proper distribution of tasks, elder advocates rebel against models of old age emphasizing withdrawal from socially useful roles.

Ageism and Sexism: The Deadly Duo

The United States is an ageist nation where paradoxically one wants to live as long as possible but not grow old. As mortality in childhood and infancy has declined, old age is increasingly associated with infirmity and death, dreaded in an individualistic, youth-conscious, and activity-oriented society such as ours. Moreover, in postindustrial societies, elders' labor is generally not needed; their wisdom has been replaced by formal education and communication technologies. Despite the current emphasis on "productive aging," few viable, respected roles are currently available to the majority of the now-old of either gender. The cultural construction of old age encourages elders to internalize their own limitations and to settle for less than their actual capacities (Philipson, 1982). Sexism and ageism form a deadly duo. Physical youth remains more central to a woman's social identity and self-esteem than to a man's. Although experience, power, and wealth associated with aging may be aphrodisiac qualities for males, current ideals of female beauty require youthful, unwrinkled faces and nubile figures of adolescence or early adulthood. Feminist scholars have noted the deeply rooted cultural ambivalence toward females of all ages, who for centuries were believed to possess magical properties. Because menstruation and birth were poorly understood until the 19th century, these uniquely female processes were regarded as indicators of fearsome supernatural powers. Magic, prophesy, healing, fertility, birth, and death were the province of women. In many cultures, the archetype of the female has also been "Mother Death": Life given by the great mother also brings seeds of death. In Norse mythology, Freya was goddess of both love and death—a common association in numerous religions. Females were often feared, as the Chinese description of female genitalia as "gateways to immortality" and "executioners of men" clearly indicates. Similarly, in traditional Maori religion with a belief in a literal, born again, reincarnation, the vagina was viewed as a "house for the dead"—a place where ghosts seeking rebirth lurk (Walker, 1988).

The Denigration of Older Women

The old woman in particular was viewed as having mystical qualities. In ancient Greece, priestesses were selected from among postmenopausal women, and only women over 60 could serve as paid ritual mourners at funerals (Banner, 1992). Indeed, the word *hag*—from the Greek *hagia,* meaning "holy one"—was once a compliment, stressing the old woman's magical qualities (Walker, 1988). By the Middle Ages, *hag* had become a pejorative term for "witch." How did this transformation come about? The answer, in part, lies in the Judeo-Christian tradition.

According to Genesis, Eve was, through her temptation of Adam, the bringer of death to humanity. Not only was the female responsible for original sin, but she exemplified salaciousness, insatiability, and enticement. As the author of Ecclesiasticus noted, "All wickedness is but little to the wickedness of a woman" (Ecclesiasticus 25:19). The dominant view of women according to the early Christian church was summarized by Tertullian in the third century, who stated that woman was "the devil's gateway, . . . the first deserter of the divine law" (Tertullian, *De cultu feminarum* ["On female dress"], quoted in Smith, 1992, p. 76). A few theologians went as far as the ninth-century monk, Odo of Cluny, who stated, "To embrace a woman is to embrace a sack of manure" (quoted in Smith, 1992, p. 76).

Female value resided only in fertility and motherhood. Once past childbearing age, a woman ceased to represent fecundity. Her sexual attractiveness was nil. In medieval and Renaissance literature, she was sometimes heavily sexualized, like Chaucer's wife of Bath, but most often, like the nurse in *Romeo and Juliet,* confined to the role of go-between in the mating game, as either romantic intermediary or sexual procurer: dangerous to social harmony in either role (Banner, 1992). Her redeeming worth was skill in caring for others in birth, illness, and death. Indeed, most villages had numerous older *medwyfs* (literally, "wise women") who eased pain in childbirth and illness. Prelates of the Church viewed these women with a jaundiced eye as possessors of forbidden knowledge—secrets of abortion, contraception, and alleviation of suffering in birth—that went against God's will to punish women for Eve's sin. By the 14th century, the Church had declared war on female healers. Although no university admitted females to study medicine, any woman who cured sickness without studying medicine at a university was a witch—a restriction not applied to men (Ehrenreich & English, 1982).

During the Inquisition, females were stamped not only as "of a different nature from men" and "more carnal than a man" (Kramer & Sprenger, 1508/1971, pp. 116-117) but as witches known to "collect male organs in great numbers, as many as twenty or thirty members together, and put them in a bird's nest" (Kramer & Sprenger, 1508/1971, p. 268). Belief in their latent uncontrollable sexuality meant that suspicion of witchcraft "fell on every old woman with a wrinkled face" (Fraser, 1984, p. 113). Available data indicate that the median age of suspected witches was between 55 and 65—hardly young, or even, for those centuries, middle-aged (Banner, 1992).

Older women as targets were financially profitable for the Inquisition as well. Well-off widows' property was impounded prior to trial; witches could also be tried after death and their property confiscated up to three generations thereafter. As many as 2 million women, primarily older, widowed, feeble, or poor, were executed. In 17th-century Puritan Massachusetts, those most likely to be condemned for witchcraft were older women, usually single, widowed, or poor, who had a reputation for annoying their neighbors (Demos, 1982).

Recent Views on Older Women

More recent theories have also labeled females of all ages as distinctly flawed. Freud's model of feminine identity echoes the views of Judeo-Christian theologians: Women have weaker superegos than men and a corrupt sense of social justice as a result of penis envy (Freud, 1961a). Freud also had scant interest in older people of either gender and made it clear in the early days of psychoanalysis that, due to the amount of material to be covered and the increasing inflexibility of the personality associated with aging, analysis was inappropriate for those aged 50 or older. Indeed, for Freud, women as young as 30 were unfit analysands due to their psychical rigidity and unchangeability; men at the same age remained youthful and pliable (Freud, 1961b).

Aging women have been of little interest to subsequent psychoanalysts. As Tallmer noted in 1989, "The common expression, the 'empty nest' syndrome, reflects the current psychoanalytic emphasis on the association between aging and loss. Psychological changes in late adulthood are generally explained as reactions to loss, and, ultimately, to the most basic fear of death" (p. 231). Yet adulthood is not merely a period of marking time between childhood and death but a period of personality change for both genders.

A notable exception to the lack of interest in female personality in midlife and beyond has been the attention paid to psychopathology attributed to menopause. By 1896, Kraepelin catalogued "involutional melancholia" as a disorder that "sets in principally, or perhaps exclusively, at the beginning of old age in men and in women from the period of menopause onwards. . . . About one third of women make a complete recovery" (Kraepelin, 1896, cited in

Greer, 1992, p. 79). Kraepelin observed, however, that emotional dullness was likely to remain, judgment and memory to deteriorate, and the course of the disease to be tedious.

The old belief that postmenopausal women were likely to be troubled by a strong sexual drive and sexual aggressiveness was echoed at the turn of the 20th century by Havelock Ellis, who commented on "old maid's insanity," a condition to which older unmarried women, career women, and lesbians were especially predisposed (Ellis, 1905/1942, p. 243). Freud, too, noted that menopause increased sexual desire in women as well as return of adolescent issues and the Oedipus complex. As late as the 1940s, psychoanalyst Helene Deutsch (1945), herself 60, viewed menopause as a woman's partial death. A listing of the perils faced by menopausal women includes reappearance of Oedipal feelings, "sublimated homosexuality of puberty," "rape" and "prostitution" fantasies, and sexual acting out. For example, Deutsch reported a case of a grandmother arrested in the park for soliciting men.

Given the level of psychopathology attributed to women at midlife and in old age, it is not surprising that theories of normal adult development have most often relied upon a male model. Whereas Erikson (1968) proposed progressive epigenetic stages leading one to become a more complex, integrated self with age, his observations, discussions, and examples were based largely on upper middle class men, as were those of Levinson (1977). For Erikson as for Freud, biology was destiny and determined personality. To the extent that they received attention, females, due to their inner space (i.e., uterus waiting to be filled), were quiet, protective, and equipped with psychological abilities to care for others. The male was the criterion for adult development. Moreover, the last stage of personality development—ego integrity versus despair—covers at least one third of one's life—a very long time to remain static in one life stage!

Feminist psychologists have challenged the assumptions made by the Freudians about the nature of female experience. As Karen Horney (1967) remarked, "Like all sciences and all valuations, the psychology of women has hitherto been considered only from the point of view of men. . . . The psychology of women . . . actually represents a deposit of the desires and disappointments of men" (p. 56).

Although they pay little attention to midlife and old age, Jean Baker Miller (1986) and other recent feminist theorists have proposed that women's desire for affiliation is key throughout their lives. Although Erikson's model of adult development assumes that identity precedes intimacy and generativity, for women these two stages are fused. Females know themselves through their relationships with others, but because valued behavior is built on male models, affiliative feminine activity is largely unrecognized and perceived passivity. Cooperation, giving, and participation in the development of others are not in direct, open pursuit of masculine goals. Females, albeit tacitly labeled as inferior beings, are more able to use their feelings of vulnerability and dependency to create a sense of internal worth. It is not penis envy that is the key to the feminine psyche but fear of ability to be "like a man"—strong, self-sufficient, and competent.

Recent contributions to role theory complement formulations of adult developmental psychology and differentiate male versus female patterns of behavior in later life. Cumming and Henry (1961), in their work on disengagement, which relies on a structural-functionalist approach, proposed that women's passage through the life course is smoother than that of men, for their roles retain an essential sameness from girlhood to death—that of homemaker, kin keeper, and nurturer. Aging men, in contrast, confront critical changes. When their instrumental role as breadwinner is lost in retirement, males lack the sources of reward upon which they have relied most of their adult lives.

More recent analyses of gender roles have emphasized discontinuity rather than sameness as characteristic of women's lives. Required to adjust to many role shifts—entry into the labor force, childbearing and child care, changes in husband's job, empty nest, career reentry, widowhood—a woman is more likely than a man to be flexible and to be able to cope with life changes (Kline, 1975; Lopata, 1971). She is also more likely to have same-gender friends upon whom she can depend for social support. Moreover, personality apparently changes in both men and women as they age; women become more aggressive, whereas men become more nurturant and affiliative—a transformation that seems to hold true cross-culturally (Gutmann, 1987).

Why do negative stereotypes about middle and old age in women's lives persist despite contrary empirical evidence? Neither menopause, the empty nest, or old age in itself correlates to decrease in well-being or to depression, although these events may be exacerbated by other negative life experiences such as poverty or poor health. The answer would seem to lie in the still-persistent belief that a woman's essence lies in her youthfulness—itself a symbol of her potential to procreate. Yet at least theoretically, once women are free of child care responsibilities, they are in a better position to be stimulated by changes, to focus on their own presents and futures, and to design their own lives. But unfortunately many now-old and soon-to-be-old women do not have this luxury. What are the life situations of older women today? What implications do their present life circumstances have for primary prevention and for social polity?

Life Situations of Older Women Today

Race, social class, religion, ethnicity, and sexual identity shape how women age. Those born in the United States, however, share common slices of history. They survived a childhood without antibiotics; at least one, if not two, world wars; the Great Depression; the Korean and Vietnam wars; the Cold War; and the current economic recession. They have witnessed numerous technological changes: inception of air travel (and perhaps the automobile); introduction of radio, TV, and computers; construction of superhighways; frozen food and microwave ovens. They have lived through the civil rights movement, the second woman's movement (and for the very old, woman's suffrage), and changes in women's roles (Hopper, 1993). As a category, immigrant women are less likely to have such commonly shared experiences, for they have brought with them the unique experiences of growing up in a variety of cultures. Many of them—for example, Latina and Asian immigrants—have arrived in this country with limited knowledge of English and different patterns of intergenerational family structures and occupational skills. Elderly Latinas, for example, share Spanish as their major common bond; their immigration histories and cultural traditions vary as widely as do their countries of origin (Markides & Levin, 1987). Latinas also represent a range of social classes from affluent or middle class to very poor, reflecting their educational attainment, wealth prior to immigration, and life chances thereafter. Asian and Pacific Island old women include Chinese, Japanese, Korean, Vietnamese, Laotian, Hmong, and Filipino, among others, with varied languages, cultures, and, very often, incidents of disaster precipitating their emigration. Despite their variation in language, country of origin, and life trajectories, these "new immigrant" women share the common themes of rigidly defined age and gender-linked roles, lesser authority of women, and precedence of the needs of the family unit over that of any individual member (Yee, 1990).

Marital Status, Family Composition, and Living Arrangements

Being married has different consequences for men and women throughout the life course. Regardless of sociodemographic characteristics, marriage appears to be more crucial for social interaction, life expectancy, and absence of depressive symptomatology among men than women in old age (Keith, 1993; Stallones, Marx, & Garrity, 1990). Married older adults of both genders may undergo less distress than the widowed, divorced, separated, or never married. Although distress levels differ among those not married, all are relatively disadvantaged compared to the married (Murrell, Himmelfarb, & Wright, 1983). Belying the notion of the traumatic effect of the empty nest on women, absence of children in the home is connected to more sharing and companionship between husband and wife in old age (Hess & Waring, 1984). Widowhood is a predictable crisis for women. Five times more females are widowed in old age than are males, and widowers are more likely to remarry, often to a younger woman. Given the high rates of widowhood and low probability of remarriage, it is not surprising that of the approximately 8.5 million older Americans living alone, women make up almost four fifths. Widows account for three out of four women aged 65 to 74 living alone, and more than four in five of those aged 75 or over (Kasper, 1988). Many elderly women living alone have no surviving children, more common among African Americans than whites. Among widows with living children, African American, Asian and Pacific Island, and Latina women are more likely to live with other family members, but widowed white females are more likely to maintain separate households (U.S. Senate, 1988). These differences in living arrangements reflect both cultural tradition (Gratton, 1987) and socioeconomic conditions. Non-Latina women are now most likely to live with their children only when they become disabled, but their minority counterparts are likely to live with family members because of economic necessity (Worobey & Angel, 1990a, 1990b). Older African Americans, Asians, Pacific Islanders, and many Latinas have lived a lifetime of oppression and devaluation by society and make up a disproportionate number of the very poor.

Regardless of marital status or children, most native-born women enter old age with a convoy of social support accumulated through social exchange throughout their lifetimes (Antonucci & Akiyama, 1987), although recent immigrants are less likely to have age-peers upon whom to rely. Never-married elders report a higher level of interaction with friends than do the married and are the most likely of any marital group to have siblings or other relatives in the household (Stull & Scarisbrick-Hauser, 1989).

The Problem of Inadequate Income

As work has become less valued as an end in itself and more esteemed for the lifestyle it makes possible—the "consumer-based good life" (Martin, 1990, p. 62)—a trend toward early retirement has increased over the last few decades. It is primarily white men who opt for early retirement, reflecting their higher wages and greater likelihood of receiving an adequate pension. Among women in the labor force at age 60 to 64, African Americans, even when they assess their health as poor, are most likely to be working. White women who similarly rate their health as poor are more likely to be retired (Belgrave, 1988).

When employed, women continue to be concentrated in a few low-paying jobs. Six in 10 of those 55 and older work in retail sales, administrative and clerical, and services—all areas with wages below the national average for all occupations (U.S. Dept. of Labor, 1989). Although female midlife career reentry has increased in recent years, women currently between 40 and 65 are at a disadvantage in the labor force; they encounter more overt sex discrimination, less opportunity for on-the-job training, and greater age discrimination than men or younger women (National Research Council, 1988).

In old age, women of every marital status have lower money incomes than their male counterparts due to lower wages, inadequate pension coverage, economic dependency on men, and widowhood. The median income in 1987 dollars—$6,425—for all old women is only 56% of that of old men ($11,544). Old women make up almost three fourths of the elderly poor, and they are far more likely to receive Supplemental Security Income.[1] Although marriage benefits both men and women economically, it is especially critical for women, who rely on the greater financial benefits accrued by their husbands.

Widowhood or divorce may mean financial disaster. Most vulnerable to poverty are widows who are very old, and members of minorities. Over half of elderly African American and Latina women not living with family members have incomes below the poverty level; half of all women aged 75 or over who live alone subsist on incomes below 150% of the poverty level.[2] Although the 1986 Tax Reform Act provides tax credits on a sliding scale to very low-income people, it eliminates the extra personal exemption previously provided to all those 65 and over—another blow for those women not in extreme poverty but with current or anticipated limited retirement incomes.

Nor is the financial situation for elderly women expected to improve in the next 30 years. Increasingly, poverty in the United States has become feminized: single mothers with young children and old women among the poorest in the nation. According to current projections, by the year 2020, two out of five elderly women will be living on incomes less than $9,500 in today's dollars (U.S. House of Representatives, 1992) and primarily dependent on Social Security and Supplemental Security Income. Clearly, they will not be among the ranks of WOOPies (well-off older persons) enjoying the growing elder consumer market!

Low-income aging women with few economic resources to cope with aging are more likely to have circumscribed lives and more physical and psychological health problems. According to one recent study, unmarried, separated, widowed, or divorced older women are subject to greater financial stress than older men—an exposure overwhelming their ability to maintain a sense of control, in turn resulting in greater psychological stress (Keith,

1993). Findings such as these are important for primary prevention, for they suggest that if older women were no more likely to brave financial strain than men, there would be no significant gender differences in their sense of mastery and psychological distress.

Carers and Cared-for in the Family

An additional hazard for the young or midlife woman is the likelihood that she will be a member of the "sandwich generation." Approximately 72% of all long-term care is provided by women (29% of whom are daughters, 23% wives, and the remainder other relatives or in-laws). Only 5% of elderly persons receive care from paid sources (U.S. House of Representatives, 1987). Just when a new, freer life lies ahead of her, unconstrained by the obligations of child care, the middle-aged or young-old woman is caught in the demands for care and support. Socialized to be a nurturer, she is trapped between a traditional sense of obligation to her parents, parents-in-law, or spouse and her hopes for individuation and self-expression.

Among aging couples, wives are almost twice as likely to be the primary caregiver (U.S. House of Representatives, 1987). That caregiving among married couples is most often performed by the wife reflects both the greater life expectancy of women and the persistence of traditional gender roles. Caregiving is rarely shared equally among family members (Chappell, 1993; Cicirelli, 1983; Seccombe, 1988). When no wife is available or healthy enough to care for her spouse, family members activate a hierarchy of caregiver selection. A daughter (or daughter-in-law, if no daughter is available) is the first choice, followed by other family members, neighbors and friends, and finally outside sources (Stoller & Pugliesi, 1988). Whether wives, daughters, or other relatives, women are much more likely than men to perform such tasks as bathing, dressing, and toileting, meal preparation, and housework. Male caregivers are likely to provide typically "masculine" services such as home repairs, transportation, financial management, and money (Kivitt, 1985; Seccombe, 1988). Hands-on caregiving is also influenced by other factors: geographical proximity, number of competing work and family obligations, feelings of indebtedness to parents, and familial and cultural norms.

The majority of disabled older persons in the community are also women, many widowed after tending an impaired spouse. A greater proportion of old women than men report difficulty on personal care activities, such as bathing and dressing. These afflictions are more marked with increasing age, although over half of the women age 85 and older say they perform all personal care activities without difficulty. Women also report greater problems in doing home management tasks, perhaps reflecting that the majority of now-old men do not perform many home management tasks—or, if they do, are more hesitant to admit disability in a survey interview! (National Center for Health Statistics, 1993). That older women have poorer functional status than men when age is held constant also reflects the lifelong association between feminine poverty and poor health throughout the life course. Poor elders are twice as likely to have health-related limitations in personal care or home management tasks (Kasper, 1988).

Caregiving and Stress

Increasingly, caregiving is an area for primary prevention. Whether the caregiver is wife, daughter, or other relative, a growing literature has documented the adverse emotional and physical effects of taking care of an elder (see, for example, Pearlin, Mullan, Semple, & Skaff, 1990; Zarit, 1989; Zarit, Reeves, & Bach-Peterson, 1980). Elderly wives with disabled spouses are often "hidden patients" (Fengler & Goodrich, 1979). Whether wife or daughter, female caregivers are likely to assess their physical health as poorer than women of the same age not providing care, and daughters are at higher risk of stress and burnout than are sons (Horowitz, 1985). The emotional impact of caregiving extends beyond the primary person charged with care, for female siblings of primary caregivers are more likely to report feeling stressed than are male sibs (Schoonover, Brody, Hoffman, & Kleban, 1988). The greater strain felt by females may come from several sources: their more intimate physical contact with day-to-day caregiving chores such as bathing, dressing and toileting; their strong socialization and involvement in nurturing (Miller, 1986); or the likelihood that men are less likely to share their feelings (Schoonover et al., 1988). The more intimate emotional links between mother and daughter described by Chodorow (1978) may also exert force on women caring for an impaired mother (Robinson & Thurnher, 1979).

Further research is needed to explore the links between gender and caregiver stress, and is also essential on ethnic variations in caregiver stress. Most immediately, one task for primary prevention is to deal with gender inequities in the division of caregiving responsibilities. A second, equally important task, is ethnic and racially sensitive interventions with potential caregivers. In many Latin cultures, the role of the wife or daughter as primary caregiver is so deeply ingrained that interventions should emphasize lightening the load of providing assistance rather than relieving a burden.

Less frequently recognized than caregiver stress is the stress felt by elders themselves when they receive care. Expectations of support from adult children vary by characteristics such as ethnicity, religion, and race. Low-income, elderly Puerto Rican women in Boston, for example, value respect from their children as the most important aspect of social support and as more important than affection (Sanchez-Ayendez, 1988). Despite the persistence of familism in Latin cultures, elderly Latinas with physical health problems are at relatively high risk of depression (Kemp, Staples, & Lopez-Aquires, 1987). Cultural traditions stressing caregiving and self-sacrifice without outside assistance among many Latina adult daughters and other female relatives may actually exacerbate dependence and disability among elderly women (Hopper, 1993).

Notwithstanding racial and ethnic variations, elders living in the homes of adult children or grandchildren are likely to have lower morale and satisfaction than elders in other living arrangements. Although their higher rates of discontent are no doubt influenced by their disabilities, the loss of autonomy among elders who have a lifelong pattern of independent living should not be belittled (Hess & Waring, 1984). Another major task, then, for primary prevention is to provide culturally sensitive emotional support for both caregivers and care recipients prior to stress and burnout.

Generational Equity: Is It Inequity?

In old age, the majority of American women have strong family ties upon which they may call in time of need. But they are also vulnerable: more likely to be poor, widowed, with functional limitations, and, at the end of life, to spend their last days in a nursing home. By the late 1970s, conservative economists began to point to the growing "burden" of supporting an elder population (Samuelson, 1978). During the recent—and current—period of fiscal constraint for social and human services, "generational equity," described by one of its leading proponents as "nothing more than the present being fair to the future" (Durenberger, 1989), became a popular theme. During the 1980s, the aged were scapegoated as greedy, getting rich at the expense of children, and receiving a disproportionate amount of benefits from federal outlays (Binstock, 1988). As a major spokesperson for the lobbying group (Americans for Generational Equity) stated, "We must recognize that there is a relationship between budgets for the elderly and budgets for the young. . . . Money that is badly needed by poor children in St. Paul is being sent to wealthy retirees in St. Petersburg" (Lamm, 1989, p. 111).

Indeed, because Americans are both living longer and having fewer children, the composition of the "dependency ratio"—currently defined as the ratio of people under age 18 and over age 64 to those between the "working ages" of 18 through 64—changed markedly during the 20th century. The average number of children per American family in 1900 was four.

Today, the average is slightly less than two. In 1900, there were 7 elders per 100 people of working age; today, there are 20 elders per 100. For the first time in history, the average married couple in the United States has more parents living than children (Preston, 1984)—a trend expected to increase, with fewer people of working age to support elders. Forgotten by proponents of generational equity concerned with cost containments is that the increase in elders to be supported is offset by an almost equal decrease in the child support ratio due to lower birth rates. The economic cost of dependent elders is balanced by reduced costs of a smaller dependent child population. Ironically, although the old have been singled out as greedy consumers of resources, no significant U.S. legislation benefiting them has been enacted since 1972. Social Security payments—the major source of income for old women—have been made taxable, and cost of living increases less gener-ous.[3] Since its inception, Medicare has continuously increased the amount of deductibles, copayments, and premiums that individuals must pay out of pocket.

Rationing of health care to American elders to contain costs (a policy already instituted in some other nations, e.g., kidney dialysis and heart transplants in Britain) has been proposed as part of the notion that older persons have an obligation to die and get out of the way (Lamm, 1989). Rationing health care specifically for the old has been advanced in greater depth by ethicist Daniel Callahan (1987), who suggested denying life-extending health care to those in their late 70s or older. Of course, we as a nation have tacitly rationed health care for some time with a two-class medical system: one for the rich, insured, and others deemed socially worthy, and the other for the poor, uninsured, or socially unworthy.

But rationing of social, economic, and health care resources for any segment of a population has profound moral and social implications, not only for those denied benefits but for the society as a whole. Most immediately, it is old women, their children, and grandchildren who are affected by the premise that the old are selfish, unwilling to pull their own weight, and depleting social resources that justifiably belong to the young. Yet propo-nents of generational equity have argued that the United States has taken an unsustainable direction in its social policies toward old people: relieving adult children from the economic support of their elderly parents and destig-matizing the concept of universal retirement, pioneering space-age trans-plants to elders, and socializing the costs of old age at the expense of children and pregnant women, one million of whom come to term without a single visit to a physician (Peterson & Howe, 1988).

Whether current American social policies on health care for pregnant women are equitable is certainly a valid question. The infant mortality rate in the United States is around 9.9 per 1,000 live births, a mortality rate twice as high as that of Japan and almost twice as high at that in Sweden (Population Reference Bureau, 1990). That a specific vulnerable class of people—in this case, the old—is identified as responsible for failure to provide care for other social categories, such as pregnant women, however, is an interesting twist on blaming one set of victims for the victimization of another set.

Little is currently being done to transfer income to the most needy of any age, and the richest fifth of the U.S. population continues to have more than 9 times the income of the poorest fifth. Increasingly, families with young children are made up of dual-earner couples: 57% of married women with children under the age of 6 and almost 73% of married women with children aged 6 to 17 were in the labor force in 1988 compared to 30% and 42% in 1970 (U.S. Bureau of the Census, 1990). Yet during the 1980s, federal and state subsidies for child care were cut dramatically, limiting access to day care for poor and near-poor families—especially those headed by single female parents (Sidel, 1986). Income tax reforms during the Reagan-Bush years assured greater wealth to those who least need it. The 1981 supply-side-based tax cuts, designed to stimulate productivity, meant that many corporations paid little or no federal income tax. By 1983, the top 10% of wealth holders owned almost two thirds of U.S. privately owned assets (Avery & Kennickel, 1989). Nor did the income tax reforms of 1986 substantially change concentration of wealth among the very rich. Between 1978 and 1987, the income of the lowest 20% of all American families declined by almost 10%, and that of the top 20% increased by more than 15% (U.S. House of Representatives, 1989). Welfare benefits for poor families with young children were reduced and eligibility was tightened. In comparison to other modern nations, the United States spends proportionately less from general revenues on social welfare programs for persons of all ages, and more of each tax dollar goes to support military programs and interest on the national debt than to social welfare programs (Children's Defense Fund, 1988).

The two major programs benefiting older persons—Social Security and Medicare—are largely self-funded: That is, contributions to these two funds are made by their eventual recipients and thus represent delayed income rather than benefits from general revenue. Paradoxically, older persons in the U.S. derive a smaller proportion of their incomes from governmental social insurance programs such as Social Security, food stamps, and Medicaid than elders in several other developed countries. Poverty rates among old people in the U.S. in general and older women in particular have been among the highest in the developed world. The minimum old age benefit provided by social programs equals only about one third of the adjusted median income for the population as a whole, far below the minimum floor of income in several European countries, Canada, and Australia (Quinn &

Smeeding, 1993). And according to a recent congressional survey, entitlements do not reach all the elderly poor: Only 30% of American elders in poverty receive Medicaid, only 56% collect SSI, and 60% obtain food stamps ("News to Use," 1993).

It seems unlikely that policies truly benefiting and enhancing primary prevention for old women will emerge until the current ideological consensus has given way to a broader focus on the vulnerability of women in all age groups. Policy debates designed to create false dichotomies, such as the rights of unborn and young children versus the rights of the old, obscure the continuing realities of economic inequality. Women, who at all ages are more likely to be poor than men, are pitted against their own self-interests. If we really care about older persons, the family, and women of all ages, issues of the feminization of poverty and structural inequality must be addressed. Racial and age discrimination, pay equity for women, job training and retraining for both genders, maldistribution of wealth, adequate income maintenance throughout the life course, including old age, and a universal health care system for people of all ages—these are all issues affecting not only the mental health and quality of life for old women but the life chances of everyone.

There is a sharp, often forgotten but vital distinction between policies based on ageist assumptions and policies that would benefit quality of life for all age groups. To neglect the rights of older women is to abrogate their past contributions to the present and to the future that they have made possible. Surely, they, their children, and grandchildren who will one day be old deserve better. Herein lies a task for primary prevention.

Notes

1. SSI, a means-tested income maintenance program for the elderly and disabled, pays an individual maximum of approximately $4,842 per year in 1988 dollars—25% below the poverty level of $5,649 for individuals in the same year.

2. In interpreting poverty levels, keep in mind that the federal government applies different income standards for those under age 65 and those 65+. At age 65, one is magically considered to need less money than when age 64.9. In 1987, the poverty index for an elderly couple was calculated at $800 less in annual income than that for a couple younger than 65. For individuals 65 or over, the index was $481 less per year.

3. Social Security in the United States is not financed from general revenues but rather is a "pay-as-you-go system" in which today's retirees are being supported by payroll taxes levied on current workers just as retirees' contributions were used to fund benefits to earlier cohorts of retired workers. Because Social Security benefits are hinged to preretirement earnings, over half of today's old women, who have had interrupted histories of paid employment, find it more advantageous to claim one half of their husband's benefits than their own. Once these women are widowed, their benefits from Social Security are reduced.

References

Antonucci, T., & Akiyama, H. (1987). Social networks in adult life and a preliminary examination of the convoy model. *Journal of Gerontology, 42,* 519-527.

Avery, R. B., & Kennickel, A. B. (1989, June). Rich rewards. *American Demographics,* 19-22.

Banner, L. W. (1992). *In full flower: Aging women, power, and sexuality.* New York: Knopf.

Belgrave, L. L. (1988). The effects of race differences in work history, work attitudes, economic resources, and health on women's retirement. *Research on Aging, 10,* 383-396.

Binstock, R. H. (1988). Aging, politics and public policy. *The World and I, 3*(11), 533-547.

Callahan, D. (1987). *Setting limits: Medical goals for an aging society.* New York: Simon & Schuster.

Chappell, N. (1993, June). *Informal social support.* Paper presented at the Vermont Conference on the Primary Prevention of Psychopathology, Burlington, VT.

Children's Defense Fund. (1988). *A children's defense budget FY 1989: An analysis of our nation's investment in children.* Washington, DC: Author.

Chodorow, N. J. (1978). *The reproduction of mothering.* Berkeley: University of California Press.

Cicirelli, V. G. (1983). A comparison of helping behavior to elderly parents of adult children with intact and disrupted marriages. *The Gerontologist, 23,* 619-625.

Clancy, C. M., & Franks, P. (1993). Physician gender bias in clinical decisionmaking: Screening for cancer in primary care. *Medical Care, 31,* 213-218.

Culpepper, E. E. (1993). Ageism, sexism, and health care: Why we need old women in power. In G. R. Winslow & J. W. Walthers (Eds.), *Facing limits: Ethics and health care for the elderly* (pp. 191-209). Boulder, CO: Westview.

Cumming, E., & Henry, W. (1961). *Growing old.* New York: Basic Books.

Demos, J. (1982). *Entertaining Satan: Witchcraft and the culture of early New England.* New York: Oxford University Press.

Deutsch, H. (1945). *Psychology of women: A psychoanalytic interpretation.* New York: Grune & Stratton.

Durenberger, D. (1989). Education and the contract between the generations. *Generational Journal, 11*(1), 5-8.

Ehrenreich, B., & English, D. (1982). *For her own good.* New York: Anchor.

Ellis, H. (1905/1942). The sexual impulse in women. In *The psychology of sex* (p. 243). New York: Random House.

Erikson, E. (1968). *Identity, youth and crisis.* New York: Norton.

Fengler, A. P., & Goodrich, N. (1979). Wives of elderly disabled men: The hidden patients. *The Gerontologist, 19,* 175-183.

Fraser, A. (1984). *The weaker vessel.* New York: Knopf.

Freud, S. (1961a). Types of onset of neurosis (Strachey, J., Trans.). In *Complete psychological works of Sigmund Freud* (Vol. 12, standard ed., pp. 1-162). London: Hogarth.

Freud, S. (1961b). Some psychical consequences of the anatomical distinction between the sexes (Strachey, Trans.). In *Collected works of Sigmund Freud* (Vol. 7, standard ed.). London: Hogarth.

Gratton, B. (1987). Familism among the black and Mexican-American elderly: Myth or reality? *Journal of Aging Studies, 1,* 19-32.

Greer, G. (1992). *The change: Women, aging and the menopause.* New York: Knopf.

Gutmann, D. (1987). *Reclaimed powers: Toward a new psychology of men and women in later life.* New York: Basic Books.

Hess, B. B., & Waring, J. (1984). Family relationships of older women: A women's issue. In E. W. Markson (Ed.), *Older women* (pp. 227-251). Lexington, MA: Lexington.

Hopper, S. V. (1993). The influence of ethnicity on the health of older women. *Clinics in Geriatric Medicine: Care of the Older Woman, 9*(1), 231-257.

Horney, K. (1967). *Feminine psychology.* New York: Norton.

Horowitz, A. (1985). Sons and daughters as caregivers to older parents: Differences in role performance and consequences. *The Gerontologist, 25,* 612-617.

Kasper, J. D. (1988). *Aging alone: Profiles and projections.* Baltimore: Commonwealth Fund Commission on Elderly People Living Alone.

Keith, V. M. (1993). Gender, financial strain, and psychological distress among older adults. *Research on Aging, 15,* 123-147.

Kemp, B. J., Staples, F., & Lopez-Aquires, W. (1987). Epidemiology of depression and dysphoria in our elderly Hispanic population: Prevalence and correlates. *Journal of the American Geriatrics Society, 35,* 920-926.

Kivitt, V. (1985). Consanguinity and kin level: Their relative importance to the helping network of older adults. *Journal of Gerontology, 40,* 228-234.

Kline, C. (1975). The socialization process of women. *The Gerontologist, 15,* 486-492.

Kramer, H., & Sprenger, J. (1971). *Malleus maleficarum: The classic study of witchcraft* (Summers, M., Trans.). London: Arrow. (Original work published 1508)

Lamm, R. (1989). Public policy for an aging America. *Generational Journal, 11*(1), 108-111.

Levinson, D. (1977). *The seasons of a man's life.* New York: Norton.

Lopata, H. Z. (1971). Widows as a minority group. *The Gerontologist, 2,* 67-77.

MacDonald, B. (1989, Spring/Summer). Outside the sisterhood: Ageism in women's studies. *Women's Studies Quarterly, 17*(1/2), 6-11.

Markides, K. S., & Levin, J. S. (1987). The changing economy and the future of the minority aged. *The Gerontologist, 27,* 273-274.

Martin, B. (1990). The cultural construction of ageing: Or how long can the summer wine really last? In M. Bury & J. Macnicol (Eds.), *Aspects of ageing: Essays on social policy and old age* (pp. 53-81). London: Department of Social Policy, Royal Holloway and Bedford New College.

Miller, J. B. (1986). *Toward a new psychology of women.* New York: Norton.

Murrell, S. A., Himmelfarb, S., & Wright, K. (1983). Prevalence of depression and its correlates in older adults. *American Journal of Epidemiology, 117,* 173-185.

National Center for Health Statistics. (1993). *Health data on older Americans, United States, 1992.* Washington, DC: U.S. Government Printing Office.

National Research Council. (1988). *The aging population in the twenty-first century: Statistics for health policy.* Washington, DC: National Academy Press.

News to use. (1993, Fall). *Update: North Shore Elder Services* [Danvers, MA], p. 1.

Pearlin, L. I., Mullan, J. T., Semple, S. J., & Skaff, M. M. (1990). Caregiving and the stress process: An overview of concepts and their measures. *The Gerontologist, 30,* 583-594.

Peterson, P. G., & Howe, N. (1988). *On borrowed time: How the growth in entitlement spending threatens America's future.* San Francisco: ICS.

Philipson, C. (1982). *Capitalism and the construction of old age.* London: Macmillan.

Population Reference Bureau. (1990). *World population data sheet, 1990.* Washington, DC: Author.

Preston, S. H. (1984). Children and the elderly in the U.S. *Scientific American, 250*(6), 44-49.

Quinn, J. F., & Smeeding, T. M. (1993). The present and future economic well-being of the aged. In R. V. Burkhauser & D. L. Salisbury (Eds.), *Pensions in a changing economy* (pp. 5-18). Washington, DC: Employee Benefit Research Institute.

Reinherz, S. (1986). Friends or foes: Gerontological and feminist theory. *Women's Studies International Forum, 9*(5), 503-514.

Robinson, B., & Thurnher, M. (1979). Taking care of parents: A family cycle transition. *The Gerontologist, 19,* 586-593.

Samuelson, R. J. (1978). Aging America: Who will shoulder the burden? *National Journal, 10,* 1712-1717.

Sanchez-Ayendez, M. (1988). Puerto Rican elderly women: The cultural dimension of social support networks. *Women and Health, 14,* 239-252.

Schoonover, C. B., Brody, E. M., Hoffman, C., & Kleban, M. H. (1988). Parent care and geographically distant children. *Research on Aging, 10,* 472-492.

Seccombe, K. (1988). Financial assistance from elderly retirement-age sons to their aging parents. *Research on Aging, 10,* 102-118.

Sidel, R. (1986). *Women and children last: The plight of poor women in affluent America.* New York: Penguin.

Smith, J. (1992). *Misogynies: Reflections on myth and malice.* London: Farber & Farber.

Stallones, L., Marx, M. B., & Garrity, T. F. (1990). Prevalence and correlates of depressive symptoms among older U.S. adults. *American Journal of Preventive Medicine, 6*(5), 295-303.

Stoller, E. P., & Pugliesi, K. L. (1988). Informal networks of community-based elderly: Changes in composition over time. *Research on Aging, 10,* 499-516.

Stull, D. E., & Scarisbrick-Hauser, A. (1989). Never-married elderly: A reassessment with implications for long-term care policy. *Research on Aging, 11,* 124-139.

Tallmer, M. (1989). Empty-nest syndrome: Possibility or despair. In T. Bernay & D. W. Cantor (Eds.), *The psychology of today's woman: New psychoanalytic views* (pp. 231-252). Cambridge, MA: Harvard University Press.

U.S. Bureau of the Census. (1990). *Statistical abstract of the United States 1990.* Washington, DC: Government Printing Office.

U.S. Department of Labor. (1989). *Report of the Secretary of Labor: Labor market problems of older workers.* Washington, DC: Department of Labor.

U.S. House of Representatives. (1989). *Background material and data on programs within the jurisdiction of the Committee on Ways and Means.* Washington, DC: Government Printing Office.

U.S. House of Representatives Select Committee on Aging. (1987). *Exploding the myths: Caregiving in America.* Washington, DC: U.S. Government Printing Office.

U.S. House of Representatives Select Committee on Aging, Subcommittee on Retirement Income and Employment. (1992). *Living in the shadows: Older women and the roots of poverty.* Washington, DC: Government Printing Office.

U.S. Senate Select Subcommittee on Aging. (Ed.). (1988). *Developments in aging.* Washington, DC: Government Printing Office.

Walker, B. (1988). *The crone: Women of age, wisdom and power.* New York: Harper.

Worobey, J. L., & Angel, R. (1990a). Functional capacity and living arrangements of unmarried elderly persons. *Journal of Gerontology: Social Sciences, 45,* S95-S101.

Worobey, J. L., & Angel, R. (1990b). Poverty and health: Older minority women and the rise of the female-headed household. *Journal of Health and Social Behavior, 31,* 370-383.

Yee, B. W. K. (1990). Gender and family issues in minority groups. *Generations, 14*(3), 39-42.

Zarit, S. H. (1989). Do we need another "stress and caregiving" study? *The Gerontologist, 29,* 147.

Zarit, S. H., Reeves, K. E., & Bach-Peterson, J. (1980). Relatives of the impaired elderly: Correlates of feelings of burden. *The Gerontologist, 20,* 649-655.

15

Promoting Successful and Productive Aging in Minority Populations

Rose C. Gibson

This chapter discusses some emerging trends in the health and family life of minority elders that will affect their successful and productive aging. Holding onto current myths and stereotypes without considering new knowledge can cause researchers, clinicians, educators, service providers, and policy makers to develop a misleading sense of reality about and overlook the potential of minority elders. Separating fact from fallacy, recognizing potential, and considering both strengths and deficits, on the other hand, will be useful in planning research, preventions, and interventions to promote productive and successful aging in the minority elderly population.

The term *minorities* refers to such groups as Asian, Native, Mexican, African, and Puerto Rican Americans. *Productive aging* means engagement over a lifetime in paid or unpaid activities that produce valued goods or services. The spouse who is caring for the Alzheimer's patient at home is no less productive than the paid worker caring for the same patient in the nursing home. *Successful aging* refers to reaching one's potential and arriving at a level of physical, social, and psychological well-being in old age that is pleasing to both self and others. Rowe and Kahn (1987) distinguished between successful and usual agers in the elderly population: Successful agers have health and functioning characteristics that resemble the mean of younger persons, whereas usual agers are characterized more by health and functioning losses generally associated with the aging process.

An integral part of the social well-being of older persons is the quality of their social relations, especially family relations and support (see, for example, Antonucci, 1985). A current problem is that we are clinging to a somewhat romanticized view of the minority family. The picture of minority elders who are immersed in extended networks in which members cater to every need may today be more myth than reality. Jacqueline Jackson (1988), in Stoller and Gibson (1993), summarized data from various published reports to illustrate the prevailing stereotype of elderly black women and their family relations:

> To illustrate with only slight exaggeration, the average old black woman lives in a blighted section of an inner city or in an isolated rural area. Poor, poorly educated, and in poor health, she is economically dependent on Social Security and other income transfer or in-kind programs (e.g., food stamps, subsidized housing, and Medicaid).
>
> This average old black woman is beset by problems, not the least of which are substandard housing in high crime areas, insufficient transportation, and inadequate access to mainstream health facilities, in part because she is stymied by and unable to cope successfully with bureaucratic institutions. If she is not gainfully employed, it is only because she is unemployed, involuntarily retired, or too ill or disabled to work. Old black women like to work because they gain dignity through working.
>
> A poor woman, she rarely uses community resources for elderly persons, such as centers for senior citizens, most often because she does not know about them nor of their eligibility requirements. . . . Extremely religious and often the matriarch of an extended family, [she] is surrounded by children, grandchildren, other relatives, or fictive kin, and by friends and neighbors who gleefully minister to her instrumental and emotional needs. "Granny" is also very happy when she is given the responsibility of rearing her grandchildren. (pp. 31-32)

Historical accounts, photographs of five-generation black families in the 19th century, and earlier work (see, for example, Gutman, 1977) suggest that such pictures of the "pampered" black elderly person were more valid in the past than they are today. To continue the archaic view is not to recognize some rather dramatic changes taking place in the contemporary black family. Although it is true that minority elders are more likely than majority elders to live in multigenerational households, recent information about these households challenges the assumption that "more" is necessarily "better." Stress and comfort seem to be doled out in equal portions to minority elders living in multiple-member households (Lynch, in press). At the same time that there are more younger members in the household to value and hold elders in esteem, these younger members have their own social problems—problems elderly persons in their households are obliged to share. Poverty, joblessness, and racial and ethnic group discrimination are all increasing in the present generation of minority youth (Gibson & Burns, 1991). It is invalid to assume, then, a better quality of social relations and social support for the minority elders from sheer numbers living in their households.

National data, in fact, indicate that the life satisfaction, happiness, and morale of black elders within multiple-generation households decrease, after a certain threshold value, monotonically as the number of people living in the household increases (Gibson, 1986a, 1986b). Thus focusing simply on numbers of people in households, as minority-majority comparative aging research frequently does, provides little information on the dynamics within these households.

Another long-standing myth is that black elders have more children available to help than white elders. To the contrary, older whites have more children available. Although more children were born to blacks than whites in today's elderly cohorts, fewer black than white children survived.

All told, the future does not portend well for the minority family and its resources for fostering productive and successful aging of its members. One of the most dramatic historical trends of our time is the aging of American society. The human life span may be extending on toward its maximum potential of about 115 years or so. These shifts in the age distribution will bring about some major changes in the composition of the minority family. For example, at the same time that population aging is having an influence, a different set of trends is also causing changes in the structure of black families.

Black female-headed households are multiplying, the economic gain of black elderly persons is slowing, large numbers of black elders are continuing to live in families rather than institutions, the number of black oldest-old women is growing much more rapidly than any other group of elderly persons, and the fertility of young black, compared with young white, women continues to be high (Gibson, 1991b). Linking these five trends, we can foresee a black family of the future that is still poor and that contains a number of young children and several generations of older women, some of whom will be the oldest old and poor in their own right.

This scenario suggests that the changing structure of the black family does not hold much promise as a future economic resource for its dependent generations, its children, and its elders. At the same time that the make-up of the black family is changing, the potentials of its resource generations are being threatened. The black family's infants, children, teenagers, and middle-aged all may be at risk as our population ages.

For example, black children, those linchpins of the black family of the future, have a 50-50 chance of growing up underprivileged, undereducated, and unemployed. They also are more likely to be physically and mentally impaired due to low birth weight and being born with AIDS (acquired immune deficiency syndrome) and cocaine addiction.

If trends in black teenage pregnancies and out-of-wedlock births continue, increasing numbers of very young black mothers, 30-year-old black grandmothers, and 45-year-old black great grandmothers will be raising children without men in the home. The issue is neither sexist nor moral; it is economic. Households containing men simply have more money.

In recent years, the homicide rate for black men aged 15 to 24 increased by an alarming 74%. This is the highest homicide rate ever for any race, sex, or age group in our society. Thus another problem to overlay on black family statistics is that the black man's emotional and economic support may be lost to black families of the future as a consequence of homicide, death by legal intervention, teenage drug abuse, incarceration, and constantly high rates of unemployment. The challenging question is how this devastation of the black manchild now is going to affect the support systems of black elders of the future—their productive and successful aging.

Middle-aged blacks also do not fare well. Their special social problem is declining labor force participation brought about by the early onset of physical limitation (Gibson, 1991c). These individuals have been called "the unretired-retired," those who are not working but who do not think of themselves as retired. These "unretired-retired" middle-aged blacks do not receive any type of retirement pay even though their work lives are probably over.

As our population ages, each of these subgroups of the black family may have competition from growing numbers of elders for preventive and inter-ventive policies, programs, and services that would address their unique social problems. If the current social ills in these groups are not made better today, a real concern is that the black family's resource generations will not have accumulated the affluence, the health, and the education to be its heads of tomorrow.

The greater tendency of the minority family to care for its elders at home is another issue that has not been factored into the equation of resources available to the minority family of the future. For example, whites compared with blacks at ages 75 to 84 are about 1.5 times more likely to be institution-alized. At ages 85 and over, whites are almost twice as likely; and at ages 100 and over, whites are about 4 times as likely as blacks to be in nursing and personal care homes (Gibson & Jackson, 1992). Thus there is an extra and often hidden economic and emotional burden of the minority family in caring for their old and very old at home.

The time probably has come to replace the romantic view of the minority family with this view of the minority family of the future, which will be top-heavy with dependents and short-handed on resources, seriously under-mining family coping capacities. The important question is, How will the ability of the black family as a matrix for productive and successful aging be compromised? It also is time to paint over the old picture with some of the more realistic, but less romantic, emerging new findings to accurately gauge the potential of the minority family as an arena for successful aging. Not to do so lures us into thinking that minority elders do not and will not need prevention or treatment programs and services to the extent of other elderly persons because their families and extensive networks are in place, stronger and more viable. Similar myths and emerging new issues in health exist concerning the successful and productive aging of minorities. We move now to these issues of physical health.

When we look at the age group 65 and over as a group, we see health differentials that favor white Americans. This is ever since health data have been collected. But if we subdivide the group into finer and finer age categories, we often see a black disadvantage in younger age groups of elderly persons that narrows, disappears, or even turns into a black advantage in older age groups (Gibson, 1994). Thus using the traditional age break of 65 and over hides some countervailing black-white health trends in younger and older groups. It is, of course, important to continue to study causes of the black disadvantage in health status, but at the same time, it is important to begin to study causes of the black health advantage. This is in the interest of better targeting prevention and treatment health care programs, promoting successful and productive aging in minority populations, and identifying the strengths as well as the deficits of minority elders.

For several years now I have observed and published on this very curious phenomenon of a decreasing black health handicap in older age groups of elders (see, for example, Gibson, 1991a, 1994). The intriguing trend is evident in multiple and diverse data sets in different parts of the country and across a variety of health measures. I also found the phenomenon in analyses of a recent social science data set collected at the University of Michigan's Institute for Social Research, Americans' Changing Lives (ACL) (House, 1986). The black health handicap on five measures—number of chronic conditions, activities of daily living, general functional limitation, self-rated health, and satisfaction with health—was larger in the 65- to 74-year-old group than in the immediately older 75- to 79-year-old group (Gibson, 1994). On two of the measures, general functional limitation and satisfaction with health, the race disparity more than narrowed in the age group 75 to 79; blacks actually gained the health advantage over whites in the percentage who were healthy.

This narrowing of the black health detriment was mainly due to sharper increases among whites than blacks in proportions of the morbid, moving from the younger to the older group of elders. This trend suggests that proportionately more diseased and disabled 65- to 74-year-old whites than blacks are entering the 75- to 79-year-old group, resulting in a more robust group of black survivors. It is interesting that when mean values of one of the measures, functional health, were graphed from the first wave of the ACL study instead of percentages who were sick, the trend was still there: The black-white gap was widest at about age 65 and narrowed considerably by about age 75. The health of whites was consistently better in each age group, but the black disadvantage was greatest at age 65 and narrowed at about age 75. A similar plot 3 years later, however, did not show the same black-white gap at ages 65 and 75. This suggests that the disparities were not age related: That is, nothing special seems to happen in the lives of blacks and whites at ages 65 to 74 and again at ages 75 to 79. However, in the Wave 2 data, the gap narrowed later, at about age 78. Thus the peculiar race disparities were observed to move along with the younger and older groups as they aged 3 years. This suggests that the age-race gap in health is cohort related rather than related to the aging process itself. In other words, members of the group aged 75 to 79 may have shared some common health-related experiences over the life course or at a particular life stage.

Similar age-by-race disparities are found in mortality data (Gibson, 1994). Differentials favor whites in younger age groups of elderly persons, but favor blacks in the older age groups. These trends are observed both in all-cause and cause-specific mortality data, in various types of studies and samples, as far back as 1900 and as recently as 1988. For example, in the ACL data discussed earlier, blacks were more likely than whites in the two youngest age groups, 55 to 64 and 65 to 74, to die out of the sample from Time 1 to Time 2. In the older age group, 75 to 79, however, whites were more likely than blacks to die.

What are some potential explanations of these odd age-by-race differences in health and mortality trends? Demographers speculate about young morbid subgroups of disadvantaged populations over the world that die out rather rapidly, leaving behind an older more highly select group of survivors. In American society, blacks are often cited as an example (see, for example, Wing, Manton, Stallard, Haynes, & Tyroler, 1985). This raises the question of whether the unusual age-by-race differentials are related to such adverse mortality selection processes.

Another explanation of the age-by-race gap in mortality is that blacks may be more susceptible to the early-onset killer diseases but more insulated, in some way, from the late-onset killer diseases, whereas the reverse is true of whites (Manton, 1982). For example, Manton found that relative risk ratios for heart disease mortality favored white men at younger ages but favored black men at older ages. The argument was that blacks are more prone to heart disease and other circulatory events of hypertensive origin. Early heart disease death is more likely to be a product of hypertension and constitutional endowment for circulatory failure. On the other hand, white men develop arteriosclerosis more rapidly and are more susceptible to arteriosclerotic forms of heart disease. Late heart disease death is more likely due to degenerative circulatory changes, mainly arteriosclerosis. Thus another possible explanation is different susceptibilities to specific diseases of blacks and whites in younger and older age groups of elders.

Other explanations of the gap might be time of measurement effects, something special about the periods in which the health questions were asked, or cohort effects, as hinted in the ACL analyses discussed earlier. The now 75- to 79-year-old black members of the 1914 to 1918 birth cohorts could be the hardy survivors of extremely noxious work environments. For example, in the early 1930s, thousands of southern black workers were lured to northern motor capitals to work in the auto plants. These black workers, however, were restricted to certain processes in the industry: Black workers usually stoked the furnaces, whereas white workers made the auto parts.

Another explanation of the gap in health may be differential exposure to certain types of risk factors for disease and dying in various age-by-race groups. An impressive and growing body of health research, in fact, is beginning to identify striking links between social and psychological risk factors and health and mortality (Kasl & Berkman, 1981; Rowe & Kahn, 1987). For example, in regard to social risk factors, elderly persons with very low levels of social relations are more likely to die out of survey samples than those elders with higher levels (see, for example, House, Landis, & Umberson, 1988). In regard to psychological risk factors, the health of older people who perceive control over their life events seems better than the health of those who perceive helplessness (see, for example, Ford, in press; Langer & Rodin, 1976; Rodin, 1986). Religion, as a risk factor, also seems to have potent positive effects on health status (Levin & Taylor, in press). In the interest of promoting successful and productive aging, it should be asked whether social and psychological factors unusually protect the health and mortality of minorities as they age. Except for a few studies (see Ford, in press), the issue of race and ethnic group differences in the influence of social and psychological factors on health and mortality has gone largely unexplored. If moderators of health and mortality could be identified, strategies to ward off poor health and premature death could be taught. Teaching preventive strategies could increase the pool of older successful agers who could be resources instead of dependents in the minority family of the future.

In short, when the age group 65 and over is disaggregated, a different picture of the comparative health and mortality of older blacks and whites emerges. This new picture challenges the prevailing myth that blacks at every age are sicker and die sooner than their white age-mates. Thus the age-race gap in health represents new knowledge that should be overlaid on old health stereotypes to promote successful aging in minority populations. Taking the new knowledge into account means that a number of older minority elders may not need certain health programs, policies, and services to the extent of their younger but sicker counterparts. It also may mean that these "successful minority agers" may be physically able to be family resources instead of family drains, and to act as helpers for their less able age-mates as well. Once again, the importance of considering the strengths as well as the deficits of the minority elders in planning for their successful aging is emphasized.

In summary, the family, social-psychological, and physical health issues discussed in this chapter urge us not to base our future preventive and interventive strategies on myth and old knowledge. The infusion of new knowledge will move forward research, planning, and policy that will increase potential and productive and successful aging. The discussions in this chapter raise several research, program, and policy issues in the interest of better prevention and intervention that will promote productive and successful aging in minority populations.

First, what research is needed to better inform minority family policies and services? What research is needed to identify the "successful agers" in minority elderly populations? How can the cognitive potential and resources of these successful agers be tapped for use in increasingly troubled minority families of the future?

Second, what services and programs should be provided to increase the resource capabilities and coping capacities of minority families now and into the future? With regard to the children, shrinking federal funding and restrictive eligibilities for the major health care, antipoverty, and educational programs that especially benefit disadvantaged minority children should be monitored. This would include programs designed to promote better prenatal care and to prevent low birth weights and infants born with drug addiction and AIDS.

With regard to minority teenagers, programs and services that provide continuing education, job training, and child care for teenaged parents could make substantial inroads into the problem and help lift these children who bear children out of poverty. Preventive counseling, vocational and academic training programs, and the creation of new jobs could help minority teenaged men.

With respect to the work and retirement dilemma of middle-aged minority workers, providing education and career training for those 55 and older is one idea. Other ideas are government-subsidized pay for these individuals as social care workers, shared jobs, or a return to cottage-type industries.

What policies are needed to strengthen the capabilities of the minority family? In the case of unretired-retired blacks at midlife, should retirement be moved to earlier ages in order to ensure benefits when work lives are in reality over? Another policy question concerns minority men who do not live long enough to collect their benefits. These two issues raise the more fundamental question of whether age-based policies generally designed for the life spans of the majority population are inappropriate for many minorities whose life spans are shortened by high death rates at midlife.

Finally, with regard to minority elders, to be sure, better health care and income support programs are needed. However, their psychological assets also need to be considered. Publicly and privately funded programs and services could encourage roles of minority elders as surrogate parents in the growing number of minority households in which the men are absent. These elderly persons have the potential for becoming one of the minority family's most valued resources.

Asking such difficult research, service, and policy questions now will help promote the successful and productive aging of both present and future generations in the minority elderly population.

References

Antonucci, T. C. (1985). Personal characteristics, social support, and social behavior. In R. H. Binstock & E. Shanas (Eds.), *Handbook of aging and the social sciences* (2nd ed., pp. 94-128). New York: Van Nostrand Reinhold.

Ford, M. E. (in press). The effects of perceived control on health care utilization among African-Americans. In Rose C. Gibson & James S. Jackson (Eds.), *Health in black America*. Newbury Park, CA: Sage.

Gibson, R. C. (1986a). Blacks in an aging society. *Daedalus, 115,* 349-372.

Gibson, R. C. (1986b). Perspectives on the black family. In A. Pifer & Lydia Bronte (Eds.), *Our aging society: Paradox and promise* (pp. 181-198). New York: Norton.

Gibson, R. C. (1991a). Age-by-race differences in the health and functioning of elderly persons. *Journal of Aging and Health, 3,* 335-351.

Gibson, R. C. (1991b). Minority families as resources for their elders. In P. Stanford & F. Torres-Gil (Eds.), *Diversity in an aging America* (pp. 4-10). San Diego: National Resource Center on Aging.

Gibson, R. C. (1991c). The subjective retirement of black Americans. *Journal of Gerontology: Social Sciences, 46,* S204-S209.

Gibson, R. C. (1994). Age-by-race differentials in health status in the elderly population: A social science research agenda. *The Gerontologist, 34,* 454-462.

Gibson, R. C., & Burns, C. J. (1991). The health, labor force, and retirement experiences of aging minorities. *Generations, 15,* 31-35.

Gibson, R. C., & Jackson, J. S. (1992). The black oldest old. In R. Suzman, D. Willis, & K. Manton (Eds.), *The oldest old* (pp. 321-340). New York: Oxford University Press.

Gutman, H. G. (1977). *The black family in slavery and freedom: 1750-1925.* New York: Vintage.

House, J. S. (1986). *Americans' changing lives* [electronic data file]. Ann Arbor, MI: Survey Research Center [Producer] and Inter-University Consortium for Political and Social Research [Distributor].

House, J. S., Landis, K. R., & Umberson, D. (1988). Social relationships and health. *Science, 241,* 540-544.

Jackson, J. J. (1988, May/June). Aging black women and public policies. *Black Scholar,* pp. 31-43.

Kasl, S. V., & Berkman, L. (1981). Some psychosocial influences on the health status of the elderly: The perspective of social epidemiology. In J. L. McGaugh & S. B. Kiesler (Eds.), *Aging, biology and behavior* (pp. 345-385). New York: Academic Press.

Langer, E., & Rodin, J. (1976). The effects of choice and enhanced personal responsibility for the aged: A field experiment in an institutional setting. *Journal of Personality and Social Psychology, 11,* 155-165.

Levin, J., & Taylor, R. J. (in press). Effects of religion on dimensions of health. In R. C. Gibson & J. S. Jackson (Eds.), *Health in black America.* Newbury Park, CA: Sage.

Lynch, S. (in press). Too much of a good thing? The negative impact of high investment in support networks on health. In R. C. Gibson & J. S. Jackson (Eds.), *Health in black America.* Newbury Park, CA: Sage.

Manton, K. G. (1982). Temporal and age variation in United States black-white cause-specific mortality differentials: A study of the recent changes in the relative health status of the United States black population. *The Gerontologist, 22,* 170-179.

Rodin, J. (1986). Aging and health: Effects of the sense of control. *Science, 233,* 1271-1276.

Rowe, J. W., & Kahn, R. L. (1987). Human aging: Usual and successful. *Science, 237,* 143-149.

Stoller, E. P., & Gibson, R. C. (1993). *Different worlds: Inequality in the aging experience.* Thousand Oaks, CA: Pine Forge Press.

Wing, S., Manton, K., Stallard, E., Haynes, C. G., & Tyroler, H. A. (1985). The black/white mortality crossover: Investigation in a community-based study. *Journal of Gerontology, 40,* 78-84.

16

Lesbians and Gay Men Also Grow Old

Douglas C. Kimmel

There is, of course, a double message in the title of this chapter. First, lesbians and gay men, like everyone else, grow old. There was a time when this was news and even experienced gerontologists were surprised to be reminded that some of the older people they worked with might be gay men or lesbians. Second, in this era of HIV/AIDS, it is important to remember that gay people do not only cope with this disease, they also grow old. There is a pressing need for research on the broad impact of this epidemic on older gay men and lesbians (Allers, 1990). On the one hand, we can assume that medical advances will allow more persons infected with HIV/AIDS to live for extended periods of time, but the physical and psychosocial effects of growing older with the disease are unknown. On the other hand, most gay men are not infected with the virus, but still are affected by the loss of friends and lovers. Lesbians, although much less frequently infected with HIV/AIDS than gay men, have also carried a major burden of coordinating and providing services to people infected with the virus, so their community has been affected as well.

In 1977, a small group who were concerned about older lesbians and gay men in New York got together and, citing Margaret Mead, noted that a community can be defined by the degree to which it cares for its vulnerable members. They focused initially on physically challenged and isolated elders and created SAGE, Senior Action in a Gay Environment, which is now a successful community organization providing a variety of services to older lesbians and gay men in New York City. Today there are a variety of organizations across the country that have been created by the lesbian and

AUTHOR'S NOTE: This chapter is revised in part from the author's presidential address, Society for the Psychological Study of Lesbian and Gay Issues—Division 44 of the American Psychological Association, August 30, 1988, and from a paper titled "Lesbian and Gay Male Aging," presented at the American Psychological Association, August 17, 1991.

gay community. Most of these organizations benefit from aging lesbians and gay men as volunteers, leaders, contributors, fund raisers, and speakers. No longer are the elders relegated to the fringes of the community. They often are courted for their expertise, their time, and their money. They are also being recognized as survivors and as sources of oral history who know a great deal about living in dangerous times.

Introduction

One of the most interesting aspects of studying older gay men and lesbians is *cohort effects*. This refers to the fact that people are born at a particular point in history and therefore are different from people born in a different period in two major ways. First, they were reared, mature, and grow old with a set of age-mates who share characteristics that may make some difference. For example, the cohort that was influenced by the civil rights movement and antiwar protests of the 1960s was at the leading edge of the struggle for civil rights for gay men and lesbians. This aspect of cohort effects means that older lesbians and gay men belong to a different cohort than do middle-aged, or younger, lesbians and gay men, and therefore important characteristics may differ between these de facto generations. For example, younger gay men and lesbians are reporting examples of discrimination that were accepted as routine by the older generation in years past.

A second aspect of cohort effects is that older people grew up and had many significant developmental experiences during a vastly different historical period. For example, nearly all studies document police harassment, arrest and imprisonment, fear of exposure on the job, and the secret society in which they lived years ago. Obviously, research on older lesbians and gay men must consider this influence and take care not to confuse aging with cohort effects.

A book of memoirs of older gay men called *Quiet Fire* by Keith Vacha (1985) quoted a respondent born in 1926 who provided a clear example of cohort effects in his life:

> I've been gay longer than it's been popular. I was gay when you had to wear red socks to be identified as gay. I walked into a bar in Chicago and had the place go absolutely dead on me because I wasn't dressed for that city. They thought I was vice. The piano player, Joy, recognized me from Hawaii and California and began playing "California Here I Come." I went to talk to her and that cleared the air. But I didn't make out that night even though I was a new face in town. Talk about harassment! The [police] backed a paddy wagon up to the back door of one of those bars and emptied everyone right

into the wagon. In those days we used to get a lot of heat and there was no such thing as entrapment. They'd just come in and bust everyone there. And get away with it! (p. 69)

Before the 1970s, many lesbians and gay men believed that they were deviant *as individuals*. However, with the advent of the lesbian and gay movement, one's personal deviance became the hallmark of one's membership in a minority group. As one old gay man phrased it recently:

When I was putting together, back in 1948 to 1950, what would become the FIRST Mattachine Society, there wasn't as yet in the minds of my fellow Queers, let alone the American society at large, even the beginnings of such a concept as that of a GAY IDENTITY. Everywhere we were constantly being told . . . that we were heteros who occasionally performed nasty acts. . . . *But we were HETEROS, we were just exactly the same as everybody else (except when we perversely insisted on performing those degenerate and WHOLLY ILLEGAL acts).* . . .

The tremendous leap forward in consciousness that was the Stonewall Rebellion changed the pronoun in Gay identity from "I" to "WE." (Hay, 1990, p. 5)

At the Stonewall rebellion, gay men (some of whom were in drag) led the revolt against police oppression after a gay bar called Stonewall was raided on a June night in 1969. This event, which has been celebrated each year since then with a public march of lesbian and gay pride, represented a paradigm shift that made possible the development of the current lesbian and gay community. Moreover, a clear example of cohort effects is that the overt gay men in the revolt were an embarrassment to many middle-aged gay men at the time, but have become role models of the gay movement today.

Two additional points must be noted by way of introduction. First, to understand aging among lesbians and gay men, we must recognize that sexual orientation is a social construct that has defined their lives in ways far greater and more subtle than their same-gender sexual preference and behavior. In that sense, there are some interesting parallels between old people in general and lesbians and gay men as a group. For example, both groups represent vast diversity among themselves: Like old people, gay men and lesbians have nothing in common except a socially defined label that has had broad and often negative ramifications. Also, many gay men and lesbians have chosen to keep their sexual orientation hidden from view because of fear. Likewise, some older people try to hide their age because the social construct of "old" is distasteful for many in our society. Moreover, old people and people who enjoy same-gender sexual relations exist in all cultures—but their status and social role varies widely across cultures.

Second, the most significant theme for understanding older lesbians and gay men is to recognize the diversity among them. Although all of the samples studied have been troubled by lack of generalizability because the population is hidden and difficult to identify, we can be confident that the actual population is even more diverse than these samples indicate. For example, many older lesbians and gay men have lived openly, often as same-sex couples, for many years. Others have spent the majority of their adult years hiding their homosexuality, sometimes in a heterosexual marriage. Many have children and grandchildren. Some are bisexual. Mix in the years of individualized attempts to come to terms with being lesbian or gay, often involving dramatic examples of oppression, stigma, and stress. Then combine lifestyle variations (such as long-term lover, serial monogamy, and living alone), racial and ethnic differences, socioeconomic status, family relations, and occupational experience. The diversity is extraordinary, and exciting. For those lesbians and gay men who have not attempted to fit themselves into the heterosexual models, there is a possibility of greater "normative creativity" because there are few set norms and expectations for lesbians and gay men (Brown, 1989).

The diversity of older lesbians and gay men clearly raises two significant research issues. The first concerns *survivor effects*. Today's older respondents have clearly lived long enough to be included in our study. Others, obviously, have died or become inaccessible to research earlier in life. The stress of living a stigmatized lifestyle may well have taken its toll in drug or alcohol abuse, accidents, violence, or suicide. Thus those we study are, by definition, the survivors and therefore likely to be different from the population of young adults from which they developed. For example, respondents in studies of older gay men usually have higher levels of education than older people in the general population. Is this because lesbians and gay men actually acquire more education or because those with greater education are the ones we are more likely to study?

Another concern is the "invisible" population of lesbians and gay men in general, and the number of "closeted" lesbians and gay men or those who are bisexual. The absence of an identifiable population reflects a very significant sampling problem (Garnets & Kimmel, 1991; Harry, 1990).

Three major themes are discussed in the remainder of this chapter: research on lesbian and gay aging, fears about aging as lesbians and gay men, and parallels between aging as a social issue and lesbian and gay issues.

Research on Lesbian and Gay Aging

In a review paper, Friend (1990) observed that the studies of older lesbians and gay men have described three differing groups:

1. *Affirmative Older Lesbians and Gay Men* who have constructed a positive identity that is individualistic and may reflect an active challenge to the heterosexist norm. It is this group who reflect the vast majority of persons who have been studied to date—perhaps they also represent a majority of older lesbians and gay men in the United States. They show a high level of self-acceptance and psychological adjustment despite the repressive social climate of their early lives.

2. *Passing Older Lesbians and Gay Men* who believe heterosexist assumptions but also marginally accept their homosexuality. They manage the resulting conflict by trying to distance themselves from stereotypically lesbian or gay activities or behavior. Some married heterosexually and attempt to keep their homosexual feelings secret. This pattern differs from bisexual marriages in which there is some degree of openness (Matteson, 1985; Wolf, 1985). A variation on this pattern would be the classic "Boston marriage," in which two unmarried women lived together and everyone assumed they were in a nonsexual relationship of convenience (Faderman, 1981).

3. *Stereotypic Older Lesbians and Gay Men* who conform to the negative images that are contained in heterosexist ideology. They tend to be lifelong loners, leading invisible lives of secrecy and even danger. Not associating with openly self-accepting gay men and lesbians, they have little chance to challenge the heterosexist belief system. Also, they tend not to associate with others because of anxiety, self-hatred, and low self-esteem. Their lives may be seen to reflect internalized homophobia.

Another review of research on older gay men and lesbians noted eight major themes:

First, it is clear that homosexuality *per se* does not cause misery, or loneliness, or any other maladjustment with aging. Even the social stigma of an unpopular sexual orientation does not seem to have much negative effect on most older gay men and lesbians—if anything, it probably has less effect on older gay men and lesbians than on younger gay men and lesbians. . . .

Second, older lesbians and gay men are a very diverse group of individuals. A sizable proportion of the lesbians and gay men in these studies are, or have been, married; some are parents and grandparents. Others are involved in long-term relationships. Some have been bereaved by the death of a lover. Some have been single for much or all of their adult lives, sometimes with occasional short-term relationships. Still others have had many relationships that have varied in duration. Many are connected with a social support network of gay and nongay friends, former lovers, relatives and neighbors; but some are relatively isolated, either as a lifelong pattern, or because they have outlived key people in their support network. A large number are open about their lifestyle, to friends if not publicly; but some are closeted.

Third, the vast majority of older lesbians and gay men remain sexually active and at least some men report that sexuality becomes more satisfying with advancing age because it is less focused on the genitals and more on the whole person. Menopause may not be as significant an event for lesbians as for nongay women, since childbearing is not as central a role for many. In general, older lesbians have more of a realistic chance of finding a sexual partner or mate than do their heterosexual counterparts since women live longer than men and lesbians tend to be attracted to women in their same age group.

Fourth, a substantial proportion of gay people are aging with levels of satisfaction comparable to other people. For example, one study of older lesbians found that nearly three-quarters of the respondents indicated that their lesbianism "had been a source of great joy and satisfaction." In addition, about two-thirds felt positive about their aging. Also, about half of the respondents felt they were as attractive as they had been earlier in life and a slightly higher proportion felt they were as sexual as they had been (Almvig, 1982). Likewise, a study of older gay men found the three factors most related to measures of self-acceptance, life satisfaction, and negatively related to depression were: "integration into the homosexual community," "satisfaction with sex life," and "commitment to homosexuality" (Berger, 1982).

Fifth, naturally, the important concerns of today's older lesbians and gay men are similar in many ways to the concerns of all older persons: good health care; a network of social support, designed by and suited for the individual; financial security; a sense of independence, dignity, and self-respect; and the freedom to live one's own life as one chooses. . . . But some of this requires more careful planning for gay men and lesbians. For example, [special issues include] wills, . . . visitation rights in hospital intensive-care units and nursing homes, . . . apartment leases, . . . and, of course, [the fact that] health insurance usually does not apply to the lover of the insured (with some notable exceptions . . .).

Sixth, there may be some positive advantages to aging as a lesbian or gay man. Many gay men and lesbians are relatively free of the sex roles that limit one's ability to perform all of the tasks required for living. There may also be more continuity in some gay lives, without children growing up and leaving home, or moving away when you were expecting them to be around to take care of you. Also, gay people often have more experience living alone than heterosexually-married people typically have, so being alone in old age is not necessarily an unaccustomed lifestyle. In addition, gay people may devote more attention to creating a network of friends who provide mutual support, including younger people. And finally, many lesbians and gay men experienced a major crisis in their lives when they had to deal with being lesbian or gay; this may help to provide a sense of "crisis competence" that allows them to cope with other crises in their lives with greater agility.

Seventh, often a *conspiracy of silence* surrounds gay issues—even with a sensitive and caring service provider. The lesbian or gay person, especially older persons who may have been "closeted" all of their lives, are often unable to disclose their lifestyle. . . .

Finally, service utilization studies indicate that older lesbians and gay men are less likely than their nongay peers to use mainstream programs such as senior centers and retirement communities. (Kimmel, Raphael, Catalano, & Robinson, 1984, pp. 69 70)

One emerging line of research from this perspective on the diversity of older lesbians and gay men is a model of "successful aging." Friend (1990) speculated that it reflects individual psychological dimensions (such as skill in coping with crises, flexibility in gender role, and ability to redefine homosexuality and aging so that they are positive affirmations of personal worth); social and interpersonal dimensions (such as redefining family to include gay and lesbian friends, and development of an intergenerational support network); and advocacy that leads one to expect and demand equal and fair treatment.

Lee (1987) proposed a different model for successful aging, based on his 4-year longitudinal study of 47 gay male respondents who ranged in age from 50 to 80 years. He compared the importance of individual psychological variables with social exchange variables and found that "the higher the social class of the respondent, the more likely he was to be among the very happy or fairly satisfied clusters on life satisfaction" (p. 59). Similarly, those men who rated themselves "well above" or "above" the average standard of living for their age—regardless of the actual dollar level—were likely to be highly satisfied with their lives. Moreover, he criticized the concept of "crisis competence" (Kimmel, 1978). Lee (1987) noted that instead of the person's developing or enhancing his life skills as a result of having to deal with a crisis about being a gay man, it was his skill in avoiding crises that was related to successful aging: "The real 'crisis competence' of the older homosexual men in my study lay in good health, social class advantage, and exchange power, often enhanced by alliance with a significant other" (Lee, 1987, p. 60).

Lee also found in his sample that the majority of men spent considerable time with younger people and preferred sexual partners at least 20 years younger. This resulted in a form of generational conflict, enhanced by the recent advent of gay liberation. Thus Lee, a sociologist, argued for a social-structural and generational conflict approach to understanding older gay men. This is a provocative perspective that differs from that of other researchers (e.g., Berger & Kelly, 1986). That is, Lee's emphasis is that gay men are similar in important ways to heterosexual men; previously, the view had been to describe and explain their uniqueness.

Differences between older lesbians and gay men are also receiving greater attention (Kehoe, 1988). Dunker (1987), who came out as a lesbian after she retired, noted that the lesbian community welcomed and provided her with a great deal of emotional support and interest that more than replaced what was lost from "the small part of the older heterosexual community that can't accept me" (p. 76). Her children, grandchildren, friends, and relatives responded to her coming out in ways "as varied as their personalities" (p. 76). Because of the lower earning power of women as compared to men, old lesbians had to develop their skills for survival. Nonetheless, there are advantages for women who are oriented toward women (instead of toward men). One involves physical aging and attractiveness. She observed: "Lesbians can reject the male standards. We can appreciate the quality of our own changes as we see what's happening to the faces and figures of the women we love. Our ideas of beauty aren't necessarily subject to male fantasies" (Dunker, 1987, p. 77).

Research on older gay men has noted the importance of maintaining a friendship network (Kimmel, 1977, 1979). Likewise, Dunker (1987) noted the importance of younger friends for lesbians because an inevitable aspect of growing older is the loss of friends: "It's imperative that older lesbians find younger friends. They need us, too. The old crone, the wise women, the witch have always been valued in many cultures. We can ensure that they are valued here, too" (p. 81).

Because lesbians and gay men are defined by their sexuality, research has also focused on sexual behavior. Pope and Schulz (1990), in a study of gay men between the ages of 40 and 77, found that 91% were sexually active but that 14% of those over age 60 were no longer active. No one reported that they had no sexual interest, however. Similarly, Raphael and Robinson (1980) reported that sexuality remained important for the 20 lesbians over the age of 50 in their study. One 72-year-old single woman who had not had a partner for 3 years, said, "I still occasionally have a wet dream" (p. 214). The dominant pattern of love relationships among respondents in this study was described as "serial monogamy," although a few respondents expressed a desire for a collective lifestyle involving nonmonogamy. Some respondents in long-term relationships expressed boredom with sexual relations. A new partner often stimulated enhanced sexuality. Kehoe (1988) reported that 53% of her 100 lesbians over age 60 were not sexually active during the past year, and 26% were very unsatisfied with their sex life. Seventy-four percent of those who were celibate indicated that it was not by choice, however.

An emerging theme in research has begun on midlife issues (Kimmel & Sang, in press). Sang's (1991) study of 110 self-identified lesbians between the ages of 40 and 59 suggested that midlife development is significant in subtle ways for this sample. For example, the majority "reported feeling more fulfilled, more self-confident and self-accepting, and more comfortable with who they are" (p. 207). They reported three main sources of meaning and satisfaction: intimate relationships, friendships, and work. Finding a balance between work and home life was difficult for many because of job demands. Some also expressed a desire to give more to their community and also to take better care of themselves. About one half reported some sort of a "midlife crisis"; those who did not often indicated a conscious decision to reshape their lives. This observation is reminiscent of Livson's (1976, 1981) finding that nontraditional women who are well adjusted tend to come into their own in midlife.

Hopefully, soon we will have a study of midlife gay men. Vaillant (1977) included one in his study, and several studies of gay men have combined midlife and aging (see Lee, 1990), but now we need to have a clearly focused study on this topic.

We also need research on older lesbians and gay men of color. The small study currently underway by Adams and Kimmel (1991) is only a modest pilot study of black gay men. It is difficult to gain access to these men because they often do not identify themselves as "gay," and, if they are willing to be interviewed, it is not possible to determine whether they are representative of the older black gay male population. Earlier research suggested that black gay men are similar to white gay men on many dimensions, but that subtle differences possibly involving vulnerability in the occupation, family relationships (especially with extended kin), religiosity, and sexual attitudes may reveal characteristics that are relevant for understanding life histories of black gay men (Weinberg & Williams, 1974). Data are also needed on African American lesbians, as well as on Asian American and Hispanic lesbians and gay men, especially across the life span.

Reflections on Selected Issues of Aging for Lesbians and Gay Men

One respondent in Vacha's book of memoirs of older gay men, a nursing home administrator, described a vivid example of social isolation that could lead to a serious problem:

At the home I noticed that there were gay people who had no one. There was Allan—though he did have a lover who would come to visit him. Poor Allan would lie there and one day he groped an orderly. The orderly came running down the hall, screaming, "You know what that old man did to me?" The nurse would say, "Look, he's senile and doesn't realize that you're a man and not a woman." Then the orderly would go back to work. One day I was walking down the hall and I heard this orderly say to Allan, "If you grab my prick one more time I'm going to bust you in the mouth." I stormed into that room, tore that curtain open and said, "You don't know it, but you are on your way out the door, go now!" Poor Allan, God love him, said, "What did I do wrong?" I said, "Honey, you were in the wrong basket." He was thrilled because now he had someone to dish with. (Vacha, 1985, p. 179)

Today SAGE, the organization providing services for older lesbians and gay men in New York City, conducts in-service training for nursing home workers and others working with aging people to increase awareness and sensitivity to the complex issues involved in situations such as Allan's. They also provide "friendly visitors" for nursing home residents and homebound elders to provide a connection between the gay or lesbian person and the community. In addition, they host a variety of social events and meetings for older gay men and lesbians. Thus SAGE provides a community and the possibility of declaring one's identity and identification with that community. Unfortunately, few places outside major urban areas offer that possibility, except on an individual basis.

In general, lesbians and gay men age very much like everyone else. The most significant concerns for older people are health, income, and loneliness; health is the most important factor in aging (Kimmel, 1990). The situation is no different for lesbians and gay men.

There is one sensitive issue worth discussing, however. Who will provide care if the older lesbian or gay man has no children? Deep in my consciousness when I began my research on older gay men was the heterosexist fear: "It may be all right to be gay when you're young; but what about when you are old and alone?"

I suspect this fear has two aspects. First, we grow up without visible role models of aging lesbians and gay men. If we are lucky, they emerge, but they may not alleviate the oppressive stereotypes of a lonely old age. Second, we live in a culture filled with negative stereotypes about old people, regardless of their sexual orientation. Anyone in our society may have watched the physical decline and dependency of a "role model" of aging that led them to fear this possibility for themselves. Also, anyone may have identified an active and vital older person as an "exception" to so-called normal aging and thereby strengthened the ageist stereotype of inevitable deterioration into a hopeless childlike state.

How do we answer this fear? Can lesbians and gay men face the distant sunset of life with enthusiasm and hope? Or must we avert our gaze and focus only on the present and short-term goals? The power of the life span approach to lesbian and gay development, it seems to me, lies in the significance of these questions.

As with many important questions, there may be no convincing answer, but let me suggest some ideas and perspectives, partly reflecting my research on aging in Japan (Kimmel, 1989). The Japanese are a people living with the deep sense of an obligation to their parents, especially their mother, who gave them so much during childhood that only one ten-thousandth can ever be repaid. We in the United States also seem to have this belief. Elaine Brody (1985), a noted gerontologist, suggested that the persisting myth that old people are not cared for by their children arises from this belief and its ensuing guilt.

> *The "truth" to which the myth speaks is that adult children cannot and do not provide the same total care to their elderly parents that those parents gave to them in the good old days of their infancy and childhood.* The roles of parent and child cannot be reversed in that sense. The good old days, then, may not be earlier periods in our social history (after all, the myth existed then too), but an earlier period in each individual's and family's history to which there can be no return. (p. 26)

Data have clearly indicated that families do care for their elderly relatives, both in the United States and in Japan, and to about the same extent. In the United States, old people are not placed in nursing homes except as a last resort; in Japan, nursing homes have long waiting lists because they are relatively scarce, but they provide care for only a small number of people in both countries because the families provide most of the care (Kimmel, 1990).

I should be clear: Women provide most of the care. In the United States it is wives and daughters who are the primary caregivers; in Japan it is wives and daughters-in-law. Men are involved in important ways—and in some cases are the primary caregivers—but it is usually the woman who makes the time or gives up her job to provide the direct physical care. Interestingly, a recent study at the Tokyo Metropolitan Institute of Gerontology (personal communication) found that adults in the United States were more willing to provide care to aged aunts and uncles, or to friends, than were Japanese adults, who reported they would provide care to their parents at a rate only slightly higher than adults in the United States. So indeed it may be worse to be old and childless in Japan than in the United States, in terms of having the family provide care—and, again, nursing homes and other types of supportive housing are quite scarce there.

The point is that much of our collective guilt about not providing enough care for elderly persons may reflect our deep sense of not being able to repay our elders for the care they gave their children. So also, our own fear of not being cared for in old age may reflect the belief that elders will be cared for only if there is some guilty offspring that can be coerced into this odious chore. If no one "owes" us this care, then we are left alone in our dotage, to "sweat out senescence" on our own.

Again, let me be explicit about the sexism involved here: It is women who provide the care, so we need a guilt-obligated daughter, or daughter-in-law, to take care of us. As nonsexist lesbians and gay men, we know that solution is not politically correct! Perhaps we might lead the way as we did by providing models of dual-career households or division of roles in relationships. We may even consider that "gay aging" points to a liberation from this sexist "solution" to the "problem" of aging.

Imagine, instead, aging free of this guilt. One would not expect to be a "burden," but rather to be an asset. Gerontologists already know that most aid flows from the elder generation to the younger generation—in the form of services, money, and assistance in emergencies (Kingson, Hirshorn, & Cornman, 1986). We also know that the vast majority of older people are independent and get along on their own in the community. It is primarily those who survive to become very old that may need the type of support and assistance we are discussing. Most of these, of course, are women. They are very likely to be widows, because they marry men (who have shorter life span on the average) and because they compound this mistake by marrying an older man.

So for lesbians and gay men, partnering someone of the same gender and of about the same age would probably reduce the chances of being alone for an extended period in old age. Likewise, partnering someone several years younger would possibly provide a likely caregiver, in case one was needed in old age. For all, consciously maintaining an age mix in one's friendship network and planning to work out an arrangement for a care partner is a sensible solution as one grows older, and especially if one survives to a very advanced age. In my study of older gay men, this strategy was frequently described and adopted. In fact, lesbians and gay men who do not have children must realize that care in old age is not automatic and plan accordingly. There is, arguably, an advantage to choosing one's caregiver, for the "automatic" care by children is of no higher quality in general than the "automatic" care of children by parents. Abuse of both age groups is gaining attention.

A remarkable book on lives of older lesbians, called *Long Time Passing*, edited by Marcy Adelman (1986), is an anthology of interviews with lesbians, some of whom are old. One respondent's comments illustrate the way care and mutual support can be worked out:

> Just because I'm old and sick and eighty-five doesn't mean I didn't have quite a gay life. You see I've loved a lot of women and a lot of women have loved me. In fact, if I weren't sick that would still be the case.
>
> But let me tell you about my life right now. My health is very poor. I no longer have a physical feeling for anyone. And I should have it because it makes you forget yourself. I miss it. . . .
>
> The most important thing in my life now is to get my health back. After all I have my sister Rebeccah that I have to take care of. She was a genius but now she has lost her memory. Sometimes she's lucid. She's in a home. I sent the home two checks today. I'm responsible for her care. . . .
>
> My family is very important to me, but I'm not very important to my family. It's not because I'm gay; it's because they have children and they're preoccupied with them.
>
> I need somebody most every day of the week. I have some people from GLOE (Gay and Lesbian Outreach to Elders), and a woman from Catholic Charities comes in once a week for $5.50 an hour. She does a good job. She cleans the house. . . .
>
> I have friends who come by and cook me dinner every now and then and I have friends who take me to my doctors appointments. These are new and younger gay friends.
>
> At one point, I thought gay people were no good. But now all these gay people are helping me. It's not my family that is taking care of me; it's my gay friends. They have been wonderful to me. (pp. 207-208)

In short, there are no guarantees. But guilt, as we know, is not the most effective motivation for high-quality care at any age. In any event, the chances of needing it are far less than the stereotype of helpless, infirm old people suggests. As with any stereotype, we must confront ageism head-on.

Look not to those occasional people who validate our stereotype, but look instead to those more frequent old people who are living the type of life we want for ourselves when we are old and find out what they have to teach us about being like them someday.

Conclusion: Some Parallels Between Aging and Lesbian and Gay Male Issues

Like race, age, and sex, sexual orientation cuts across all dimensions and experiences of human life. Gay people have no more in common with each other than do other groups such as blacks, women, or old people. But, like old people, no one is born into a gay lifestyle, though there may be biological factors in both conditions. Like being old, being lesbian or a gay man takes some living and some experience to become established, and there is no "cure." Like being old, being a gay man or lesbian is both romanticized and stigmatized. We call this "ism" *ageism*. One distinction, however, is that old age is a stigma available to anyone who lives long enough.

Although old lesbians and gay men may not have any "secrets" to impart, they have survived. Some may need our help, and organizations such as SAGE are a wonderful benefit, but many elders may have something to teach us about living. As lesbians and gay men, they may also have something to teach about the history of our community. This "oral history" is often the only history that exists.

Most of all, they pose a challenge to us: Look ahead and live, for as long as you have. There are no guarantees. But there are a lot of possibilities, if you do not let the "isms" get to you. If you live long enough, you also will be old. If not, that is one "ism" you will not have to face. But, for me, challenging "isms" is a lot more interesting than the alternative, given the chance. That is the opportunity that gay aging provides no matter what age we are: to live all the years of our lives with the integrity and courage of the pioneers that we are.

References

Adams, C. L., & Kimmel, D. C. (1991, November 23). *Older African-American gay men.* Paper presented at the meetings of the Gerontological Society of America, San Francisco.

Adelman, M. (Ed.). (1986). *Long time passing: Lives of older lesbians.* Boston: Alyson.

Allers, C. T. (1990). AIDS and the older adult. *The Gerontologist, 30,* 405-407.

Almvig, C. (1982). *The invisible minority: Aging and lesbianism.* Utica, NY: Utica College of Syracuse University.

Berger, R. M. (1982). *Gay and grey: The older homosexual man.* Urbana: University of Illinois Press.

Berger, R. M., & Kelly, J. J. (1986). Working with homosexuals of the older population. *Social Casework, 67,* 203-210.

Brody, E. M. (1985). Parent care as a normative family stress. *The Gerontologist, 25,* 19-29.

Brown, L. S. (1989). New voices, new visions: Toward a lesbian/gay paradigm for psychology. *Psychology of Women Quarterly, 13,* 445-458.

Dunker, B. (1987). Aging lesbians: Observations and speculations. In Boston Lesbian Psychologies Collective (Ed.), *Lesbian psychologies* (pp. 72-82). Urbana: University of Illinois Press.

Faderman, L. (1981). *Surpassing the love of men: Romantic friendship and love between women from the renaissance to the present.* New York: William Morrow.

Friend, R. A. (1990). Older lesbian and gay people: A theory of successful aging. *Journal of Homosexuality, 20*(3/4), 99-118.

Garnets, L. D., & Kimmel, D. C. (1991). Lesbian and gay male dimensions in the psychological study of human diversity. In J. D. Goodchilds (Ed.), *Psychological perspectives on human diversity in America* (pp. 143-192). Washington, DC: American Psychological Association.

Harry, J. (1990). A probability sample of gay males. *Journal of Homosexuality, 19*(1), 89-104.

Hay, H. (1990, April 22-28). Identifying as gay—there's the key. *Gay Community News,* p. 5.

Kehoe, M. (1988). Lesbians over 60 speak for themselves. *Journal of Homosexuality, 16* (Whole Nos. 3/4).

Kimmel, D. C. (1977). Psychotherapy and the older gay man. *Psychotherapy: Theory, Research and Practice, 14,* 386-393.

Kimmel, D. C. (1978). Adult development and aging: A gay perspective. *Journal of Social Issues, 34*(3), 113-130.

Kimmel, D. C. (1979). Life-history interviews of aging gay men. *International Journal of Aging and Human Development, 10,* 239-248.

Kimmel, D. C. (1989, Spring). Aging in the United States and Japan. *Kaleidoscope, 5,* 8-11. (Published by the City College of New York/CUNY).

Kimmel, D. C. (1990). *Adulthood and aging: An interdisciplinary, developmental view* (3rd ed.). New York: John Wiley.

Kimmel, D., Raphael, S., Catalano, D., & Robinson, M. (1984). Older lesbians and gay men. In F. H. Schwaber & M. Shernoff (Eds.), *Sourcebook on lesbian/gay healthcare* (pp. 69-70). New York: National Gay Health Education Foundation, Inc.

Kimmel, D. C., & Sang, B. E. (in press). Lesbians and gay men in midlife. In C. J. Patterson & A. R. D'Augelli (Eds.), *Lesbian and gay identities across the lifespan: Psychological perspectives.* New York: Oxford University Press.

Kingson, E. R., Hirshorn, B. A., & Cornman, J. M. (1986). *Ties that bind: The interdependence of generations (a report from the Gerontological Society of America).* Washington, DC: Seven Locks.

Lee, J. A. (1987). What can homosexual aging studies contribute to theories of aging? *Journal of Homosexuality, 13*(4), 43-71.

Lee, J. A. (Ed.). (1990). Gay midlife and maturity. *Journal of Homosexuality, 20* (Whole Nos. 3/4).

Livson, F. B. (1976). Patterns of personality development in middle-aged women: A longitudinal study. *International Journal of Aging and Human Development, 7,* 107-115.

Livson, F. B. (1981). Paths to psychological health in the middle years: Sex differences. In D. H. Eichorn, J. A. Clausen, N. Haan, M. P. Honzik, & P. H. Mussen (Eds.), *Present and past in middle life* (pp. 195-211). New York: Academic Press.

Matteson, D. R. (1985). Bisexual men in marriage: Is a positive homosexual identity and stable marriage possible. *Journal of Homosexuality, 11*(1/2), 149-173.

Pope, M., & Schulz, R. (1990). Sexual attitudes and behavior in midlife and aging homosexual males. *Journal of Homosexuality, 20*(3/4), 169-177.

Raphael, S. M., & Robinson, M. K. (1980). The older lesbian: Love relationships and friendship patterns. *Alternative Lifestyles, 3,* 207-229.

Sang, B. E. (1991). Moving toward balance and integration. In B. Sang, J. Warshow, & A. J. Smith (Eds.), *Lesbians at midlife: The creative transition* (pp. 206-214). San Francisco: Spinsters.

Vacha, K. (1985). *Quiet fire: Memoirs of older gay men.* Trumansburg, NY: Crossing.

Vaillant, G. E. (1977). *Adaptation to life.* Boston: Little, Brown.

Weinberg, M. S., & Williams, C. J. (1974). *Male homosexuals: Their problems and adaptations.* New York: Oxford University Press.

Wolf, T. J. (1985). Marriages of bisexual men. *Journal of Homosexuality, 11*(1/2), 135-148.

17

Comparative Perspectives on Successful Aging

Charlotte Ikels
Jeanette Dickerson-Putman
Patricia Draper
Christine L. Fry
Anthony Glascock
Henry Harpending
Jennie Keith

Though economics is widely known as the "dismal" science, gerontology cannot be far behind. Some scholars would argue that gerontology's dominant paradigm, the "misery perspective," can be attributed to the hard facts of life faced by most elders in the West until quite recently, but Tornstam (1992) argued that the origins and persistence of this view of old age are rather more sinister and derive from our hidden contempt for weakness. He also pointed out that researchers are continually befuddled when their own data disconfirm hypotheses based on the misery perspective. Be that as it may, the misery perspective has certainly contributed to our own apprehensions about old age and the hope that maybe, somewhere, older persons are doing much better than they are presumed to be doing in the West. The data presented in this chapter attempt to address this slippery question ("Where are elderly persons doing best?") and, more important, to identify the variables that contribute to positive outcomes in old age.

Project AGE

Project AGE was a coordinated comparative study carried out by seven anthropologists working in seven sites to determine the meaning of successful aging and to chart the pathways that different cultures provide to achieve a successful old age.[1] The project was carried out in two phases during 1982-83 and 1987-88. Findings on successful aging from the first phase are

304

reported in Keith, Fry, and Ikels (1990). Here the findings from both phases are presented.

Sample

Located in four countries, the seven sites involved in Project AGE were selected to ensure broad representation in terms of scale, complexity, subsistence pattern, residential mobility, and population structure. Brief descriptions of each of the sites are provided in Ikels et al. (1992). From least to most complex the populations or communities studied were

1. The !Kung of Botswana, who are better known in the anthropological literature as the Bushmen (e.g., Lee & DeVore, 1976). Though currently a settled population, the older members spent their childhoods and most of their adult years as hunter gatherers.
2. The Herero of Botswana, a settled pastoral population. For a fuller description of the Herero, see Gibson (1956, 1959, 1962).
3. Clifden, a rural seacoast community in Connemara in the west of Ireland. For an overview of the historical and contemporary circumstances of Irish rural life, see Arensberg and Kimball (1968), Fox (1979), Kane (1968, 1979), Messenger (1969), and Scheper-Hughes (1979).
4. Blessington, a small town being transformed by in-migration into a suburb of Dublin, the capital of the Republic of Ireland.
5. Momence, Illinois, a small town with an agricultural hinterland located 50 miles south of the Chicago Loop.
6. Swarthmore, Pennsylvania, a college town and upper middle class community, most of whose residents commute to work elsewhere.
7. Hong Kong, a densely populated enclave under British control on the southeast coast of China. Hong Kong is a commercial and industrial hub whose economy is tightly linked to international markets. Four neighborhoods varying in socioeconomic characteristics constituted the sampling frame for the study. For a fuller description of the social characteristics of Hong Kong, particularly as they affect aged persons, see Chow (1990, 1992), Ikels (1983, 1989), Mitchell (1972), and Phillips (1992).

In each of the sites, the sampling goal was to obtain approximately 200 interviews, including, where possible, an oversampling of the population over 60. The minimum age for inclusion in the study was whatever the local population estimated as the beginning of adulthood. In five of the sites, random sampling techniques were utilized to obtain respondents, whereas in the Botswana sites efforts were made to interview at least one person from every household in the settlements that were included in the study.

Methodological Issues

A cross-cultural study such as Project AGE involves a delicate balancing act. The problem that researchers have to keep constantly in mind during both the data-gathering and the data-analysis phases is how to satisfy the need for comparability without violating the integrity of the data from any one of the sites. Project AGE's solution to this dilemma was, first, to require that each investigator agree to address a set of key questions using the same or appropriately adapted instruments; second, to adopt multiple strategies to investigate these key questions; and third, to focus on the interpretation of measurements rather than on the measures themselves.

Another more global concern was how to compensate for the impact of cultural differences on the research process itself. Norms of interaction, expressive style, perceptions of the research instruments, and period effects all impinge on the very act of gathering data. Every society has norms for interaction, such as rules about how to participate in a conversation, rules governing the roles of participants of different status, and rules of propriety governing what one may ask and what one may disclose. As a result of their experience in Project AGE, Draper and Glascock (1989) presented a paper entitled "Can You Ask It?" that pointed out how asking culturally inappropriate questions or requiring a laconic informant to elaborate on answers can affect rapport and even lead to termination of the interview. For example, Draper learned that any question including the phrase "a good old age" was an inappropriate question for the !Kung, who do not view a good old age as a possibility.

Differences in expressive style take many forms. Among the !Kung, with their strong ethic of sharing, playing up one's needs or complaining of neglect is a legitimate discourse style, and a public interview provides a perfect setting in which to shame those who have not shared their resources. On the other hand, but for the very same reason, the Herero, for whom many !Kung work, have a major incentive to understate their resources. Along these same lines, Glascock found that the Irish maintain a stiff upper lip in the face of adversity, giving themselves high scores on life satisfaction, for example, because "[you] just have to put up with what [you] have" or responding, "No complaints—things are going quite well." Finally, the Chinese, in keeping with Confucian norms of moderation in all things, tend to avoid extremes, insisting that "some are better off than I and some are worse off—I'm in the middle." In the face of such disparate expressive styles, it would be ludicrous to accept life satisfaction scores, even when obtained by the same instrument, at face value. As mentioned above, culturally sensitive interpretation of measurements is critical for understanding comparative data.

Perceptions, or rather misperceptions, of research instruments can easily lead to surprising responses. This problem, though not insurmountable, surfaced early in the Hong Kong research, in which, in accordance with the findings of pilot interviews and the Project dictum to adapt instruments, the Cantril Self-Anchoring Ladder (Cantril, 1965) was transformed into a flight of stairs. Unfortunately, however, on seeing the stairs, many Hong Kong informants thought they were being asked how well they could climb them. When, in a subsequent research project, Ikels employed the flight of stairs with elderly residents of Guangzhou (Canton) in China, informants leaped to the conclusion that they were being asked which floor they would like to live on! This different but equal misperception of the question can be attributed to the fact that Guangzhou was in the midst of housing reform, and many households were expecting to move imminently. Though they could seldom choose the building into which they were being moved, they could express preferences for a particular floor. Ladder placement in Swarthmore, however, seemed to be guided by an implicit assumption that the scale measured goal attainments. If one was just starting out, one would have few accomplishments and therefore could not realistically place oneself very high on the ladder. Similarly, to place oneself at the very top of the ladder would be to suggest that one had attained all one's goals and that nothing was left to do, an unacceptable option to Swarthmore's strivers. Putting oneself at the top could also be viewed as bragging or, worse, as tempting fate.

As the Guangzhou case illustrates, local events at the time of the interview can easily color the content of people's responses. Economic concerns, for example, are central to life satisfaction in many of the sites, but the concrete expression of those concerns is shaped by local economic conditions. Thus in 1982-83 Momence was enduring high unemployment rates, and Hong Kong was on tenterhooks awaiting the outcome of political negotiations about its future that were being carried out by British and Chinese officials in Beijing. Similarly, in 1987-88 Botswana was in the seventh year of a major drought, a fact of overwhelming concern to the !Kung and the Herero. These period effects are often overlooked by researchers when only a single site is being investigated, but a comparative study cannot afford to ignore them.

All of the issues raised in this section point up the dangers of relying on a single methodology or a single instrument to investigate a multidimensional topic like successful aging. Although in this chapter we report primarily on the findings from the interviews with our aggregate sample, we also have life histories from a subsample of the older informants, data gathered from participant observation in community organizations and public spaces, interviews with key informants (community leaders, professionals in the field of social service, etc.), and the previously published works of other researchers. Our interview schedule also included a number of different strategies for tapping informant beliefs and feelings about aging in their societies.

These interview strategies included a card sort (referred to as the Age Game) requiring informants to arrange into groups a set of up to 48 cards describing typical individuals in terms of a cluster of attributes, such as marital, parental, residential, and employment statuses,[2] and the Cantril Self-Anchoring Ladder with appropriate modifications. The card sort was used to elicit the following information: (a) an abstract or generalized depiction of the adult life course, (b) personal preferences—the informant was asked to identify which age group he or she would most or least like to be in and why, and (c) concrete examples of older individuals personally known who were considered to be having a good (successful) or bad (unsuc-cessful) old age and the criteria used for assessing goodness or badness. The Cantril Self-Anchoring Ladder was used to determine how satisfied the individual informant was with his or her own life at the time of the interview (as well as several years earlier and later) and the criteria on which the satisfaction was based. The more internally consistent the data from a given site, the more confidence we could have that we had indeed correctly identified local definitions of the good life and of a good old age. Inconsistent data would require further analysis. The data from each of these questions are presented below.

Findings

Perceptions of the Adult Life Course

We asked people of all ages to describe the adult life course because we felt that descriptions of old age in isolation from the rest of the life course would provide only a truncated image of life in the societies in the project. To hear, for example, that everything is terrible for elderly persons when, in fact, everything is terrible for everyone can be very misleading, as can be hearing that things are good for elders when, in fact, they are much better for everyone else. Therefore, for each age group or stage identified, inform-ants were asked to describe the good and bad points or best and worst things about being in it.

Detailed site analyses of the life courses informants provided are available in Ikels et al. (1992). Here we will discuss only the overall analysis. There are both commonalities and some important differences in the themes that people in the sites use to talk about the life course. Vitality and strength versus frailty is a relevant continuum everywhere. The mapping of social-level complexity onto the individual life course is shown clearly in the differing numbers and types of themes used in addition to this one, especially if we consider the sites from lowest to highest in scale. The !Kung define every life transition in terms of physiological change. For Herero, and all the other groups, kinship and domestic statuses assume relevance as well. Reproductive status and the shifting ratio of freedom to responsibility are the key themes in all the groups except the !Kung. In addition, starting with Clifden, employment status is singled out as a significant marker. In the cases of Clifden, Blessington, Momence, and Hong Kong, discussion of employment tends to focus on the distinction between employment and unemployment as well as on the location of the workplace, in or outside of the community. In Swarthmore, however, employment is discussed more in terms of a career trajectory.

Although informants in all sites were able to generate some version of an adult life course and to describe its various stages, it was very clear that to do so seemed normal and easy in some but foreign and awkward in others. In short, some populations, especially the !Kung and long-time residents of Clifden, found the whole question of a staged life course inappropriate and irritating. We think that there are five reasons for this: (a) characteristics of the social field, (b) education, (c) cultural salience of age categories, (d) predictability of life events, and (e) variability in timing of normative social or work roles. These points are developed further in Ikels et al. (1992).

Age Group Preferences

Once informants had described the adult life course and had indicated which group they personally belonged to, they were asked to indicate which group they would most like to belong to and which group they would least like to belong to. The choice of groups and the criteria used to select them could be checked against the generalized descriptions of the life course provided earlier. Informant responses are presented below in Tables 17.1 through 17.3.

Because informants conceptualized the adult life course differently—that is, some divided it into as few as 2 stages whereas others saw 11, Table 17.1 separately displays the preferences of people who perceived from 3 to 6 stages (the vast majority of people in all the sites). Even a brief glance at Table 17.1 reveals the unpopularity of membership in the oldest age group. Few individuals select old age, the last category in each series of groups, as the group they would most like to belong to, whereas most readily identify it as the group they would least want to belong to.

The data on the very first line rapidly disconfirm the popular Western belief that aging in a Chinese society is preferable to aging almost anywhere

TABLE 17.1 Age Group Preferences Across Sites

	Most Preferred Group by Number of Groups					Least Preferred Group by Number of Groups				
	1	*2*	*3*			*1*	*2*	*3*		
Hong Kong	29	14	1			2	7	34		
Swarthmore	4	11	6			7	1	8		
Momence	14	16	9			15	3	21		
Blessington	19	20	9			13	3	29		
Clifden	2	4	1			2	0	5		
Herero	11	7	0			2	0	16		
	1	*2*	*3*	*4*		*1*	*2*	*3*	*4*	
Hong Kong	28	11	6	1		4	2	9	26	
Swarthmore	1	9	15	9		14	0	1	15	
Momence	12	22	13	2		17	0	1	30	
Blessington	19	16	5	4		11	2	5	27	
Clifden	6	6	3	1		4	0	3	9	
Herero	12	20	19	3		6	4	3	41	
	1	*2*	*3*	*4*	*5*	*1*	*2*	*3*	*4*	*5*
Hong Kong	20	5	10	4	1	2	7	3	2	21
Swarthmore	3	12	22	17	6	17	0	2	3	32
Momence	9	20	18	5	0	8	0	2	2	40
Blessington	8	7	10	5	3	15	2	0	2	14
Clifden	5	8	2	0	0	1	0	1	0	12
Herero	4	3	3	1	0	0	1	0	1	9

	1	*2*	*3*	*4*	*5*	*6*	*1*	*2*	*3*	*4*	*5*	*6*
Hong Kong	12	9	5	1	0	0	0	0	2	0	5	14
Swarthmore	5	12	5	13	6	3	12	0	1	2	1	23
Momence	6	8	8	5	7	2	14	2	1	0	4	14
Blessington	7	12	5	2	4	0	7	2	0	1	3	16
Clifden	1	2	4	2	1	1	1	0	0	2	0	7
Herero			N.A.						N.A.			

else. Only 1 out of 44 Hong Kong informants who divided the adult life course into three stages (youth, middle age, and old age) preferred to be old, whereas 29 preferred to be young. When the responses of those who viewed the life course as consisting of four, five, or six stages are added in, the same picture emerges: Only 3 out of 157 people would choose to be in the oldest group, whereas 89 would prefer to be in the youngest. These preferences contrast most dramatically with those of Swarthmore, where old age is evaluated more positively than youth (though the middle stage of the life course is, in fact, the most preferable).

The reasons for this differential evaluation of youth are quite straightforward. Most Hong Kong informants described the first stage in their life course sequence as the interval between completion of school and marriage. In Hong Kong, these young people have money of their own for the first time and few expenses. They still live at home, and their mothers still cook their meals, wash their clothes, and generally fuss over them. In short, it is a time of self-indulgence, made sweeter by the knowledge that marriage and parenthood (responsibility) will put a permanent end to it. In Swarthmore, by contrast, one is expected to be self-supporting by this stage, to have landed that first good job on the career ladder or to have gotten into a good graduate school, and to be independent in mind and action. In short, it is a time of great responsibility and of great vulnerability because critical decisions have to be made at a stage of life when one has quite limited experience and, indeed, may not even know what one really wants to do.

These different experiences of youth also shape informant choices of the least desirable stage of life. Selections of the least desirable group take the form of a J-shaped curve: That is, a few people think being young is undesirable, almost no one finds middle age undesirable, and the vast majority find old age undesirable. Those societies requiring their young people to make major employment decisions, particularly when associated with relocation from one's home community, show the greatest ambivalence about youth: In Momence, Blessington, and Clifden almost as many people reject it as prefer it. Swarthmore remains the most negative toward youth, whereas Hong Kong and Herero respondents rarely select youth as the least desirable stage of life. None of this discussion, however, should be allowed to obscure the fact that old age is the least desired stage in all of the societies. Old age may have its compensations, but they are seldom enough to make it a desirable time of life. Chronic disease, physical frailty, material insecurity, and anxiety about one's support system (all characteristics predominantly associated with old age) are simply too daunting for most people to find old age attractive.

Because a person's knowledge base derives partly from books or what others say and partly from personal experience, we hypothesized that an individual's own placement in the life course was likely to influence perceptions and evaluations of its stages. In Table 17.2, we attempt to control for this variable and present the aggregate responses across all the sites.

Figures appearing along the diagonal indicate the numbers of people who selected their own age group as the most or least desired. Figures above the diagonal signify the number of people who selected a group older than their own, whereas figures below the diagonal signify the number of people who selected a group younger than their own. The conclusions to be drawn from this table are somewhat more heartening than those drawn from Table 17.1. First, in all societies and in almost every case, the modal preferred age group

TABLE 17.2 Aggregate Preferences by Own Age Group

Own Group	Most Preferred Group by Number of Groups						Least Preferred Group by Number of Groups					
	1	*2*	*3*				*1*	*2*	*3*			
1	30	8	0				2	1	35			
2	34	41	1				12	6	55			
3	17	27	26				27	7	23			
	1	*2*	*3*	*4*			*1*	*2*	*3*	*4*		
1	22	6	2	0			2	2	5	22		
2	21	41	8	2			15	1	8	46		
3	22	21	36	0			12	2	7	53		
4	13	16	15	18			27	3	2	27		
	1	*2*	*3*	*4*	*5*		*1*	*2*	*3*	*4*	*5*	
1	9	4	1	0	0		0	0	2	1	11	
2	14	27	12	5	0		5	4	3	4	39	
3	12	7	28	4	0		9	3	0	2	34	
4	5	9	15	17	0		16	0	0	1	27	
5	9	8	9	6	10		13	3	3	2	17	
	1	*2*	*3*	*4*	*5*	*6*	*1*	*2*	*3*	*4*	*5*	*6*
1	11	1	1	0	0	0	0	1	0	0	3	9
2	7	19	3	0	0	0	0	0	1	3	4	18
3	3	12	17	3	1	0	11	0	0	1	1	17
4	4	1	2	16	2	0	6	0	3	1	1	10
5	4	6	3	0	13	0	8	1	0	0	2	13
6	2	4	1	4	2	6	9	2	0	0	2	7

is one's own. This finding is true even of elderly people! It is important to note, however, that the modal category does not necessarily contain the majority of responses: For example, if we look at those who divided the adult life course into five age groups and put themselves into the last age group, we find that 10 (the modal response) accounts for only 24% of the preferences. It is also the case that, with only three exceptions, those preferring the oldest age group are themselves old. This finding suggests that upon reaching old age one discovers that it is not so bad as one expected. The second, and less heartening, observation is that informants who do not select their own age group are much more likely to prefer membership in a younger than an older group—that is, to be more comfortable with a known than an unknown experience.

The modal least desired stage of life is, as we saw above, old age, but one's own placement in the life course does make a difference. Elderly persons are the least likely of all respondents to choose old age as the worst time of life; in fact, among those older persons identifying three or six stages, youth is rejected more than old age. A close examination of Table 17.2 reveals that there is a subtle, not entirely consistent, shift in the balance of negative preferences as one moves through the life course. The proportion of people holding strongly negative views of old age drops with increasing age.

The above observations are based on aggregate data. To learn about intersite variation, we need to look at Table 17.3, which displays the preferences of older people by site. Although the sample size is quite small,[3] especially in the case of Clifden, several points can be made. The first is that, in comparison with other elderly persons, older people in Swarthmore account for a disproportionately high amount of the positive views of aging and a disproportionately low amount of the negative views. That these figures have something to do with characteristics of Swarthmore rather than simply the characteristics of the United States is obvious when the percentages from Swarthmore are juxtaposed with those from Momence. The second is that elders in Ireland are just as likely to view old age as desirable as undesirable, a finding that is equally true of both Irish sites. Finally, old age is most negatively evaluated by elderly persons in Hong Kong (four times as many elderly Chinese see old age as undesirable as see it as desirable), followed closely by the Herero. These findings are discussed further in the discussion section.

Examples of Successful and
Unsuccessful Elderly Persons

Only data from Hong Kong are available, and in view of the negative evaluations of aging held by so many Chinese residents the news is good. A majority of Chinese informants personally know elderly individuals whose situations they consider desirable: That is, if they were in this person's shoes, they would be very satisfied. Seventy-three percent of women and 55% of men identified a positive case, a few examples of which are provided below.

> The man living opposite us. He has run several shops. His children furthered their studies abroad and have come back. Now he does not run a business. He has closed his shops and is enjoying the happy lot [an idiomatic expression used to describe the contentment of one who has no responsibilities and is enjoying the social and material rewards of his years of labor]. (Said by a 56-year-old man of his 65-year-old neighbor)

TABLE 17.3 Elderly Age Group Preferences (in Percentages)

| | Own Group Most Desirable | | Own Group Least Desirable | |
	%	Total N [a]	%	Total N [a]
Hong Kong	17	18	69	16
Swarthmore	51	45	26	35
Momence	22	58	45	58
Blessington	31	48	36	47
Clifden	33	9	33	3
Herero	20	15	67	15

a. Total N indicates the number of elderly who answered the question. In Hong Kong, for example, a total of 40 elderly were interviewed, but only about half were able to play the Age Game. Of the 18 elderly who indicated a preference, only 3 (17%) said they would prefer to be in their own age group.

She does her best for the family. The children are persuaded by her and are filial to her. She is over 70, but she can still bear the responsibility of the family. She does not know many characters [i.e., is only semiliterate] yet she is open-minded. She is the happiest one among my relatives. (Said by a 38-year-old woman)

My father worked hard and struggled to raise us. When he teaches us, he does not punish. He is very attentive to the family and makes us feel family warmth. He doesn't gamble. (Said by a 25-year-old man of his 65-year-old father)

Though she is old she can still walk, and she helps those other old people who need assistance. She still has value and can help to lessen the problems of others. Thus she makes use of her own time to replenish and enrich herself [spiritually]. She is not like others who only know how to make unhappy sighs and say that they are bored. (Said by a 29-year-old woman of a 65-year-old relative)

One of the most interesting aspects of the examples provided by Hong Kong informants is their focus on social attributes. It is almost as if the informant interpreted the question as "What is a good old person" rather than as "What is a good life for an old person" (Ikels, 1989; Keith et al., 1990). This focus on social attributes probably has its origins in Hong Kong's high rates of intergenerational living and in the fact that most Hong Kong Chinese believe that a quarrelsome, demanding older person is unlikely to have a good situation because dependence on the younger generation is the primary means to a good old age.

Fewer people, but still about half (55% of women and 43% of men), were able to provide examples of elders doing poorly (unsuccessful elders). Two examples of elders doing poorly are given below.

> Problems of health: old people's disease, heart trouble. The sickness doesn't have a name. It is due to growing old. (Said by a 60-year-old man of a 75-year-old)

> Her children are not filial to her; they cannot get along with her. For example, when it rains, she tells her son to carry an umbrella, but he rebukes her and says he doesn't like to carry an umbrella. (Said by a 35-year-old about a 75-year-old)

Men provided fewer examples either positive or negative than women. Many said they simply did not know the situation of any particular elder well enough to comment on them. In most such cases, the men explained their unfamiliarity as a consequence of their long work hours: "I just go to work and come back. I don't know the circumstances of the people around here." Men and women also differ in the types of cases they call to mind, again reflecting male work role experiences: That is, they focus on labor force participation and working ability much more than women as a basis for evaluation. Women are more likely to mention support issues, such as presence or absence of caregivers, companionship, or income adequacy.

Life Satisfaction

Our final strategy for investigating the topic of successful aging was to measure well-being, conceptualized more in terms of life satisfaction than of mental health status. Life satisfaction has come to be viewed as a more stable variable than happiness (or mood) and to involve a more cognitive component (Campbell, Converse, & Rodgers, 1976; George, 1981; Horley, 1984; Larson, Mannell, & Zuzanek, 1986). We asked each individual to assess his or her life compared to his or her definition of the best life possible and, as indicated above, employed modifications of the Cantril Self-Anchoring Ladder. The modifications or adaptations included a reduction in the number of rungs on the original ladder from 10 to 6 in five sites and to 5 in two sites. In addition, in Hong Kong the ladder was replaced by a flight of stairs and among the !Kung and Herero by the five fingers of the interviewer's hand.

In order to learn the bases on which respondents assigned themselves a score, we asked several questions designed to tap the domains of greatest personal salience. Depending on the particular site, these questions required the informant to specify the nature of the "best possible life" and the "worst

TABLE 17.4 Distribution of Well-Being Scores

	Site						
Score	!Kung (N = 102)	Herero (N = 186)	Clifden (N = 129)	Bless. (N = 170)	Mom. (N = 207)	Swarth. (N = 201)	H.K. (N = 192)
1.0			1	3	1	1	4
1.2		38					
1.5	20						
2.0			3	3	3	4	13
2.4		56					
3.0	33		10	16	21	11	68
3.5							18
3.6		64					
4.0			30	51	66	40	49
4.5	8						2
4.8		19					
5.0			56	58	73	86	26
5.5							1
6.0	41	9	29	39	43	59	11
Means	4.0	3.1	4.7	4.6	4.6	4.9	3.7

NOTE: The !Kung self-ratings have been converted from a 5-point scale on which the lowest rating was not allowed to a 6-point scale. This omission of the lowest possible rating on the scale leads to an upward skewing of the scores. The Herero self-ratings have also been converted from a 5-point scale to a 6. In this and all subsequent tables, the means are based on the converted scores.

possible life" in the community, the reasons for assigning him or herself a particular score, what score the informant would assign to his or her life of 5 years ago and for what reasons, and what score he or she anticipated assigning to his or her life 5 years from the time of the interview and for what reasons. Among the !Kung and the Herero, no past and future well-being scores as such were sought. Instead, informants were asked simply whether their past life (10 years ago) was better or worse than their present, and the Herero were also asked about their expectations of life (better or worse in the future).

For the purpose of comparison, informants' reasons for their well-being were grouped into four major categories or domains: those referencing physical, material, social, or personal sources of well-being. The first three domains are reasonably self-explanatory. *Physical* generally includes references to health, functionality, or the need for care. *Material* generally includes all references to subsistence-related activities and economic resources—from having one's cattle die, to losing one's job, to buying a house—whereas *social* encompasses references to family, friends, other

TABLE 17.5 Mean Well-Being Scores by Sex

				Site			
Sex	*!Kung*	*Herero*	*Clifden*	*Bless.*	*Mom.*	*Swarth.*	*H.K.*
Males	3.8	3.2	4.6	4.7	4.6	4.7	3.6
	(*N* = 51)	(*N* = 66)	(*N* = 61)	(*N* = 80)	(*N* = 94)	(*N* = 82)	(*N* = 99)
Females	4.3	3.0	4.8	4.6	4.7	5.0	3.8
	(*N* = 51)	(*N* = 112)	(*N* = 69)	(*N* = 90)	(*N* = 113)	(*N* = 119)	(*N* = 93)

people, and wider social issues. The fourth category, *personal,* was intended to capture the more egocentric types of responses, such as references to states of mind, personality attributes, goals, and interests. A fifth category of general, that is, non-domain-specific, statements, such as "everything is good," was also used but is not displayed in the tables below. Depending on the goals of any particular analysis, of course, individual subcategories, such as "states of mind," "circumstances of descendants," or "retirement," can be broken out for separate analysis.

Table 17.4 displays the distribution of well-being scores. Given our earlier discussion of the impact of expressive styles on people's statements, it should be obvious to the reader that these scores, however interesting, cannot be accepted at face value: That is, they cannot be interpreted as valid indicators of the relative rank of the societies in terms of how well they meet the needs of their members. Nevertheless, these scores can be usefully compared for two purposes: (a) intrasite variation and (b) patterning across sites. Tables 17.5 through 17.7 display the effects of gender, age, and health status on well-being.

As Table 17.5 shows, in all the sites gender has only a minor effect on average scores: In only one population (the !Kung) does the difference amount to even one half a point. In five of the sites, women give themselves slightly higher ratings than men, whereas in Blessington and among the Herero, men give themselves slightly higher ratings than women.

Each researcher was asked to divide the study population into three age ranges broadly defined as young, middle-aged, and old. Variations by age exceed those by gender (Table 17.6). Though in Clifden there is scarcely any difference by age, in the other sites the differences range from a high of 1.4 points among the Herero to a low of 0.4 in Hong Kong. Patterning by age is not consistent. Among the !Kung, Herero, and Chinese, elderly persons view their present circumstances more negatively than do the young, whereas in Blessington, Momence, and Swarthmore the reverse is the case. In all sites, with the exception of the !Kung and Momence, among whom the middle-

TABLE 17.6 Mean Well-Being Scores by Age Category

Age Category	Site						
	!Kung	*Herero*	*Clifden*	*Bless.*	*Mom.*	*Swarth.*	*H.K.*
Young	4.1	3.7	4.8	4.2	4.2	4.5	3.9
	(N = 21)	(N = 47)	(N = 23)	(N = 57)	(N = 53)	(N = 50)	(N = 54)
Middle-	4.3	3.1	4.7	4.7	4.8	4.9	3.6
aged	(N = 50)	(N = 78)	(N = 47)	(N = 53)	(N = 62)	(N = 79)	(N = 107)
Old	3.6	2.3	4.7	4.9	4.7	5.1	3.5
	(N = 31)	(N = 53)	(N = 59)	(N = 60)	(N = 91)	(N = 72)	(N = 31)

NOTE: For site-specific reasons, the chronological ages defining the boundaries of these ranges vary slightly. Among the !Kung, Herero, and Chinese, the ranges are under 30, 30 to 59, and 60 or older. In Clifden they are under 36, 36 to 64, and 65 or older. In the case of Blessington and Swarthmore, the ranges are under 40, 40 to 64, and 65 or older, whereas in Momence, they are under 35, 35 to 59, and 60 or older.

aged claim the highest life satisfaction, the relationship between age and life satisfaction is linear, that is, straight down or straight up with increasing age.

Because health status is often assumed to have a major impact on life satisfaction (and even, perhaps, to be the mechanism underlying variation by age, especially when life satisfaction declines with age), we looked separately at the relationship between subjective health and well-being. As can be seen from the means in Table 17.7, this relationship is the strongest one so far: In all cases, those in the poorest health have the lowest mean scores, and each improvement in health status is accompanied by an improvement in well-being. Further support for the importance of health status comes from our data on sources of well-being. As can be seen in Table 17.8, in every site, those in poor health are more likely than those in average or excellent health to reference health-related (physical) reasons as a basis for their self-rating.

From Table 17.8 we can see that there are two distinct patterns of domain salience. The African and Chinese populations are overwhelmingly concerned with material issues—worrying about livestock, earning a living, and financial security. The second most salient domain for both the !Kung and the Herero is the physical—probably reflecting the fact that in both populations physical strength and endurance are essential to success in subsistence activities. In Hong Kong, however, the next most frequently mentioned domain is the social, which in this case usually means the family unit. In the American sites and Blessington, what is distinctive is the lack of any overwhelming preponderance of references to any particular domain. Although the rank order of the four categories varies within these three sites, all four categories are referenced by at least 20% of the respondents in each of the sites, and no category is mentioned by a majority of respondents. Clifden falls between these two patterns: That is, in terms of variation within

TABLE 17.7 Mean Well-Being Scores by Health Status

Health				Site			
Status	*!Kung*	*Herero*	*Clifden*	*Bless.*	*Mom.*	*Swarth.*	*H.K.*
Poor/fair		2.2	4.4	4.3	4.2	4.4	3.4
		(N = 50)	(N = 39)	(N = 32)	(N = 40)	(N = 17)	(N = 16)
Aver./	N.A.	3.2	4.8	4.5	4.6	4.7	3.4
Good		(N = 55)	(N = 59)	(N = 80)	(N = 90)	(N = 74)	(N = 81)
Excellent		3.7	5.0	4.9	4.8	4.9	4.0
		(N = 69)	(N = 31)	(N = 58)	(N = 77)	(N = 109)	(N = 95)

NOTE: In four sites a 4-point scale was used and in a three 5-point scale. The actual labels used to describe the points on the scale varied somewhat from site to site.

Clifden, the social domain is relatively prominent but not nearly so prominent as the material domain among the Africans and Chinese.

Discussion

The findings from the four sources of data (perceptions of the adult life course, membership preferences, examples of successful and unsuccessful elders, and life satisfaction) considered in this chapter are remarkably consistent in what they reveal about the variables that make for a good old age. As a species, human beings seem to have a hierarchy of needs (Cantril, 1965). Not until the material issues of life are satisfactorily resolved *and* one is not disturbed by health problems can one afford to think about other issues: to evaluate social relationships more in terms of affective than instrumental needs, to ponder whether one is in the right job as opposed to merely having a job, and to consider whether one is developing to one's full potential.

Elderly people rank themselves highest in those societies in which they are most able to continue to rely on an independent source of income to meet their material needs. In Swarthmore, the independent income includes substantial accumulated assets along with pensions and government supported programs such as Social Security. In Clifden, Blessington, and Momence, government income support (and other) programs provide a cushion that under normal circumstances is sufficient to meet the self-perceived needs of most elders. Among the !Kung and the Herero and in Hong Kong, however, most older persons do not have an independent source of income. None of them, or only a modest percentage, in these societies receive pensions, and government income support programs range from nonexistent to those providing pocket money. The basic assumption of individuals and governments in these societies is that income support is a family responsibility. Yet when

TABLE 17.8 Domains by Health Status (in Percentages)

Domain	!Kung (P = 24) (A = 31) (E = 30)	Herero (P = 44) (A = 50) (E = 68)	Clifden (P = 39) (A = 55) (E = 31)	Bless. (P = 31) (A = 81) (E = 57)	Mom. (P = 40) (A = 91) (E = 77)	Swarth. (P = 23) (A = 60) (E = 107)	H.K. (P = 17) (A = 138) (E = 27)
				Site			
Physical	39	24	22	20	35	43	15
Poor/fair	50	27	36	32	65	52	29
Aver./good	32	18	13	20	30	33	14
Excellent	37	26	19	12	25	46	11
Material	68	91	21	41	49	44	70
Poor/fair	63	95	10	45	35	43	82
Aver./good	77	96	18	44	51	40	72
Excellent	63	85	39	35	53	47	56
Social	16	19	39	37	31	49	29
Poor/fair	25	20	38	23	20	43	35
Aver./good	10	20	35	47	32	55	26
Excellent	16	18	48	30	34	48	41
Personal	6	0	10	21	27	31	20
Poor/fair	8	0	10	13	10	30	6
Aver./good	3	0	13	21	29	38	21
Excellent	7	0	3	25	35	26	26

NOTE: The numbers listed in parentheses under each of the column headings refer to the number of informants who rated their health poor/fair (P), average/good (A), or excellent (E). Thus, for example, among the 85 !Kung who answered this question, 24 rated their health as poor/fair (P = 24), 31 as average/good (A = 31), and 30 as excellent (E = 30). The figures in the body of the table represent percentages. Thus in the row "Poor/fair" under "Physical," the figure 50 in the first column means that 50% of the !Kung who rated their health as poor or fair (i.e., 50% of 24) mentioned a physical or health-related reason to explain their level of life satisfaction.

families are themselves poor, they can provide only the most minimal type of security to elderly members. In this context, the most effective way to help older persons may be indirect: helping their families raise their standard of living. If the elder can somehow be a means to that end—for example, by operating or assisting in a small business (Tout, 1989)—so much the better.

Though all people are concerned about their material standard of living, the content of what constitutes an adequate standard is subject to enormous variation. At the most basic level, for example, a !Kung will be delighted with a quality of accommodation that would be totally unacceptable to most Irish and Americans. Because of these enormous differences in cultural standards and the fact that people nearly always prefer to emigrate to places with higher standards of living, it will be difficult for Americans (given our definitions of an acceptable standard of living) to find that special someplace else to have a more satisfactory old age. Similarly, whereas elderly Chinese may find three-generational households desirable (and many do not), it is unlikely that most Americans would prefer this arrangement for themselves.

One point on which social gerontologists seem to agree is that subjective well-being is the product of expectations and experience (Bearon, 1989; Campbell, 1981; George, Okun, & Landerman, 1985; Nydegger, 1980; Whitbourne, 1985). People develop a notion of desirable and possible goals and, on the basis of their own and others' experiences in moving toward these goals, conclude that they are doing well or poorly. The significance of this phenomenon in terms of the production of specific cohort-centric world views is potentially enormous.

When a society undergoes rapid change, particularly when, for example, the standard of living rises precipitously, younger and older people will almost inevitably have very different ideas of what constitutes an acceptable standard of living. Older people, recalling that their parents and grandparents had no indoor plumbing or no financial resources in old age beyond those provided by immediate kin, are likely to be favorably impressed by such basics as running water and indoor toilets or by state welfare provisions for aged persons, however modest. Young people, though, are more likely to take such provisions for granted. Similarly, older people whose young adult lives were disrupted by war or civil unrest generating unemployment or famine are likely to view social and political stability favorably even if the stratification system is discriminatory and the political system oppressive, whereas younger people are more likely to view this same stability as stagnation and to be distressed by the unequal opportunities they face.

By emphasizing analyses of the relationships among synchronic variables, researchers have essentially ignored the role of historical factors in establishing the baseline expectations against which different cohorts measure their current status. In order to understand age differences in life satisfaction, researchers must consider the historical contexts in which individuals develop their definitions of the good life.

Notes

1. The team was coordinated by Christine L. Fry of Loyola University of Chicago, who conducted research in Momence, Illinois, and Jennie Keith of Swarthmore College, who conducted research in Swarthmore, Pennsylvania. Other team members, their current academic affiliations, and their research sites are: Jeanette Dickerson-Putman, Indiana University at Indianapolis, Blessington, Ireland; Patricia Draper, Pennsylvania State University, !Kung, Botswana; Anthony Glascock, Drexel University, Clifden, Ireland; Henry Harpending, Pennsylvania State University, Herero, Botswana; and Charlotte Ikels, Case Western Reserve

University, Hong Kong. The research was supported by grant AG0 3110 from the National Institute on Aging and published as *The Aging Experience: Diversity and Commonality Across Cultures* by Keith, et. al. (Sage, 1994).

2. Card descriptions were read aloud to some nonliterate informants in Hong Kong and to almost all informants in Herero villages, most of whom could read but very slowly. Among the !Kung, the card sort was abandoned, whereas in Clifden it was used with fewer than half of the participants. Those who could not or would not play the Age Game in these sites were asked to provide the terms used to describe people of increasing age starting with adulthood. Once a set of named categories was supplied, the person was asked the same set of questions as for those who played the card version of the Age Game.

3. Even in those sites in which the card sort generally worked, elderly people had the most difficulty with it. People who could not play the Age Game in any form could not be asked to express their preferences for membership.

References

Arensberg, C., & Kimball, S. (1968). *Family and community in Ireland* (2nd ed.). Cambridge, MA: Harvard University Press.

Bearon, L. B. (1989). No great expectations: The underpinnings of life satisfaction for older women. *The Gerontologist, 29,* 772-778.

Campbell, A. (1981). *The sense of well-being in America: Recent patterns and trends.* New York: McGraw-Hill.

Campbell, A., Converse, P. E., & Rodgers, W. L. (1976). *The quality of American life: Perceptions, evaluations, and satisfactions.* New York: Russell Sage.

Cantril, H. (1965). *The pattern of human concerns.* New Brunswick, NJ: Rutgers University Press.

Chow, N. (1990). Ageing in Hong Kong. In B. K. Leung (Ed.), *Social issues in Hong Kong* (pp. 164-177). Oxford: Oxford University Press.

Chow, N. (1992). Hong Kong: Community care for elderly people. In D. R. Phillips (Ed.), *Ageing in east and south-east Asia* (pp. 65-76). London: Edward Arnold.

Draper, P., & Glascock, A. (1989, February). *Can you ask it?* Paper presented at the annual meetings of the Society for Cross-Cultural Research, New Haven, CT.

Fox, R. (1979). The visiting husband on Tory Island. *Journal of Comparative Family Studies, 10,* 163-190.

George, L. K. (1981). Subjective well-being: Conceptual and methodological issues. In C. Eisdorfer (Ed.), *Annual review of gerontology and geriatrics* (pp. 345-382). New York: Springer.

George, L. K., Okun, M. A., & Landerman, R. (1985). Age as a moderator of life satisfaction. *Research on Aging, 7,* 209-233.

Gibson, G. D. (1956). Double descent and its correlates among the Herero. *American Anthropologist, 58,* 109-139.

Gibson, G. D. (1959). Herero marriage. *Rhodes Livingstone Journal, 24,* 1-37.

Gibson, G. D. (1962). Bridewealth and other forms of exchange among the Herero. In P. Bohannon & G. Dalton (Eds.), *Markets in Africa* (pp. 617-639). Evanston, IL: Northwestern University Press.

Horley, J. (1984). Life satisfaction, happiness, and morale: Two problems with the use of subjective well-being indicators. *The Gerontologist, 24,* 124-127.

Ikels, C. (1983). *Aging and adaptation: Chinese in Hong Kong and the United States.* Hamden, CT: Archon.

Ikels, C. (1989). Becoming a human being in theory and practice: Chinese views of human development. In D. Kertzer & K. W. Schaie (Eds.), *Age structuring in comparative perspective* (pp. 109-134). Hillsdale, NJ: Lawrence Erlbaum.

Ikels, C., Keith, J., Dickerson-Putman, J., Draper, P., Fry, C. L., Glascock, A., & Harpending, H. (1992). Perceptions of the adult life course: A cross-cultural analysis. *Ageing and Society, 12,* 49-84.

Kane, E. (1968). Man and kin in Donegal: A study of kinship functions in a rural Irish and an Irish-American community. *Ethnology, 7,* 245-258.

Kane, E. (1979). The changing role of the family in a rural Irish community. *Journal of Comparative Family Studies, 10,* 141-162.

Keith, J., Fry, C. L., & Ikels, C. (1990). Communities as context for successful aging. In J. Sokolovsky (Ed.), *The cultural contexts of aging* (pp. 245-261). Westport, CT: Greenwood.

Larson, R., Mannell, R., & Zuzanek, J. (1986). Daily well-being of older adults with friends and family. *Psychology and Aging, 1,* 117-126.

Lee, R. B., & DeVore, B. I. (1976). *Kalahari hunter-gatherers.* Cambridge, MA: Harvard University Press.

Messenger, J. (1969). *Inis Beag Isle of Ireland.* New York: Holt, Rinehart & Winston.

Mitchell, E. (1972). *Family life in urban Hong Kong.* Taipei: The Orient Cultural Service.

Nydegger, C. (1980). Measuring morale. In C. Fry & J. Keith (Eds.), *New methods for old age research* (pp. 127-145). Chicago: Loyola University, Center for Urban Policy.

Phillips, D. R. (1992). Hong Kong: Demographic and epidemiological change and social care for elderly people. In D. R. Phillips (Ed.), *Ageing in east and south-east Asia* (pp. 45-64). London: Edward Arnold.

Scheper-Hughes, N. (1979). *Saints, scholars, and schizophrenics.* Berkeley: University of California Press.

Tornstam, L. (1992). The quo vadis of gerontology: On the scientific paradigm of gerontology. *The Gerontologist, 32,* 318-326.

Tout, K. (1989). *Ageing in developing countries.* New York: Oxford University Press.

Whitbourne, S. K. (1985). The psychological construction of the life span. In J. Birren & K. W. Schaie (Eds.), *Handbook of the psychology of aging* (2nd ed., pp. 594-618). New York: Van Nostrand Reinhold.

Name Index

Subject Index

About the Contributors

George W. Albee, Ph.D., is Professor Emeritus of Psychology at the University of Vermont, past president of the Vermont Conferences on Primary Prevention of Psychopathology (VCPPP), and general editor (with Justin Joffe) of the series of volumes published by VCPPP. He is a past president of the American Psychological Association (1969-1970) and Chair of the Board of Social and Ethical Responsibility in Psychology (BSERP). He chaired the Task Panel on Prevention for President Carter's Commission on Mental Health. He received, among numerous distinguished awards, the American Psychological Association's Gold Medal Award for Life Contribution by a Psychologist in the Public Interest in 1993.

Lynne A. Bond, Ph.D., is Professor of Psychology at the University of Vermont and President of the Vermont Conferences on Primary Prevention of Psychopathology (VCPPP). Her research has focused on early child development, family interaction, and strategies for optimizing parent and child development and interaction. She is co-principal investigator of Listening Partners, a preventive/promotive intervention to foster the cognitive and socioemotional development of isolated rural mothers and their children. She has chaired a number of the Vermont Conferences on the Primary Prevention of Psychopathology and was principal investigator of a clinical training grant designed to train trainers of primary prevention.

Neena L. Chappell, Ph.D., a sociologist, was the founding director of the Research Centre on Aging at the University of Manitoba and is the first director of the Centre on Aging at the University of Victoria. She has an established history of conducting research and publishing in gerontology, particularly in the areas of informal support, formal support, interfaces between the different systems of care, and social policy. She has published three books and over 100 articles. She orients her research to community-relevant questions.

Stephen J. Cutler, Ph.D., is Professor of Sociology, the Bishop Robert F. Joyce Distinguished University Professor of Gerontology, and Director of the Center for the Study of Aging at The University of Vermont. He is the past editor of the *Journal of Gerontology: Social Sciences* (1990-1993) and Chair of the American Sociological Association's Section on the Sociology of Aging. His principal gerontological research interests include transportation, voluntary association participation, sociopolitical attitude change, caregiving, everyday cognitive problems, anticipatory dementia, and ethical issues.

Jeanette Dickerson-Putman, Ph.D., is Assistant Professor in the Department of Anthropology at Indiana University at Indianapolis. She earned her Ph.D. from Bryn Mawr College and has conducted research on the role of women in development in Papua, New Guinea, as well as on aging in Ireland.

Roger A. Dixon, Ph.D., is Professor of Psychology at the University of Victoria, in British Columbia, Canada. From 1981 to 1986, he was a Research Scientist at the Max Plank Institute in Berlin, Germany. He is the author or coauthor of numerous articles, chapters, and reports and has served on several editorial boards. His major research interests are in the psychology of aging, with special focus on the interplay between expertise and compensation in maintaining competent functioning throughout adulthood.

Patricia Draper, Ph.D., is Professor of Anthropology and Human Development at Pennsylvania State University. She earned her Ph.D. from Harvard and has a particular interest in the biocultural underpinnings of sex roles.

Christine L. Fry, Ph.D., is a Professor of Sociology and Anthropology at Loyola University of Chicago. She earned her Ph.D. from the University of Arizona and has a long history of interest in culture and aging. Along with Jennie Keith, she was the moving force behind the National Institute on Aging grant that funded the research that underlies the chapter she coauthored in this volume.

Margaret Gatz, Ph.D., is Professor of Psychology at the University of Southern California, where she developed the doctoral track in clinical psychology and aging. She is Associate Editor of *Psychology and Aging*. In collaboration with colleagues ranging geographically from Stockholm to South Pasadena, her funded research includes a study of dementia in Swedish twins and a longitudinal investigation of three-generational families. She has an abiding interest in sense of personal control and autonomy, and a recurring impulse to scrutinize well-known assumptions that may have little empirical basis.

Pearl S. German, Ph.D., is Professor in the Department of Health Policy and Management in the School of Hygiene and Public Health at The Johns Hopkins University, with a joint appointment in the Department of Medicine, School of Medicine. She is Assistant Director for Gerontology Studies in the Health Services Research and Development Center and has long and varied experience in health services research, particularly in research with older populations. She was responsible for the establishment of an interdepartmental program in gerontology that she directs. She has been principal investigator and co-investigator on several large community-based studies, and has been actively involved with the aging network at local, state, and national levels. She was a member of the Institute of Medicine Plan on Prevention in the Elderly, and chaired the Task Force on Disease Prevention and Health Promotion of the Gerontological Society of America.

Rose C. Gibson, Ph.D., is Faculty Associate at the Institute for Social Research and Professor, School of Social Work, at the University of Michigan, where she teaches the Sociology of Aging and Research Methodology on Minority Populations. She is the author of *Different Worlds: Inequality in the Aging Experience, Health in Black America, Blacks in an Aging Society,* and numerous other publications on age, race, and health in the elderly population. She is Editor-in-Chief of *The Gerontologist.*

Anthony Glascock, Ph.D., is Professor and Head of the Department of Psychology/Sociology/Anthropology at Drexel University. He has utilized the resources of the Human Relations Area Files as well as his own fieldwork to develop hypotheses about the treatment of the aged. He has carried out research in Somalia as well as in Ireland.

Armin Grams, Ph.D., is Professor Emeritus in the Department of Human Development Studies and an affiliate of the Center for the Study of Aging at the University of Vermont. He has served as president of the Association for Gerontology in Higher Education (1992-1993) and Chair of the National Center on Rural Aging. A past member of the Board of Directors, he serves on the President's Advisory Committee of the National Council on the Aging. He has been very active in local networks on aging and has developed and implemented training programs for Vermonters working or preparing to work in the field of aging.

Henry Harpending, Ph.D., is Professor of Anthropology and Human Development at Pennsylvania State University. He earned his Ph.D. from Harvard and has a special interest in demography.

Jon Hendricks, Ph.D., is Professor and Chair of the Department of Sociology at Oregon State University. Coauthor of the well-known book *Aging in Mass Society: Myths and Realities,* now in its fourth edition, he has authored and edited over 16 other books and scores of journal articles and chapters in the field of gerontology. He serves as co-editor of *The International Journal of Aging and Human Development,* and is a past Chair of the Behavioral and Social Sciences section of the Gerontological Society of America and of the Section on Aging of the American Sociological Association.

Charlotte Ikels, Ph.D., is Associate Professor in the Department of Anthropology at Case Western Reserve University. She has conducted research on social and health-related aspects of aging among Chinese populations in the United States, Hong Kong, and China. For much of the past decade she has been involved in a multistage, multisite project funded by the National Institute on Aging investigating the relationship between age and culture—in particular, how aging in a particular culture shapes the experience and meaning of old age. Her most recent work examines the impact of China's post-Mao economic reforms on the elderly in 200 urban households in Guangzhou, China's sixth largest city. She recently edited a special issue of the *Journal of Cross-Cultural Gerontology* entitled "Home Health Care and Elders: International Perspectives."

Jennie Keith, Ph.D., is Provost and Professor of Anthropology at Swarthmore. She has a long history of interest in the impact of community context on the experience of aging. Along with Christine Fry, she was the moving force behind the National Institute on Aging grant that funded the research that underlies the chapter she coauthored in this volume. She is the senior author of the book *The Aging Experience* (Sage), the major product of the research.

Douglas C. Kimmel, Ph.D., is Professor of Psychology at City College, City University of New York, and author of the textbook *Adulthood and Aging.* His research on older gay men led him to become a co-founder of SAGE, a program for older lesbians and gay men, in 1977. He is past president of Division 44 of the American Psychological Association (Society for the Psychological Study of Lesbian and Gay Issues) and co-editor with Linda Garnets of an anthology of research entitled *Psychological Perspectives on Lesbian and Gay Male Experiences.* He is currently studying older African American gay men with Clarence Adams.

Neal Krause, Ph.D., is Professor in the School of Public Health and a Research Scientist in the Institute of Gerontology at the University of Michigan. He is currently working on three major projects that examine the measurement of social support, the relationship between stress and well-being, and cross-cultural issues in aging (directed by Jersey Liang), each of which is funded by the National Institute on Aging. He has published extensively in these and related areas.

Elizabeth W. Markson, Ph.D., is Associate Director of the Gerontology Center at Boston University and is on the faculty of the Kantor Family Institute. Much of her current research focuses on gender and aging. She has recently completed an analysis of gender-specific social and medical risk factors for nursing home placement, a study on gender-specific correlates of depressive symptoms in old age. Her book *Older Women* received a Book of the Year Award from the *American Journal of Nursing.* She is former book editor of *The Gerontologist,* served on the Publications Committee of the Gerontological Society of America, and is on the international editorial board of *Revista de Gerontologie.*

Phyllis Moen, Ph.D., is the Ferris Family Professor of Life Course Studies and of Sociology at Cornell University. She is also Director of Cornell's newly formed Life Course Institute. While on leave from Cornell, she spent several years as Director of the Sociology Program at the National Science Foundation. She has published numerous books and articles on women's roles, health and well-being, families, the life course, and policy. She has been a member of the American Sociological Association Family and Aging Section Councils, and associate editor of numerous journals in her field.

James A. Mortimer, Ph.D., is Associate Director of the Minneapolis Veterans Administration Geriatric Research, Education, and Clinical Center and Associate Professor of Epidemiology and Neurology at the University of Minnesota. Among his three books and 140 scientific publications is *The Epidemiology of Dementia.* He has been Chair of the Mental Disorders of Aging Review Group at the National Institute of Mental Health and the Executive Convener of the Fourth International Conference on Alzheimer's Disease and Related Disorders held in 1994.

Jason T. Newsom, Ph.D., is a statistical consultant at the University Center for Social and Urban Research at the University of Pittsburgh. He received his Ph.D. in social psychology at Arizona State University. His interests include social cognitive theory in aging and health, functional status and mental health, measurement of perceived control, and applications of structural equation modeling techniques.

Eric T. Poehlman, Ph.D., was Associate Professor of Medicine at the University of Vermont at the time he wrote his chapter. Currently, he is in the Division of Gerontology, Department of Medicine, University of Maryland at Baltimore. His research interests primarily focus on the impact of physical activity on the regulation of body composition, metabolic rate, and sympathetic nervous system activity in older men and women. His more recent research has focused on the development of guidelines to predict caloric requirements of healthy elderly and Alzheimer's patients. His research has been funded by the National Institute of Aging and the Alzheimer's Association.

John W. Reich, Ph.D., is Professor of Psychology at Arizona State University. His research interests are in person/situation interaction processes, attribution theory, aging, and applied social psychology. Currently he is studying how congruence in control beliefs affects the mental health of women with rheumatoid arthritis and how anxiety affects control responses in anxiety-inducing social situations.

Eleanor M. Simonsick, Ph.D., is an epidemiologist in the Epidemiology, Demography, and Biometry Program of the National Institute on Aging (NIA). Before coming to the NIA, she was a research associate in the Division of Gerontology in the Department of Epidemiology and Preventive Medicine of the University of Maryland School of Medicine, and subsequently a postdoctoral fellow in the Department of Mental Hygiene of The Johns Hopkins University School of Hygiene and Public Health.

Michael A. Smyer, Ph.D., was Professor of Human Development at Pennsylvania State University at the time he wrote his chapter for this volume. Currently he is Professor of Psychology, Dean of the Graduate School of Arts and Sciences, and Associate Vice President for Research at Boston College. A licensed psychologist, he has focused his research on the development, implementation, and evaluation of health-related interventions for older adults and their families. He has been president of the

Division of Adult Development and Aging of the American Psychological Association.

Alex J. Zautra, Ph.D., is Professor of Psychology and Director of Clinical Training at Arizona State University. He earned his Ph.D. in clinical psychology in 1975 from the University of Utah and received postdoctoral training in social psychiatry and public health at Columbia University. His extensive research and writing focus on the contributions of psychological and social factors to the health and well-being of those with chronic illness.